Just Business Practices in a Diverse and Developing World

Also by Frederick Bird

INTERNATIONAL BUSINESS AND THE CHALLENGES OF POVERTY IN THE DEVELOPING WORLD

INTERNATIONAL BUSINESSES AND THE DILEMMAS OF DEVELOPMENT: Case Studies in South Africa, Madagascar, Pakistan, South Korea, Mexico and Columbia

THE MUTED CONSCIENCE: MORAL SILENCE AND THE PRACTICE OF ETHICS IN BUSINESS

GOOD MANAGEMENT: Business Ethics in Action

Also by Manuel Velasquez

BUSINESS ETHICS

Just Business Practices in a Diverse and Developing World

Essays on International Business and Global Responsibilities

Edited by
Frederick Bird and Manuel Velasquez

First published 2006 by
PALGRAVE MACMILLAN
Houndmills, Basingstoke, Hampshire RG21 6XS and
175 Fifth Avenue, New York, N.Y. 10010
Companies and representatives throughout the world

PALGRAVE MACMILLAN is the global academic imprint of the Palgrave
Macmillan division of St. Martin's Press, LLC and of Palgrave Macmillan Ltd.
Macmillan® is a registered trademark in the United States, United Kingdom
and other countries. Palgrave is a registered trademark in the European
Union and other countries.

ISBN 13: 978–1–4039–2130–7   hardback
ISBN 10: 1–4039–2130–X   hardback

This book is printed on paper suitable for recycling and made from fully
managed and sustained forest sources.

A catalogue record for this book is available from the British Library.

Library of Congress Cataloging-in-Publication Data
Just business practices in a diverse and developing world : essays on
international business and global responsibility / edited by Frederick Bird
and Manuel Velasquez.
        p. cm.
    Includes bibliographical references and index.
    ISBN 1–4039–2130–X
    1. Social responsibliity of business–Developing countries. 2. International
business enterprises–Moral and ethical aspects–Developing countries.
3. Business ethics. I. Bird, Frederick B. (Frederick Bruce), 1938– II. Velasquez,
Manuel G.

HD60.5.D44J87 2006
174'.4–dc22

                                                                2005056374

10   9   8   7   6   5   4   3   2   1
15   14   13   12   11   10   09   08   07   06

Printed and bound in Great Britain by
Antony Rowe Ltd, Chippenham and Eastbourne

Contents

**Part III   Acting Responsibly in the World As It Is and
As We Hope It Will Become**   197

Preface

Today more people worldwide than ever before enjoy comfort and affluence, yet one in three human beings lives in poverty. Though globally interconnected, our world is enormously heterogeneous, not only in religions, political ideologies and ethnic customs, but also in terms of the diverse settings in which people work to support themselves and their families. People work in rural and urban areas, as part of industrialized and pre-industrialized economies. At the same time we live in a world where more people than ever before live out their work lives in businesses as organized social institutions, and where businesses play increasingly influential roles in almost all societies.

Over the past six years we have been conducting research to explore ways in which businesses operating internationally manage their relationships with local cultures and social economies in developing areas, and the possible ways in which these businesses could promote local development while pursuing their own legitimate objectives. We have conducted this research primarily through case studies of particular firms in specific developing areas. Together with a large team of co-researchers, we have conducted studies of more than four dozen businesses in 20 countries. In each study we have attempted initially to gain a good historical sense of the conditions of each developing area as a background for understanding the possibilities and limitations that these firms faced. We have sought to learn from their experiences, attending as much to the ways in which they have constructively interacted with the societies in which they operated as to their mistakes and missed opportunities.

The impetus for this research project began several decades ago when I was working to help organize anti-poverty programmes in the Chinatown and the downtown areas of San Francisco in the 1960s. Later, in order to gain perspective on these local anti-poverty programmes, I wrote a very long doctoral thesis on how Americans in general had perceived and responded to poverty from 1885 to 1970. While continuing my interest in this topic and beginning initial studies of development and underdevelopment, I moved to Montreal, where I taught comparative ethics in the Religion Department at Concordia University. In the process, I became very interested in the quite different ways in which people in different religious and cultural traditions have thought about ethics. I became convinced that it was important to interpret the ethics of other peoples through their own traditions and not primarily through our own Western ethical philosophies. In the 1980s, in response to an invitation to collaborate from Jim Waters, I began to apply this general interest in the comparative, sociologically informed study of ethics to the topic of business ethics. In the early 1990s Manny Velasquez and I began conducting case-based field research on business ethics in practice as evidenced in targeted North American firms. In the meantime, Manny had become increasingly interested in international business ethics. We eventually saw that we could combine and integrate our several research interests – poverty reduction, comparative ethics, business ethics and international business ethics – through the kind of research we eventually initiated six years ago.

This research has been furthered by organizing a team or network of researchers who were prepared to conduct case-based field research investigations for particular developing areas, where they had interests, contacts and linguistic abilities. Eventually, an international network of 36 researchers from 12 countries has participated in this project. They have conducted studies of more than 50 firms in 20 countries. In order to foster collaboration and shared understanding, we have organized five research workshops hosted by Concordia University, as well as one co-hosted by the Centre for the study of International Businesses at Dalhousie University in Halifax, Nova Scotia.

The members of this research team have thus far published two books of case studies with Palgrave Macmillan, based on research in Nigeria, Uganda, Ghana, South Africa and Madagascar in Africa; in Pakistan, Vietnam and South Korea in Asia; and in Guyana, Colombia, Guatemala, Mexico and Northern Canada in the Americas. Our research group expects to publish two further volumes of case studies through the *Journal of Business Ethics*, extending the research as well to studies in Brazil, Chile, Sudan, Malaysia, Indonesia and Fiji.

I would like to thank all of the following people who have been connected with this research team and network: Sylvie Babarik, Dr Thomas Beschorner, Dr Ding Bocheng, Dr Hevina Dashwood, Dr Russell Daye, Magda Donia-Sousa, Dr William Flanagan, Dr Titus Fossgard-Moser, Dr Margaret Griesse, Rifai Pipip Hasan, Dr Stewart Herman, Dr Stephanie Hiss, Dr William Holder, Dr Bakr Ibrahim, Dr Jan Jorgensen, Katherine Jorgensen, Dr Bassem Khalifa, Dr Farzad Khan, Dr Peter Koslowski, Dr Elise Kotze, Dr Kobus Kotze, Dr David Krueger, Jean-Baptiste Litrico, Dr Terri Lituchy, Jacqui MacDonald, Dr Alhaji Marong, Marco Mingarelli, Ander Riel Muller, Ida Mutoigo, Dr Rabia Naguib, Dr Robert Nixon, Dr Nelson Phillips, Brenda Plant, Dr Bill Puplampu, Dr Emmanuel Raufflet, Dr Samuel Sejjaaka, Dr Joseph Smucker, Dr Manuel Velasquez, Dr William Westley, Dr Gail Whiteman and Dr John Williams.

I would especially like to thank Martine Montandon and Munit Merid, the secretaries at the Religion Department of Concordia University, for their assistance in helping to organize this research team and the workshops we held. I would like to thank Audrey Bean and Fred Louder for their invaluable assistance preparing these manuscripts for publication. Finally, I would like to thank the Social Sciences and Humanities Research Council of Canada for their generous financial support for this research project.

Frederick Bird

Foreword by Dr Kirk Hanson

The rise of China and India, as well as the emergence of the Southern Hemisphere as an economic power, will shift the global economic paradigm and assumptions that have driven the global economy in the last half of the 20th century. The United States and Western Europe, which have recently dominated the global economy, will share influence with these new powers and later may well be dominated by them. The dominance of western global corporations will be challenged by the rise of powerful Chinese and Indian corporations, by new alliances of corporations and economic interests in other parts of Asia and in Southern regions assumed by some to be permanently 'at the bottom of the pyramid'.

Similarly, 20th century ethical paradigms about the role of the corporation in the world will be supplanted by new 21st century formulations. The debate over global ethical standards and the search for 'a global ethic' has been, arguably, dominated by the intellectual traditions of Western civilization, most recently Enlightenment thinking. During the past 20 years, Asian scholars and political and economic leaders have resisted purely Western thinking about ethics, human rights and social justice. In the 21st century, ethical studies grounded solely in Western thinking will be challenged as never before by religious and philosophical perspectives of Hinduism, Confucianism and Islam, and even by a resurgent Christianity of the Southern Hemisphere. The authors of the essays in this book take these possibilities seriously.

The authors seek to advance the dialogue regarding ethics and economics beyond questions regarding how Western and Enlightenment formulations of human rights, or international codes of behaviour composed by moral activists and corporate executives exclusively from Western civilization, should guide corporations. Whether future attempts will reach back to a pre-Enlightenment natural law tradition, to various forms of justice analysis, to a melding of religious moral traditions, or to other sources is not as clear as is the central insight that we must seek for new ways of thinking about ethics in a truly global society.

The role of religion in global economic, military and communication systems is the focus of increasing scholarly focus.[1] Religious traditions and sensibilities are being encountered daily by corporations seeking to do business in countries with religious traditions quite unlike our own. The worldwide firestorm over the publication of cartoons of the Muslim Prophet Mohammad well illustrate this. The moral settings of individual countries are unique and belie simple assumptions that the world – or ethical theory – are 'flat'.[2]

While speaking to Chinese executives last year about why they should embrace certain international codes of conduct, it was suddenly clear to me that the integration of Chinese companies into global economy, in part accomplished by their adoption of international codes, is but a way-station to the development of something more revolutionary, more of a paradigmatic break with our current ways of thinking about global ethical corporate behaviour.

By the middle of the 21st century, Chinese and Indian companies may dominate the globe. At a minimum, their financial and economic power will rival that of American and Western European companies. These new companies, joined by others located in a resurgent Southern Hemisphere, will drive a new ethical synthesis about global ethics and about the global ethical behaviour of business and nation-states. This book is an important step in the creation of the new synthesis made necessary by these developments.

Notes

1. See, for example, Hanson, Eric O. (2006) *Religion and Politics in the International System Today* (New York: Cambridge University Press).
2. See Friedman, Thomas L. (2005) *The World is Flat: A Brief History of the 21st Century* (New York: Farrar, Strauss and Giroux).

List of Contributors

Sylvie Babarik received her BA at McGill University in Montreal, where she majored in Political Science. She is currently completing a master degree's in Religious Studies at Concordia University in Montreal. Between August 2001 and May 2002 she spent nine months in Guatemala working for COVERCO, where she edited and translated reports, and coached factory monitors on reporting techniques. In addition to her studies and work in labour rights, she has been working as a freelance journalist since 1997.

Frederick Bird holds the Concordia University (Montreal) Research Chair in Comparative Ethics; for the 2005–2006 academic year he is on leave from Concordia and teaching at the University of Wisconsin in Madison. Besides co-editing the three volumes of this series, he is the author of *The Muted Conscience: Moral Silence and the Practice of Ethics in Business* (1996, 2002) and co-author of *Good Management: Business Ethics in Practice* (1990). Among his numerous published articles are 'Early Christianity as an Unorganized Ecumenical Movement' (2002), 'Good Governance' (2001), 'Justice and Empowerment' (1999), 'Moral Universals as Cultural Realities' (1996), and 'How Do Religions Affect Moralities?' (1989). Dr Bird is a graduate of Harvard College, Harvard Divinity School, and the Graduate Theological Union in Berkeley, California. In the 1960s he helped organize anti-poverty programmes in downtown San Francisco.

Hevina S. Dashwood is Associate Professor in the department of Political Science, Brock University, St. Catharines, Ontario. Her research and publications have been primarily in the area of international development, with a focus on Africa. She is the author of *Zimbabwe: The Political Economy of Transformation* (University of Toronto Press, 2000). Her current research on Canadian mining companies is being funded through a research grant from the Social Sciences and Humanities Research Council of Canada.

Russell Daye is a minister of the United Church of Canada serving in Halifax, Nova Scotia. In 2002 he received a PhD in comparative religious ethics from Concordia University in Montreal for his research on South Africa's reconciliation process. From 2002 to 2004 he taught ethics and theology at the Pacific Theological College and worked with the federal government and NGOs in Fiji on that country's reconciliation process. He has also lectured at Concordia University and McGill University, Montreal. He is the author of *Political Forgiveness: Lessons from South Africa* (Orbis Books, 2004) and a number of published papers on post-conflict reconciliation and the role of multinational corporations in the developing world.

Kirk Hanson is Director of the Markalla Center for Applied Ethics at Santa Clara University, California.

Joseph Smucker is Emeritus and Adjunct Professor in the department of Sociology and Anthropology at Concordia University in Montreal. He obtained his PhD from Michigan State University. His research and publications have been primarily in the areas of industrialization, economic development, management philosophies and labour markets. He is the author of *Industrialization in Canada* (1980), editor (with Axel van den Berg) of *The Sociology of Labour Markets* (1997), and co-editor with Frederick Bird and Emmanuel Raufflet of *International Business and the Dilemmas of Development* (2004), the second volume of this series.

Manuel Velasquez is Charles J. Dirksen Professor of Business Ethics at Santa Clara University, where he holds appointments in the department of Management and the department of Philosophy. Dr Velasquez is Past President of the Society for Business Ethics. He is the author of *Business Ethics: Concepts and Cases* (6th edition, 2005), as well as numerous articles and cases studies; his current research is focused on international business ethics.

Introduction

Frederick Bird and Manuel Velasquez

International businesses operating in economically developing areas face a number of challenges. These areas experience very high rates of poverty and malnutrition. More than half of the population in these areas lives in poverty, defined as income of less than $2 per day per person. Literacy levels are lower and mortality rates higher than in more developed parts of the world. The physical and social infrastructures are much less advanced. Moreover, catching up with the world's economically developed areas is not a simple matter, since the organized structures for public administration are typically weaker, credit is difficult to obtain and public debt levels are high. Although, to be sure, the economies of a number of developing areas – especially those in East and South Asia and parts of Latin America – have grown during the last third of the 20th century, the situation of the least developed areas has not been promising. The economies of these areas – many rural areas in the most populated Asian countries like China, India, Bangladesh, Pakistan and Indonesia, most Sub-Saharan Africa, targeted regions in Latin American countries and slums areas all over the world – have not prospered.

International businesses seem to be well positioned to make a difference in these areas.[1] They already have operations in many developing areas. Compared with many of the governments and local businesses found in developing areas, international businesses seem to possess access to extensive resources and power. The largest transnational businesses – firms like British Petroleum, IBM, Wal-Mart, Royal Dutch/Shell and Allianz – have annual budgets greatly in excess of most developing countries. Of the 100 largest economies in the world, half are represented by countries and half by businesses.[2] International businesses have access to markets and technologies that can be utilized to help developing areas expand their own economies. They provide contexts in which workers from developing areas can develop personal and business skills. They are in position to create jobs and increase tax revenues. Today foreign direct investment transfers considerably larger revenues to developing areas than are provided by foreign aid and private-sector charity (Culpeper and Whiteman, 1998). International businesses today possess considerable resources in the form of wealth, organizational know-how, international liaisons and access to technological innovations. These resources are sufficient to affect the populations and economies of many developing areas in ways that can make a difference for good or ill.

The critical questions turn on how international businesses will now choose to utilize their capacity to make a difference in developing areas. Will they continue to increase their investments? And will they do so in constructive ways responsive to the diverse cultural settings in which they find themselves?

In answer to the first question, some economists have observed a general reluctance to invest in the most impoverished areas. This reluctance stems from perceptions that assume the return on investment in these areas is lower, governments less stable and operations less secure (Group of Lisbon, 1995, ch. 2). Because those areas that are least interconnected internationally are also among the most impoverished in the world (Legrain, 2002, ch. 2), a strong argument can be made that it is important to find ways of attracting international businesses to work in these areas. A number of recent studies have demonstrated how businesses can succeed while operating in culturally diverse, low-income regions (Fairbanks and Lindsay, 1997). Citing numerous examples, Forstater, MacDonald and Raynard (2002) illustrate how businesses can make profits by engaging the poor in developing areas as consumers, employees and entrepreneurs. Citing other well-researched cases, Prahalad (2005) argues that businesses can make their fortunes in developing countries, so long as they use their imaginations and remain responsive to local circumstances. Many international firms will, no doubt, continue to invest in these areas simply because they seek minerals, agricultural products and inexpensive labour especially found in these areas.

What matters most, then, is the manner in which international businesses establish their operations in developing areas. In answer to this question, many critics assume that international businesses cannot be trusted to invest in these areas in constructive ways.

Just as the British and Dutch East India companies exercised sovereign authority over large parts of the Indian subcontinent and Indonesia in the 18th and 19th centuries, so in the 20th century firms like Union Minière in the Congo, the United Fruit Company in Guatemala and Ranger Oil in Angola have directly intervened to influence political processes (Drohan, 2003, ch. 4, 7; Litvin, 2003, ch. 1, 2, 4). In important but less overt ways, international businesses exert indirect influence in developing areas by the ways their operations affect domestic prices, labour markets and inter-group relations. In dozens of locales, the presence of international firms has aggravated income inequalities, occasioned speculative labour migrations, exacerbated inter-tribal conflicts, polluted environments and encouraged corruption. In many areas, these firms have acted to shape public policies to their own advantage by lobbying to gain favourable tax rates, tax credits, access to mineral rights and right-of-way concessions. In a number of areas they have aligned themselves with autocratic regimes by using government troops to meet their security needs.

Many critics of international businesses regard such questionable actions as typical, given the basic character of most international businesses. Bakan (2004) makes a strong case for distrusting any and all corporations. A corporation, he argues, is a business institution that is legally designed to 'pursue relentlessly and without exception its own self interest regardless of the often harmful consequences it might cause to others'. He further maintains that all corporations are characterized by '[an] obsession with profits and share prices, greed, lack of concern for others and a penchant for breaking the rules'. They are 'compelled to cause harm, when the benefit of doing so outweighs the cost' (pp. 1, 58, 60).

While fully recognizing that international businesses have aggravated the situation in many developing areas, the essays in this book assume that international businesses can act constructively in some settings. By virtue of their direct presence, or through their partnerships and supply chains, international businesses have created millions of jobs; they have paid royalties and taxes, supported local enterprises, provided settings for workers to learn new skills, transferred advanced technologies and have thus helped variously to foster economic growth in developing areas. Nor are they entirely free to 'pursue relentlessly and without exception' their own self-interest. As societies have industrialized, most businesses have been steadily subjected to an increasing number of governmental regulations regarding working conditions of their employees, minimum wages, external audits of their finances, truth in packaging laws regarding their products and advertising, pollution standards regarding their wastes and so forth. Indeed, most businesses, in practice, probably do not define their best interests as enterprises as narrowly as Bakan assumes; rather they variously pursue their best interests by seeking to realize the distinct purposes that they are in business to realize – producing, extracting, marketing, serving, educating and so forth – and by seeking to conserve and enhance their overall assets. Although they often invoke the highly ideological rhetoric of profit-making, most businesses pursue this aim along with many others. In practice, firms variously seek to measure how well they are realizing their best interests by gauging returns on investments, productivity, share prices, market share and the realization of other particular purposes. From this perspective, profit-seeking is an indirect (though not always accurate) general measure of how well businesses are utilizing their assets over time. Over the long haul, most boards and executives know that to realize their best interests they must find ways of gaining the most effective long-term working relationships with their stakeholders – workers, suppliers, creditors, managers, partners, community groups, consumers and governments – as well as with their investors.

As to the role of international businesses in developing areas, it seems reasonable to assume that, in ways not greatly different from most humans, these firms are capable of both morally responsible and irresponsible actions. If we hope to understand both the possibilities and limitations of what international businesses can do in developing areas, it is probably best not to demonize them, nor to regard them as morally neutral; neither to overlook their possibilities nor to expect too much of them. It helps to recall that they are in various ways legally regulated and challenged by advocacy groups and unions. They are also reminded from time to time to pursue the overall best interests of their organizations as a whole, rather than the private interests of particular executives. Understood in these terms, international businesses can make a difference.

Nonetheless, in order to make a constructive difference in developing areas, international businesses must find ways of operating within cultural and economic contexts quite different from those found in developed European countries. Many employees in these settings have had little experience working in relation to time-clocked schedules. Negotiations typically proceed through a gradually unfolding sense of personal relationships rather than by the point-form logic of contractual stipulations. Working environments are often structured more in terms of personal authority and patrimonial largesse than in terms of bureaucratic rules. Economic infrastructures in the form of regular commercial exchanges as well as banking and credit systems are frequently underdeveloped. As a result, international firms are challenged to find new ways of operating, which both link with the diverse institutional and cultural patterns they meet in these areas and yet are consistent with the overall policies of their organizations.

While conducting research on more than 50 different internationally connected businesses, we have learned a good deal both about the practices of particular firms as well as the opportunities and difficulties of specific developing areas. In others books we have reported on these findings.[3] The essays in this volume reflect more generally on some of cross-cutting themes that emerged as part of this research. The book is divided into three parts, each of which covers a distinct challenge that seems to be especially important in determining whether international businesses in developing areas are in a position to make a constructive difference.

The first challenge has to do with balancing the need to respond to and respect local customs and moral conventions while still operating with a common perspective about the responsible ways of engaging in business. Many international businesses have complicated their operations in developing areas either by failing to take account of local cultural values or by simply yielding to apparent local customs in ways that diverged seriously from core corporate guidelines. The apartheid regime in South Africa occasioned this kind of dilemma for many international firms doing business there. Was there any alternative between divesting and accepting *de facto* the apartheid rules as the laws and customs of the country? The essays in Part I explore ways that businesses operating in diverse cultures can take account of cultural differences while also continuing to operate in terms of common points of reference. Without either insisting on relative or absolute norms, these essays both express and advocate the use of three complementary strategies for balancing these contrasting concerns.

The first strategy is to foster genuine, respectful, attentive, reciprocating communications with employees, partners, community groups and government representatives in developing areas. The second strategy involves learning from the experiences of other firms and precedents established by regional and international agreements. The third strategy counsels businesses to begin to identify their basic ethical responsibilities in terms of particular valued ends or 'goods', and then to recognize that people can follow somewhat different norms or rules while still working to promote these ethical values.

The second challenge that these businesses face is to find ways of balancing their social responsibilities with their business interests. Many international businesses, as well as many critics of these firms, identify these responsibilities and interests as separate concerns. These essays take an alternative perspective. In particular, they look at the responsibilities of international businesses from the perspective of developing areas. From this perspective, what often matters most is the way these businesses add economic value by creating jobs and supporting local commerce. The essays in Part II assume that the nature of these responsibilities will change over time as the relationships between international businesses and the government of a given country changes, as the social role of the government evolves and as businesses themselves alter their interactions with the local society. These essays argue that the initial social responsibilities of firms are to their varied stakeholders, without whose ongoing interactions they cannot operate; these social responsibilities are interwoven with their business interests. In addition, however, international businesses possess social responsibilities occasioned by the way they are embedded in the societies in which they operate: (a) legal duties as beneficiaries of legal systems that provide the public context for their operations; (b) social obligations as contractual partners of governments; and (c) civic responsibilities as beneficiaries of existing public order. In many cases international firms have decided to assume their social responsibilities more vigorously because they realized this was a better way to manage their risks as well as their reputations. However as they identify and pursue their social responsibilities, these firms also face the additional challenge of monitoring their own practices, not only to track their own operations effectively but also to build social capital by identifying and learning from their mistakes. The last two essays in Part II explore different strategies for conducting these kinds of social and ethical audits.

A third challenge arises out of clashes between idealists who demand that international business in developing areas should give priority to social responsibility and the realists who are conscious of the larger obstacles, difficulties and constraints which these businesses face. Often idealistic critics and realistic defenders of the status quo talk past each other. The problem is that both tend to adopt a too restrictive view of current realities. The essays in Part III variously address these concerns. Although written from perspectives that seem alternatively pragmatic or visionary, as a whole these essays call for a larger understanding of the world as we find it in order to help bring into being a world less unbalanced and more just.

While assuming that international businesses should act primarily as businesses and not as social welfare agencies, the essays in this book explore ways that businesses can make a constructive difference by developing their assets, responding to their opportunities and working collaboratively with their stakeholders. As they are read together, these essays also demonstrate the advantage of encouraging continuing conversations between sociological analyses of the situations businesses find themselves in and ethical protests and challenges to operate businesses more humanely. Rather than complaining about these strongly different views and attempting to mute them, it makes sense to view these exchanges as provocative and potentially instructive.

These three challenges facing international businesses as they operate in developing countries correspond to three perennial challenges that any viable ethic must address. First, it must be able to articulate moral standards that allow people to act responsively to contextual and historically contingent circumstances, while maintaining a basic common moral perspective that remains authoritative for all. This ongoing challenge has been vari-ously debated by those who favour more principled or more situational approaches to ethics; by those who, like Habermas (1993), distinguish between ethics as such, which is universalistic, and pragmatic applications, which are contextual. Second, a viable ethic must find ways of balancing categorical moral claims (i.e., that people ought to act in certain ways pre-eminently out of respect for such claims) with the ulterior benefits of acting morally. Kant, who insisted that people ought to act morally strictly out of a sense of moral obligation, also recognized in his *Critique of Practical Reason* (1788) that a viable ethic also made implicit promises that life would go well for those who so acted. He ultimately invoked belief in God, whose existence could not be demonstrated in rational terms, as the assurance for this promise. Although Kant rejected their solutions, both Stoics and Utilitarians provide alternative ways of balancing these claims and promises.[4] Third, a viable ethic must also find ways of making it seem credible that moral programmes they favour can work to transform the world as it is. Ideals that cannot connect with realities remain figments of imagination. Any viable ethic must find ways of connecting the world as we find it to the world as we hope it to become.

Notes

1. With reference to developing areas and countries, we use the term 'international businesses' to refer to any local firms connected internationally with other businesses either as subsidiaries, partners or suppliers.
2. These data are cited in an unpublished essay by Wesley Cragg (2005).
3. Some of these case studies have appeared in the two volumes already published in this series: *International Businesses and the Challenges of Poverty in the Developing World*, F. Bird and S. Herman (eds) (2004); and *International Business and the Dilemmas of Development*, F. Bird, E. Raufflet and J. Smucker (eds) (2005). Others will appear in two forthcoming special issues of the *Journal of Business Ethics*.
4. For further discussion, see Green (1978) and Bird (1990).

References

Bakan, J. (2004) *The Corporation: The Pathological Pursuit of Profit and Power* (Toronto: Penguin Canada).

Bird, F. (1990) 'How Religions Affect Moralities: A Comparative Analysis', *Social Compass*, vol. 37(3), pp. 291–314.

Bird, F. (2004) 'International Trade as a Vehicle for Reducing Poverty: The Body Shop's Community Trade Programme', in F. Bird and S. Herman (eds), *International Businesses and the Challenges of Poverty in the Developing World* (London: Palgrave Macmillan), chapter 12.

Bird, F. (2005) 'Preparing to Mine: The Rio Tinto Venture in Madagascar', in F. Bird, E. Raufflet and J. Smucker (eds), *International Business and the Dilemmas of Development* (London: Palgrave Macmillan), chapter 6.

Cragg, W. (2005) 'Toward the Creation of a Canadian Business Ethics Research Network', unpublished report, *Social Science and Humanities Strategic Research Cluster Design Project*, Toronto: York University.

Culpeper, R. and Whiteman, G. (1998) 'The Corporate Stake in Social Responsibility', in M. Hibler and R. Beamish (eds), *Canadian Development Report 1998: Canadian Corporations and Social Responsibility* (Ottawa: North-South Institute).

Drohan, M. (2003) *Making a Killing: How and Why Corporations Use Armed Force to do Business* (Toronto: Random House Canada).

Fairbanks, M. and Lindsay, S. (1997) *Plowing the Sea: Nurturing the Hidden Sources of Growth in the Developing World* (Boston, MA: Harvard University Press).

Forstater, M., MacDonald, J. and Raynard, P. (2002) *Business and Poverty: Bridging the Gap* (London: The Prince of Wales International Business Leaders Forum).

Green, R. M. (1978) *Religious Reason: The Rational and Moral Basis of Religious Belief* (New York: Oxford University Press).

The Group of Lisbon (1995) *Limits to Competition* (Cambridge, MA: MIT Press).

Habermas, J. (1993) *Justification and Application: Remarks on Discourse Ethics* (Cambridge, MA: MIT Press).

Kant, I. (1788) *Critique of Practical Reason* translated by L. W. Beck (Indianapolis: Bobbs Merrill Educational Publishing).

Legrain, P. (2002) *Open World: The Truth About Globalisation* (London: Abacus).

Litvin, D. (2003) *Empires of Profit: Commerce, Conquest and Corporate Responsibility* (New York: Texere).

Prahalad, C. K. (2005) *The Fortune at the Bottom of the Pyramid: Eradicating Poverty through Profits* (Upper Saddle River, NJ: Wharton School Publishing).

Part I

Searching for Common Standards in a Morally Diverse World

Introduction

Frederick Bird and Manuel Velasquez

International businesses operate in countries all over the world with diverse cultures and deeply different moral traditions. Ethical ideas are attached to widely different religious and political systems, legal traditions and philosophical ideas. These moral cultures hold clashing views regarding all sorts of issues from the legitimacy of abortion to the use of indentured workers, from ideas about acceptable interest rates to the place of women in the workforce, from assumptions about legitimate inequalities to beliefs about professionally manageable conflicts of interests. In some areas of the world, especially in farming areas, for example, it is acceptable for children to work alongside their parents, though outsiders might regard this practice as intolerable. Many feel it is acceptable to raise the levels of executive compensations greatly in excess of the increases in the overall productivity of their firms, though critics might strongly disagree. Many businessmen believe that as long as they adhere to local laws they can legitimately flare gases or pollute streams, even though these practices may be against the law in their home countries. Other business people feel these practices are unconscionable. Existing ethical traditions are often not much help in resolving these kinds of conflicts, because these traditions differ in so many fundamental ways, not only with respect to practical norms but also in their views of the ultimate ends of human life and what constitutes valid and reliable reasoning about these ethical principles and human ends (McIntyre, 1988).[1]

This ethical diversity seems inescapable. As they develop their feelings of social identity and even their own particular understandings of common sense, human beings have been deeply affected by specific moral traditions. In modern industrialized countries, widely held liberal secular views have not gone unchallenged by those who uphold or are influenced by sectarian beliefs and traditional religious values. It is within the context of these distinct moral cultures that people typically gain and reinforce their sense of conscience, develop moral vocabularies and cultivate their social loyalties. Some moral cultures are thinly spread over wide areas, like political liberalism or the conventional economic ethic associated with free-enterprise market systems. Other moral cultures are much more deeply embedded in particular populations, ethnic groups and religions. People may well be influenced by several moral cultures at once. Furthermore, moral cultures are rarely monolithic. Dissent and divisions exist within almost all moral cultures.

For long periods of time, in many areas, moral diversity has not constituted much of an ethical problem. People lived in keeping with their own mores and typically either ignored, disdained or vaguely tolerated other moral ideas, most of which had little real impact on their everyday lives. To be sure this situation changed for conquered peoples who were forced to submit to the standards of their conquerors but these are instances of moral imposition not moral diversity. Moral diversity has become more problematic to the extent that people from different cultures are obliged regularly to interact as fellow citizens within multi-ethnic and multilingual states and empires, whether as trading partners connected by international commerce, as immigrants from foreign cultures or as ideological opponents in culturally pluralistic political communities.

Moral diversity occasions a number of difficulties. It gives rise to seemingly intractable moral disagreements which, like current debates over same-sex marriage and abortion, seem very difficult, if not impossible, to resolve. Moral diversity also gives rise to the notion that all moral ideas are in some sense accidental or arbitrary – the social constructs of the community in which one happens to have been raised, or philosophical fads that have caught the fancy of intellectuals, the social elite or some other minority. This apparently contingent diversity encourages some people to adopt a 'consumer' orientation toward ethics, viewing all received moral traditions as collections of more or less appealing and compelling ideas among which people may feel free to make a personal choice. In the process, fundamental moral ideas may well lose the authority they seem to possess when they are regarded as grounded in reason, ancient traditions, human nature or divine revelation.

Cultural relativists counsel us to accept this moral diversity as the basic human moral situation. For example, early 20th-century anthropologists and sociologists like Ruth Benedict (1934) and William Graham Sumner (1906) point to the wide variation in social conventions and folkways. They argue that attempts to identify moral universals are, for the most part, efforts to impose particular moral ideas on others. More recently, Clifford Geertz, in his studies of Indonesia, notes that the ideas about justice and law found in Hindu, Muslim and Malay traditions (all of which survive in contemporary Java) differ not only in how they define basic norms but also in their conceptions of the juridical practices that might reliably be used to resolve practical conflicts about these matters (Geertz, 1983, ch. 8). Geertz argues that we cannot hope to solve the many current problems this diversity aggravates by seeking to identify some supposed lowest common denominator of moral values – what he calls 'bloodless generalization' (Geertz, 1963; 1973, ch. 1, 6, 10). Rather, he urges that 'through comparison ... of incomparables' we can attempt to foster relevant problem-solving communication (Geertz, 1983, p. 233).

Taking this suggestion seriously, most international businesses recognize that they cannot effectively operate in countries with different cultures without an appreciation of cultural differences. They cannot reach viable business agreements unless they make the effort to understand what particular gestures, phrases and customs mean to those with whom they are negotiating (Adler, 1981; Hampden-Turner and Trompenaars, 1993; see also chapter 10). Many international businesses have therefore made efforts to learn, for example, about occasions when they are expected, as a matter of courtesy, to make gifts to business partners, and other occasions when such gifts might instead be interpreted as inappropriate attempts to buy influence. They have sought as well to learn the culturally appropriate ways of dealing with political leaders, marketing retail products, negotiating with indigenous elders, or even declaring their earnings for tax purposes (Velasquez, 1996).

International businesses, however, cannot address all of the issues occasioned by moral diversity simply by endeavouring to be 'culturally sensitive'. They cannot realistically operate with markedly different standards in every country where they do business; nor can they condone practices their own moral systems deem blatantly unacceptable, even if such are seemingly acceptable in the local culture – such as forced labour, off-budget gifts extorted by public officials, or overt discrimination against women.[2] They need to develop some common frame of reference, which will still allow them to exercise cultural sensitivity in fitting ways. To re-state this challenge in fuller terms, international businesses must find coherent ways of addressing ethical issues that allow them at the same time to operate at two levels: (a) invoking common standards and points of reference; and (b) identifying, appreciating, sometimes criticizing but still working with diverse local moral traditions that are nonetheless in keeping with these common elements.

A number of authors have proposed ways of addressing this challenge. One approach has been to set forth a universally relevant foundational ethic, which might serve as a basis for evaluating, criticizing or appreciating various culturally specific ethics. In practice, proponents of this approach have formulated a new ethic, or else reformulated an old ethic as a comprehensive system by which to identify central moral affirmations, which in turn can serve appropriately to appreciate, evaluate or critique other moral ideas.[3] Brown (2004) has attempted to develop such a comprehensive ethic, which looks at business practices from an environmental perspective in relation to the traditional belief in reverence for life. A number of advocacy groups have championed ideas about human rights as providing a moral credo for businesses operating in diverse cultures. In the 1990s, Donaldson and Dunfee worked to construct a comprehensive ethic for businesses in relation to social-contract theory. A recent version of their model proposes a number of vaguely defined, universally valid 'hypernorms', set forth as procedural, structural and substantive standards. Although Donaldson and Dunfee do not name or explicate these standards, they argue that such standards can be presumed to exist and can be inferred, in practice, from various international codes and statements of principles, which make over-lapping references to the common normative standards against bribery, gender discrimination, intentional deception, unsafe working conditions and other unjust practices. Donaldson and Dunfee then argue that such hypernorms can be applied in evaluating local moral customs. Although they acknowledge the importance of the diverse ethical traditions with which people identify so strongly in local cultures, they reject as inauthentic all local moralities which are either not accepted by majorities, are not consonant with their hypernorms, or do not allow for principled dissent (Donaldson and Dunfee, 1999). Many local moralities are thereby in practice dismissed, including a large number that call for differential treatment of women as well as all those (such as existentialism and many other personal ethics) embraced only by minorities.

In practice, comprehensive ethics manage the tension between local moral cultures and common standards by emphasizing the priority of the latter. Relativists emphasize the priority of the former. They tend to regard statements of comprehensive ethics as expressions of moral imperialism. In any case, as Walzer (1994) has argued, people ordinarily think and communicate about moral issues by using the vocabularies and sentiments attached to these local moral cultures. In contrast, the common elements found as aspects of these local moral systems are culturally and morally thin. Walzer argues that it is a mistake to think we can invoke these common elements as moral absolutes around which we can easily develop strong ethical convictions among diverse peoples. At best, people from diverse cultures can invoke these common elements to facilitate communication (Walzer, 1994).

The essays in this book address the moral issues facing international businesses neither from the perspective of comprehensive ethics, nor from a relativist standpoint. All of the essays take the view that although there are common values that can be used to evaluate the moral appropriateness of local practices, nevertheless because diverse cultures can achieve these values through diverse moral practices and institutions, these diverse local practices must be taken seriously as morally legitimate approaches to the common values. The two following essays seek in different ways to identify elements that might be included in the common values that can readily and practically be utilized to address the moral issues faced by international businesses in diverse cultural settings. Each attempts also to develop an approach that recognizes the moral legitimacy of diverse local practices.

In chapter 1, 'Natural Law in International Business Ethics', Manuel Velasquez argues that utilitarianism and human rights theory, the prevalent approaches to international business ethics, are based on assumptions that are present in Western cultures but that are absent from many non-Western cultures. Labelling these approaches as 'ethnocentric', he claims that an adequate approach to cross-cultural ethics must not be based on these Western assumptions of equality and individualism. Instead, Velasquez proposes that we turn to the natural law approach to ethics that was developed prior to the rise of the modern egalitarian and individualistic culture of Western Europe and North America. Such a natural law approach, he claims, proceeds by identifying the basic human goods or purposes that are sought or realized through the social institutions of all societies and that each society seeks through its own distinct set of institutions and through the differentiated norms embedded in these institutions. These basic human goods, he argues, provide a useful and commonly available framework for evaluating some institutions as being better or worse than others; however, to the extent that a society's institutions succeed in securing the basic human goods, they must be respected as morally legitimate, no matter how different they may be from ours, or how unappealing they may be to our own moral sensibilities. The international manager, in discussion and interaction with local cultures, must understand how the institutions of such cultures can be morally legitimate.

In chapter 2, 'Justice in International Businesses', Frederick Bird attempts to articulate the outlines of a theory of justice that takes into account the fact that diverse ethical traditions have diverse views on justice by tying his account of justice to the diverse ends or purposes organizations have. Bird first distinguishes three forms of justice in terms of the basic practices business organizations engage in: justice in exchanges, justice in distribution and justice in adjudication. He argues that the end of these business practices is to enable the organization to grow its assets and realize its purposes, while enabling the parties to its various exchanges to feel that those exchanges are mutually beneficial. This implies that justice in exchanges requires that the parties to exchanges should be fully and honestly informed; that businesses should support the public goods that let them make these exchanges; and that the benefits to the parties be proportionate to their contributions, risks and efforts. Justice in the distribution of organizational resources means that resources should be distributed so as to secure the interests of the organization as a whole; that all organizational members should have equal opportunity to access organizational positions; and that resources should be fittingly and effectively used. Lastly, justice in the adjudication of intra-organizational conflicts requires that conflicts should be resolved by an appropriate use of formal due process procedures, informal resolution processes and open debate and negotiation. Bird ends by noting that 'just business practices help businesses to realize their ends as businesses'.

Without leaning too far toward foundational ethics, on one hand, or relativistic ethics, on the other, both these essays presuppose or directly employ three basic strategies for arriving at justifiable ethical positions in situations of moral diversity. As long as they are not regarded as being definitive and authoritative, these strategies will be helpful, problem-solving ways of addressing ethical issues in a world that will doubtless remain morally pluralistic.

The first strategy approaches ethics from the perspective of dialogue or discourse. If businesses are to negotiate agreements with their diverse stakeholders, including especially those, such as unions, competitors, governments or advocacy groups, with whom there may be tense relations, then they must adhere to certain basic procedural guidelines. In order to develop viable ethical positions regarding local customs that differ markedly from those back home (as Velasquez proposes), businesses need to consult with appropriate members of the local culture. They must take the time to foster reciprocating discussions, attentive to what others explicitly and implicitly say (Bird, 1996b, ch. 7).

The second strategy approaches ethics through historical precedents that differing parties might well find instructive, and possibly compelling, for both of their respective cultures. Precedents provide weighty arguments rather than absolute and definitive answers: they help identify common terms of reference; they allow parties to acknowledge shared assumptions; and they offer instructive models for thinking about issues at hand (Jonsen and Toulmin, 1988). As a major example, Velasquez cites the natural law teachings of Aquinas, which for several centuries have been effectively applied to the resolution of conflicting moral claims. Another example is the 1992 Rio Conference on sustainable development, to the principles of which many environmentally concerned business people (as well as their critics) make reference today. Still another example is the stakeholder model of the firm, with its emphasis on shared ideas, to which Bird makes reference.

The third strategy approaches ethics from what might best be described as a revised view of natural law ethics. From this perspective, the initial efforts to find common moral grounds are embodied not in attempts to identify universal norms but rather in steps to identify the valued ends or moral 'goods' toward which particular human institutions or social practices tend. Velasquez identifies these valued ends or moral goods broadly with respect to the ends of human societies: social order, knowledge and family life. These valued ends may be identified more circumspectly, as Bird does when he writes about the 'good' or best interests of businesses, interactive exchanges and the adjudications of ethical conflicts within businesses. From the perspective of this revised view of natural law ethics, moral deliberations then move on from the identification of valued ends to the recognition both of minimal expectations needed to realize and further these ends and of the diversity of ways in which these minimal requirements can be met.

Notes

1. For a much more extensive discussion of these kinds of fundamental moral differences, see Bird (1996a), ch. 6, especially pp. 99–104.
2. Klitgaard (1998) argues that one of the most insidious forms of ethnocentrism occurs when persons who ethically oppose a particular practice in their own country (such as bribery) condone the practice in a foreign country where the people regard it as acceptable. To be morally consistent, Klitgaard argues, we should voice our opposition in both contexts but withhold any judgement of moral blame in the settings where the local culture tolerates the objectionable practice.
3. One very influential example of this 'comprehensive' approach to ethics is the effort to distinguish between, on one hand, a basic economic ethic (such as the ethic associated with a utilitarian view of economics), which should govern all business practices, and, on the other hand, diverse local customs, which though they are to be respected, are to be regarded merely as the means of contextualizing this fundamental economic ethic, which remains dominant. For a philosophical critique of this ethic see Brown (2000); for its defence, see Friedman (1962) and Gilder (1981).

References

Adler, N. J. (1981) *Cross-cultural Management Bibliography, 1971–1980: A Review of Twenty-four Journals* (Montreal: McGill-Queen's University Press).

Benedict, R. (1934) *Patterns of Culture* (Boston: Houghton Mifflin).

Bird, F. (1996a) 'Moral Universals as Cultural Realities', in F. N. Brady (ed.), *Ethical Universals in International Business* (Berlin: Springer).

Bird, F. (1996b) *The Muted Conscience: Moral Silence and the Practice of Ethics in Business* (Westport, CT: Quorum Books).

Brown, P. G. (2000) *Ethics, Economics and International Relations* (Edinburgh: Edinburgh University Press).

Brown, P. G. (2004) 'Are There Any Natural Resources?', *Politics and Life Sciences*, vol. 23(1), December, pp. 11–20.

Donaldson, T. and Dunfee, T. W. (1999) *The Ties That Bind: A Social Contract Approach to Business Ethics* (Boston: Harvard Business School Press).

Friedman, M. (1962) *Capitalism and Freedom* (Chicago: University of Chicago Press).

Geertz, C. (1963) *Peddlers and Princes: Social Change and Economic Modernization in Two Indonesian Towns* (Chicago: University of Chicago Press).

Geertz, C. (1973) *The Interpretation of Cultures* (New York: Basic Books).

Geertz, C. (1983) *Local Knowledge: Further Essays in Interpretive Sociology* (New York: Basic Books).

Gilder, G. (1981) *Wealth and Poverty* (New York: Bantam Books).

Hampden-Turner, C. and Trompenaars, A. (1993) *The Seven Cultures of Capitalism: Value Systems for Creating Wealth in the United States, Japan, Germany, France, Britain, Sweden and the Netherlands* (New York: Doubleday).

Jonsen, A. R. and Toulmin, S. (1988) *The Abuse of Casuistry: A History of Moral Reasoning* (Berkeley: University of California Press).

Klitgaard, R. (1988) *Controlling Corruption* (Berkeley: University of California Press).

Sumner, W. G. (1906) *Folkways: A Study of the Sociological Importance of Usages, Manner, Customs, Mores and Morals* (Boston: Ginn and Company).

Velasquez, M. (1996) 'Ethical Relativism and the International Business Manager', in F. N. Brady (ed.), *Ethical Universals in International Business* (Berlin: Springer).

Walzer, M. (1994) *Thick and Thin: Moral Argument at Home and Abroad* (Notre Dame, IN: University of Notre Dame Press).

1

Natural Law in International Business Ethics

Manuel Velasquez

Moral diversity and the international business manager

It is a truism that business today has been globalized. Even the smallest firm in the most local market is now affected by the forces of supply and demand in distant parts of the world. The boy gathering cardboard on the streets of Mexico City is affected by the worldwide price at which cardboard is trading in the commodity markets of Japan.

While many companies today still operate completely within a single nation and export their products for sale abroad, most large companies involved in international activities are now multinational enterprises that own and operate productive assets – factories, mines, banks, design centres and the like – in several countries. Multinationals expand production into foreign countries primarily to derive the advantages of market proximity but also to exploit local cost or resource advantages as well as to overcome trade barriers.[1]

The rise of the multinational enterprise has given us a new figure: the expatriate manager who leaves his or her native culture and inserts himself or herself into a foreign host culture in order to operate a subsidiary of the company for which he or she works. There the manager comes face to face with the issue of moral diversity. Since cultures differ widely on the morality of practices such as child labour, bribery, discrimination, euthanasia, homosexuality, infanticide, nepotism, patricide, polygamy, pornography, slavery, suicide or cruelty to animals, (to name just a few), what the expatriate manager may judge to be immoral from the perspective of his or her own culture, might be viewed as morally permissible by members of his new host culture; conversely, what the manager and his home culture may see as morally permissible, the host culture may condemn as unthinkably immoral and perverse.

Moral diversity is not just a theoretical problem for the international business manager; in both the firm's internal and external environments, it creates significant managerial problems. Internally, the international manager is faced with the task of getting expatriate managers and local employees with diverse moral beliefs to communicate and work together; externally, the international manager must somehow do business in a culture where government officials require bribes, purchase agents ask for kickbacks, suppliers use forced labour or child labour, labour laws require discrimination against women and minorities or employees engage in nepotism – dealings that violate the manager's deepest moral convictions.

In many cases, of course, it is possible to run a business successfully without giving in to local norms with which one deeply disagrees; but in many other cases it is not possible, unless one goes along with the host country's moral practices. It is these hard cases that we want to talk about, cases where business can be conducted only on the condition that one engage in activities that seriously violate one's own moral convictions.

To focus our analysis, let us describe a concrete example of the sort of case we have in mind. The case is set in the decade of the 1970s in Saudi Arabia, formerly a country of Bedouin desert nomads and now the world's largest exporter of oil (Nyrop et al., 1977; Nawwab et al., 1980). Although the description of Saudi Arabian practices below is couched in the past tense, many of these practices endure to the present day.

During the 1930s, when petroleum had already become a strategic military and economic resource for the United States, Standard Oil of California (which was later joined by Texaco) founded Casoc, a subsidiary formed to drill for oil in Saudi Arabia. The company was renamed Aramco in 1944 and continued to operate under that name until 1980, when it was acquired by the Saudi Arabian government. By 1970, when the productivity of US oil fields peaked and began to decline, access to Saudi oil became an absolute necessity. During the crucial decade of the 1970s, when Standard Oil and Texaco ran Aramco, the company's managers had to operate in an Islamic culture whose practices clashed sharply with their own moral beliefs.

Saudi Arabia has been described as 'an Islamic theocracy' that does not recognize what Westerners refer to as 'the separation of church and state'.[2] The nation's legal, political and social systems then, as now, were based on Islamic law and so were accepted by Saudi citizens as divinely inspired. The government repeatedly stated that it disagreed with Western notions of moral rights and that it viewed the law of Islam as the only legitimate source of morality and of political authority. Saudi citizens were in complete agreement with these declarations. Indeed, the government could not have endured without their support and its policies were acceptable only if consistent with their strict Islamic values. According to Sandra Mackey, an American who lived in Saudi Arabia during the 1970s:

... the newly Western-educated elite continued to accept Islam as the central focus of life, contributing to the power that Islam holds over the people of Saudi Arabia. ... A Saudi's emotional identification with Islam is rooted in the fact that Islam is not just a religion, it is a civilization and a culture; it is fundamental to a Saudi's perception of who he is and what his world is about. Even with their exposure to foreign influences, the Saudis held tenaciously to their traditions defined by religion. This reality created a situation in which every move toward modernization made by the government had to be justified in religious terms. (Mackey, 1987, p. 104)

Saudi Arabia was ruled by a hereditary Muslim monarch. Throughout the decade of the 1970s the king and his princes and officials ruled through a system of public audiences where subjects presented petitions or grievances and in which the king was the ultimate decision-maker. Aside from this right to an audience, Saudis had no right to participate in the nation's political process – not, at least, as participation is understood in the West. For example, Saudis had no voice in electing their leaders, nor in the processes through which laws and regulations were established. Saudi Arabia, in fact, had no elective political institutions. The legitimacy of the government depended on the extent to which the people of Saudi Arabia believed that the monarchy had remained true to the teachings of Islam.

The judicial system of Saudi Arabia then, as now, was based on Islamic law, which does not recognize either the right to a trial by jury or by an impartial judiciary bound by Western rules of evidence and procedure. Saudi courts, instead, were staffed by Islamic judges who based their decisions on the Koran or the Hadith (sayings of the prophet Muhammad). There were no other written laws, and no appeal to legal precedents. In a criminal case, the state gathered the evidence and prosecuted the case while the accused waited in jail without bail and, often, without access to anyone. Trials were often closed to the public and defendants had no attorney. When a person was convicted of a crime for which penalties were not explicitly mentioned in the Koran, judges set sentences at their discretion. The Koran, for example, explicitly stipulates amputation of the hand for crimes of theft and execution by beheading or by stoning for more serious crimes such as rape and murder. However, when imposing sentences for less serious crimes such as adultery, drunkenness or other violations of the behavioural standards of Islam, it was up to the judge to decide how severe the flogging would be.

Saudi Arabia did not recognize the right to freedom of speech or the associated right to freedom of the press. In fact, the law expressly prohibited any criticism of Islam, a prohibition that Saudis supported.

The suppression of news in Saudi Arabia is remarkably easy since there is no perceptible public pressure on the government for disclosure. This absence of the demand for the right to know reflects the culture as much as it does the repressive nature of censorship. In a society where the self-esteem of the individual and the privacy of the family are paramount, censorship is almost self-imposed. It is secrecy, not disclosure, that is the virtue. Security for the individual, group and nation is thought to reside in unity behind stated values and ideals, not in the divisiveness created by a free press. (Mackey, 1987, p. 273)

Journalists, in their reports, had to uphold Islam, oppose atheism and promote the culture of Saudi Arabia. Government censors removed any articles they found offensive. All television and radio stations were owned by the government, which censored all programmes to remove any reference to non-Islamic religions, mention of alcohol or sexual innuendo.

Saudi society also did not recognize the Western right to freedom of religion. Although Islamic law recognizes the rights of foreigners to follow other religions, every Saudi citizen had to be Muslim and the law strictly forbade public non-Muslim religious services of any kind. The law also prohibited wearing religious symbols in public. It was and remains, a crime for a Saudi citizen to convert to another religion – a crime punishable by death.

Islamic laws and customs, at least as interpreted by the Wahhabi sect of Islam, require systematically that women be treated in ways that Westerners would characterize as discriminatory (Alireza, 1987; Mernissi, 1975; Esposito, 1982). Although women could own and inherit property it had to be managed by a male relative. Although they could receive elementary, secondary and higher education, they could not study 'male' subjects such as engineering or architecture. They could not work alongside men, nor could they be placed in managerial positions above men. All employees were segregated by sex and women, whatever their positions, were allowed to contact male clients only by telephone, letter, or through an intermediary. For a woman to wear 'immodest' clothing was punishable as a lesser crime. It was both immoral and illegal for an unmarried woman to be in the company of a single male to whom she was not related unless accompanied by an adult male relative. It was illegal for a woman to drive an automobile. In buses women had to sit in special sections and enter by the rear door. A woman could not travel within Saudi Arabia or abroad unaccompanied and when travelling had to carry a letter from her husband or father stating the reason for her travel. In court, the testimony of one man equalled that of two women.

Other groups besides women were also subjected to discrimination. Because Saudi Arabia's pool of skilled labour was relatively small, it was forced to open its borders to large numbers of foreign workers, mostly skilled workers from the United States, India, Pakistan and parts of Africa. But discrimination against these workers, particularly Africans and Asians, was widespread and explicitly sanctioned by the government. Shi'a Muslim citizens were prohibited from employment in the well-paying oil industry and had limited access to social services. Foreigners could not travel beyond the limits of the city where they were employed without their employer's permission. Nor could a foreign worker take a different job without the permission of his previous Saudi employer.

Finally, Saudi Arabia did not recognize the right of free association. Labour unions were forbidden, as were strikes or collective bargaining of any sort. As mentioned earlier, non-Muslim religious gatherings of any kind were prohibited. And women could not gather unless their meeting was supervised by an adult male.

Westerners frequently criticized many of these Saudi practices as violations of human rights, particularly of the rights cited in the United Nations Universal Declaration of Human Rights. But Saudi Arabia had deliberately abstained from voting for the Declaration in 1948 and as of July 1982 had not ratified any of the UN multilateral human rights instruments other than those against genocide and slavery (US House Foreign Affairs Committee, 1983, pp. 63n. and 622–3). The Saudis claimed that the Koran and the Hadith stipulated the basic moral relationships that should obtain among men and women and apart from these, moral standards had no validity.

The case of the American managers of Aramco is what is sometimes called a hard case – a case where the moral norms and practices of the local host culture significantly offend the international manager yet where the manager has no choice but to deal with these practices. Aramco managers had to deal with Saudi practices because the strategic importance of Saudi oil forced them to remain in Saudi Arabia and confront these moral differences. Should company managers abide by the discriminatory norms governing the treatment of women? Should the company quietly accept the government's refusal to recognize the right to freedom of speech, the right to participate in the political process, the right of free movement, the right of association, the right to unionize, the right to freedom of speech and freedom of the press and the right to a fair trial? Should the company raise objections to the punishments and police processes that in the light of Western moralities appear immorally excessive, even barbaric? Should it object to the absence of freedom of religion and the officially sanctioned persecution of minority Islamic groups such as Shi'a Muslims? Or should the company quietly condone these practices?

Ethicists have proposed two main responses to these kinds of questions: 'absolutism' and 'relativism'. The term 'absolutism' here is a technical term and does not mean excessively rigid or unenlightened. Instead, absolutism refers to any view that holds that there are certain moral principles (however enlightened those principles might be), which everyone should live by regardless of their culture, and regardless of whether all cultures recognize these principles. International managers, the absolutist would hold, must remain true to these principles (whatever they might be) and should refuse to condone behaviour that violates the principles. The relativist, on the other hand, holds that there are no moral principles that everyone everywhere should live by. According to the relativist, managers should respect and adapt to the moral norms and behaviours of the local culture since there are no grounds for preferring the manager's own morality. We will examine both of these approaches in the two following sections of this essay. We will try to show that the most prevalent forms of absolutism are mistaken, and we will argue that relativism too is deficient. Finally, we will propose a distinct way of approaching hard cases, a way that is based on what we call 'common morality'.

Absolutism and moral diversity

Ethicists who have approached issues in international business ethics generally have taken an absolutist approach. An absolutist approach to ethics is one that claims that there are certain moral standards that it is wrong for any person to transgress, even if that person's culture – or the person himself or herself – does not recognize those standards.[3] These universally valid principles are presumed to be foundational standards ('first principles'), knowable by all reasoning humans and applicable in all settings. Utilitarians, for example, claim that it is morally wrong for a person to behave in a way that is contrary to the utilitarian principle of securing 'the greatest good for the greatest number', regardless of that person's culture or morality. Proponents of human rights approaches claim that it is morally wrong for one person to violate another's rights regardless of either person's culture. We will look carefully at absolutism of the human rights variety and then, more briefly, at the utilitarian form of absolutism since, we will argue, the cross-cultural problems that plague human rights theories also debilitate utilitarian theories.

Many absolutists who have written on ethics and international business have claimed that there is a set of moral rights that are universally binding on all people everywhere and they have applied these rights to situations like that of the American managers in Saudi Arabia. This rights approach to ethics in international business is evident in the United Nations Draft 'Norms on the Responsibilities of Transnational Corporations and Other Business Enterprises with Regard to Human Rights' (2003), as well as in other international documents produced primarily by Western experts such as the OECD 'Guidelines for Multinational Enterprises' (2000) and the ILO 'Tripartite Declaration of Principles Concerning Multinational Enterprises and Social Policy' (1977). The strength of the human rights approach, of course, is that it provides the manager with a basis for evaluating the ethics of behaviours in diverse cultures: certain behaviours are wrong and should be suppressed or reformed when they violate people's human rights, regardless of the culture in which those behaviours take place. The human rights approach is an approach that some philosophers have taken when discussing international ethics in business (Shue, 1980).

A good example of a philosopher who has adopted this approach is Thomas Donaldson, who in his book *The Ethics of International Business* (1989), claims that international ethical issues can be solved by appealing to a 'minimalist' ethic consisting of ten 'fundamental international rights' which are supposed to be obligatory across all nations provided the rights are 'affordable in relation to resources, other obligations and fairness in the distribution of burdens' (Donaldson, 1989, 1992). Donaldson's preferred list of fundamental international rights includes the rights to:

1. Freedom of physical movement
2. Ownership of property
3. Freedom from torture
4. A fair trial
5. Non-discriminatory treatment
6. Physical security
7. Freedom of speech and association
8. Minimal education
9. Political participation
10. Subsistence

Donaldson argues that these principles are justified because they are the principles that would be chosen by rational individuals forging a social contract with one another.

More recently, Donaldson, in collaboration with Thomas Dunfee, added a layer of complexity to this theory. Donaldson and Dunfee argue that morality, particularly from an international perspective, should be understood as having two parts: a set of universal 'hypernorms' arrived at through a universal social contract and a set of less fundamental local norms based on local or regional social contracts (Donaldson and Dunfee, 1994). These universal hypernorms, they argue, would include the rights mentioned in Donaldson's list, while local norms would include whatever norms groups might agree to in light of their religious, philosophical, historical or other cultural characteristics. In spite of this apparent concession, however, Donaldson and Dunfee claim that such local norms must be consistent with Donaldson's preferred list of fundamental moral rights. Although some of Donaldson's own more recent writings suggest he may have qualified his views on the role of rights in international business (Donaldson, 1996), we will here consider only his and Dunfee's earlier writings as illustrative of an approach to international ethics that takes rights as basic.

Donaldson and Dunfee's moral rights standards imply the Saudi cultural practices described above are clearly and seriously immoral. Saudi Arabian cultural practices violate Donaldson's preferred rights to freedom of physical movement, a fair trial, non-discriminatory treatment, political participation and freedom of speech and association. These violations are so egregious, in fact, that it would be seriously immoral for a manager to go along with them.

But an unqualified rights approach to international ethics – like Donaldson's – carries with it several significant problems. Cultural differences place important limits both on Donaldson's attempt to articulate such universal moral rights principles and on his attempt to provide a social contract justification for them. We turn now to arguing for these claims.

The fundamental problem with the rights approach is that it is ethnocentric: it is based on the moral categories and particular conceptual framework of a particular kind of culture. To understand this ethnocentrism, consider the well-known cultural categories first researched and identified by the psychologist Geert Hofstede. Having studied some 114,000 workers in 40 different countries Hofstede argued (using factor analysis) that his data indicated the existence of four basic kinds of variations or 'dimensions' in the cultural attitudes of the workers he studied (Hofstede, 1980, 1991). Although Hofstede's study has been criticized (Kim et al., 1994) we can here presume to use his dimensions heuristically; two of these dimensions are especially important for our purposes. Hofstede found that cultures differ, first, in what he called 'power distance' or the extent to which the members of the culture accept inequality. Some nations' cultures are egalitarian and minimize status differences, while others are more authoritarian and endorse centralized and hierarchical decision-making and hierarchical status. (The United States and Australia, for example, are relatively egalitarian, while Malaysia, Mexico and Saudi Arabia tolerate, or even embrace, certain inequalities.) Second, cultures differ in terms of what he called 'individualism versus collectivism', or the extent to which the individual identifies with the group. Some cultures are collectivist and emphasize identification with groups, such as the family, tribe or nation. Others are individualistic and emphasize personal independence and freedom, the pursuit of personal goals and individual fulfilment and the nuclear family. In such a culture the individual is of supreme value and society is only a means to the fulfilment of the individual. (The United States, for example, is highly individualistic, while Saudi Arabia and Indonesia are collectivist.)

The central problem with an approach like Donaldson's is that his ten moral rights principles derive from the conceptual structure of a Western individualistic and egalitarian culture – his own local culture. Indeed, that explains why his moral rights probably feel to many readers, as they do to me, as so fundamental, so compelling and so obviously valid that everyone should submit to them; yet they are ethnocentric.

First, Donaldson's moral rights principles derive from an American culture that is deeply individualistic, a culture with its roots in the individualism of 19th century England and America and one which is based on assumptions about self-identity, individual autonomy and the priority of the individual that are alien to collectivist cultures. Rights principles like Donaldson's imply that individuals have entitlements and that these entitlements derive not from the group but from the individual's own inherent dignity and thus permit the individual to seek his or her own interests free from interference by the community. The very notion of an individual right necessarily assumes that individuals have an identity, a sense of who they are, which is independent of their place in any community and that the interests of this independent self may take priority over the interests of the community.

The moral standards of a collectivist culture are based on the completely different assumption that both the identity and the value of the individual derive from his or her relationship to the larger community (Wong, 1984). I am not John Smith; I am rather a member of the Smith family; and that family, that group of mine, is the source of my identity. It was there before I was and so the dignity and value I have derives from and depends on the status and dignity of my family group. In such collectivist cultures the idea that individuals have moral rights that are prior to the local community and can stand in judgement of its practices makes little sense.

Second, the moral rights that Donaldson proposes derive from an egalitarian American culture, which assumes that the status of the individual is independent of his or her place in a hierarchy. From the egalitarian point of view, no individual is inherently or naturally subordinate to any other individual and this natural equality is prior to the artificial inequalities that develop in a society. Inequalities therefore should be minimized, especially status inequalities that are based on race, sex, religion or ethnic background and such inequalities are characterized as unjust discrimination. On the other hand, non-egalitarian cultures assume that there are 'natural' hierarchies and the status of each person derives from his or her place in these hierarchies. The caste system of India is a perfect example, as is the male-female hierarchy of Saudi Arabia. In these cultures, the natural hierarchy comes before the person. From this non-egalitarian perspective, people are fundamentally unequal and they merit unequal treatment according to their status in the natural hierarchy. Inequalities should not be suppressed, since they are natural and fundamental. Discrimination according to status is morally legitimate and equal opportunity violates the natural inequalities of persons.

Thirdly, and perhaps most importantly, the underlying social contract justification that Donaldson articulates in support of his list of rights is a justification which, though deeply embedded in the moral framework of American culture, is deeply flawed. Donaldson argues that everyone, everywhere, must accept and live by his list of rights because there is a group of imaginary rational individuals that would agree to live by these rights. It is difficult to see, of course, why the supposed agreements made by an imaginary group of rational individuals would show that any real person in the real world is bound by those agreements. But apart from this flaw, Donaldson's social contract argument appeals to concepts that are alien to a communal culture like that of Saudi Arabia. First, the social contract argument envisions the contractors as atomistic individuals who are unrelated to each other and who are each seeking their own individual self-interest. And second, the social contract argument assumes that moral obligations are a human construct, the outcome of an agreement voluntarily entered into. From the perspective of a collectivist or inegalitarian culture, neither of these assumptions makes sense. A collectivist culture can make little sense of the idea that people are unrelated to each other, or that the pursuit of self-interest can dominate the harmony and welfare of the group. And an inegalitarian culture holds that moral obligation derives from one's status and position in a hierarchy that has its basis in 'nature', in the way things are, not in voluntary agreements.

A rights-based ethic such as Donaldson's, then, with its commitment to Western ideals of equality and individual rights, proposes as universally binding, moral standards that derive from assumptions that are proper to our local culture and not universal at all. So a rights ethic disregards the values rooted in other kinds of cultures. For these reasons, then, we believe that a rights ethic such as Donaldson's has to be rejected as ethnocentric.

Other normative approaches that are popular in the West are also deeply ethnocentric. In particular, utilitarianism, the main alternative to human rights theories in Western ethical traditions, is also deeply embedded in a system of conceptual assumptions that make little sense in many non-Western cultures (Velasquez, 2000). While there are many varieties of utilitarianism, utilitarian theories in general claim that everyone, regardless of his or her culture, must either act so as to maximize utility in each particular action (so-called 'act utilitarianism') or must follow rules that if generally followed will maximize utility (so-called 'rule-utilitarianism'). Whatever their form, however, all utilitarian theories have in common the assumption that the proper bearers of utility – and so of all value – are individuals. All utilitarian theories claim that it is the aggregation of these individual utilities that must be maximized. Utilitarian theories, then, even more so than human rights theories, assume that it is individuals, not collectives, that are the proper vessels of value and that morality must be judged by the extent to which individuals, not collectives, are allowed to achieve their ends. Thus utilitarianism, much like human rights theories, make essential use of the conceptual assumptions of an individualistic culture – assumptions that, we have argued, make little sense in a collectivist culture like that of Saudi Arabia.

In addition, utilitarian theories assume that individuals have desires and satisfactions that are identifiable independently of the community around them. Thus, to the extent that these desires define the individual (and from the perspective of utilitarian theory the individual is wholly defined by his or her desires and their satisfaction), utilitarianism is based on an atomistic individualism. While the surrounding community may affect the extent to which an individual's desires are satisfied, utilitarianism presumes that the quantity of satisfaction – the utility – an individual experiences, can be measured (or at least estimated or inferred) without that measurement being affected by the individual's relationship to the community. Utility – the key value in utilitarianism – is conceived in atomistic terms that are foreign to a collectivistic culture that attributes value to the relationships themselves that constitute the collective.

Finally, utilitarian theories also invoke the egalitarian assumptions that, we have argued, are characteristic of Anglo-European cultures but not of hierarchical cultures like that of Saudi Arabia. In aggregating the utilities of individuals, utilitarians assume that the utility of any single individual is to be given no greater nor lesser weight than the quantitatively equal utility of any other individual. Consider, for example, the slogan that John Stuart Mill attributes to the father of utilitarianism, Jeremy Bentham: 'Everybody to count as one, nobody for more than one' (Mill, [1863] 1961). This assumption flies in the face of a number of cultures, which are founded on hierarchical relationships such as societies influenced by Confucian ideas of right relationships, Hindu caste culture, as well as Saudi culture. For these cultures it is axiomatic that some individuals are by nature ranked above other individuals and that their utility has greater weight than the utility of others. Utilitarianism is thus rooted in the egalitarian assumptions of our local culture. These assumptions make little sense in non-egalitarian cultures.

The two main absolutist approaches to ethics that prevail in the West, then, are incapable of adequately resolving the dilemmas of moral diversity that confront the international manager. Both of these approaches are ethnocentric.

Relativism and moral diversity

Confronted with the ethnocentrism of Western absolutist ethics, many have turned to moral relativism, the theory that the only standards available for making moral judgements are the local standards that prevail within a given culture (Harman, 1975; Wong, 1984). Each cultural community, the relativist holds, has its own moral traditions and values and members of a community must rely on their own traditions and values to resolve the moral questions they face and not on abstract moral absolutes.[4]

Early 20th-century anthropologists such as William Graham Sumner (1906), Margaret Mead (1928) and Ruth Benedict (1934), as well as linguists such as Benjamin Whorf (see Carroll, 1956) and later anthropologists such as Clifford Geertz (1973) advanced such views.[5] So have a number of more recent relativist philosophers such as David Wong (1984), Gilbert Harman (1975) and Richard Rorty (1993). In addition, many recent 'particularist' approaches to ethics have advanced theoretical positions that are difficult to distinguish from relativism.[6] Some 'communitarians', for example, have claimed that certain preferences generated by life within a community, with its special traditions and culture, can morally override the supposedly universal obligations of abstract justice (Taylor, 1985; Sandel, 1982); some virtue theorists have claimed that moral judgements must be based on the sensibilities and character traits inculcated by life within a particular community (MacIntyre, 1981); and advocates of 'partiality' have claimed that preferring the interests of members of one's community (friends, family, or tribe) can legitimately override the claims of universal moral principles (Williams, 1981).

The advice of the relativist to the international manager is straight-forward: when in Rome, do as the Romans do. Since there are no absolute moral standards to which the American manager in Saudi Arabia can appeal, it is illegitimate for the American manager to conclude that those Saudi practices that conflict with American moral standards are in some sense 'worse' or 'more unjust' or 'more immoral' than American practices; there is nothing more to be said, other than that Americans and Saudis differ. American managers should therefore accommodate themselves to Saudi practices and demonstrate tolerance and respect for those practices. It is, of course, a historical fact that this is what American managers operating in Saudi Arabia did before and throughout the 1970s. Their initial agreement with Saudi Arabia stipulated that company 'employees shall not interfere with the administrative, political, or religious affairs within Saudi Arabia. The penalty of breach of this provision will be deportation of the employee so offending and after such employee shall have been punished according to the laws of the country' (Robertson, 1979, p. 128). Company handbooks subsequently repeatedly stressed the importance of demonstrating 'tolerance and respect' for Saudi practices and beliefs (Lebkicher, Rentz and Steineke, 1960).

For most anthropologists and philosophers who openly advocate moral relativism, the key argument in favour of relativism is an empirical fact: the existence of moral diversity (Wong, 1984; Harman, 1975). Impressed by the fact that cultures differ on the morality of a wide variety of practices, the relativist concludes that there are no moral principles that can be said universally to obligate the people of all cultures (Harman and Thomson, 1996). Many absolutists respond to this argument by claiming that the relativist has the facts wrong and that in actuality there exist a wide variety of moral standards that are universally present in all cultures (Edel, 1968; Brown, 1991; Bowie, 1990). These include obligations of reciprocity; regulations governing sexual activities, specifically including prohibitions of incest; obligations to keep one's promises; prohibitions against murder, rape and violence toward members of one's community; obligations of parents to care for their children; prohibitions against theft; prohibitions against holding persons responsible for injuries that are unintentional or not under one's control (Brown, 1991; Hockett, 1973; Pinker, 2002).[7]

However, careful consideration of the issues will quickly show that absolutist, as well as relativists, are mistaken when they appeal to the existence or non-existence of universally recognized moral standards as proof or disproof of their respective theories. The absolutist, for example, holds that there are moral standards that are absolute in the sense that everyone, even those whose cultures do not accept those standards, is obligated to follow those standards. Consequently, the absolutist can consistently hold that these absolute standards need not be universally recognized; the absolutist may hold, for example, that some cultures are victims of 'affected ignorance' and so do not recognize these absolute standards, which, nevertheless obligate them (Moody-Adams, 1997). Absolute standards need not be universally recognized standards. On the other hand, the relativist claims that people are obligated to follow only the moral standards that are prevalent in their own culture and that there are no absolute standards that obligate those whose cultures do not accept those standards. Consequently, the moral relativist can consistently hold that although there may be some standards that all cultures happen to hold, nevertheless these standards are not absolute because they would not obligate a person whose culture did not hold them. Universal recognition of a standard does not by itself imply that the standard is an absolute standard.

The implication of these considerations is that moral relativists are mistaken in supposing that if they can demonstrate empirically that there are no moral universals, they have thereby demonstrated that absolutism is false. But absolutists are equally mistaken in supposing that they have shown moral relativism is false if they can demonstrate empirically that moral universals exist. Widespread agreement or disagreement about moral matters is insufficient to establish that moral relativism is either true or false (Rachels, 1980, 1986).

Although the supposed existence of moral universals may be insufficient to disprove moral relativism, there are other reasons to question whether moral relativism is an adequate approach to the moral problems that confront the international manager. The moral relativist claims that people are obligated to follow only the standards of their own culture and that there are no absolute standards that can be used to criticize or evaluate the behaviours of people in other cultures. But this advice of the relativist does not respond to the real problems that moral diversity creates for the international manager. The business manager is confronted with disputes between persons or groups – disputes that are rooted in their conflicting moral standards. A group of Americans, for example, may feel that women in a plant should be promoted just as men are, while Muslims may assert that it is immoral for female managers to be promoted over men. One group may feel that all workers should have an equal opportunity to be hired for the most desirable jobs, while another group of workers may feel that such jobs should be distributed through family or ethnic connections. One group may see nothing wrong with hiring children to work in a factory, while another may find that abhorrent. To suggest in such cases that international managers should simply apply their own culture's standards is pointless, since the problem is that of trying to referee differences between cultures. When one cultural standard must be chosen over another, the relativist can offer no moral criteria for making that choice and abandons the manager to his or her own devices.

Moreover, there is an inescapable arbitrariness at the core of the relativist approach. The relativist holds that people are obligated to follow only the prevailing moral standards of their own culture, and that outsiders have no legitimate basis for criticizing these cultural standards as morally good or bad. The relativist, of course, faces crippling problems when trying to define who is 'outside' or 'inside' a given culture or when trying to deal with the fact that cultures evolve, and that within any culture there are people inevitably who hold dissenting views (Moody-Adams, 1997; Zechenter, 1997). And there is an obvious inconsistency in the relativist's claim that although there are no moral standards that bind everyone, nevertheless everyone is morally obligated to demonstrate tolerance by 'respecting' the moral standards of other cultures.[8] But more importantly, the relativist's claim that each person is obligated to follow the standards of her particular culture (whatever 'culture' is supposed to encompass), as well as the claim that others are obligated to respect the standards of alien cultures, are both arbitrary. Why are Saudis (or Americans) obligated to follow the standards of their own culture simply because it is 'their' culture? Without appealing to an absolute moral standard such as loyalty, the relativist can provide no explanation why people are obligated to follow the standards of their own cultures. Nor can the relativist logically provide any argument why 'outsiders' should 'respect' and not criticize, undermine, or obliterate the moral standards of other cultures. In the absence of such arguments, there is no reason to think that a person is justified in following the moral standards of her culture, nor is there any reason to think that others should respect the standards of an alien culture. The values that underlie a Sicilian or Russian gangster culture, for example, are not necessarily to be followed merely because one is a Sicilian or Russian gangster; nor should outsiders avoid criticizing these gangster values merely because they themselves are not gangsters. Blind allegiance to the values of one's group cannot justify adherence to a local morality.

Natural law and moral diversity

What we want to do now is suggest a way of overcoming the ethno-centrism of moral rights theories without falling into the incoherence and arbitrariness of moral relativism. To do this, we will harken back to a historical period that preceded the rise of the individualistic and egalitarian forms of culture which produced modern rights-based, utilitarian and social contract theories of ethics. In doing so, we will rediscover an ethical approach that seems to provide a better basis for an approach to international ethics than do moral rights or social contract theories. I am referring to the natural law tradition of ethics.

There are, of course, many versions of natural law theory. Natural law can refer to the Stoic doctrine that humans ought to live according to nature (as found, for example, in the views of Epictetus and Cicero), the enlightenment doctrine that the moral law has an objective basis (many, for example, cite Kant as a natural law ethicist), the social contract doctrine that certain moral rights originate in the state of nature (such as the natural rights views found in the writings of Hobbes, Locke and Rousseau), the doctrine that morality is part of the essential nature of law (the subject of a classic debate between H. L. A. Hart and Lord Devlin) and the odd view that morality is based on the natural functions of living organisms and their parts (the Roman Catholic view, for example, that homosexuality is sinful because it deviates from the natural function of sex). None of these are the kinds of natural law theory that we want to discuss.

The tradition of natural law we have in mind is the tradition that derives from the moral theory developed by Thomas Aquinas in the 13th century and since developed in a tradition that extends to the present (Velasquez and Brady, 1997). In this tradition, natural law is based on the idea that all human beings and societies everywhere pursue certain basic human goods through their social institutions.[9] Among these basic human goods that all societies pursue and without which humans beings cannot flourish, Aquinas stressed four: first, the preservation of individual life and health; second, the reproduction of society through human procreation and care of the young; third, the transmission and development of knowledge and technology; and fourth, the maintenance of an orderly society through norms that coordinate our activities and adjudicate our differences. Undoubtedly there are other human goods such as, for example, friendship and communication; for now, however, we can restrict ourselves to these four, which, for the sake of brevity, we can refer to as the goods of life, family, knowledge and social order. These common ends are such that all human beings everywhere normally view them as good, while their destruction is normally seen as bad. The natural law theory, then, is first, the claim that there is a set of fundamental goods, which are universally recognized in every society, including, at a minimum, life, family, knowledge and social order. In normal circumstances these are recognized as good and so should be pursued and in normal circumstances their destruction is recognized as bad and so should be avoided (Aquinas [1947] I–II, Q. 94, a. 4).

But although natural law theory sets out a single set of basic human goods it claims are sought by people in all cultures, it also claims that there are many different means that cultures may adopt to pursue these goods. According to Aquinas, 'practical reasoning is concerned with what our actions can bring about and such things can be brought about in more than one way' (ibid.). The goals are the same for all, but the cultural means for attaining those goals are many and so subject to historical and geographical variability (Aquinas [1947] II–II, Q. 170, a. 1, obj. 3). Consequently, Aquinas argues, we must recognize that morality has a two-part structure: it can be organized into what he called 'primary' and 'secondary' levels. At the primary level are the basic human goods that are pursued through the institutions of all societies and so are 'unchanging' moral absolutes. At a secondary level are the varying norms that are embedded in the particular institutions of each particular culture. These are the ordinary and familiar or 'common' moral norms, which surround a person within a culture and against which the behaviours of the members of that culture are judged. Toward these secondary norms Aquinas took a relativist stance.

We propose, then, that we take from natural law theory the insight that morality has a two-part structure: (1) a set of basic goods that the institutions of all societies are designed to achieve and which humans need in order to flourish; and (2) a system of norms embedded in the institutions through which each particular society attempts to achieve these goods, but which vary from one society and time to another.

What exactly does it mean to say that different cultures may adopt different institutional norms to achieve the same fundamental goods of the natural law? The various natural law goods are ordinarily pursued by means of the institutions that each culture has developed to pursue those goods. Each society's particular political, legal, social, religious and cultural institutions provide the means through which its members pursue what is necessary for human life, for the establishment of families and the raising of children, for the pursuit of knowledge and for the establishment of an ordered society.[10] And different cultures adopt different institutions to pursue these goods.

The basic goods are achieved not only through institutions like the state, but also through the family, property systems, contractual systems, the conventions of friendship and so on and these are humanly constructed and evolve over time (Berger and Luckmann, 1966). As Searle (1995, 1998) has argued, institutions are not 'brute facts' but 'institutional facts' that are 'observer-dependent' because their very existence depends on those human 'activities and attitudes' through which institutions are constructed and maintained. In this respect institutions are unlike the fundamental goods toward which humans are naturally drawn. The drives to preserve life, to form families, to pursue knowledge, to develop technology and to seek order are naturally given drives: they are brute facts of human nature, which orient us toward the goods we then seek to achieve through our socially constructed institutions.

Moral and non-moral norms are integral to, and constitutive of, the social institutions through which societies pursue the basic goods. Institutions emerge when humans engage in interactions that continue over time and which are structured by shared understandings about what these interactions are for and shared expectations about how they will proceed. Such interactions may be as simple as those by which people regularly greet each other with handshakes or embraces, or as complex as those by which people constitute and sustain families or corporations or governments. With respect to games and etiquette, the governing expectations may be set down in explicit rules, while the expectations that shape everyday interactions between acquaintances may be communicated through less clearly defined gestures and signals (Goffman, 1967). These shared expectations are norms and institutions consist of systems of such norms.

The norms that make up the fundamental social institutions through which a group pursues the basic human goods, are local moral norms. Unlike relativism (and unlike Donaldson's social contract theory), which cannot explain why people should adhere to their own local norms, natural law theory has a straightforward explanation for the binding nature of one's local morality. These local moral norms are morally binding on the members of the culture because these norms constitute or support the very institutions through which the members of that culture must pursue the basic goods. But although morally binding on the members of the given culture, these secondary institutional norms are not morally binding on the people of other cultures who may pursue the basic goods through other institutional means.[11]

By basic institutions we mean those institutions that seem to be generically human although they may vary from one culture to another in the particular way they are structured. For example, everywhere humans communicate with each other using the institution of language; yet language structures and vocabularies are highly varied. In a similar manner, humans everywhere live as families in complex social units; yet the forms those families assume vary immensely. To some degree everywhere humans recognize the institution of property; yet what may be claimed as one's own and what one is or is not entitled to do with what one owns varies not only from one culture to another but also from one period to another in the same culture's history. And everywhere people recognize the institution of promising, although again the nature and extent of obligation vary from culture to culture. The particular characteristics of a generic institution, then, depend on elements within the culture.

In the institutions of an individualistic culture we can expect that individual rights will reign supreme, while in the institutions of a collectivist culture, we can expect that the interests of the group will dominate over the goals of the individual. In the institutions of an egalitarian culture, justice will consist of equal opportunity regardless of status, while in the institutions of a non-egalitarian culture, justice will consist of treating people in accordance with their position in a hierarchy. In contrast with a rights-based ethic, then, a natural law ethic will not condemn as immoral all inequalities embedded in a culture's institutions, no matter how much they may offend our Western sensibilities; nor will the natural law tradition condemn as immoral institutions that suppress individual rights in favour of the interests of the group.

This does not mean, however, that 'anything goes' as a moral relativist might suggest. For a culture's institutions are means, and some means can be evaluated as better or worse than others. A culture's institutions and its embedded moral norms, then, can be evaluated by asking how well they succeed in providing for all their members the goods of life, family, knowledge and social order. When the institutions of a culture fail in their basic purpose of providing these goods for all their members, they are inadequate and should be reformed.

From the natural law perspective, then, there are two crucial questions to be asked by the global manager as he or she confronts moral diversity. First, do the various institutions of a given foreign culture – its political institutions, family institutions, legal framework, its court system, cultural practices and so on – succeed in securing the goods of life and health for all its people? Do they provide conditions in which families can form and children can be nurtured and cared for? Do they ensure the establishment of order and stability in society and do they allow for the expansion of knowledge on which social progress can build? If the answer to these questions is yes, then these institutions and their associated norms are not to be rejected as immoral, although they may clash profoundly with our own deepest intuitions about the values of equality and of individual rights.

Secondly, the global manager should ask: do these institutions and their associated norms of justice achieve the basic human goods for all their members in the best possible way, given the circumstances in which the society finds itself? This, we believe, is often a very difficult question to answer. Many of us from a liberal culture tend to believe that the 'democratic' values of liberalism are the only legitimate values and that all cultures should accept, for example, our liberal notions of equality and individual moral rights. But given the high levels of social stability evident in most cultures, given the widespread and high levels of fulfilment that most members of other cultures derive from their own cultural practices and institutions; and given the apparent support and agreement with their own cultural practices that the people of most societies exhibit, it is not clear that liberal institutions would in fact be better for other cultures than those institutions they currently have in place.

What will a natural law ethic say about the cultural practices of Saudi Arabia? First, it seems to us that unlike a rights-based ethic, it will not condemn as simply immoral the inequalities and forms of collectivism embedded in its cultural institutions. Although such cultural features, particularly as related to the treatment of women, deeply offend our Western sensibilities, a natural law ethic will not necessarily condemn them.

The crucial questions for the natural law ethicist, as we said, are two. First, do the various institutions of Saudi Arabian culture – its theocracy, its family institutions, its legal framework, its court system, its cultural practices and so on – succeed in securing the goods of life and health for all of its people? Do they provide conditions in which families can form and children can be nurtured and cared for? Do they ensure the establishment of order in society? And do they allow for the expansion of knowledge and technology on which social progress can build? If these questions are answered affirmatively, then these institutions and their constitutive norms are not to be rejected as immoral, no matter how profoundly they may clash with our own deepest convictions about the values of equality and of personal rights. Based on the observations of those who have studied the Saudis, as well as the testimony of the Saudis themselves, we believe that these questions do in fact have affirmative answers. Observers note, for example, that traditional Saudi institutions, particularly the family, are effective in providing for the material needs of all society's members.

> [Despite] all its meddling, the [Saudi] family never leaves a member in need. Traditionally, the extended family system has taken care of the problems of the needy, the sick, the handicapped and the aged. ... A blood relative left in material or physical need is a personal disgrace to the rest of the family. And unlike in the West, nepotism is a virtue. Intolerable shame would fall on any Saudi who refused to give a job to a relative. (Mackey, 1987, p. 119)

Family institutions, in spite of the (to Western eyes) repressive treatment of women, are perceived by Saudi women as effective arrangements for providing for their needs. S. Altorki, who interviewed the female members of 13 Saudi families spanning three generations, notes that 'men and women alike view this arrangement as a protection of women from the distress and inconveniences of the public arenas and not as a restricting dependence upon men' (1986, p. 65). Altorki quotes the 'educated wife of a man of the younger generation' as stating the 'thinking of her age group':

> I think that in our country men have a better position than women. On the other hand, the women don't have to be exposed to many inconveniences and to the struggle for living that they face in other countries. We don't have to slave to support a family – that burden falls on the man. We don't even have to be troubled by running around getting gro-

ceries or other necessities – the men do that. We do have our responsibilities, but they are different, though not less important, than those of
men. Where would a family be without a mother in the house? What
kind of children would a society have without the care given them by a
full-time mother? It is not true that men control our lives. (Ibid.)

Saudi family institutions, then, even as perceived from the viewpoint of
women, seem to provide their members with the basic material and emotional goods characteristic of fulfilling family life in which both men and
women can flourish.

One might be tempted to argue that these institutions can be criticized
for failing to treat women with the respect they are due as human beings
whose dignity is equal to men's. But such an argument, we believe, would
implicitly appeal to a western interpretation of what equal dignity means
and requires and so would be ethnocentric. Alternatively, one might try to
argue that the greater good of Saudi society would be served by more liberal
institutions, perhaps by securing wider acceptance and so greater stability.
But given the high levels of social stability evident in Saudi Arabia, given
the widespread and high level of fulfilment that most Saudis derive from
their Islamic institutions and given the apparent support and agreement
with their Muslim practices that the people of Saudi Arabia exhibit, it is not
clear that liberal institutions would in fact be better than those currently in
place. S. Mackey, for example, who lived in Saudi Arabia during the oil
boom of the 1970s and who is harshly and vehemently critical of the position of women in Saudi culture, nevertheless admits:

> [Saudi] women themselves appear unwilling to struggle for their stake in
> the new society. From a Western point of view, women show an alarm-
> ing obedience to the basic presuppositions of the Saudis' traditional
> culture. Although there are pockets of resistance, the vast majority of
> women continue to accept their imprisonment at the hands of men.
> (Mackey, 1987, p. 132)

The reason for this acquiescence is that Saudi people, women as well as
men, feel they derive from their institutions a high level of personal satisfaction and fulfilment, even those who have lived in and are familiar with
Western liberal societies.

> That most of the younger-generation [Saudi] women who have been edu-
> cated abroad do not contribute to a more radical departure from tradition
> must be understood in terms of the advantages they perceive in their
> society. Women of the younger generation see advantages in the relative
> freedom of choice that liberated Western women enjoy in the countries
> they visit. Nevertheless, this realization has not geared them toward open

defiance of traditions, except in rare and isolated cases. ... Whereas they complain about parental control and restrictions on their mobility, many see advantages in the financial and emotional security that their networks of kin and friends grant them. (Altorki, 1986, p. 136)

Thus, even those Saudi women who are familiar with Western practices seem to prefer their own close-knit collective institutions to the individualistic and atomistic institutions of the liberal West.

The intense efforts Saudi Arabia has expended on building schools and institutions of higher education and on importing Western technology, suggests that Saudi institutions are also capable of sustaining a drive toward the good of knowledge. As oil funds flowed into the country, Saudi rulers have pursued successive 'Five-year Development Plans,' which have invested heavily in education and technology development. This dedication to knowledge and technology is not new. L. Davidson argues most educated Muslims respect scientific research as something approved by God, often citing the Hadith passage that reads: 'the Messenger of Allah [Muhammad] said, "He who goes forth in search of knowledge is in the way of Allah till he returns",....''the seeking of knowledge is obligatory upon every Muslim."' (Davidson, 1998, p. 116).

Saudi institutions, then, should not be criticized as morally backward or defective. Instead, the international manager should accept them as fundamentally justified because they are one society's response to the natural law imperative to seek life, family, social order and knowledge.

Finally, one might try to argue that some Saudi practices are inconsistent with some of the deep values of Islam embedded in their own institutional structures. Such arguments, we believe, might succeed.

[W]hile Islamist women reject Western standards and the 'commodification' of women's bodies (turning them into a commodity through advertising and entertainment) and reassert the primacy of 'family values', many women also call for a reinterpretation of the Quran to purge from society and law restrictive and abusive attitudes toward women. These women point out that such policies as female circumcision, the seclusion of women, the isolation of women from economic activity and even restrictions on women attending the mosque are not really Islamic in origin. They are cultural add-ons that have come to be identified with Islam over the centuries. (Davidson, 1998, p. 79)

But if such arguments are to succeed, they will have to see Saudi institutions and their constitutive norms from within and judge their morality in terms of the values embedded within those very institutions. And it is clear, we hope, that it is the point of this article to recommend exactly such an approach.

We conclude, then, that the American managers of Aramco were not morally mistaken when, as we noted earlier, they agreed not to 'interfere' with the administrative, political, or religious practices of the Saudis, in effect condoning these practices (Robertson, 1979, p. 128). And they were right to stress the importance of demonstrating 'tolerance and respect' for Saudi practices and beliefs (Lebkicher et al., 1960). Toward the local moral norms and practices of the Saudis, the managers of Aramco correctly adopted a relativist stance.

Conclusion

Let us end by suggesting that the natural law approach to ethics that we have sketched is not vulnerable to the same ethnocentric problems that plague a rights approach, nor does it fall into the difficulties that affect a relativist position. Natural law theory allows the manager to critically evaluate the institutions and associated practices of a culture in terms of common basic goods that cultural institutions and practices are established to achieve; these institutions can be evaluated as being better or worse means for pursing those goods. But natural law theory also avoids the pitfalls of moral absolutism because it holds that there are a range of cultural institutions and practices that are effective and therefore legitimate means of achieving these goods. Natural law theory holds, therefore, that behaviours that may be wrong in terms of the institutional norms of one culture, may be perfectly moral in terms of the institutional norms of another culture.

Natural law theory, then, takes the position that local norms and practices are generally valid sources of obligation for members of the local culture, because such obligation is grounded on the value of the basic goods such norms and practices secure for those members. They can, however, be criticized as being more or less effective means for pursuing the common ends of human nature, or as being incoherent or otherwise irrational means for pursuing those ends.

Finally, we should point out that we are not arguing that Western approaches to ethics ought to be rejected or abandoned. It is clear that Western cultures share some common moral convictions and a theory of moral rights can appeal to those shared Western values to articulate and justify moral judgements of practices within Western cultures. Perhaps the claim can also be made that such Western values are the most effective and logically coherent means for pursuing our common ends. If so, then such claims would support attempts to reform other cultures when such cultures stand in opposition to these Western values, as well as support attempts to persuade other cultures to change. But these claims are not self-evident truths. We cannot presume the universal validity of Western moral rights theories that are rooted in an individualistic and egalitarian culture that is itself not universal.

Notes

Portions of the first part of this paper, particularly the Saudi Arabia case developed in this first part, are based on a talk delivered at Washington and Lee University in Lexington, Virginia, July 1996. My thanks to Washington and Lee University for allowing me to reuse portions of that case here.

1. Export trade, in fact, remains today the largest and fastest growing form of international economic activity, now averaging about $4 trillion a year.
2. Esposito (1992, p. 198ff.) has argued that the main reason why members of Western cultures find Islamic fundamentalism so objectionable is that most Westerners subscribe to the principle that church and state should operate in separate spheres, a view that derives from a European history marked by a series of religious wars.
3. Note that the absolutist does not claim that there is a set of moral standards that are actually recognized in every culture, or would be universally accepted if only everyone carefully considered them. The absolutist claim is simply that there are certain arguments with true premises, which logically imply the conclusion that every human being has certain moral obligations. It does not follow from this that this conclusion will be universally accepted, since not everyone may be aware of the arguments for it; nor that everyone would accept the arguments once they have considered them, since some may challenge or reject the premises and their assumptions; nor even that everyone would accept the conclusion once they have accepted the arguments, since even if everyone accepts the arguments and accepts the truth of the premises, simple weakness of will – what Moody-Adams (1997) calls 'affected ignorance' – may prevent some from accepting the conclusion. It is important also to note that there is a distinction between saying that what a person has done is wrong and saying that the person is to blame for doing wrong. A person may do something that is wrong, but his or her action may be excusable for a number of reasons such as ignorance that what he or she was doing was wrong or inability to do otherwise. So when the absolutist claims that a person of another culture is behaving wrongly, this claim does not imply that the person is to blame for this behaviour.
4. Apart from these standards, which have only local validity, there are no moral standards that it would be wrong for every person to transgress, including those persons whose own culture does not recognize those standards.
5. Subsequent research has overturned many of the empirical claims on which these relativist theories were based. For example, Freeman (1983) criticized Mead's claims that Samoan attitudes, particularly toward adolescent sex, child rearing and religion, differed substantially from Western attitudes. Malotki (1983) criticized Whorf's claims that Hopi time conceptions are radically different from ours. Nevertheless, the relativist theories put forward by these anthropologists had an enormous influence on the relativist views of the later 20th century.
6. A particularist approach to ethics claims that moral questions should be resolved by appealing to the actual moral traditions and practices of that particular social group to which one belongs (see O'Neill, 1996, pp. 11–13). Many, if not most, particularists would resist being characterized as 'relativists' of course.
7. While it is possible to identify many such 'universals', it should be noted that these assume diverse local expression and this diversity raises heated debate over their true 'universality'.

8. The inconsistency that is commonly attributed to the relativist is that while relativism claims that there are no absolute standards, nevertheless the relativist's plea for 'tolerance' assumes that toleration is an absolute value and that everyone, regardless of his or her culture, is obligated to adhere to the standard of toleration by not criticizing the moral practices of alien cultures (see for example, Zechenter, 1997).

9. Similar teleological conceptions of values are common in the social sciences. For example, Schwartz (1994) suggests that '[Human] values represent, in the form of conscious goals, three universal requirements of human existence to which all individuals and societies must be responsive: needs of individuals as biological organisms, requisites of coordinated social interaction and survival and welfare needs of groups'. For a fuller explanation of his view, see Schwartz (1992).

10. Aquinas discusses the conventional and changeable nature of private property and of slavery at (1947) I–II, Q. 94, a. 5, reply 3. On the conventional and changeable nature of marriage institutions see Aquinas (1947), Supplement, Q. 65. In these discussions Aquinas makes it clear that institutions are established to serve basic human needs and should be reformed or abandoned when they fail to serve these needs; see, for example, his discussion of the institution of private property at (1947) II–II, Q. 32, a. 5.

11. Aquinas's most important discussion of cultural variability concerns the moral norms embedded in the different kinds of family institutions found in different cultures. Aquinas was aware that while Christian Europe had adopted monogamous family institutions, both Islamic and early Hebraic cultures had adopted polygamous family arrangements. Aquinas concludes that these do not violate the natural law, since polygamous marriages, much like monogamous marriages, achieve the natural law good of preserving the species through procreation and of providing care for the resulting offspring. However, he argues polygamous institutions are not as well suited for achieving these ends as is monogamy, since polygamous families provide more occasions for discord among the marriage partners than do monogamous families (Aquinas [1947], Supplement, Q. 65).

References

Alireza, M. (1987) 'Women of Saudi Arabia', *National Geographic*, vol. 172(4), pp. 423–53.

Altorki, S. (1986) *Women In Saudi Arabia: Ideology and Behavior Among the Elite* (New York: Columbia University Press).

Aquinas, T. (1947) *Summa Theologica* [1266–1273], tr. Fathers of the English Dominican Province, 3 vols. (New York: Benziger Brothers); also available online at http://www.ccel.org/a/aquinas/summa/home.html.

Benedict, R. (1934) *Patterns of Culture* (Boston: Houghton Mifflin).

Berger, P. L. and Luckmann, T. (1966) *The Social Construction of Reality* (Garden City, NY: Doubleday).

Bowie, N. E. (1990) 'Business Ethics and Cultural Relativism', in P. Madsen and J. M. Shafritz (eds), *Essentials of Business Ethics* (New York: Penguin Books), pp. 366–82.

Brown, D. E. (1991) *Human Universals* (Philadelphia: Temple University Press).

Carroll, J. B. (ed.) (1956) *Language, Thought, and Reality: Selected Writings of Benjamin Lee Whorf* (Cambridge, MA: MIT Press).

Davidson, L. (1998) *Islamic Fundamentalism* (Westport, CT: Greenwood Press).

Donaldson, T. (1989) *The Ethics of International Business* (New York: Oxford University Press).

Donaldson, T. (1992) 'Individual Rights and Multinational Corporate Responsibilities', *Phi Kappa Phi Journal*, vol. 72, pp. 7–9.

Donaldson, T. (1996) 'Values in Tension: Ethics Away From Home', *Harvard Business Review*, September–October, pp. 48–61.

Donaldson, T. and Dunfee, T. W. (1994) 'Toward a Unified Conception of Business Ethics: Integrative Social Contracts Theory', *Academy of Management Review*, vol. 19, pp. 252–84.

Edel, M. and Edel, A. (1968) *Anthropology and Ethics: The Quest for Moral Understanding* (Cleveland: Press of Case Western Reserve University).

Esposito, J. (1982) *Women in Muslim Family Law* (Syracuse, NY: Syracuse University Press).

Esposito, J. (1992) *The Islamic Threat: Myth or Reality?* (New York: Oxford University Press).

Freeman, D. (1983) *Margaret Mead and Samoa: The Making and Unmaking of an Anthropological Myth* (Cambridge, MA: Harvard University Press).

Geertz, C. (1973) *The Interpretation of Cultures* (New York: Basic Books).

Goffman, E. (1967) *Interaction Rituals* (New York: Doubleday).

Harman, G. (1975) 'Moral Relativism Defended', *Philosophical Review*, vol. 84, pp. 3–22.

Harman, G. and Thomson, J. J. (1996) *Moral Relativism and Moral Objectivity* (Oxford: Blackwell).

Hockett, C. F. (1973) *Man's Place in Nature* (New York: McGraw-Hill).

Hofstede, G. (1980) *Culture's Consequence: International Differences in Work-Related Values* (Beverly Hills, CA: SAGE).

Hofstede, G. (1991) *Cultures and Organizations* (London: McGraw-Hill).

Kim, U., Triandis, H., Kagitcibasi, C., Choi, S. and Yoon G. (1994) *Individualism and Collectivism* (Thousand Oaks, CA: SAGE).

Lebkicher, R., Rentz, G. and Steineke, M. (1960) *Aramco Handbook* [No Location], Arabian American Oil Company.

MacIntyre, A. (1981) *After Virtue* (Notre Dame, IN: University of Notre Dame Press).

Mackey, S. (1987) *The Saudis: Inside the Desert Kingdom* (Boston: Houghton Mifflin).

Malotki, E. (1983) *Hopi Time: A Linguistic Analysis of the Temporal Concepts in the Hopi Language* (Berlin: Mouton).

Mead, M. (1928) *Coming of Age in Samoa* (New York: Morrow).

Mernissi, F. (1975) *Beyond the Veil: Male-Female Dynamics in a Modern Muslim Society* (Cambridge: Schenkman Publishing).

Mill, J. S. (1961) 'Utilitarianism' [1863], in J. Bentham and J. S. Mill, *The Utilitarians* (New York: Doubleday).

Moody-Adams, M. M. (1997) *Fieldwork in Familiar Places* (Cambridge, MA: Harvard University Press).

Nawwab, I. I., Speers, P. C. and Hoye, P. F. (1980) *Aramco and Its World* (Washington, DC: Arabian American Oil Company).

Nyrop, R. F., Benderly, B. L., Carter, L. N., Eglin, D. R. and Kirchner, R. A. (1977) *Area Handbook for Saudi Arabia* (Washington, DC: U.S. Government Printing Office).

O'Neill, O. (1996) *Towards Justice and Virtue: A Constructive Account of Practical Reasoning* (Cambridge: Cambridge University Press).

Pinker, S. (2002) *The Blank Slate: The Denial of Human Nature and Modern Intellectual Life* (New York: Viking).

Rachels, J. (1980) 'Can Ethics Provide Answers?', *Hastings Center Report*, vol. 10, pp. 33–9.

Rachels, J. (1986) *Elements of Moral Philosophy* (New York: Random House).

Robertson, N. (1979) *Origins of the Saudi Arabian Oil Empire: Secret U.S. Documents, 1923–1944* (Salisbury, NC: Documentary Publications).

Rorty, R. (1993) 'Human Rights, Rationality and Sentimentality', in S. Shute and S. Hurley (eds), *On Human Rights: The Oxford Amnesty Lectures* (New York: Basic Book), pp. 111–34.

Sandel, M. J. (1982) *Liberalism and the Limits of Justice* (Cambridge: Cambridge University Press).

Schwartz, S. H. (1992) 'Universals in the Content and Structure of Values: Theoretical Advances and Empirical Tests in 20 Countries', in M. Zanna (ed.), *Advances in Experimental Social Psychology* (Orlando, FL: Academic Press).

Schwartz, S. H. (1994) 'Beyond Individualism/Collectivism, New Cultural Dimensions of Values', in U. Kim, H. Triandis, C. Kagitcibasi, S. Choi and G. Yoon (eds), *Individualism and Collectivism* (Thousand Oaks, CA: SAGE), pp. 85–119.

Searle, J. (1995) *The Construction of Social Reality* (New York: Simon & Schuster).

Searle, J. (1998) *Mind, Language* and *Society* (New York: Basic Books).

Shue, H. (1980) *Basic Rights: Subsistence, Affluence* and *U.S. Foreign Policy* (Princeton, NJ: Princeton University Press).

Sumner, W. G. (1906) *Folkways* (Boston: Atheneum).

Taylor, C. (1985) 'Atomism', in *Philosophy and the Human Sciences: Philosophical Papers*, vol. 2 (Cambridge: Cambridge University Press), pp. 187–210.

U.S. Congress, House of Representatives. Committee on Foreign Affairs (1983) *Human Rights Documents: Compilation of Documents Pertaining to Human Rights* (Washington, DC: U.S. Government Printing Office).

Velasquez, M. (2000) 'Globalization and the Failure of Ethics', *Business Ethics Quarterly*, vol. 10(1), pp. 343–52.

Velasquez, M. and Brady, N. (1997) 'Catholic Natural Law and Business Ethics', *Business Ethics Quarterly*, vol. 7(2), pp. 83–107.

Williams, B. (1981) *Moral Luck* (Cambridge: Cambridge University Press).

Wong, D. (1984) *Moral Relativity* (Berkeley: University of California Press).

Zechenter, E. M. (1997) 'In the Name of Culture: Cultural Relativism and the Abuse of the Individual', *Journal of Anthropological Research*, vol. 53(3), pp. 319–47.

2
Justice in International Businesses
Frederick Bird

Introduction

What does it mean to say that international businesses in developing countries should be just? Businesses are not governments, or social welfare agencies, or civil society organizations. In what ways then should we expect them to be just? Furthermore, if we expect them to be just, or at least not unjust, as most people do, then how precisely should they balance concerns for justice with their responsibilities as businesses?

Consider several examples.

Think about the individuals and pension funds that bought shares in a firm like Enron. Investors were clearly outraged when they found their shares greatly depreciated in value because management had not forthrightly communicated the company's current financial worth. They felt Enron executives had acted irresponsibly and perhaps illegally to maximize their own benefits while treating other investors unfairly. Other firms typically feel unfairly disadvantaged when competitors are able to secure contracts on the basis of what seem like special and questionable relationships with governments. Local managers and employees in developing countries feel unjustly treated when expatriates are able to gain excessively high salaries, supposedly because of the higher costs of living in their countries of origin. Consider further examples. Many local residents in developing countries have felt unfairly treated when little or none of the wealth generated by international mining, petroleum or forestry companies exploiting their lands has benefited them directly. Many workers and observers have protested against the long hours and almost forced labour conditions on many of the primary-producer work sites currently found in developing countries.

In Uganda, British American Tobacco (BATU), which purchases dried tobacco leaf from almost 50,000 small farmers, treats these suppliers in ways that seem unjust to many observers. It forbids the farmers to produce for other companies; it provides the sole basis for judging the quality and cash value of their crops; and it pays them so little that they can never accumulate any savings or capital (Sejjaaka, 2004). In northwestern Guyana, Barama Forestry built forest roads, which remained open after the company completed its own logging operations. Although these roads, for the most part, met the environmental standards of Guyana's Forestry Stewardship Council, their existence facilitated the travel of hundreds of fortune-seeking small mining operators, who, without any property claims to the area, ravaged the lands and the villages of the indigenous peoples. These peoples, by long cultural tradition, felt the land was theirs and thus felt unjustly abused (Whiteman, 2004). From 1960 to the present, the people of the Niger Delta have watched as the Royal/Dutch Shell affiliate in Nigeria extracted more than $180 billion worth of oil from under their lands. For the most part, these people's lives did not improve as a result; in many ways, conditions grew worse. People had lower real incomes and worse still, less access to potable water. Many felt that a basic injustice had been dealt them.

It might be useful as well to consider examples where businesses themselves feel unjustly treated, cases where otherwise responsible firms have been expropriated by national governments or have suffered from sabotage by local guerrilla groups. Many firms in developing countries complain that their goods are charged excessive tariffs when they try to market them in the industrialized countries. Other firms complain about workforces that are disorderly and regularly tardy, as well as about governments that set unfair prices or levy unfairly excessive taxes.

In practice, public attention to questions about just business practices initially emerges in settings like those just described. Where people feel unfairly treated, the experience of injustice correspondingly gives rise to thoughts and discussions of justice. However, given the circumstances in which these particular discussions of injustice are occasioned, it has typically been easier to speak about and identify injustice in terms of specific instances than to articulate broadly accepted standards of justice that would in turn seem fitting and compelling to all of those involved in any of the kinds of conflicts to which I have just referred (Cahn, 1949; Wohlgast, 1989). However, without being able to refer to common perspectives, protests against particular injustices as well as corresponding calls for justice are likely to seem arbitrary and to reflect particular points of view.

In writing this paper I propose to address two serious challenges. The first challenge consists in attempting at once to set forth a common framework for just business practices while still respecting the fact that diverse ethical traditions have thought about justice quite differently. Even within the ethical traditions of the North Atlantic countries, we see that liberals, conservatives, social democrats and communitarians think about justice in quite different ways. These traditions variously invoke distinct ideas about individual rights and equal opportunity, social equality and the common good, equal status and community order. Ways of thinking about justice become even more variegated when we consider other ethical traditions. For example, many religious traditions typically think about these matters in relation to beliefs about God's judgement and justice. The classical cultures of India and China approached issues of justice from quite different perspectives. There are, for example, no direct equivalents to the Western notion of justice in Indian and Chinese cultural traditions, although ideas of comparable importance can be found in the social arguments and rules developed in these cultures according to the concept of Dharma in India or of the Tao and 'right relationships' in China (Dumont, 1972; Weber, [1922] 1951; Weber, [1922] 1958). Thus, whether we make reference to clashing civilizations, opposing ideologies, or cultural differences, it is quite evident that humans have thought about justice quite differently (McIntyre, 1988; Huntington, 1996). The challenge here has two sides. On one hand, we are challenged to identify common elements in spite of these differences; on the other, we are challenged to state these common elements in ways that still respect the cultural traditions which supply the values, vocabularies and modes of expression in terms of which people in diverse settings typically think and communicate.

The second challenge consists in finding ways to persuade business people why as managers, entrepreneurs, governors, trustees and executives they should be interested in just business practices. They may well be concerned about justice as citizens, taxpayers, customers and employees. But why should people care about whether their businesses are just?

In the remainder of this essay I will set forth a model of just business practices, which I hope will answer these challenges. This model identifies common features of justice and demonstrates how they can be integrated with diverse traditions of ethical discourse. In the process, I will indicate how this model can be utilized to think about and respond practically to the typical issues of perceived injustice facing businesses in various cultural and economic contexts. I will also attempt to demonstrate why firms have a vested interest in seeking to operate in keeping with just business practices.

Questions of justice

Most people would probably agree that justice, broadly understood, is realized to the extent that each person receives his or her due, as enunciated by Aristotle in Book Five of the *Ethics* (Thomson, 1953); and this broad definition applies equally to groups, or human organizations. Or to express this idea more fully, in situations of uncertainty, risk and limited resources as well as situations of real and potential conflicts to act justly is to act in ways so that each is accorded the opportunities, benefits, hardships and rewards that they merit. Generally, when we think about justice, we are considering alternative ways of ordering or arranging human interactions such that the life chances of human beings and human institutions, seem appropriate in terms of who they are, what they have done and/or what they may be expected to do. For the most part, we tend to think of justice in terms of the fitting order in human relations determined in keeping with our notions of merit.

Such ideas about merit and fitting order, however, vary enormously. While many probably would endorse general ideas about equal human dignity, most humans nonetheless assume that other opportunities and burdens ought to be allocated in relation to more specific and hierarchically graded criteria, such as achievement, seniority, responsibility, culpability, honour or kinship. Many debates about justice revolve around the criteria for determining relevant criteria and how these criteria should be interpreted and applied.[1]

In practice, what matters to most people is not justice abstractly defined but justice with respect to particular activities, domains or questions. I will therefore subdivide the larger field of justice with regard to business practices into three dimensions, representing ways in which questions of justice have frequently been raised; for the purposes of this essay, they represent three ways of looking at recurrent issues that business people face and in relation to which they must invoke notions of justice. My three-part account of types or approaches to justice corresponds to distinctions made by Aristotle in Book Five of the *Ethics* (Thomson, 1953).

1.   The first dimension of justice asks: how should we distribute benefits and burdens, opportunities and risks, rewards and deprivations among members of any group, however small or large? This is the fundamental question of *justice with respect to fitting and fair distributions*, whether these distributions occur within a business organization, voluntary association, nation or other human collectivity. Traditionally, this dimension has been considered under the rubric of distributive justice.

2.   Questions of justice are often posed from a slightly different perspective, in which the focus of attention shifts from concerns about overall allocations to concerns about the character of the interactions and exchanges between and among people and organizations. In interactions between two or more parties, whether employers and employees, firms and suppliers, donors and recipients, businesses and community groups, what ways of acting seem just and which ways of acting seem unjust? This is the question of *justice with respect to fair and fitting exchanges*. Traditionally, this question has been discussed under to the seldom-used rubric of 'commutative justice'. It is this dimension of justice that I will primarily consider in this essay.

3.   Questions of justice arise in cases where there has been a real or apparent violation of the basic rules or expectations that govern human interactions. Questions then arise about the appropriate ways to determine

whether wrongs have been committed, what sorts of wrongs these are, what should be done in response and how offenders should be appropriately treated. Our third question, then, concerns *justice with respect to the fair and fitting adjudications* of conflicts involving perceived wrongs. Because discussions about this question have often revolved around ways of treating real or accused offenders, these discussions have sometimes proceeded with regard to concerns about 'retributive justice'. I have deliberately excluded this rubric because it is much too restricted; it focuses only on a part of the larger process of adjudication (namely fitting ways of treating offenders) and also takes only one particular view of how to treat these offenders.[2]

Other observers have developed various approaches to questions of justice in business organizations. Some have distinguished between distributive and procedural justice (Deutsch, 1985; Folger, 1987; Folger and Konovsky, 1989; Greenberg, 1996; Cropanzano, 1993; Sheppard et al., 1992). For most of these authors the distinction lies in the procedures that organizations employ in dealing with questions of justice, and such procedures influence the degree to which eventual judgements and policy decisions are accepted more than do the substantive principles and rules they apply in their decisions. While I am sympathetic to this argument, I have followed a more traditional account of different types of justice, first of all because I think that it is important to call attention to the quite different range of concerns associated with our three traditional dimensions of justice. It is possible to examine these dimensions both substantively, in terms of principles and purposes they seek to honour, and formally, in terms of the processes and procedures they seek to follow. These procedural questions arise quite differently, depending upon whether the question concerns just distributions, exchanges, or adjudications. In any case, in this essay I will discuss each of these three dimensions of organizational justice with regard to their ends and minimal expectations and also to their purposes and procedures.

A practical strategy for ethical deliberations

I have developed this model of just business practices using ethical strategies similar to those associated with the natural law tradition and with contemporary discourse ethics. As in the natural law tradition, I propose that the search for common standards begins by considering the ends or the practical good of the human institutions or practices we are concerned about. In keeping with discourse ethics, I propose that this process be conceived as one involving ongoing communicative interactions.

I arrive at common standards with respect to justice by undertaking sequentially several related but different exercises. The preliminary exercise consists in acknowledging that those who are involved practically in thinking about justice are likely to hold a range of quite different views both about the relevant standards of justice and about the actual institutional practices of justice in their societies. These differences will persist throughout the deliberations. However, to the extent that such deliberations are successful – meaning that those involved are able to arrive at some mutually respectful understandings – these differences are likely to assume less weight and significance.

The initial exercise in this process of deliberating consists in the activity of identifying common assumptions about the end or the good of the practice of justice. Although we can undertake this exercise with respect to the practice of justice generally, we can also do so with respect to any particular sphere of justice, such as justice in the courts, justice with respect to education or just negotiations. Walzer (1983) begins his discussion of several different spheres of justice (membership, social honour, friendship, welfare, etc.) by examining in each case particular values that we seek to enhance and honour in these different areas. This exercise is most appropriately thought of as a communicative activity, whether or not others are directly involved, as it consists in attempting to identify formulations of the end or good of justice – its core concern and, in practice, its ultimate purposes – in ways most likely to gain general support of others.

This initial exercise focuses on seeking to identify the end or good associated with the practice of justice, rather than seeking to identify relevant norms. This procedure asks us to reflect on our experiences as well as the experiences of others and to keep in mind what various people have said about justice. People may engage in this initial exploration by thinking intuitively, logically or historically about this question of the end or good of justice. This initial exercise parallels the approach taken by the Roman jurists when they sought to formulate their *ius gentium* ('law of nations', i.e., the set of legal guidelines common to all groups) by discerning and formulating common elements in the varied customs and rules of the diverse peoples who became part of their empire (Maine, 1879, ch. 3). The aim here is not to arrive at definitive and timeless definitions, but rather to set forth at particular moment in time workable formulations that allow ongoing discussions and deliberations to proceed. The initial objective is to seek rough consensus, recognizing that the different parties to a given discussion may articulate their formulations in somewhat different but equivalent or corresponding expressions. I assume that as we move from initial efforts to set forth our views about these ends or practical goods, we can revisit this topic, informed by subsequent deliberations and seek greater clarity and firmer consensus.

The next exercise in this process of deliberating requires those involved to identify the minimal expectations that would have to be met in order to realize the envisioned end or practical good. For example, in order for two people to engage in a conversation that might lead to an agreement that both would voluntarily support, both minimally must agree to take turns listening and speaking, to speak honestly and keep the conversation alive until both are willing and able to consent to accept the terms for the agreement they have thereby reached (Bird, 1996, ch. 7). Typically, then, minimal expectations identify necessary but not sufficient bases for realizing envisioned objectives.

What especially characterizes minimal expectations is that, in spite of other, often serious differences, they represent standards that most parties to any negotiations or deliberations can adopt.

The strategy for practical ethics I am proposing calls for us, first, to formulate statements both about the valued end/the practical good of justice; second, to spell out the minimal expectations that need to be honoured to realize this end; and, third, practically and imaginatively to pursue these formulations in ways likely to gain the consensus of others, including especially others from diverse moral traditions.

Basic business practices

Before beginning to outline my proposed model for just business practices, it will be useful to sketch very briefly the basic practices that businesses engage in as social organisms. The account that follows is descriptive not normative: it highlights those features of businesses that are characteristic of any and all businesses and this will be useful in identifying the basic valued goods or ends of businesses as social institutions. I then attempt to identify feasible standards of justice for businesses by determining those minimal normative expectations that must be honoured across diverse cultures in order to realize these basic ends. This approach parallels the natural law ethical strategy developed by Velasquez in chapter 1.[3]

Businesses are variously established to undertake a wide range of economic activities: they buy and sell, manufacture, invest, in transport and deliver tangible or intangible goods and services. They also consume goods and services, offer jobs, generate incomes and create debts. In addition to these basic economic activities, they provide places for people to meet, to gain recognition, to use their imaginations and so forth. Thus business organizations continually engage in interactive exchanges with diverse constituencies, which variously invest in, lend to, purchase from, work for, sell to, collaborate with, provide infrastructures for, govern or manage the firms themselves. Recognizing that firms can only do business by engaging in these overlapping interactions, a number of observers have argued that firms constitute and reconstitute themselves in an ongoing process of initiating and maintaining relationships with their several stakeholders (Freeman, 1984; Hill and Jones, 1992; Clarkson 1995; Wheeler and Sillanpaa, 1997). This view, though widely cited, does not quite fully represent the fundamental character of firms as social realities, as it seems to treat each firm as an autonomous unit with distinct boundaries (Oliver, 1993).

However, without its ongoing interactions with its stakeholders, not only would a firm be unable to continue to do business; it would not be able to carry on the basic activities – buying, selling, investing and producing – by which it constitutes itself as a business. Rather than saying that firms *have* stakeholders, it makes more sense then to say that *by means of their ongoing interactions with diverse stakeholders, firms constitute and re-constitute themselves as businesses.*

Several economists have proposed a different but, I think, complementary model, which defines the social reality of a firm as a nexus of contracts or treaties (Jensen and Meckling, 1976; Williamson, 1990). This model also defines businesses in terms of ongoing interrelationships. However, this account too mis-describes firms, in part because it seems to define them in terms of formal contracts, thereby overlooking all those interactions which are not associated with formal agreements; and also because it identifies the social reality of the firm in terms of formalized statements rather than in terms of ongoing activities and interactions – not all of which have to do with formalized statements. Also missing from this economic account is the recognition that what all of these interactions succeed in accomplishing (to the degree that any firm is able to remain in business) is that they serve as means of utilizing human and natural resources to create the economic and social value that firms, as social institutions, are established and maintained to realize. Using this economic model as a point of departure, therefore, we can best describe a firm as *an overlapping nexus of negotiated asset-creating interactions that involve varied constituents or stakeholders, including managers, employees, creditors, suppliers, investors, customers and communities, among others.*

Firms foster their basic interests by initiating, maintaining and protecting diverse sets of asset-creating interactions in ways that allow them to further the particular purposes they have chosen to pursue. The *assets* and *purposes* of firms differ, but are related. These purposes may be variously understood and stated depending upon the degree to which any particular firm is organized to retail, manufacture, farm, transport, communicate, consult, train, invest or save, among other things. Configurations and constellations of purposes differ for every firm and its sense of identity is often closely associated with how it envisions and seeks to realize its purposes, which it may redefine or reorder over time. For example, many of the large petroleum firms have redefined their identities as extractors, refiners and marketers of petroleum and its products to being 'energy companies' utilizing and conserving, as well as developing, multiple sources of energy.

The assets of firms include all the resources on which they can draw in order to further their purposes and interests. Broadly understood, assets are resources, which, when appropriately utilized, serve as means to store and add economic value. In terms of business operations, assets assume several typical forms:

- Financial assets, including investments, credit that can be accessed and tax benefits
- Productive assets, including machines, working spaces, information systems, access to energy and organizational structures
- Human assets, including the skills of workers, their dispositions with respect to work and their capacity for innovation
- Social assets, including the trust, goodwill and networks linking people and safe and reliable social orders
- Natural assets, including not only available natural resources but also the access to clean air and potable water

Firms attempt to gauge how well they are performing in relation to their purposes and assets. There are a number of options. Mission-based organizations, especially community groups and governments, often measure their performance with respect to their successes in realizing and furthering particular programmes or initiatives: a national defence department measures its success in terms of military operations (rather than budget objectives); a school system measures its success in terms of educational goals achieved and benefits to students. Some businesses gauge their performance in relation to sales, productivity growth or return on investment. Each gauge tends to highlight certain interests, while obscuring or ignoring others; and it may well be a matter of debate as to which measures are most fitting. It is well to observe that a firm's profit margin represents a particular measure, defined in terms of interests of one particular constituency, rather than the overriding purpose for varied business activities. It is, in any case, a measure of the assets of firms and of financial assets in particular, rather than a way of identifying and gauging the realization of a broader social mission.

Governing boards, executives and senior managers bear particular responsibilities with respect to the activities of firms as a whole. How well firms perform clearly depends on how well they utilize the assets available to them and how effectively they manage all of the overlapping and intersecting interactions that are integral to their businesses. For the most part executives and senior managers initiate and undertake negotiations with diverse stakeholder groups on behalf of the firm as a whole, while each stakeholder undertakes a single set of negotiations to determine its relationship with the firm in question. Executives and senior management undertake multiple negotiations with all the relevant and diverse stakeholders. The boards of large corporations are expected to review the activities and strategies of their organizations as well as the overall state of their assets and to exercise guiding and critical judgements, with the aim of promoting the best interests of their firms. The board is expected to hold executives accountable for managing the firm in ways that further these overall interests, i.e., in general realizing their purposes, and protecting and enhancing their assets.

Table 2.1 Justice in International Businesses

A. Justice with respect to interactive exchanges	B. Justice with respect to distributions	C. Justice with respect to adjudications of perceived wrongs
1. Choices are voluntary	1. Fair apportionments of resources	1. Fair hearings for cases involving violations of strict obligations
2. Choices are based on honest communication	2. Fair access to offices and opportunities	2. Fair resolutions of cases involving moral failings and questionable practices
3. Exchanges respect and do not undermine relevant public goods dilemmas	3. Fair utilization of resources	3. Fair discussions and negotiations and dissent in cases involving moral
4. Parties may bargain so that benefits are roughly proportionate to contributions and costs		

With this general picture of basic business practices in mind, we can now address normative questions about the basic interests or ends of these business practices. Depending upon the character of particular businesses and the priorities identified by their executives and board, their basic interests may be more closely associated with realizing purposes, strengthening assets or both. Similarly, specific constituencies connected with a firm – its employees, executives, investors, customers and suppliers are likely to define their own interests with regard to particular purposes and assets from which they stand to benefit. For the moment, however, it is useful simply to observe that the basic interests of a firm are connected with two different kinds of considerations: the specific set of purposes and products it is designed to realize and the assets its activities exploit, protect and create (Bird, 2001).

1. Just exchanges

In order to carry out their work as businesses, firms engage in a variety of ongoing interactive exchanges with a number of specific constituencies, each of which is in a position to make legitimate demands that the firm consult and negotiate with them about such interactions. Not all the groups actually affected by the activities of a particular business are in this position; as a number of indigenous peoples and advocacy groups have learned over time, groups have gained this legitimacy historically, by achieving public recognition and by effectively gaining the attention of firms through demonstrations and boycotts and by effecting changes in the law. Each of these constituencies puts itself at risk as it engages in these interactions.

In the most general terms, we can assume that each of these interactive exchanges is working well (1) to the extent that the interactions function in ways that enable the firm to protect and enhance its assets and to realize its purposes and (2) to the degree that those immediately involved feel that the interactions benefit each in appropriate ways. The good of any interactive exchange is realized, then, to the extent that the exchange fulfils its purposes and does so in ways that are regarded as mutually beneficial to the parties involved.

The principles of voluntary choice and honest communication

Traditionally, two standards have been invoked as guides for fair and fitting exchanges. These standards state that parties to exchanges (1) should be able to act voluntarily and (2) should be fully and honestly informed with respect to all information relevant to the exchange. If an exchange is to be fair, the parties ought to be able to enter into it freely without any kind of coercion or excessive constraint on the choices they make as they negotiate the terms of their exchange. Ordinarily, parties are assumed to act voluntarily if they are able to make choices among alternatives. It is also generally accepted that the parties cannot negotiate freely unless they are reliably informed as to the nature of the exchange they are transacting; neither party has the right to misinform the other. These standards are regularly used as guidelines for business transactions. When businesses negotiate with each other or with creditors, suppliers and workers, they may, depending upon fluctuations in supply and demand or upon their own priorities as to goals and needs, arrive at quite different estimations of costs and benefits and correspondingly require or agree to quite different terms and conditions in exchanges with different groups and at different times. Whether or not the terms of agreement are considered just, in keeping with the standards of just exchange, depends not on the substance of these terms but rather on whether the discussions leading up to the agreement were undertaken freely and openly – that is, based on accurate and reliable access to any relevant information related to the terms of the exchange.

For businesses these are indeed important standards. Typically, when people protest against information asymmetries, lack of transparency, lack of full and open disclosure or information deliberately withheld (as in exchanges involving illegal payments, manipulated negotiations, bribery or extortion), they are asserting that their freedom to bargain has been compromised.

With respect to negotiations, it is important to keep in mind two considerations. First, there is an important ethical difference between intentional deception in what one overtly communicates (in other words, lying) and withholding information to protect confidences and privileged information (in other words, keeping secrets), which may be morally or even legally required. Insofar as the withholding information does not put the other persons at serious risk or result in irreversible harm, keeping secrets is ordinarily justified (Bok, 1978, 1984). Second, negotiations, by their very nature, take place over time. At the outset, the parties involved may withhold information about their final bargaining positions and as negotiations proceed, they may privately adjust these positions in response to information they receive from those with whom they are bargaining. Hence, as negotiations unfold, the parties incrementally disclose their final bargaining positions.

There are widespread feelings of resentment among many of the indigenous peoples in developing areas who have been contacted by international businesses seeking to mine or log in their regions. Many of these groups feel that the international firms have not really listened to their concerns and have not genuinely entered into two-way consultations (Whiteman and Mamen, 2002). To be sure, each side in these discussions often experiences difficulties in comprehending the other's concerns, because of their cultural differences and the commitment of each side to its own agenda. Both sides have been given to stereotyping and both, at times, have been reluctant to allow time enough for really reciprocal exchanges (Bird, 1996, ch. 3). Nonetheless the indigenous peoples have suffered overwhelmingly. In the course of the larger research project with which this book is associated, we have found several positive examples of satisfactory consultations between international firms and indigenous groups, including the consultations between the Raglan Mine and Inuit in northern Quebec (Bird and Herman, 2004, ch. 12), the exploratory discussions between Rio Tinto and Malagasy in southeastern Madagascar (Bird et al., 2005, ch. 6) and the collaborations initiated by a small overseas petroleum firm with indigenous groups in Colombia (Bird et al., 2005, ch. 13).

If these conversations are to be free and based on reliable and non-deceptive information, they need to be genuinely open-ended and reciprocal. For the most part these discussions take place over time as the parties make and respond to offers and counter-offers, formulate and reformulate their positions. In order for these conversations to proceed in ways that are genuinely satisfactory, those involved need to listen attentively to what others say and respond in ways that indicate the responders have taken into account what the others have said. They also need to be willing to continue the discussions until all involved agree to a common position. In practice communication does not always occur in this manner. Many such discussions are characterized by what the psychologist Jean Piaget (1951) referred to as 'bypassing monologues'. The discussants in these cases fail to listen attentively to each other. Interactive communications are also undermined whenever one of the parties seeks prematurely to close off further discussions. To the degree that actual communications fail in these ways to be reciprocal, one or another of the parties is likely to feel, even if they eventually consented to the agreement, that the information used as basis for the agreement is not as full as it ought to be and that their consent is in fact less than fully free. These parties are likely to harbour feelings of resentment and to comply only half-heartedly, even with agreements they have formally accepted.

Interacting exchanges are inevitably affected by arrangements of power: both by the differential power exerted by the parties themselves as well as various third parties, including governments, local and international financial institutions, community groups and other businesses. Power represents the capacity to realize objectives even in the face of opposition or resistance (Weber, [1914] 1978, p. 53). In the case of these interactive negotiations, power is especially embodied in actions and existing rules that affect the outcome, apart from the arguments and information freely set forth by the parties involved. Parties can also exert power by physical coercion, economic sanctions, public demonstrations, legal suits, strikes, boycotts and the withholding of valuable information. In principle, how businesses interact with their constituents and others should not be shaped by which parties can exert the most power. They should rather be determined in keeping with relevant laws and by the voluntary choices of those involved, based upon current and reliable information and their assessments of their own interests. Nonetheless, the parties characteristically do use the power available to them to influence the course of their negotiations. When and in what ways do these exertions of power prevent parties involved from interacting in ways that correspond to fair exchanges? Short of physical coercion, how much power can parties exert in ways that can legitimately be regarded as fair? Without attempting a detailed and exhaustive answer, we can, I think, arrive at some practical minimal answers to these questions. The key here is to consider what factors make it possible for the negotiations to proceed so that parties can establish, review or renew their interactive exchanges. Thus it seems reasonable to argue that it is illegitimate to use power to break off negotiations permanently. On the other hand, it seems reasonable to argue that it is legitimate to exert power to balance or neutralize the power already exerted by others. Such exercise of countervailing power seems to be not only fair but also functional, in that it allows negotiations to proceed in setting where one party might otherwise feel overpowered (Galbraith, 1952). It also seems justifiable for any one party to exercise power with the aim of pressuring the others involved in negotiations, either to continue or resume two-way negotiations that otherwise might lapse or falter, or to pay greater attention to certain arguments and information that otherwise might not receive sufficient attention. Using these guidelines, it is possible both to recognize that power inevitably affects interactive exchanges and to identify those exercises of power that seem legitimate and even necessary if such exchanges are to be just.

These two basic standards for just exchanges – the norms for voluntary choice and the open and reliable access to relevant information – remain fairly robust. They incorporate almost all of the concerns raised by the recent discussion of procedural justice in organizations, which has focused primarily on employee relations. This same concern for procedural justice, articulated broadly in keeping with these two standards, can also be invoked to guide and to criticize the ways businesses interact with all of their stakeholders. These standards for just exchanges seem both morally compelling and practically effective. Businesses cannot operate without developing and sustaining ongoing interaction with a number of different groups. However, by themselves these standards overlook and take for granted other considerations that directly affect whether any interactive exchange is in fact fair, appropriate and just. In the paragraphs that follow I will discuss and defend two additional standards.

The principle respecting public goods

Parties to interactive exchanges are obliged to support and maintain the specific sets of public goods that make it possible for them to initiate, transact and benefit from their exchanges. Such exchanges do not take place in social vacuums. People are able to enter into financial, commercial, labour and organizational transactions with respect to business practices because governments and communities provide legal frameworks, protect against violence, create and sustain infrastructures, promote social order, establish training programmes and develop social confidence. Private exchanges, in short, take place within the context of public goods. In the absence of these public goods – in 'frontier' settings where random violence, social disruption and opportunism are commonplace and public authority may be entirely absent – it is much more difficult to initiate and maintain ongoing interactive exchanges. How well these larger social arrangements are institutionalized affects, in turn, the capacity of firms to initiate and maintain the varied interactions integral to their businesses.

The public goods that facilitate the interactive exchanges central to business may vary considerably between less economically developed societies and modern societies with well-developed welfare systems, voluntary sectors or civil societies. These public goods include minimally the following:

• Laws governing commercial transactions, labour practices and property claims
• Rudimentary physical, social and commercial infrastructures
• A reasonable degree of social order
• Educational, apprenticeship and training programmes by means of which parties to these transactions can develop the skills and capabilities to perform their duties in relation to these exchanges

These public goods are established and supported by government legislation and public taxes, and by the philanthropic gifts or initiatives of men and women of good will. They are also supported by the deference and respect of all those who use and honour them. Depending upon the society in question, its history, the overall state of its economy and the overt commitments of its citizens, these kinds of public goods may be adequately or inadequately supported.

Businesses are called upon to support and not to undermine public goods insofar as these particular public goods enable them, directly or indirectly, to engage reliably in the varied interactive exchanges related to their business practices.[3] We can spell out the obligations of businesses with respect to these particular public goods in three points.

1. Minimally, businesses are legitimately required not to disrupt or degrade the public goods from which they benefit. If they benefit from the use of roads or available water, they are duly obligated not to degrade excessively, but rather to maintain, these public goods. If they benefit from various services of local governments, then they are correspondingly obligated not to undermine these governments by evading or unduly minimizing their payment of local taxes.

2. Besides paying taxes, businesses are called upon to support these diverse public goods in various other ways that seem appropriate. Thus, insofar as they benefit from them, businesses can be expected to obey local laws, support local commerce and foster civil society.

3. In order appropriately to fulfil their obligations to support those public goods that make it possible for them to do business, firms must exercise judgement. It is impossible to spell out all of these obligations in law, as no legal system can identify all of the public goods from which businesses benefit. Insofar as businesses benefit from social order, public confidence and local commerce, they need to explore various ways by which they can help to support and not diminish the value of these public goods. They may undertake a range of initiatives, including expanded efforts to purchase supplies locally, collaborative business and social ventures with local businesses and community groups and the support for employee volunteer programmes – not fundamentally as expressions of philanthropy but as social investments put forth to support and invigorate the public goods that make business activities possible. Insofar as businesses fail to support the public goods that make it possible for them to engage in the interactive exchanges integral to their operations, they act as freeloaders on these public goods.

The principle respecting proportionality in exchanges

Business exchanges are just to the extent that the negotiated benefits that parties gain by virtue of these exchanges are considered by the parties to be roughly proportionate to a reasonable combination of their contributions, risks and efforts. This principle of proportionality, though an important and necessary feature of just exchanges, is essentially a traditional standard associated only loosely with ideas about commutative justice. It is not, however, a precise standard. It probably more closely approximates a standard of excellence, which parties should aspire to realize, rather than an absolute obligation that must be met no matter what. Nonetheless, minimally stated, exchanges can be described as just only if the parties, in the course of their negotiations, have duly considered issues of proportionality, mutually acknowledged their moral weight and committed themselves to actions that will, as far as possible, realize this standard.

According to the principle of proportionality, when parties make large investments, undertake significant risks, exert considerable efforts or exercise valuable skills or capacities, it is reasonable for them to expect that they will reap corresponding benefits (barring intervening factors beyond the parties' control). When we attempt to assess what parties bring to an exchange, we have to take into account (1) their actual contributions, gauged in relation to efforts, skills, impacts and outcomes, as well as the time they invested; (2) the alternative opportunities they have foregone and the costs they have already invested in the choices they have made;

and (3) the specific risks they face as a result of their involvement in these interactions. For example, we need to assess the role of employees in exchanges not only with regard to their actual work and its contributions but also in relation to their costs in terms of education, housing and the commitments of other family members.

Similarly, when we attempt to assess the benefits parties gain, we need to take account of a wide variety of possible outcomes, including (1) benefits in the form of direct payments, deferred payments, opportunities for learning and career development, security with respect to employment and investments, social contacts and opportunities to engage in purposive activities, as well as (2) costs they have experienced in the form of lost opportunities as well as work-related stress and injuries. Thus, for example, with respect to employees, 'overall benefits' includes not only income and fringe benefits but also job security, as well as opportunities for skill development, advancement and constructive work. At the same time, though the level of wages for particular work is inherently influenced by market conditions, particular wage levels should also be related to the extent and quality of the work actually accomplished and risks actually assumed.

The relationship between what parties bring to exchanges and what they can reasonably expect to gain from them is inevitably subject to several important contingencies. For example, the values which are assigned to the contributions, benefits and costs of these exchanges are always affected by culturally influenced assessments, as well as by market variations in supply and demand of the goods, services, activities and funds the parties contribute and from which they benefit. At the same time, these exchanges may or may not turn out as expected because of a number of not easily controllable historical factors, including political changes, alteration in currency values, changes in overall organizational strategies and shifts in the national or international economies, as well as unexpected natural disasters.

The principle of proportionality provides a way of thinking about these variables, rather than a fixed answer. This principle encourages parties in business interactions to explore how benefits should ideally be connected in fitting ways to the parties' contributions and costs. Correspondingly, although the types and value of the benefits those parties receive are inevitably affected by contingencies associated with cultural, market and political factors, from the perspective of the principle of proportionality these factors must not be regarded as absolute.

The principle of proportionality calls for parties to make persuasive, evidence-based claims indicating how various factors are interrelated; it further requires that each party should consider seriously the arguments of other parties with respect both to what they bring to, and take from these exchanges. Moreover, as a standard of excellence, this principle treats the negotiations with respect to interactive exchanges as being in principle open-ended or renegotiable: that is, notions of proportionality can be appropriately invoked not only to guide preliminary discussions with respect to new agreements but also to review and re-assess actual agreements and to judge the degree to which the outcomes of such agreements match the parties' expectations.

As a set of normative standards for business practices, the model of justice with respect to exchanges assumes that businesses and the parties they interact with will actively pursue their own interests and will bargain as effectively as they can to secure these interests.

Why should businesses adhere to these standards? They should do so, first, because just exchanges foster conditions of trust. Businesses must engage in ongoing interactions with multiple parties, they ought to adhere to the standards for just exchanges out of respect for those with whom they interact, as well as to obtain their willing collaboration. Second, just exchanges create what analysts now refer to as 'social capital', a non-material but real asset, which fosters cooperation, facilitates negotiation and ensures communication. When businesses violate these standards, they occasion suspicions, resentment and reluctance to cooperate. When parties feel they might be taken advantage of, might be deceived or manipulated into accepting less than optimal terms, they are much more likely to respond slowly, to seek short-term advantages, call into question the motives of others, haggle over details and act in other ways that add to the overall transaction costs involved in reaching agreements (Lin et al., 2001; Putnam et al., 1993). To the degree that businesses ignore or violate the standards for just exchanges, they tend to treat particular negotiated interactions as singular exchanges not likely to be repeated. They tend therefore to seek immediate advantage rather than cultivate viable long-term relations. However, when businesses recognize that they are likely to develop long-term interactions with a number of different constituent groups, they are more likely to follow the principle of just exchanges as a way of fostering trust in these relationships (Axelrod, 1984; Frank, 1988).

A third reason why businesses ought to adhere to the standard for just exchanges is that in so doing they are much more likely to foster organizational learning. Businesses put themselves at needless risk to the extent that they impede the ordinary flow of communication among parties with whom they interact. However, if they consider their interactions to be just exchanges, they are likely to remain more conscientious and this in turn enriches communications with new ideas, useful feedback and timely sharing of advice in problem areas.

The fourth reason why businesses ought to adhere to the principle of just exchanges is that they are likely thereby to obtain and enhance productive cooperation from and among the parties with whom they interact. Recent studies of organizational commitment and organizational citizenship behaviour among employees provide an interesting illustration of this point. When workers feel little commitment to the firm for which they work, they are much more likely to absent themselves from work, show up for work late, look for other employment and do as little work as they can, or else do it grudgingly. Such behaviour is very costly for firms, which often feel compelled as a result to hire additional workers or waste valuable time and resources on productivity improvement or fighting absenteeism (Mowday et al., 1982). Firms therefore have an interest in exploring ways to enhance the organizational commitment of their workers. For the most part, efforts to raise attendance levels and improve workmanship by policing workers or running attendance-management programmes do not work very well. Two organizational initiatives, however, seem to be particularly successful. One involves reorganizing the workplace so as to reduce surveillance and allow workers more discretion over the pace and character of their own work. The other refers to all of those forms of organization that allow workers to see that their work adds real value (Glisson and Durrick, 1988). What is noteworthy about each of these initiatives is the way interactive exchanges between workers and managers have been altered to foster trust, respond workers' concerns and build in intrinsic work-related rewards for workers in ways that make these benefits seem fittingly proportionate to what the workers in fact contribute.

2. Just distributions

For the purposes of this study, I will sketch a model for distributive justice primarily within organizations, recognizing that a different and perhaps larger question concerns the role of businesses with respect to distributive justice within societies. To be sure, how businesses allocate resources and rewards internally in turn affects their impact on the larger society. As in the discussion of just exchanges, I will attempt to articulate a model that can, I think, be invoked or adopted as a core feature within culturally different models of distributive justice.

In terms of their own operations, businesses tend particularly to raise questions of distributive justice when they consider how the varied resources to which they have access should be allocated and distributed. Questions about allocation of resources arise in many different ways; for example, what portions of organizational resources should be assigned for wages, executive salaries, research, marketing, training programmes, auditing or new technologies? Should old plants be renovated or new plants built? Should workforces be cut, or should compensation systems be reduced? Should the business invest in new product lines, combine departments, retrain redundant workers or spend less on advertising?

Questions bearing upon fitting resource allocations take many shapes in part because organizational resources themselves are embodied in diverse forms. These resources include buildings, access to credit, properties, income tax credits, skilled workers and goodwill, among other things. For heuristic purposes, we can, as I have noted earlier in this essay, identify five major groupings of organizational resources:

1. Financial assets
2. Productive resources
3. Human resources
4. Social assets
5. Natural assets

In order to make a full accounting of organization resources, we must take into account not only current assets but also potential assets and opportunities. Liabilities, or negative assets, may include tax burdens, debts, foregone opportunities, unresolved conflicts, threatened boycotts or excessive sunk costs in particular technologies. Businesses can be expected to view the allocation and utilization of assets and liabilities from a strategic perspective; that is, they can be expected to invest in and allocate varied resources with the aim of advancing their overall best interests.

Issues with respect to just distribution within businesses need to be viewed from three different but complementary perspectives. The first looks at these issues from the top down, in terms of how organizational resources are apportioned among different units and activities. The second looks at these issues from the bottom up, in terms of the access of individuals to resources. The third perspective looks at these issues horizontally, inquiring about how effectively and appropriately resources are put to use. Each perspective is a way of examining whether the distribution of resources in fact serves the business's best interests: that is, whether it serves to realize the basic purposes and to protect and augment the fundamental assets, of the business as a whole.

The question of just apportionment

Businesses must determine how to allocate their resources among various competing groups, units, projects and parties. It can be useful at times to think of these various units as competitors in internal organizational markets. They describe their needs, goals and prospects and seek to promote their own interests while also promising to advance the best interests of the organization as a whole (Hallal et al., 1993). Critical decisions as to allocations of resources are made in different ways and at different times – often at formal strategy or budget meetings. But such decisions are often made incrementally, in response to the efforts of particular departments or projects to seek more assistance. Because it is difficult to determine ahead of time which ways of apportioning organizational resources will in fact promote its best interests, the organization's leaders may rely on past experiences, current trends and their sense of the strengths and competencies of their organization (Selznick, 1957). In practice, many other factors influence this decision-making process, not all constructively, including personal ambitions, exaggerated claims, reluctance to change and much more.

A just apportionment of organizational assets, then, involves distributions, which while honouring the principles of just exchanges, also best serve the interests of their organization as a whole. Negatively stated, unjust apportionments may fittingly be described as being unbalanced: that is, favouring the interests of particular parties, programmes or individuals in ways that run contrary to the overall interests of the organization. In *Permanently Failing Organizations* (1989), Meyer and Zucker describe a number of firms that unduly favoured the interests of particular constituencies – customers, employees or community groups. In all cases, the firms used up more resources than they generated.

How international businesses in developing areas choose to compensate expatriate employees often occasions aggravated debates about the just apportionment of organizational resources. On the one hand, as a matter of a fair exchange, employees expect to receive benefits comparable to, or higher than, they would have received if they had stayed at home. However, if their local levels of pay far exceed those of local employees, this difference gives rise to feelings of resentment; it seems as if excessive amounts of organizational funds are being diverted to pay expatriate employees. Clearly, it is in the interest of these firms to balance these claims in a way that seems fair to all concerned. How businesses choose to allocate funds for executive salaries represents another controversial issue. For many businesses, compensation packages for executives have risen much faster than either inflation or the share value of their firms. Questions arise not only whether or not these benefit levels represent fair exchanges for services rendered, given the current status in the market for valued executives, but also whether this allocation of organizational resources best serves the interest of the firm as a whole. This is not only a matter of strategy; it is also a matter of justice, since the diversion of resources to serve particular interests or the failure to utilize resources effectively in response to contingencies necessarily deprives some parties, programmes or policies of the means to realize their legitimate purposes. It is also easier in retrospect to see when a firm has overtly favoured particular parties or programmes at the expense of the organization as a whole than it is to anticipate and avoid these problems. Nonetheless there are several fairly reliable strategies that businesses can adopt to prevent these problems and promote their best overall interests.

1. They can obtain a reliable and accurate picture of their current assets by engaging auditors to render a comprehensive accounting of organizational resources. The well-defended tradition to assess the overall resources of firms in terms of financial assets makes sense from the perspective of investors and creditors. More broadly, it is argued that this approach is as well both feasible and largely justifiable, because it is possible to calculate other resources roughly in terms of financial assets. Moreover, it has been asserted that viewing the overall state of assets in terms of financial returns

to investors makes sense because, in principle, investors are expected to receive only the residual returns after the business has first met all its other obligations (Daniels and Morck, 1996; Hansmann, 1996; Jensen and Meckling, 1976). Others have criticized this perspective because it tends in practice to over-emphasize the ways firms create wealth by attracting investments and it overlooks the extent to which firms increase their wealth in terms of how well they utilize as well their human and social assets (Blair, 1995, 1996). The tendency to focus restrictively on financial assets also results, in part, from the legal responsibilities of many boards, especially in British and American firms, to look after the financial interests of investors. However, because these interests can be materially affected by how firms utilize human, social, productive and natural assets; it can be argued investors have a corresponding material interest in knowing how well such assets are performing. This is another reason why firms need to maintain a lively sense of the condition and potentials of all of their varied assets. The more narrowly they view their resources, the more likely they are to become strategically unbalanced.

In order to address the problems occasioned by narrowly assessing a firm's assets primarily in financial terms, a number of recent critics have called for what they refer to as 'triple bottom line' accounting, in which firms assess their social and environmental performances in addition to their financial performance. While the triple bottom line approach broadens the way organizational assets are viewed, it is still open to criticism, since it tends to overlook (or at least does not focus on) productive and human assets as such, and also tends to view environmental and social assets separately from, and after, the financial bottom line evaluations (Norman and MacDonald, 2004).

2. Businesses are more likely to reach balanced decisions to utilize resources in their best interests if those making decisions maintain lively communications with all stakeholders. It is important that all units and parties be well represented in the strategic decision-making processes. Those making decisions are then better able to determine both the performance and potential of units able to speak on their own behalf. To the degree that multiple parties and programmes are able to advocate for themselves, those making decisions can put each of these claims in perspective when assessed alongside the claims of others. Open and forthright communication matters also because it provides those making strategic decisions with up-to-date information on how current and past strategies have affected variously organizational units as well as the company as a whole. In practice, organizational communications are often less than optimal.

3. Businesses are more likely to apportion their resources more fairly if they are able to find ways of distinguishing and strengthening the role of the directors and managers whose duty it is to exercise good judgement on behalf of the organization as a whole. These organizational decision-makers

are required to innovate and at the same time to conserve organizational assets; to respond creatively to external contingencies; to keep track of internal developments; and to inspire and manage their subordinates. As managers and executives are especially expected to administer and to lead, governing boards are especially expected to exercise judgement. In the process, they are expected to keep track of the interests of their firm as whole, to evaluate whether current strategies serve these interests and to explore alternatives. In many smaller firms and family businesses, this governing function is often performed as well by senior executives. In either case, the practice of exercising judgement is an important organizational activity, in which the firm consciously reviews its use of resources, deliberates over policy initiatives and holds executives accountable in serving the best interest of their organizations (Bird, 2001).

In practice, governing boards often fail to rise fully to this task; instead they become too closely identified with the executives and their particular interests, or else with the interests of particular investors. Board members are often ill prepared for their deliberations. Some become distracted with micro-managing particular programmes and budget details. Nonetheless, if the governing board serves as a locus for critical deliberations and organizational judgement, it is likely to act in ways such that organizational resources will be fairly apportioned so as to further the best interests of the firm as a whole.

In these several ways, organizations seek to apportion resources fairly. This goal remains somewhat elusive, and it is impossible to propose a single principle or formula that can reliably apportion organizational assets. Nonetheless, there are, as I have indicated several procedural principles that can and have served as approximate guidelines for actions.

Questions of just access

From a second perspective we can view how well organizations fairly distribute resources internally by looking at the opportunities they provide for their members and employees to gain access to organizational positions. An organization may be considered just to the degree that it allows all members to compete for these positions freely and without discrimination based on factors such as gender, age and race, which are unrelated to the job requirements of these positions. Businesses are just from this perspective to the extent they adhere to the traditional liberal principles regarding equal opportunities.[4]

In practice, businesses deviate from this standard in numerous ways. Women and visible minorities are under-represented in senior positions in ways that would not occur if the principle of equal access were fully honoured. The actual factors that tend in practice to impede access to these positions are not always overt; sometimes they reflect the subtle ways in which information about opportunities is miscommunicated and the strength of particular employees is overlooked. Frequently, firms favour certain suppliers solely because of a longstanding business relationship and overlook the offers of competitors who might well deliver better goods and services at a lower cost or in an equally timely manner.

In a number of ways it ought obviously to be in the interest of businesses to ensure fair access to positions. They are likely thereby to benefit from higher-quality performances by highly motivated employees; they are likely also to reduce or eliminate potential resentment among workers, suppliers, managers and customers whose claims and past contributions would otherwise have been ignored and slighted.

Questions of just use

Often questions of use are viewed in relation to notions of efficacy and conservation rather than justice. Nonetheless, how effectively and fittingly organizations use the resources at their disposal is also a matter of justice. When given resources are wasted, horded, or misused, those resources are not available for others to utilize for valued alternative purposes; and others are thereby denied opportunities they might otherwise enjoy. At the same time the organization as a whole loses out. In the early 1990s I conducted research at a university hospital, which was in the midst of a number of overlapping discussions about allocation of hospital health care resources. On the surface, the most pressing questions seemed to focus on how to choose between different parties and programmes, all of which presented compelling cases about their needs, their promise and their importance. Ironically, several of the most helpful responses at the time were initiated by those concerned with the fair utilization of existing resources: one such response by the purchasing department explored ways to reduce costs through cooperative purchasing arrangements developed with other hospitals. Another creative response concerned efforts to involve families more directly in the care of their own members, thereby dramatically reducing the need for hospital resources. A third initiative involved efforts by physicians and nurses to collaborate more fully in decision-making about the delivery of clinical services. All of these initiatives proposed more effective and fitting use of hospital resources; what is more, they indirectly expanded the pool of resources available for distribution to other projects and units.

From the perspective of distributive justice, resources are used fairly and fittingly when they are utilized in terms of their own character, strengths and limitations. Businesses best utilize human resources when they employ workers on jobs that exercise and develop their talents, skills and discretion, while respecting their liabilities, the limits of their strength or attention and their need for feedback and recognition. Businesses best use natural resources by utilizing them in ways that can be sustained over time as long as possible. Finally, insofar as possible, they best interact with all resources by viewing these – including the goodwill of those with whom they interact – as assets to be conserved rather than as resources to be consumed.

3. Just adjudications

We gauge whether or not businesses are just, not only with regard to the interactive exchanges they engage in and the overall distribution of organizational resources, but also with regard to how they resolve or adjudicate conflicts with respect to ethical standards. Although these conflicts may assume diverse forms, they most obviously arise whenever anyone violates a moral or legal standard acknowledged as binding or obligatory by the firm in question. In these cases, we become especially concerned about how to manage justly both complaints of wrongdoing as well as actual hearings about wrongdoings. How these and other kinds of ethical conflicts are resolved measurably affects the extent to which an organization's members feel their organization is just.

At the outset it is important to determine the character of the ethical issues or conflicts in question. Different kinds of issues call for quite different responses and responding in ways that seem inappropriate occasions additional feelings of injustice. Consider the following sets of examples.

Type One: Cases involving violations of obligatory standards

1. In violation of its own published code of practices, accountants at a British overseas firm calculated transfer prices for goods and services used by their divisional plant in Argentina in excess of ordinary costs, with the result that the local plant seemed to be operating barely above the break-even point. As a result the local firm paid very low taxes:

2. In violation of his company's code, an expatriate executive used mechanics and custodians from the plant he managed in Guatemala to undertake major renovations on his house.

Type Two: Cases involving questionable practices and moral failings

1. Because a number of managers failed in the past to provide adequate feedback to certain poorly performing subordinates, a new supervisor faced the dilemma of having to fire or retain employees who never received candid accounts of how well they had been performing:

2. In opposition to company purchasing guidelines and the recommendation of the purchasing officer, the manager at a particular production site continued to use his discretion as unit supervisor to buy certain chemicals at costs 14 per cent higher than their fair market value from a long-time supplier who had also become a personal friend.

Type Three: Cases involving genuine moral dilemmas or debates

1. Unlike many other American firms and in opposition to a petition by a minority of investors, Otis Elevator decided to continue its operations in South Africa in the 1980s and 1990s. It defended this position arguing that it could offer important opportunities for employment and promotion of blacks, while working from inside the country to oppose the apartheid system.

2. In order to overcome past injustices, a large international firm deliberately sought to hire indigenous employees and even promote them to senior positions, even when in some cases non-indigenous applicants probably were more qualified.

3. In violation of overt company rules, but in keeping with local practices, company employees at dockside warehouses paid warehouse agents undeclared facilitation fees to reduce by more than half the time involved in off-loading their supplies from ships to local transport vehicles.

All these cases involve ethically questionable practices; all have given rise to ethical conflicts. Most have occasioned complaints. Yet in ethically important ways, these cases differ in the kinds of issues they raise. In the paragraphs that follow I will discuss each of the different categories of ethical issues or conflicts and I will suggest appropriate ways of adjudicating these types of cases.

In the Type One cases listed above, someone working for a firm has acted in violation of an obligatory standard stipulated by the firm itself. The two cases cited above involving transfer pricing and 'liberal' use or abuse of executive perks may seem a bit ambiguous, since in some settings these practices have indeed been excused as customary. It is possible to imagine less ambiguous instances: overtly misrepresenting production output, harassing employees or bribing public officials and purchasing agents. In all of these cases, one or more parties have been accused of wrongdoing because they have violated a strict organizational standard. If justice is to be done in ways that seem fair in these cases, it is necessary to follow a set of fairly well-known due-process procedures designed to protect both the accusers and the accused from reprisals and malicious complaints. At the outset, it is important to recall that it is possible for accusers to make their complaints before legal courts if they feel that the suspected wrongdoing warrants such a response. Due-process systems for internal hearings in businesses are especially designed to adjudicate accusations of wrongdoings using procedures developed for this purpose within specific organizations. In most cases, these procedures take place confidentially rather than publicly in order to protect the repute of accusers and accused from unsubstantiated claims. In all cases, those accused must be clearly informed of complaints against them and must be able to defend themselves adequately against these accusations. In some instances complaints about employees violating obligatory codes can be managed by routine intervention on the part of the employees' immediate supervisors. However, in cases involving accusations against supervisors, it is necessary to establish hearing procedures that involve third parties. Although it is not excessively difficult to establish due process procedures within businesses, few businesses have in fact done so (Ewing, 1989).

Type Two cases concern questionable practices and moral failings, usually involving departures from moral codes regarded as standards of excellence rather than strict obligations. The failure to provide adequate feedback and the fudging of purchasing rules are both apt examples of this 'slippage' from ideals. Other examples might be: the use of exaggerated and misleading information in advertising; careless supervision over new employees; padded expense accounts; or failure to disclose information about potential conflicts of interest. For the most part ethical issues of this type are not dealt with best by accusations of wrongdoing and formal hearings. In most instances, these kinds of cases can be resolved and adjudicated by an informal and interactive process that allows those involved to reconsider how they might best formulate the issues at hand in ways that are practical as well ethically demanding and that allows those missing their ethical marks to save face while acknowledging their shortcomings. Leaders can call for increased dedication; colleagues can confer, work to resolve differences and seek support each other's efforts; and those involved in the wrongdoing can seek to learn from their mistakes and renew their commitment to moral excellence. To treat these kinds of cases as outright violations – treat standards of excellence as if they were standards of obligation – is to misrepresent the character of the relevant ethical principles. This can have several additional adverse consequences. One response is simply to tolerate these kinds of moral failings as if they were acceptable, or overlook them as insignificant, since the perceived alternative of instituting formal hearings seems not only morally excessive but also a waste of organizational resources. Another typical response is to deal selectively and arbitrarily with some instances of wrongdoing, while ignoring others. To many, these kinds of response seem hypocritical, because certain easily identified acts are morally censured while other, possibly much more serious acts evoke no overt ethical response (Waters and Bird, 1989).

Type Three cases concern genuine moral dilemmas, about which people have been able typically to develop different and often quite contradictory ethical responses. People took opposing ethical views about whether businesses ought to have remained in South Africa in the 1980s, whether particular affirmative-action strategies were morally acceptable and whether the payment of facilitation fees was morally justified. Some have argued that each of these actions was egregiously wrong and have rallied groups to pressure international businesses to change their ways. Others at the same time mounted opposing moral arguments, justifying in ethical terms decisions of businesses to remain in South Africa, to discriminate in favour of minorities and to pay facilitation fees. We can add to the list of Type Three cases a number of additional moral dilemmas faced by businesses: debates or ethical conflicts about the uses of nuclear energy; the use of educational retreats for doctors as marketing strategies for pharmaceutical companies; the use of children as part-time workers in developing countries; and decisions to conduct businesses in countries with oppressive regimes that have committed numerous human rights abuses. In all these examples it has often been difficult for proponents of one view (whether opposing or condoning such practices) to recognize that their opponents have mounted credible, albeit quite different, moral arguments. These kinds of ethical conflicts are best viewed as genuine dilemmas rather than as violations of moral obligations, instances of moral failings or questionable practices. They are best resolved through debates and negotiations. To be sure, within reasonable limits parties to these debates may mount demonstrations in support of their positions. In many such controversies, differences cannot easily be resolved over the short term.

How should businesses respond to such ethical conflicts over their practices? As we have reviewed the examples cited above, it has become clear that finding fitting and fair ways of managing these cases involves considerations of substantive principles and purposes as well as appropriate procedures. Choosing the appropriate procedure depends, first, upon the character of the perceived moral conflict and, second, upon the purposes that it seems appropriate to pursue in each instance. Typical discussions of procedural justice tend to focus on guidelines for due-process and this is certainly useful. Where the perceived wrong seems to involve a violation of important ethical obligations, then the overriding purposes correspondingly revolve around correctly identifying offenders and offences through informal and formal hearing procedures that follow these guidelines. However, where the perceived wrongs seem to involve moral failings, the overriding purpose is different and the response shifts toward objectives related to motivating those involved to act with greater moral attention and commitment. Appropriate procedures for realizing these objectives, include altered intra-group interactions, personal counselling, adequate feedback and altered reward systems. Where the perceived wrong involves issues about which there are genuine moral disagreements, adequate responses are likely to be quite different, allowing those involved to acknowledge and respectfully (often quite forcefully) present opposing moral points of view. Appropriate procedures in these cases would provide for debate and negotiation, as well as dissent.

Conclusion: why just business practices matter

In this essay I have developed a model of justice that is not overtly aligned with any specific ethical tradition. To be sure, in places I have commented, usually in the notes, on how this model approaches certain questions of justice in ways similar to moral traditions associated with natural law, discourse ethics, Aristotle and contemporary authors such as Rawls, Walzer and Nozick. However, for the most part I have attempted to arrive at guidelines for just business practices by thinking about fitting ways by means of which businesses as social institutions could behave justly in situations that called for them to engage in ongoing interactive exchanges, allocate organizational resources and risks and adjudicate conflicts. I have approached questions of justice from this institutional perspective because, in a world of moral diversity, it is important to be able to share ideas and intuitions about justice. This model sets forth such ideas of justice as applied to businesses, rather than proposing a new master theory of justice. It develops these ideas by reviewing common institutional features of business readily recognizable by business people whether their businesses are family firms or corporations, large international businesses or small enterprises, operating in Uganda or Korea, Italy or the United States. We might well refer to this as an institutional model for justice in international businesses.

Businesses operating in diverse cultures need not suppose that all ideas about just business practices are impossibly relative; nor do they need to adopt absolute ideas of justice from a particular moral tradition. From the perspective of the model I have presented, international businesses, to some degree, can both honour local traditions and seek to identify common moral perspectives. They can further elaborate on, modify and justify their support for this institutional model of justice by making reference either to local moral traditions or more comprehensive ethical theories.

My discussion has indicated several reasons why businesses should be just with respect to interactive exchanges, the distribution of risks and resources, and the adjudication of moral conflicts. I will now conclude this essay by reviewing, adding to and reformulating these reasons, invoking both ethical and pragmatic arguments.

Businesses should act with justice because it is the right thing to do. Businesses should foster justice in the ways I have described because by acting in this way they express and embody genuine respect toward others. Respecting others means paying enough attention to them and to their communications so that we have a good sense of their concerns, perspectives and points of view. Paying attention in this way is vital for negotiations as well as adjudication. When others are treated with respect, they are more likely to respond to invitations to cooperate and collaborate. Additionally, business should practice justice because in the process they are more likely to conduct their operations in ways that seem reliable and expected, rather than arbitrary.

For understandable reasons justice has in the European traditions long been associated with law and order because when people adhere to norms of justice, they are more likely to act with regularity and due process. Businesses should act with justice because, for the most part, that is how they expect others to act. To be sure, no one expects others always to act this way. Most of us know that others at times will act in self-serving or even ruthless ways. Furthermore, we have established various systems of courts, regulatory agencies and independent external financial audits as proximate but not completely effective means to limit the most egregious forms of self-interested or self-aggrandizing behaviour. And we are fair warned to remain alert, expecting that some people, as they pursue their own advantage, will dissimulate, violate confidences, contravene rules and put others at needless risk. Nevertheless, these behaviours outrage most of those involved in businesses, whether managers, investors, consumers or workers, because we expect others most of the time to honour the common normative expectations associated with justice. Hence, as a matter of simple reciprocity, businesses should act with justice because that is how they hope and expect others to act most of the time. It is realistic, I think, to assume that humans are likely to be moved simultaneously by altruism and self-interest; by the capacity for industry and cooperation and the capacity for greed and self-deception. Any realistic business ethic must assume the possibility that all these moral sentiments are likely to come into play. A realistic ethic would help us find ways to attend to and limit possibilities for self-aggrandizing conduct and to appreciate and encourage the possibilities for moral behaviour.[5]

Businesses should practice justice because it is in their own best interests. Just business practices help them realize their legitimate ends in several ways. A concern for just distribution reminds businesses to focus on allocating their resources in ways that best serve to realize their purposes, and conserve and enhance their overall assets. The norms associated with fair exchanges and fair adjudications likewise help businesses to act in ways that facilitate both the ongoing interactions integral to business operations but also the satisfactory resolution of internal and inevitable organizational conflicts. To the degree that businesses operate in keeping with standards associated with fair exchanges, distributions and adjudications, they also thereby operate in ways that foster trust and reduce resentment.

Finally, just business practices function to conserve and enhance the overall goodwill and social capital of business organizations operating in developing countries.

Notes

1. In Western societies, justice has been variously associated with a balanced and fundamentally good social order, fairness, acting in keeping with law (especially natural law or divine law), equal opportunity and social equality.

2. Questions of justice and businesses have also been raised with respect to a fourth, cross-cutting concern, namely the fair and fitting use of armed force. Many businesses, especially those located in conflict zones, have had to consider how they can best protect their operations from armed attack (Drohan, 2003; Moser and Bird, 2004). The question of justifiable use of police force thus does arise, at least for some business firms. However, since most businesses do not face these kinds of threats, I will not consider questions regarding the just uses of armed force in this essay. This essay was written primarily on the basis of research on international businesses in developing areas. However, the model for just business practices is as relevant for domestic as for international businesses.

3. Of the various models of distributive justice, perhaps the most influential are those developed by John Rawls (1971) and Michael Walzer (1983). The model I develop in this essay reflects Walzer's concerns about how notions of justice vary in different sectors of society; however my approach is not incompatible with Rawls. While this study focuses on justice within businesses, chapters 4 and 8 discuss issues related to the just practices of businesses within societies.

4. Rawls (1971) has set forth a model of distributive justice that calls for fair equality of opportunity. According to this model, not only should discrimination be eliminated in the competition for positions but any differences in rewards and or opportunities should be structured in ways that work to the benefit of those who are least advantaged. Whether this model can be applied to businesses may depend upon which groups – low-skilled contractual workers, low-skilled suppliers or low-income customers – might count as least advantaged within businesses and on whether it is possible to guard their opportunities to compete fairly for access to valued organizational resources.

5. For a fuller statement of these assumptions see especially two classic works by Reinhold Niebuhr, *The Nature and Destiny of Man* (1941) and *The Children of Light and the Children of Darkness* (1944).

References

Axelrod, R. M. (1984) *The Evolution of Cooperation* (New York: Basic Books).

Bird, F. (1996) *The Muted Conscience: Moral Silence and the Practice of Ethics in Business* (Stamford, CT: Quorum Books).

Bird, F. (2001) 'Good Governance: A Philosophical Discussion of the Responsibilities and Practices of Organizational Governors', *Canadian Journal of Administrative Studies*, vol. 18(4), pp. 298–312.

Bird, F. and Herman, S. (eds) (2004) *International Business and the Challenges of Poverty in the Developing World* (London: Palgrave Macmillan).

Bird, F., Raufflet, E. and Smucker, J. (eds) (2005) *International Business and the Dilemmas of Development* (London: Palgrave Macmillan).

Blair, M. M. (1995) *Ownership and Control: Rethinking Corporate Governance for the Twenty-first Century* (Washington, DC: Brookings Institution).

Blair, M. M. (1996) *Wealth Creation and Wealth Sharing: A Colloquium in Corporate Governance and Investment in Human Capital* (Washington, DC: Brookings Institution).

Bok, S. (1978) *Lying: Moral Choice in Public and Private Life* (New York: Vintage Books).

Bok, S. (1984) *Secrets: On the Ethics of Concealment and Revelation* (New York: Vintage Books).

Cahn, E. (1949) *The Sense of Injustice* (New York: New York University Press).

Clarkson, M. B. E. (1995) 'A Stakeholder Framework for Analyzing and Evaluating Corporate Social Performance', *Academy of Management Review*, vol. 20(1), pp. 92–117.

Cropanzano, R. (ed.) (1993) *Justice in the Workplace: Approaching Fairness in Human Resource Management* (Hillsdale NJ: Lawrence Erlbaum Associates).

Daniels, R. J. and Morck, R. (1996) 'Canadian Corporate Governance Policy Options', Discussion Paper No. 3 (Ottawa: Industry Canada); also available on line at http://strategis.ic.gc.ca/epic/internet/ineas-aes.nsf/en/ra01011e.html.

Deutsch, M. (1985) *Distributive Justice* (New Haven: Yale University Press).

Drohan, M. (2003) *Making a Killing: How and Why Corporations Use Armed Force to Do Business* (Toronto: Random House).

Dumont, L. (1972) *Homo Heirarchicus: The Caste System and Its Implications* (London: Palladin).

Ewing, D. (1989) *Justice on the Job: Resolving Grievances in the Non-Union Workplace* (Boston: Harvard Business School Press).

Folger, R. (1987) 'Distributive and Procedural Justice in the Workplace', *Social Justice Research*, vol. 1(2), pp. 143–59.

Folger, R. and Konovsky, P. (1989) 'The Effects of Procedural and Distributive Justice on Reaction to Pay Raise Decisions', *Academy of Management Journal*, vol. 26, pp. 115–30.

Frank, R. H. (1988) *Passions within Reasons: The Strategic Role of the Emotions* (New York: Norton).

Freeman, R. E. (1984) *Strategic Management: A Stakeholder Approach* (Boston: Pitman).

Galbraith, J. K. (1952) *American Capitalism* (Boston: Houghton-Mifflin).

Glisson, C. and Durrick, M. (1988) 'Predictions of Job Satisfaction and Organizational Commitment in Human Service Organizations', *Administrative Science Quarterly*, vol. 37, pp. 161–81.

Greenberg, J. (1996) *The Quest for Justice on the Job: Essays and Experiments* (Thousand Oaks, CA: SAGE).

Hallal, W. E., Geranmayeh, A. and Pritchard, J. (eds) (1993) *Internal Markets: Bringing the Power of Free Enterprise Inside Your Organization* (New York: John Wiley and Sons, Inc.).

Hansmann, H. (1996) *The Ownership of Enterprise* (Cambridge, MA: Harvard University Press).

Hill, C. W. L. and Jones, T. M. (1992) 'Stakeholder Agency Theory', *Journal of Management Studies*, vol. 29(2), pp. 127–54.

Huntington, S. P. (1996) *The Clash of Civilizations and the Remaking of World Order* (New York: Simon and Schuster).

Jensen, M. C. and Meckling, W. H. (1976) 'Theory of the Firm: Managerial Behaviour, Agency Costs and Ownership Structure', *Journal of Financial Economics*, vol. 3, pp. 305–60.

Lin, N., Cook, K. and Burt, R. S. (eds) (2001) *Social Capital: Theory and Research* (New York: Aldine de Gruyter).

Maine, H. S. (1879) *Ancient Law* (New York: Henry Holt and Company).

McIntyre, A. (1988) *Whose Justice? Which Reason?* (Notre Dame, IN: University of Notre Dame Press).

Meyer, M. W. and Zucker, J. A. (1989) *Permanently Failing Organizations* (London: SAGE).

Moser, T. and Bird, F. (2004) 'Managing Security Through Community Relations', in F. Bird, E. Raufflet and J. Smucker (eds), *International Businesses and the Dilemmas of Development* (London: Palgrave Macmillan).

Mowday, R., Parker, W. and Steers, R. (1982) *Employee-Organizational Linkages: The Psychology of Commitment, Absenteeism and Turnover* (New York: Academic Press).

Niebuhr, R. (1941) *The Nature and Destiny of Man* (New York: Charles Scribner's Sons).

Niebuhr, R. (1944) *The Children of Light and the Children of Darkness: A Vindication of Democracy and a Critique of its Traditional Defense* (New York: Charles Scribner's Sons).

Norman, W. and MacDonald, C. (2004) 'Getting to the Bottom of "Triple Bottom Line"', *Business Ethics Quarterly*, vol. 14(2), pp. 243–62.

Nozick, R. (1974) *Anarchy, State and Utopia* (New York: Basic Books).

Oliver, C. (1993) 'Organizational Boundaries: Definitions, Functions, and Properties', *Canadian Journal of Administrative Sciences*, vol. 10(1), pp. 1–17.

Piaget, J. (1951) *The Language and Thought of the Child* (New York: Humanities Press).

Putnam, R., Leonardi, R. and Nanetti, R. F. (1993) *Making Democracy Work: Civic Traditions in Modern Italy* (Princeton: Princeton University Press).

Rawls, J. (1971) *A Theory of Justice* (Cambridge, MA: Harvard University Press).

Selznick, P. (1957) *Leadership in Administration* (New York: Harper and Row).

Sheppard, B., Roy, H., Lewicki, J. and Minton, J. W. (1992) *Organizational Justice: The Search for Fairness in the Workplace* (New York: Lexington Books).

Thomson, J. A. K. (1953) *The Ethics of Aristotle* (Middlesex: Penguin Books).

Walzer, M. (1983) *Spheres of Justice: A Defense of Pluralism and Equality* (New York: Basic Books).

Waters, J. A. and Bird, F. (1989) 'Attending to Ethics in Business', *Journal of Business Ethics*, vol. 8, pp. 493–7.

Weber, M. ([1914] 1978) *Economy and Society*, 2 vols., G. Roth and C. Wittich (eds) (Berkeley and Los Angeles: University of California Press).

Weber, M. ([1922] 1951) *The Religion of China* (New York: The Macmillan Company).

Weber, M. ([1922] 1958) *The Religion of India*, H. H. Gerth and D. Martindale, D. (tr.). (New York: The Free Press).

Wheeler, D. and Sillanpaa, M. (1997) *The Stakeholder Corporation* (London: Pitman).

Whiteman, G. and Mamen, K. (2002) 'Examining Justice and Conflict between Mining Companies and Indigenous Peoples: Cerro Colorado and Ngabe-Bugle', *Journal of Business and Management*, vol. 8(3), pp. 293–310.

Williamson, O. E. (1990) 'The Firm as a Nexus of Treaties: An Introduction', in M. Aoki, B. Gustafson and O. Williamson (eds), *The Firm as a Nexus of Treaties* (London: SAGE).

Wohlgast, E. H. (1989) *The Grammar of Justice* (Ithaca and London: Cornell University Press).

Part II

Global Perspectives on Corporate Social Responsibility

Introduction

Frederick Bird and Manuel Velasquez

Business people have long assumed that they have social responsibilities. Ever since the late 19th century, through service organizations and fraternal orders, church groups and private philanthropy, executives and managers have contributed to innumerable civic enterprises and public causes. Although the concern for socially responsible business practices is not new, in recent years businesses have been called upon, perhaps more than ever, to be 'socially responsive', to exercise 'social responsibility' and to be 'good corporate citizens'; they are challenged to follow 'sustainable business practices' and review their performance in relation to the 'triple bottom line'. Although each of these terms expresses the social responsibilities of businesses from a somewhat different perspective, they all assume that businesses ought to act in keeping with ethical concerns above and beyond making profits. There has certainly been a marked overall increase in the volume and attention given to spelling out the social and ethical responsibilities of businesses. Major corporations, industry associations, consultancies and advocacy groups have all developed codes of practice, which businesses are expected to follow. Seminars and courses are offered by a host of new business ethics institutes, and there is now a vast library of books, learned journals, articles, tapes and videos devoted to the subject. Business people have taken up the cause through organizations like Businesses for Social Responsibility and the World Business Council for Sustainable Development. Professional associations of both academics and consultants have been developed to foster this concern. An ever-expanding number of social or ethical investment firms have been established to encourage responsible business practices through targeted investment strategies. Even the United Nations has acted to foster responsible business practices through the Global Compact Initiative.

What is the significance of the contemporary expanded interest in socially responsible business practices? In chapter 3, 'Pursuing Corporate Social Responsibility in Changing Institutional Fields', Joseph Smucker draws on the American experience to examine the oscillating shifts between business and governments in occupying positions of power and influence over civil society. Currently, he argues, business and the logic of the market place dominate the 'institutional field' in American society. As a result, he claims, social demands that once were made of government are now aimed at business. Three aspects of business organizations, however, make it difficult to meet these demands. First, managers' ability to respond to social demands is constrained by the necessity of serving the interests of shareholders. Second, most shareholders, particularly the large pension funds, demand first and foremost a higher return on investment. Third, businesses are being transformed from large, centrally controlled organizations into decentralized networks of legally independent firms, which cannot be easily controlled. Some companies have adopted practices that respond to these demands for corporate social responsibility because they can justify these practices in terms of higher profits; others have adopted and published detailed codes of conduct. Smucker asks whether or not businesses now should be expected to pursue broader social objectives in the name of corporate responsibility, above and beyond ethical behaviour in the pursuit of business objectives: 'Corporate social responsibility ... is a contingent term; contingent on the degree of influence of business interests in civil society relative to other institutions, especially the state or government.'

In a recent essay prepared for a special issue of *The Economist,* Clive Crook (2005) roundly criticizes the current enthusiasm for promoting responsible business practices. He argues that businesses are not well designed to function as social philanthropies; rather they are designed to utilize natural and human resources to increase economic value in ways that benefit both their immediate stakeholders and the larger societies in which they operate. To meet this challenge effectively, businesses require (a) effective and decent management, and (b) appropriate, even in some cases stringent, government regulations and interventions. Crook argues that the codes of ethics, social investment projects and public rhetoric associated with the corporate social responsibility movement rarely address these basic responsibilities.

How valid is Crook's criticism? Should we listen instead to critics like the 'social investment consultant' Michael Jantzi (2005), who argues that corporate social responsibility is 'the most important issue of the century ... so far'? We have been concerned in this book, as in our two preceding volumes, with the challenges facing international businesses, especially when operating in developing countries. We have, therefore, attempted to assess their practices in terms of how they affect the inhabitants and institutions of those developing countries. We have learned a number of things in the process.

We have learned, for example, that businesses need to be responsive to cultural differences and historical contingencies (see chapters 1 and 10). One common theme is the importance of respecting the moral standards of local cultures. It is necessary to underline the extent to which people continue to be influenced by multiple moral cultures today, given the current fashion of thinking that economic globalization is making all people alike. Proponents of this idea invoke visions of a borderless, 'flat' world where all peoples are not only increasingly interconnected but also increasingly moulded by common values of efficiency, individual choice and personal or organizational self-realization (Friedman, 2005). Yet despite the reality and multifaceted influence of today's interconnected global culture, people's diverse local cultures, for the most part, are *not* disappearing. All over the world, people remain influenced both by diverse major ethical traditions, associated especially with religions, political and economic ideologies and dominant philosophical ideas – as well as by thousands of smaller local moral cultures, each of which, in its own way, encourages moral sentiments, fosters ethical ideals and champions social norms. Even when they differ from the ethical standards familiar to foreign business people, these moral cultures represent (a) social realities, which influence how people act and cannot therefore be ignored; and (b) social resources, which can be called upon to encourage those virtues that businesses indeed value, such as integrity, honesty, loyalty and industry.

We have further learned that businesses operating in developing areas typically face a number of perplexing dilemmas – associated with security issues, labour relations and questionable payments, among other things – which rarely admit of simple right-or-wrong solutions (Khan, 2005). Although codes of ethics may provide guidelines in some ambiguous situations, what business people especially need to do, if they are to act responsibly, are (a) to cultivate effective, reciprocating communications with many different people in the countries where they operate; and (b) to develop their own capacities to exercise effective judgement (Bird, 2005).

In chapter 4, 'Toward a Political Ethic for International Businesses', Frederick Bird further develops this line of argument. This essay focuses on the political aspect of the larger topic about the social responsibilities of businesses. Using the examples of Shell in Nigeria, Talisman in Sudan and Rio Tinto in Madagascar, Bird examines issues related to how international firms ought to interact with the governments in the countries in which they are doing business. Instead of the traditional political ethic for businesses, which primarily indicates, all too narrowly and statically, what they should *not* do, Bird develops an account that considers more fully the legal duties, contractual obligations and civic responsibilities of businesses in relation to governments. In particular Bird elaborates on the vital necessity of exercising judgement in concrete situations. For example, if an international business engages in any social investment projects, it should do so out of respect for the principle of civility, which requires all civic entities (including business organizations) to act to support the public goods that make their particular activities possible. This political ethic is not a matter of corporate charity, but the appropriate consequence of an analysis of the of the business's embeddedness in the society in which it operates.

In chapter 5, 'Global Initiatives to Promote Corporate Social Responsibility in the Mining Sector', Hevina S. Dashwood examines the history of the Global Mining Initiative (GMI), a union of nine multinational mining companies dedicated to developing and promoting sustainable mining practices and, more generally, socially responsible corporate behaviour. In 1999, when the GMI was launched, multinational mining companies had a bad reputation – in some cases deservedly acquired. Non-governmental organizations were playing an increasingly prominent role in an emerging global civil society and societal norms were shifting in favour of greater corporate social responsibility. In response, the GMI initiated research on sustainable mining practices and sponsored regional meetings of government, the mining industry, NGOs and other interest groups. Member companies agreed to implement ethical business practices, integrate sustainable development considerations into their decision-making process, uphold human rights and improve environmental performance. Dashwood notes that although some mining companies were motivated by the desire to lower risk, increase their reputational capital or avoid government regulation, others, such as Placer Dome and Noranda, were motivated by their newfound commitment to social responsibility. According to Dashwood, the significance of the GMI 'lies in the fact that a process of dialogue and learning is occurring amongst major mining companies'.

In chapter 6, 'Fostering Social Responsibility in Businesses: The Role of Ethical Auditing', Frederick Bird reviews a number of different approaches for monitoring the social performance of businesses. Bird suggests that the ethical standards and codes developed by companies, industry groups, NGOs and civic associations in recent years have little value unless efforts are made to ensure compliance with these standards through some form of 'ethical auditing'. Bird distinguishes six approaches to ethical auditing that have developed in the last several years: (1) legally-mandated public audits; (2) investigative exposés by media, civic associations and academics; (3) diagnostic surveys using standardized checklists; (4) custom-designed diagnostic audits; (5) active organizational listening; and (6) developmental evaluations. Bird notes that there is no one 'best' approach, since each has strengths and weaknesses and the effectiveness of any particular approach will depend on situational contingencies. Moreover, the approaches are not mutually exclusive, and often several can be brought to bear on the same issue.

Social audits play a vital role in fostering responsible business practices. If we expect businesses to operate in ways that are socially responsible, then we must explore how different approaches to monitoring businesses affect their actual social performances. In chapter 7, 'Monitoring Labour Conditions of Textile Manufacturing: The Work of COVERCO in Guatemala', Sylvie Babarik reports on the work of COVERCO, a non-governmental organization created to monitor the extent to which local manufacturers of apparel for major American retail brands were complying with the ethical requirements of the companies they supplied. COVERCO interviewed workers and managers of Guatemalan apparel factories, inspected these factories and reported back to the American brand-name company any violations of the company's labour code as well as violations of any national labour laws or international labour treaties. Babarik describes how this monitoring activity – certainly a form of ethical auditing – became a crucial mechanism for adjusting the demands of codes formulated in industrialized nations to the moral aspirations, needs and values of locals in developing nations. COVERCO conducted mediating discussions among factory managers, workers and brand-name company representatives on such troubling ethical issues as worker abuse, the treatment of women, wages, workplace health and safety and unionization.

Why should businesses seek to be socially responsible? Of course how we answer this question largely depends upon the sorts of questions we raise about the social responsibilities of businesses. Nonetheless we can identify several common features of what might be called the 'conventional answer' to this question. In the conventional view of things, businesses are called upon to exercise social responsibility with respect to normative expectations that may differ from, or at least do not necessarily coincide with, their core economic interests, which are usually defined in terms of return on investment, profits, market share and other financial concerns. Ideally, every socially responsible business would respect the human rights of its employees, eschew questionable payments, refrain from polluting, support worthy community activities, work against discrimination and make philanthropic contributions. Whatever these moral standards may be, businesses are expected to meet them, according to the conventional perspective, because it is both ethically correct and worthy of moral esteem; or because such actions are expected by many business people and business critics; and because such actions are good for the business's reputation.

Should businesses be socially responsible merely because it is 'good for business'? Working from the conventional perspective, some authors have attempted to build a persuasive business case for responsible business practices anecdotally, by recounting tales of socially responsible companies that seemed also to flourish economically. They also cite case studies that seem to indicate that socially responsible businesses are usually better positioned to manage uncertainties. Others have attempted to compare how large numbers of businesses score quantitatively in terms of their social responsibilities and their financial performance. Despite the diversity of indicators employed for both variables (some studies score the social responsibility of firms simply by reputation), more than 127 studies have discovered some measure of positive correlation. However, when examined more closely, these results seem much less certain. No single set of indicators was used consistently among these studies (surely reputation is an unreliable indicator in any case), nor were the correlations statistically significant in many cases. But the correlations, even to the extent they have proven to be significant, may actually exist because firms are more likely to be in a position be socially responsible if they are financially successful in the first place. The 'business' case for socially responsible business practices thus remains weak (Margolis and Walsh, 2003). As Zadek has recently observed, while describing Nike's path to becoming a socially responsible business, 'There is no universal business case for being good, despite what we might wish' (Zadek, 2004, p. 6).

From the conventional perspective, firms ought to be socially responsible merely because it is good to be socially responsible, and because it may be advantageous (or at least not disadvantageous) for business in general.

In the essays published in this book, as in the case studies published in our two previous volumes, we have approached the topic of responsible business practices somewhat differently. In thinking about international businesses from the perspective of developing countries with their high rates of poverty, we conclude that the major social responsibility of businesses is to pursue their legitimate activities so as to foster sustainable economic development. International firms contribute toward economic development not so much by direct social investments as by the jobs and skill training they offer, the credit they make available, their utilization of local suppliers, their interconnections with local commerce and other business activities (see chapter 8). In developing countries, therefore, international businesses should be judged by the degree to which they have added to or depleted the overall stocks of financial, productive, human, social and natural assets with which they interact. We refer to this non-conventional perspective as an 'asset development' rather than a 'cost minimization' view of business interests, and as a value-added rather than benchmarking approach to business ethics (Bird, 2004). We begin by assuming that the fundamental social responsibilities of firms are not extras or add-ons to their business activities (Norman and MacDonald, 2004). Rather, as Freeman (2004) has recently argued, the social responsibility of businesses is simply a way of acknowledging the fact that businesses as social institutions can operate only by working with the resources made available for them through interactions with their several stakeholders. In a somewhat different formulation (see chapter 2), Bird has argued that firms are responsible for protecting and enhancing their overall assets as effectively as possible, and must do so in keeping with notions of fair exchanges. In addition because of the way they are socially embedded, businesses become as well civil agents with various legal duties, contractual obligations and civic responsibilities (see chapter 4). We regard other statements of the social responsibilities of businesses – with respect to working conditions, social contributions and so forth – as secondary to these basic principles. From this perspective the business case for socially responsible practices can be stated, not in terms of financial results or other objective performance indicators, but rather in terms of actual practices that can be viewed as being intrinsically valuable to a given business's operations. For example, if workers are treated with respect, if their work is valued in obvious ways and close surveillance is avoided, their organizational commitment is likely to improve and their productivity to increase (Bird, 1999; Glisson and Durrick, 1988). Insofar as businesses bargain fairly with their suppliers, customers, creditors and other stakeholders, they are likely to foster trust, minimize resentment and reduce aggravated transaction costs (see chapter 2; also Axelrod, 1984; Frank, 1988). Insofar as Boards and Directors exercise effective oversight, they are more likely to make sure that their company operates in terms of its core competence to protect and enhance assets overall (Selznick, 1957; Bird, 2001; Blair, 1995). Insofar as businesses seek to pursue their objectives through commercial links with other businesses in their communities, they tend to strengthen local webs of social interconnection, which operate indirectly to enhance their own ability to achieve their objectives (Fossgard-Moser and Bird, 2005).

References

Axelrod, R. M. (1984) *The Evolution of Cooperation* (New York: Basic Books).
Bird, F. (1999) 'Empowerment and Justice', in J. J. Quinn and P. W. F. Davies (eds), *Ethics and Empowerment* (Houndsmill, Basingstoke, Hampshire: Macmillan).
Bird, F. (2001) 'Good Governance: A Philosophical Discussion of the Responsibilities and Practices of Organizational Governors', *Canadian Journal of Administrative Studies*, vol. 18(4), pp. 298–312.
Bird, F. (2004) 'Ethical Reflections on the Challenges Facing International Businesses in Developing Areas', in F. Bird and S. Herman (eds), *International Businesses and the Challenges of Poverty in the Developing World* (London: Palgrave Macmillan), chapter 1.
Bird, F. (2005) 'Dilemmas of Development: Managing Socially Responsible International Businesses in Developing Areas', in F. Bird, E. Raufflet and J. Smucker (eds), *International Business and the Dilemmas of Development* (London: Palgrave Macmillan), chapter 1.
Blair, M. M. (1995) *Ownership and Control: Rethinking Corporate Governance for the Twenty-first Century* (Washington, DC: Brookings Institution).
Crook, C. (2005) 'The Good Company: A Survey of Corporate Social Responsibility', *The Economist* (22 January), pp. 1–22.
Fossgard-Moser, T. and Bird, F. (2005) 'Managing Security Problems through Community Relations: A Comparative Study of Petroleum Companies in Colombia', in F. Bird, E. Raufflet and J. Smucker (eds), *International Business and the Dilemmas of Development* (London: Palgrave Macmillan), chapter 14.
Frank, R. H. (1988) *The Passions within Reasons: The Strategic Role of the Emotions* (New York: Norton).
Freeman, R. E. (2004) 'The Stakeholder Approach Revisited', *Zeitschrift für Wirtschafts- und Unternehmensethik*, vol. 5 (3), pp. 228–41.
Friedman, T. L. (2005) *The World is Flat: A Brief History of the Twenty-first Century* (New York: Farrar, Strauss and Giroux).

Glisson, C. and Durrick, M. (1988) 'Predictions of Job Satisfaction and Organizational Commitment in Human Service Organizations', *Administrative Science Quarterly*, vol. 37, pp. 161–81.

Jantzi, M. (2005) 'The Most Important Issue of the Century ...So Far', *Management Ethics* (Spring) (Canadian Centre for Ethics and Corporate Policy), pp. 1–5.

Khan, F. R. (2005) 'Hard Times Recalled: The Child Labour Controversy in Pakistan's Soccer Ball Industry', in F. Bird, E. Raufflet and J. Smucker (eds), *International Business and the Dilemmas of Development* (London: Palgrave Macmillan), chapter 7.

Margolis, J. D. and Walsh, J. (2003) 'Misery Loves Companies: Rethinking Social Initiatives by Business', *Administrative Science Quarterly*, vol. 48, pp. 268–305.

Norman, W. and MacDonald, C. (2004) 'Getting to the Bottom of "Triple Bottom Line"', *Business Ethics Quarterly*, vol. 14(2), pp. 243–62.

Selznick, P. (1957) *Leadership in Administration* (Berkeley: University of California Press).

Zadek, S. (2004) 'The Path to Corporate Responsibility', *Harvard Business Review* (December) Reprint R0412J.

3

Pursuing Corporate Social Responsibility in Changing Institutional Fields

Joseph Smucker

Introduction

In 1971 Jules Cohn reported the results of his survey of 247 business firms and a case study of a single firm, all of which were engaged in ameliorating what were thought to be the major causes of inner-city decay and social unrest in the United States. Some three years earlier, after the riots in the Watts district of Los Angeles, many major business firms had announced with much fanfare that they were ready, with government support, to initiate programmes designed to address these problems. Subsequently a variety of projects were undertaken, including purposive hiring from the inner city, providing job training and apprenticeship courses, contributing expertise for small local businesses and providing materials and expertise for community rebuilding projects.

Cohn's research discovered considerable disillusionment and disappointment among business executives. The endeavours were costly and seemed to show very few positive results. After listing more specific causes for the failures, Cohn noted the difficulties of applying a business-oriented, technologically driven logic to the solutions of inner-city problems. The basic problem as he saw it was a failure to recognize that 'the central issues in community problems are political rather than technological'; that business firms can probably 'serve the public interest best by continuing to play a limited role in urban affairs, cleaning their own houses through expanded employment and training programmes, and providing revenues for the cities through taxes and donations' (Cohn, 1971, pp. 109–110). If they wished to be more directly involved, business firms would do best by financially supporting other organizations that had the expertise to deal directly with these social problems.

Cohn's diagnosis was made during the waning years of the welfare state in the United States, when government agencies played a dominant role in advancing public welfare and business was regarded as a resource to aid in their policies.[1] Since then, the configuration of institutions has changed in nearly all of the advanced market economies. While these changes have not been the same in all respects, what has been similar is the increased influence of business interests on their respective polities. In response, an increased number of non-institutionalized social movements and special interest groups have emerged, expressing their concerns and demands directly at business interests. In effect, civil society has been 'awakened' as governments have been either unable or unwilling to deliver public services or to respond directly to citizens' demands, at least in the manner in which they have done so in the past (Tadashi and Ashizawa, 2001; Zadek, 2001).

It is the thesis of this essay that the business corporation[2] has become the dominant force in the institutional landscapes of the advanced market economies, as the roles of governments in the marketplace have either receded or have been redirected along lines favouring free-market principles (Bradshaw and Vogel, 1981; Yergin and Stanislaw, 1998; Schwartz and Gibb, 1999; Wilson, 2000; Pearson and Seyfang, 2001). However, the position of power and influence which business corporations now occupy has also rendered them more vulnerable to demands from groups of diverse interests from within 'civil society'.[3] As Schwartz and Gibb (1999) have put it, 'the shift of power from nation-states means that the public in general requires more accountability from other powerful actors, such as business, and expects them to respond directly to the demands of public opinion rather than waiting for that opinion to be mediated by government in the form of legislation or regulation'.[4] Allen observes that in the UK, 'More strategically minded business figures have recognized that the post-1989 ideological triumph of capitalism has, at least in part, had the paradoxical effect of enhancing expectations of corporate social responsibility' (2001, p. 85).

In contrast to the time when Cohn carried out his study, business interests are less subject to limiting regulations of the state (Boyer, 1996). Rather, they have become a dominant force, influencing in direct ways not only economic but also social policies. It may not be too extreme to argue that business interests have usurped the role of the state, and that the economic principles of 'the market' have become the principal source of legitimation and justification. This shift means that interest groups in the remainder of 'civil society' must direct their demands to business interests. These demands have gone beyond merely economic matters; they include expressions of social concerns, ranging from the preservation of the natural environment to concerns for public health, poverty reduction, social equity, and freedom from want and fear. Demands for greater corporate social responsibility, then, are coming from groups within civil societies that are very much aware of the changed and diminished role of governments, especially as constitutive agencies, in defining the premises, rules and responsibilities of actors in advanced market economies. Of course, since each market economy is the outcome of unique historical processes and cultural characteristics, these issues vary in their content and forms of expression, and in their modes of response.

The shift in dominance from government to business interests is not an evolutionary process. Rather, viewed historically, and in different national settings, the relationship between business and government has been an oscillating one, with influence passing back and forth between the two institutions. At times, particularly among 'late developing' economies, the interests of both have been nearly fused together. The nature of the power relationship between these two institutional sectors influences the modes of expression of vested interest groups in the larger civil society and in some cases even the opportunity to express their needs.

In the following pages, I first present a brief historical review of the shifting nature of the relationship between government and business interests, as illustrated by the American experience. I conclude this section with the argument that business interests are now dominant and thus provide the 'template' by which even public services are provided. Next, I argue that this shift has provoked the growth of social movements and interest groups with social welfare agendas aimed directly at challenging present-day business interests. I then suggest that the response of business interests, especially business corporations, is complicated by their own organizational structures. Three features of the contemporary American business corporation are especially significant here: (1) the role of managers, (2) the current orthodoxy about the business objectives which managers should pursue, and (3) the organizational changes which have emerged in meeting these business objectives. I note two tactical responses of corporations in meeting these challenges: (1) converting the concerns of social movements into niche marketing, and (2) adopting and publicizing codes of conduct as a means to promote positive public reputations.

I conclude with a return to a consideration of the influence of institutional configurations in defining the range of issues over which corporations can reasonably be expected to be 'responsible'. This raises the longstanding philosophical question as to whether the idea of corporate social responsibility is to be restricted to ethical behaviour in attaining business objectives, or whether the business enterprise as a social institution, should be expected to pursue broader objectives of 'social virtue'. If business interests represent the dominant orientation of societal institutions, they can expect increased pressure from groups within civil-society demanding that they play a greater role in ameliorating social injustices. However, since this is likely to infringe on their ability to pursue their own economic objectives in open market economies, they will eventually require the state, or a similar regulative institution, to reassert an independent role in providing for the general social welfare – unless, of course, the government allies itself with business interests and restricts the expression of civil dissent (see also Block, 1994). (An extreme expression of this institutional arrangement would constitute a fascist state.)

Business interests, the state and social responsibility

Economic systems are governed in widely differing ways among different nations and societies – from outright government or state control in defining the rights of citizens and the rules of economic behaviour, as well as allocating resources for production and distribution, to market-centred systems where business interests dominate the institutional structures and government serves primarily a regulative and facilitative role (Fligstein, 2001). More specifically, within the general framework of market-centred economies, the relationships between business interests and governments vary among different nation-states. They also vary over time within single nation-states (see for example, accounts of these relationships in Asian societies in MacIntyre, 1994). One important consequence of these often shifting relationships is their effects on civil society and the ability of elements within civil society to influence both the state and business interests. Figure 3.1 provides a simple illustration of these relationships.

In this model, simplified for heuristic purposes, the three institutional areas should be seen as moving forces in continual dynamic tension.[5] In some societies, and in some periods, business interests and government have been almost fused together; the development strategies of Japan,

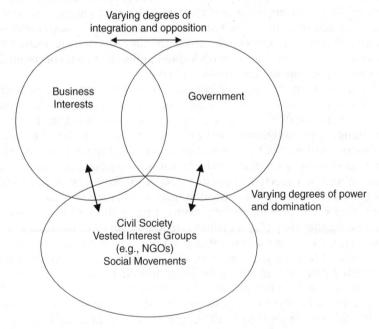

Figure 3.1　Conceptualized relationships among business interests, government (the state) and civil society

South Korea and Taiwan are examples of this near-fusion. In socialist economies, the government sector dominates. In western market economies, especially the United States, business interests currently dominate the institutional fields. In contemporary industrialized and industrializing countries, the ebbs and flows of influence between these two institutional sectors shape the nature of civil society and the forms of expression of citizens' concerns. Currently the international presence of large corporations, the international flows of capital and the perspectives of major international regulatory bodies add even more weight to the influence of business interests, in contrast to national governments, on the character of civil societies.

The relationship between business and government in market-based economies is an uneasy one. Markets may be efficient in the allocation of resources, but they require the state to enforce the rules that make orderly transactions possible. What is not so well defined, however, is the locus of responsibility for the welfare of the general public. Are those principles of the market that emphasize free choice sufficient to ensure the welfare of individual members of civil society? Or are governments the best means to define and ensure the rights and responsibilities of citizens? What sorts of relationships between business interests and governments are best able to promote the well-being of civil society? These questions imply the larger question of how the general social welfare in market economies is to be guaranteed. What type of institutional configuration best serves this function? How are markets themselves to be constructed?[6]

In his historical account of the manner in which business interests in the United States have defined their social responsibilities, Heald (1970) notes the continual tension between business interests and government, and the shifts of power and influence between the actors in these two sectors. In the late 1800s, in the United States, laws governing working conditions were being passed in the various states as a result of pressures from a wide variety of civic groups and labour organizations.[7] They were often supported by employers if they were persuaded that such legislation would improve workers' productivity and reduce potential costs. For example, early laws providing for workmen's compensation not only provided benefits, however modest, to injured workers but they also 'promised to reduce costly litigation that occurred under the employers' liability laws' (Nelson, 1975, p. 141). Enforcement of such laws was uneven, and employers often disregarded them (ibid.); but what is of special interest, for our purposes, is that interest groups from civil society, of which there were many, including labour unions, made their appeals to state governments rather than directly to business interests. Once such social legislation was passed, government inspectors, in order to gain compliance, often stressed the idea that conformity with the laws would in the long run, advance the economic interests of business firms (ibid., p. 177).

According to Heald's account, business interests grew in power and influence following the depression in the 1890s, and occupied a dominant position in American society during the 1920s. In effect, business firms themselves had evolved from a powerful interest group in 19th-century civil society, to a dominant institution in the 20th century. They promoted the virtues of open markets free of government regulation, and the idea of a unity of interests among labour, stockholders, customers and the community at large (Heald, 1970, p. 176). The prevailing notion was that the general social welfare could be served best if each of these interests were subject to the discipline of the market. While social welfare agencies might be required to temporarily assist those citizens who might suffer setbacks and failures, these services were to be highly restricted since dependency rather than productivity could be the final outcome if they were allowed to expand. The most that business could do in this regard was to provide philanthropic gifts to agencies offering short-term welfare services. Indeed, different forms of philanthropy played a major role in the attempt to convey the imagery of a community of common interests.[8] The philanthropy of 'captains of industry' (or 'robber barons') like Carnegie and Rockefeller, who personally owned and managed their giant firms, provided a model of the role philanthropy could play in gaining public support for business activity.

With the coming of the Great Depression in the 1930s, what had once been described as the great virtues of a market economy for society as a whole came to be seen as forces of destruction. The business rhetoric about the 'community of interests' in a market economy rang hollow as unemployment soared and poverty deepened. The earlier assumption that the welfare of business also ensured the welfare of the community now, in the 1930s, required that business firms also accept responsibility for failure. (Heald, 1970, pp. 149, 190–8).[9] In the midst of an increasingly hostile public and as a result of the passage of Roosevelt's New Deal, following Keynes' analysis of the causes of the Depression and his proposed solutions, business enterprises were faced with a 'fundamental challenge' to their primacy in American society. Increasing proportions of the population especially from among the urban middle class viewed the government programmes of the New Deal as necessary checks to what they regarded as the self-serving nature of business interests (Fine, 1967, p. 47). The appeals to socialism were also gaining favour especially with signs of its apparent success in the Soviet Union.

In response, big business mounted public relations campaigns arguing, in effect, that adherence to free-market principles would in the long run benefit society as a whole. Amongst themselves, however, business leaders called for an examination of their own behaviour and for greater sensitivity to community needs. Donaldson Brown, vice-president of General Motors, argued in 1935 that corporations, like individuals, cannot 'hope to thrive' if they are 'surrounded by degeneracy and squalor' (quoted in Heald, 1970, pp. 155–6). In business-oriented publications the most common theme was that while executives should focus on business objectives they needed to be aware of the social consequences of their actions (for references to business publications and public statements see Heald, pp. 174–202).

It is apparent from Heald's historical analysis that there has been a long-standing ambivalence among business executives about the relationship between the business enterprise and the rest of society. During the first half of the 20th century, two themes appear to have dominated their interpretations about this relationship. The first sought to lay stress upon the 'community of interests' among the business enterprise, its labour force, its investors and its surrounding community. The second emphasized the need to cultivate societal support more aggressively in order to fend off increasing government regulations and combat the growing influence of organized labour. Of course there also remained the argument that business executives had no responsibilities other than to manage their firms in an efficient and effective manner. According to this perspective, pursuing the interests of the firm was, in the long run, the best guarantee of a vibrant and egalitarian society.

In practice, business executives wavered between active engagement in programmes of social welfare, of which philanthropy played a major part, or simply mounting public relations campaigns that justified conventional business practices. Behind these initiatives was the constant concern over the consequences of increasing government incursions into the market that included social security legislation, minimum-wage laws and labour rights. These policies and other forms of government regulations were seen as threats to the 'fundamental principles essential to the maintenance of a free and competitive economy' (General Motors policy statement, quoted in Heald, 1970, p. 196).[10]

During the Second World War, these apprehensions were largely held in abeyance as both business interests and the government combined forces in the war effort. At the end of the war, the government in the United States emerged as the dominant institutional sector, playing an active role in attempting to guide the direction of the economy and ameliorate its weaknesses. Similar developments occurred in Great Britain and Western European countries while in the Soviet Bloc, the state gained supreme rule. Throughout the Western world the 'welfare state' became well established, with governments regulating minimum standards of income and establishing programmes to ensure acceptable levels of health and safety, education and housing as defining attributes of citizens' rights (Wilensky, 2002, p. 281). Governments also expanded basic infrastructures and regulated utilities, transportation and communications systems as services essential to the public interest (Bauman, 1998; for essays on the Canadian experience in creating a welfare state, see Moscovitch and Albert, 1987).

Markets might be an efficient means to allocate resources but government interventions were seen to be necessary to ensure their smooth operation. Business, it was thought, could lend at least benign support to the welfare state as long as its welfare policies ensured a healthy and productive labour force and labour unrest was held to a minimum. Further, business interests could support the government's fiscal and monetary policies as long as they promoted economic growth while maintaining market stability.

In the United States throughout the 1960s, the government continued to play a major regulative role in the economy. In most Western European countries, governments played an even more prominent role with outright control of utilities, communications and rail and air transportation. Many social analysts and commentators, including Heald (1970, p. 299), argued that the welfare state represented a mature state of industrial development, a permanent feature of advanced capitalism in which the state would ensure a high level of social welfare for everyone.[11] As business interests were the generating force of wealth and prosperity, so government services were the means to ensure that the whole of civil society benefited. Equality of opportunity was to be the principle by which these benefits could be assured; government would provide the means by which individuals could prepare themselves to participate in the economy through its funding of the education system and by providing support for the unemployed and those in need. The market and business interests, in turn, would provide the structures of opportunity through the organization of occupations and distribute the rewards to individuals depending on their abilities and commitments to the work ethic. During this period of near-fusion of objectives between business and government, Eells imagined the possibility of the corporation becoming more 'socially oriented, more gregarious, more civic-minded and more cosmopolitan'; such a corporation could be viewed as a 'metro corporation' 'thereby underlining its maternal concern for a numerous brood' (Eells, 1960).

But just as the virtues of business became its vices during the Great Depression, so too did the lauded programmes that governments had initiated from the early 1930s through the 1960s suffer the same fate. Disillusionment began during the 1960s and continued through the 1970s (see for example, O'Connor, 1973; Offe, 1984).[12] Significant changes occurred in the United States, the United Kingdom and to a lesser extent in Western European countries by the late 1970s and through the 1980s. Social welfare programmes and regulated industries, established in the past to serve the public good, had been based on the assumption of a self-sufficient nation-state that could maintain rates of economic growth in excess of increased costs of social welfare. The eventual 'crisis' of the welfare state was the inability to sustain extensive social welfare policies in the face of slower economic growth and increased economic competition from foreign firms.[13]

Business interests argued that government regulations that had been designed to serve the public interest had contributed, along with other government policies, to their inability to operate successfully in an era of intense international competition (Boyer, 1996; Yergin and Stanislaw, 1998, pp. 109–22). Labour market policies became the focus of criticism of government welfare programmes. The 'social contract' guaranteeing relatively secure employment could no longer be sustained when production could be made more efficient in foreign localities and advanced technology could take over more labour functions (Pearson and Seyfang, 2001; for descriptions of the effects of the dismantling of government labour support programmes in Canada, see Panitch and Schwartz, 1988). Unemployment insurance schemes, minimum wage laws, health and safety standards came to be defined as handicaps to business firms' competitive success.

Meanwhile, at the very time that the significance of labour declined in the production process, business interests increased their emphasis on the importance of the work ethic. Their leverage was the threat of the loss of employment to cheaper labour elsewhere while their rhetoric extolled the virtues of a new 'creative', multi-tracked, multi-career labour force committed to 'life-long learning'. Managers of corporations prided themselves in becoming 'lean and mean'– even as they imposed greater responsibilities upon the lower echelons, while reducing the ranks of middle management.[14] At the very time government support services were most needed, it was claimed that such services were costs which society could no longer afford in an intensely competitive world market. Much of what had once been viewed as social investments in a more productive labour force now came to be seen as costs (Bauman, 1998, p. 32). These were persuasive arguments and contributed to a renewed interest in 'the market' as the principal means of allocating resources in industrialized societies while fostering a renewed sense of individual freedom. Costs could be contained and efficiencies regained as equity in the distribution of social benefits came to be based on individuals' contributions to economic production rather than on their rights as citizens. While this put the burden of responsibility on the individual, the concept of 'freedom' was its persuasive ideological justification.

Neo-liberalism and concepts of social responsibility

In the 1970s, amidst the criticism of the seemingly intrusive nature of government regulations and the waste of government bureaucracies, the economic inefficiencies of the Soviet Bloc were frequently cited as examples of what could evolve should the current role of the government persist. These issues were most clearly articulated in the United Kingdom, where the structure of political parties provided the institutional means by which this dissent could find clear expression. In 1979, the election of Margaret Thatcher as prime minister was the culmination of growing disillusionment with 'big government' and the adoption of a market-oriented perspective. Her election further influenced the turn toward 'neo-liberalism', already articulated by Hayek (Hayek, 1960, 1967) and given further weight by the well-known arguments of Friedman from the 'Chicago School' of economics (Friedman, 1982; for a counter-argument, see Blinder, 1987). The election of Ronald Reagan in 1980 can be interpreted as the political expression of a growing belief that a bloated government bureaucracy had contributed to the faltering US economy.

In the United States, an aggressive campaign mounted by business interests and the Republican Party capitalized on the growing disenchantment with the welfare state. It was claimed that federal government policies rooted in the liberal ideology of the New Deal era were the main obstacles to continuing economic growth, and indeed were the main causes of increasing inflation and unemployment; that individual initiative had been stymied by overly generous welfare policies; and above all, that welfare was a right to be earned rather than guaranteed.[15]

Since the late 1970s, those adhering to a belief in the cleansing properties of regulation-free markets have been relatively successful in reducing government strictures and regulations, in dismantling costly welfare programmes and in incorporating private enterprise in delivering services formerly operated by the state. The formula runs something like this: economic well-being for the individual provides the basis for liberty and free choice, which, in the aggregate, benefit the quality of life for everyone. It is through consumption that this freedom of choice is exercised and the market is sustained. The unfettered competitive dynamics of the market ensure that these functions are carried out efficiently. In effect, the political rhetoric of neo-liberalism is one of production, markets and freedom expressed through consumption.

Indeed the ideology of market-based principles has been advocated as a fit model for government itself, its agencies and public service organizations (Osborne and Gaebler, 1993). Deregulation and privatization were dominant themes during the 1980s and 1990s, with many of the public services formerly provided by governments taken over by private firms. In the United States, private corporations have assumed control of the administration of health care, the administration of a number of elementary and secondary schools, the administration of prisons and even many of the functions previously carried out by the military.[16]

This institutional transformation, with its emphasis on individualism and the virtues of the marketplace as a metaphor of the 'good society', has resulted in a redefinition of the rights of the citizen. Individuals are defined as clients and consumers who are free to make their own economic choices in a constant effort to better themselves (Osborne and Gaebler, 1993).

Social progress tends to be equated with consumerism, and choices made in consumption supposedly provide evidence of freedom for the individual. The products of consumption, in turn, become measures of social success, blunting the social costs of class and inequality. The individual is held responsible for success or its absence (Fine and Leopold, 1993, p. 300; Cross, 2000). The means to achieve these rewards is through adherence to a work ethic that stresses self-discipline in employment, which then enables free choice in consumption (Bauman, 1998).

These changes in institutional configurations and their associated ideological justifications, not foreseen in their scope some 30 years ago, have exalted the corporation to iconic status as the guarantor of efficiency and effectiveness, while the idea of the competitive market conveys the image of freedom and distributive justice to 'deserving' participants. Business interests have regained their prominence lost during the Great Depression. Insofar as their social responsibilities are concerned, the emphasis has shifted from the notion of a 'community of interests' and social obligations to the idea of providing the conditions for maximizing free choice among individual actors. The ideal expression of free choice is that of the consumer in the marketplace (Schor, 1998; Cross, 2000). Indeed, it has been an easy step to equate free choice in consumption with the political freedoms imagined in ideal democracies. In this association there is a tendency to forget that historically the movements toward democracy preceded the market-based economy.

If the freely choosing consumer has become the defining attribute of the citizen in the 'good' society, it suggests that the citizen-as-consumer is free to speak for 'the public' and to demand that business interests play a role in improving the general social welfare. Clark (1996) notes that, 'paradoxically the attempt to eviscerate the social democratic conceptions of the public and narrow it to a nation of consumers has had the effect of opening up representational "spaces" in which increasing numbers of groups and agencies have attempted to lay claim to speak for "the public interest"' (1996, p. 78). It is in the name of the 'public interest' that demands have been directed to corporations for greater social responsibility. As the operations of business firms have become increasingly international in scope, so too have the demands expanded from groups representing civil society. Increasingly these demands express concerns for upholding human rights. Yet the definitions of what these human rights should entail tend to mirror the institutional values of the West rather than those of indigenous nation-states (see chapter 1).

It remains of some significance that the increasing chorus of demands for corporate social responsibility is so often couched in consumer terms, an additional indication of the current hegemony of business interests over civil society. In effect, this hegemony is being turned back upon business interests themselves. Thus consumers may demand coffee, but they may also demand that it is 'fair trade' coffee (Müller, 2005); they may demand cheap clothing, but not if it is produced in sweat shops by child labour; they may demand oil, but they may also demand that refineries do not pollute nor engage in unethical dealings with local governments. If freely choosing consumers and clients are a hallmark of capitalist societies, their choices are not limited merely to products and services. Their choices also include how the goods and services are created. Thus, somewhat paradoxically, the very shifts in institutional arrangements that have made neo-liberalism possible have also created a 'market' for socially responsible corporate behaviour (Lewis, 2002). There is now a 'market' for information on corporate integrity; a 'market' for monitoring services on ethical practices; a 'market' for devising codes of conduct; a 'market' for 'reputation'.

But the notion of 'markets' for each of these issues implies self-interest and fails to recognize the importance of cooperation and community (see Etzioni, 1988; Bauman, 1998; Putnam, 2000). When considering the role of corporations in developing economies, there is the tendency to assume that traditional communal practices need to be converted into contemporary Western competitive market behaviour (Marglin, 2003). But even markets, in order to remain viable, require cooperation and trust. Further, societies differ in the ways they define the basic rights of their citizens; and these differences are reflected in the institutional configurations of each society (see chapter 1). A simple question of whether the government should ensure that 'no one is in need' results in considerable variations in response among Western capitalist societies and is reflected by the variation in their welfare programmes (see for example, the results of national surveys reported in *The Economist*, 8 November 2003).

Structural constraints to corporate response

> For anyone in charge of a large quoted company, the level of outside scrutiny – whether by government, consumer groups, the press or the financial markets – is far beyond anything a corporate leader would have been subjected to in the past. For many bosses, this sense of managing in a goldfish bowl has become particularly onerous. *The Economist*, 25 October 2003

How business firms respond to pressures from civil society depends on the nature of their relationships with government and civil society. But the structures of business firms themselves also influence the nature of their responses. The changing nature of the structure of the corporation provides a good example of these issues. The corporate form of business organization has long been the main form of business enterprise that has influenced the operations and strategies of business interests as a whole.[17] But it is not a static form; rather it comprises different vested interests, which have influenced its strategy as well as its structure over time. Further, theories of good management have been in constant flux and the boundaries of jurisdiction defining the responsibilities of senior managers remain poorly defined.

In the recent past, three interrelated factors have been especially prominent in shaping the response of corporations to demands for assuming greater social responsibility: (1) the role of professional management; (2) the increased influence of shareholders in forming corporate policy; and (3) the shift in forms of corporate structure from multifunctional bureaucracies to 'networked' firms.

Consider first the role of managers. The individual manager is accountable to those who have vested interests in the corporation and is, in effect, an employee hired for his or her expertise. That expertise requires skills both in mapping out corporate objectives and in gaining the trust and cooperative efforts of employees further down the levels of command. But managers, even senior managers, do not have the freedom to make decisions for the firm that owner-managers enjoy. A 19th-century American tycoon or the family head of a Korean *chaebol* conglomerate could decide on his own initiative how his companies were to be run and what strategies were to be pursued. Managers of public corporations, on the other hand, must be able to negotiate the demands of diverse constituencies within the corporate structure as well as the demands from government regulatory bodies. In addition, they must anticipate and evaluate the strategies of their competitors (Fligstein, 1997, p. 19).

For example, within the corporation, the objectives of engineering departments may have to be compromised in order to meet the demands of marketing departments. Wage increases may have to be contained in order to remain competitive. Personnel may have to be laid off for the cause of greater efficiency. Definitions of what constitutes good management may have to change, as successful competitors adopt new methods of production and new methods of financing their operations. In effect, the manager is expected, and indeed trained, to apply his or her skills for the well-being and enrichment of the corporation, even as the definitions of these objectives change (for an example of these changes, see Smucker, 2005). These decisions often require a detachment by the individual manager from his or her own sense of moral integrity (Jackall, 1988).

For most of the history of the American corporation, managers were left to deal with these issues without interventions by shareholders. Certainly the concept of 'stakeholder', denoting any group whose interests might be affected by the corporation, was unknown. Competitors, labour unions, government legislation, and perhaps consumer groups have always had to be taken into account of course, but shareholders and boards of directors tended to assume that the expertise of managers themselves need not be questioned as long as steady gains were achieved.

A second factor shaping the responses of corporations to pressures from the social environment is the increased influence of shareholders, especially those representing financial institutions. In 1957, Adolf Berle saw the beginnings of radical change in the relationship between boards of directors and managers. Berle observed that corporations were in fact controlled by managers, and would continue to be controlled by them unless an oligarchic power were to emerge from among the then dispersed shareholders. Berle saw such an 'oligarchic power' beginning to emerge as pension funds increasingly invested in corporate stocks. These funds, Berle argued, must meet payouts to be determined at a later date. Since future inflation trends as well as prices and wages cannot be accurately predicted, pension funds are drawn to equities that reflect shifting market values (Berle, 1957, pp. 7–12). What Berle saw emerging, Fligstein (1990) and Useem (1993) have documented: managers are no longer able to assume that their shareholders will be passive and that their boards will simply support their decisions. The financial institutions that have invested in such equities demand continual profitable returns. Managers can no longer assume autonomy from shareholders.[18]

Meanwhile, financial institutions have become dominant forces among shareholders. They have also become major influences on policy decisions of managers (Useem, 1993). The fact that managers must focus on continual positive returns for these shareholders makes them unusually sensitive to a wide range of factors that would influence their profit levels. Indeed, the hackneyed use of the expression 'bottom line' reflects this emphasis. In following this objective, the firm itself becomes defined as a bundle of assets to be bought and sold as short-term financial returns may dictate (Fligstein, 1997, p. 30).[19]

While social interest groups may challenge firms on their mode of operations, it is really investment institutions that are more directly influential. Until it can be shown that involvement in projects of social relevance will generate positive financial returns, corporate management will remain constrained in its responses to such demands.

This development leads us to the third complicating factor influencing a firm's responsiveness to demands from special interest groups. That is the growing prevalence of networked forms of business enterprises. Alfred Chandler's model (1966) of the multi-unit firm once provided the standard description of corporate objectives and behaviour. Chandler argued that the modern multi-unit corporation emerged as a rational solution to reducing the costs of market-based transactions. This form of corporate structure, labelled by some authors as 'Fordism', is well suited to standardized production for mass markets that are self-contained and have relatively stable and uniform production costs. In the past, these conditions were insured by a more active regulatory role of governments in the economy. But since the 1970s, with increased government deregulation and with increased competition from foreign producers, this organizational form has given way to contractual arrangements among independent production units (Powell, 1990). These network arrangements allow for greater flexibility as marketing has shifted from mass to 'niche' or specialized markets. Technological advances that provide access to lower cost producers in other national economies eliminate many of the administration and capital costs within a single corporation.

If greater financial returns can be gained by dismantling the corporation's component parts, the responsible and rational manager would be expected to follow this path. The once solidly unified multi-unit corporate organization is now defined as a conglomerate of potentially saleable assets to be replaced by negotiated contracts with suppliers operating at lower costs. If mergers and acquisitions are undertaken they are done so as a means to maintain profit levels through diversification of products and services rather than as a means to achieve economies of vertical integration.

The growing complexity in the organization of the production process makes the problem of establishing responsibility and accountability more difficult, especially when the organizational components involve diverse cultures and different institutional configurations. Is the transfer of one phase of production to a foreign firm a socially responsible act? Perhaps it benefits the host area, and even the consumer; but what social benefits does the move offer to the previous employees? In considering the scope of social responsibility the question emerges as to the priorities to be assigned to the relevant constituencies or stakeholders of each of the subcontractors along the path of production. In contrast to an affluent community, for example, a community in a developing area may be willing to endure environmental pollution in return for well-paid employment. Thus, it can be argued that the scope of social responsibility and the nature of the stakeholders varies among different social contexts (Pearson and Seyfang, 2001).

A sense of the intricate patterns of influence and response to civic demands is illustrated by Hoffman's account (2001) of the interaction among vested interest groups, the US government and American corporations in the chemical and petroleum industries. In the 1960s, according to Hoffman, industry representatives tended to dismiss the concerns raised by environmental groups as merely minor technical matters. From 1970 to 1982, public reaction to major industrial accidents and the threat of increased government regulations caused the industries to react in a defensive manner. It was at this time that the Nixon administration, in an effort to placate public concern, supported the creation of the Environment Protection Agency (EPA).

With the decline of government influence during the Reagan administration and, significantly, the weakening of the EPA, business interests were expected to devise their own solutions to environmental pollution. But this proved difficult to implement, given the lack of will and the complexity of commitments of the corporations to their own constituencies throughout the world. Meanwhile, failures to respond to these issues resulted in increased militancy amongst environment protection groups. The backlash of public opinion against the Reagan administration's weak environmental policies served notice to the petroleum and chemical industries that concern for the environment was pervasive and persistent, and that these concerns included foreign operations and subcontractors. By the late 1980s, according to Hoffman, the intensity of demands from organized groups in the wake of major environmental disasters (such as the Bhopal incident in India) eventually influenced institutional investors, who, along with the insurance companies (whose own financial interests were at stake), put pressure on the petroleum and chemical corporations to include environmental protection in their business strategies.

Hoffman describes the transition in the role of government as one in which the Nixon administration attempted to reach a compromise with environmental groups by creating the Environment Protection Agency. The Reagan administration viewed the EPA and government regulation in general as impediments to business interests, and set about weakening federal regulatory agencies. An aroused public then challenged industry directly and corporate managers realized that the environmentalist cause would not disappear (Hoffman, 2001, p. 155). Indeed, the pattern of response of chemical and petroleum corporations in an era of weakened government intervention follows closely the cycles of strength of public opinion on these issues as measured by public opinion polls. Over the nearly 30-year period from the 1970s through the 1990s, as the proportion of the population who favoured stricter environmental controls increased, firms in these industries responded by changing their manufacturing processes. As public attention around these issues declined, the standards that these corporations actually followed became more lax (Hoffman, 2001, pp. 114, 117, 144).

It is finally important to point out how financial interests played a crucial role in transforming the corporations' responses to environmental demands. With the increased influence of financial investors on management decisions, reputation became a major concern in marketing the corporations' products as well as in attracting investments.[20] Strategies for dealing with environmental pollution problems came to be seen as reputation issues which in turn influenced consumer and investor behaviour. Reputation thus became a competitive issue with financial returns to be reaped by demonstrating that new and less wasteful practices were being adopted. Further, there emerged a sort of herd-like response as individual firms became aware that their competitors were adopting environmental standards as an integral component of their business strategies. Equipment designed to protect the environment came to be seen as good investments rather than as non-recoverable costs. As Hoffman puts it, 'the "win-win" scenario replaced pollution prevention and waste minimization as the dominant rhetoric and logic'. He further notes that in a 1995 *Times Mirror* poll, '69 per cent of Americans believed that environmental protection and economic development could work together' (ibid., p. 156).

Consistent with our contention that government agencies have become relatively weak in relation to business interests is the finding by Hoffman of a shift in government policies, away from acting as a protector of the public good to its role as arbiter between citizen groups and business interests. Government regulations did at one time contribute toward more environmentally responsible business practices; but with the growth in influence of business interests, they became relatively weak and unstable in their enforcement.[21]

Business interests, despite their present dominance of civil society, have also become more vulnerable to demands that go beyond their economic objectives. Managers have become increasingly concerned about their corporations' reputations as responsible citizens since this has a direct bearing on their profit margins. Indeed, it can be argued that the current proliferation of corporate codes of conduct is part of a strategy for marketing corporate reputation (Klein, 2000; OECD, 2001).[22]

It would seem that these developments provide unique opportunities for those who would advocate more demonstrations of social responsibility by business firms. Yet movements for greater social responsibility must compete with maximizing financial returns. Such appeals for greater social responsibility are likely to be effective only if it can be shown that they will enhance financial returns or provide a favourable image for attracting investors. With many government agencies themselves operating on business models of 'cost recovery' services, and with political parties casting themselves as guardians of the 'market', there remain few institutional avenues for socially concerned groups to pressure firms to practice greater social responsibility without first demonstrating its economic value.[23]

Meanwhile, corporations remain active in attempting to shape the social environment in ways that will further their objectives. If local business interests are threatened by foreign competitors, they have not been averse to seeking protection through government intervention. On the other hand, they have not been shy in attempting to impose their models on foreign economies. These movements also raise questions about the social responsibility of corporations. If France, for example, defines the small farmer as a distinctive cultural entity that requires government protection, it would arguably be socially irresponsible for foreign corporations to insist that subsidies to preserve them be removed. Similarly, it would be socially irresponsible for foreign firms to insist that publicly funded health care in a given country constitutes an unfair subsidy of labour costs. In both cases, to insist that these support systems be removed would be to insist that institutional alignments conform to one model – a model that serves corporate interests rather than the welfare of the general population as defined by citizens in sovereign states.[24]

Ethical practice or social responsibility?

In the ideal imagery of market-based economies, the primary objective of the business firm is to sell goods and services in order to maximize profitability or 'owner value' over the long term. It pursues this objective in a competitive environment while 'respecting distributive justice' and 'ordinary decency' (Sternberg, 2000). The question of corporate social responsibility is a question of the range of consequences of the corporation's operations for which it should be held accountable. It is also a question of the social obligations the corporation owes as a 'citizen' of its host society.

Hoffman notes that firms will incorporate environmental issues into their policies when these can be converted into terms that improve business operations and returns:

> [When] buyers and suppliers impose environmental pressures on the firm, these pressures become framed as an issue of operational efficiency through resource acquisition, processing and sale. When imposed by banks, shareholders, and investors, such pressures become framed as an issue of capital acquisition. When consumers begin to consider environmental concerns in their purchasing decisions, the issue becomes framed as an issue of market demand. When trade associations see opportunities in presenting a unified front on environmental affairs, the issue becomes one of industry reputation or external and government relations. And when academic and religious institutions begin to impose environmental concerns, the issue becomes framed as one of human resource management regarding personal values and corporate culture. (Hoffman, 2001, pp. 208–9)[25]

But to address issues of social responsibility in these terms reinforces the assumption that the dominance of the market model is justified. It further restricts the scope of corporate social responsibility. The problem is captured by the following comments in a speech made by Geoffrey Chandler:

> Let me be clear that I am not talking of the economic justification for sustainable activities, but of the currently popular use of the business case as a reason for moral behaviour. There is, of course, a business case for doing right; it is fundamental to reputation. But as a point of departure, as a justification for doing right, it is ... part of the problem, not part of the solution. (Cited in Forstater et al., 2002)

If the justification for acting in socially responsible ways is that it is, in the end, profitable for the corporation, then no appeal can be made to moral claims. If such a justification is maintained then one cannot argue, for example, that providing cheaper drugs for AIDS victims in sub-Saharan

Africa is a moral responsibility, unless it can be shown that this will somehow improve the drug companies' economic returns. What is at issue here is the assumption, well argued by Sternberg (2000), that business interests can only be responsible for those social issues that have a direct bearing on their role as value-maximizing structures. From this perspective, business firms might 'do well by doing good'; but attempting to do good is irresponsible if it detracts from the firm's efforts to maximize its economic returns, however these may be defined.

According to this view, business can respond only to consumers' choices between competing products or services. If consumers are offended by the operations of a business enterprise, it is their responsibility not to invest in it, or work for it, or purchase goods and services from it (Sternberg, 2000). This approach assumes that consumers have adequate information about the firm and that those affected by its operations make rational judgements based on that information. One might argue that as 'transparency' is absolutely necessary in order for consumers to make informed decisions, exercising transparency, in addition to following rules of distributive justice and ordinary civility, is all that is really required for firms to meet their social responsibilities. By this line of reasoning, a firm that offers substandard wages need only make its wage policies known; it is then up to job-seekers and consumers to decide if its business practices are acceptable or not. However, this does not ensure a solution for an existing social problem; it merely shifts the moral choice to other parties.

One response to this problem is to revive the notion that safeguarding the public welfare is the proper function of governments, essentially a functionalist argument. Such an argument, however, does not take into account the shifts in power and influence among societal institutions. To say that the moral concerns of business interests should be restricted to the pursuit of maximizing owner value and that to take on other responsibilities is a misallocation of resources is to assume that other institutions will ensure the proper and ethical functioning of civil society. Clearly, this cannot be expected where other institutions are relatively weak. As Margolis and Walsh put it, 'If no other institutions are positioned or equipped as well as business organizations to respond, then concerns with misallocation look quite different from the classic case in which a more efficient response is available' (2003, p. 293). Forty-five years ago, Davis (1960) argued that as business interests increase their social power, so should their social responsibilities be expanded. Failure to do so would only invite more government intervention.

If institutional alternatives are absent, citizens and vested interest groups can only appeal directly to business interests in seeking to create 'just societies'. But being virtuous by taking on added social responsibilities cannot be sustained in a competitive market environment as long as the key objective of any corporation is to maximize owner value. Only if all firms take on these responsibilities can socially responsible firms remain competitive.[26]

The contingent nature of corporate social responsibility in market economies

It has been the contention of this essay that there exists in market economies an ongoing tension between the institutions of the state (political power) and those institutions representing business interests (economic power). The distribution of power and influence between these two institutional sectors varies greatly across different nation-states. It also varies historically within each nation-state. But this is not to deny the potential power and influence emanating from civil society. South Korea, for example, is currently experiencing a rise in influence of interest groups within its civil society described by some as movements of 'democratization'. In effect, these groups have emerged to fill the vacuum left by the growing division between business interests and government policies and the uncertain outcome of this division. Of course, extreme weakness of both government and business institutions or, in some cases, religious institutions, can result in civil chaos.

Questions about corporate social responsibility, and the manner in which such questions are framed, depend in large part on the nature of the relationship between business interests and governments. If business interests dominate the institutional field, they will also be faced with greater demands for ameliorating social problems than will be the case where the government plays a dominant role. On the other hand, in order for them to respond, it seems necessary to couch those demands in economic terms. But in framing the issues in this manner, questions that require moral judgements are left unaddressed.

Forms of government support of public services that are channelled through private delivery services merely reinforce the dominance of economic values and a 'contractarian' ideology. Under these conditions, moral responsibilities again become subject to economic returns. As Barber points out, to privatize services is to remove their accountability to the 'sovereign' public (Barber, 2002, p. 270).

If other institutional sectors are weak, functionalist arguments that assert that business enterprises should be concerned only with wealth creation (in an ethical manner, of course) cannot be sustained. Under these conditions, one can only argue for a stronger government to protect civil society, or argue in support of the 'virtuous' corporation. This latter approach would define the corporation as itself a 'responsible citizen' (Megone, 2002). It would emphasize the importance of creating its goods or services and marketing them in a manner that improves the social well-being of the population. But unless all firms assume these added responsibilities no single firm is likely to do so unless it can be shown that this will increase its competitive advantage (Zadek, 2001, p. 222). Indeed, to extend corporate social responsibility to all possible stakeholders under competitive market conditions would soon destroy an enterprise.[27]

Corporate social responsibility then is a contingent term; contingent on the degree of influence of business interests in civil society relative to other institutions, especially the state or government. Not only is the range of issues influenced by these institutional alignments, but so too is the manner in which these issues are expressed. Cohn's comments in 1971 regarding the limits of the abilities of corporations to solve social problems were based on the assumption that other more competent institutional mechanisms were available. With the absence of many of these mechanisms, where else but from the business sector are the solutions to these problems to be expected?

Perhaps when pressures for corporate social responsibility become especially severe, when managers are at a loss in attempting to work out a balance between economic objectives and meeting demands for greater social responsibility, we shall see a return of government-funded services and monitoring agencies at both the national and international levels. Perhaps, as Wallerstein has suggested, a consequence of weakened and discredited governments might be a period of chaos with debates and battles among groups at local levels creating 'complex and flexible' alliances, 'workable only if we keep in front of our minds the egalitarian objectives' (Wallerstein, 1995, p. 271). Perhaps we shall see a continued development of the 'third way', in which, though market principles become embedded in political governance, a balance is struck between free choice and social responsibility (Giddens, 1998, 2001; for a critical view, see Allen, 2001). And among the social movements now proliferating throughout the world, it is not beyond the realm of possibility to suggest that the communitarian component of viable civil societies might gain greater importance relative to the demands of disconnected groups of individual consumers and profit-maximizing firms (Etzioni, 1988; Putnam, 2000; Mintzberg et al., 2002).

Notes

1. Over the past 30 years a huge volume of literature on the 'welfare state' has accumulated. Esping-Anderson, a leading voice on the concept, argues that it should not be confused with simply an array of government-sponsored social programmes. Rather, it conveys the idea that the nation-state has made a binding commitment granting citizens basic social rights, including the right to make claims on the government. The government of a welfare state guarantees that it will uphold the well-being of the entire social community, or 'civil society'. The focus is on the nature of these commitments rather than on the array of discrete social policies. Esping-Anderson (1994) estimates that this definition would probably cover only the OECD countries following the Second World War. However, measures used in historical and comparative research on the evolution of welfare states and their similarities and differences tend to be based on rates of government expenditure on particular social programmes. Further, one cannot discount the piece-meal manner in which the welfare state has emerged historically, nor the way in which it has been 'weakened', 'dismantled' or 'transformed' – depending on one's perspective – since the late 1970s.

For a survey of the variety of interpretations of the extent of changes and altera-
tions of the 'welfare state' see Gilbert (2002, pp. 9–31); or compare, at one
extreme, Esping-Anderson, who claims that only marginal adjustments to the
policies of welfare states are being made (1996, p. 265), to the other extreme,
represented by Zijderveld (1999), who argues that since the 1980s the role of the
state has been greatly diminished in favour of 'the market', and that European
countries are following the lead of the United States.

The important issue, however, is not so much the relative size of state
expenditure on social welfare projects as the manner in which the funds are
spent. Government funding of welfare programmes may be similar in two different countries, but one may allocate those funds through government agencies
designed to carry out specific welfare functions, while the other may contract
those services to private agencies. In the latter case, the government's role is
significantly altered and, many would argue, considerably diminished as the
value of efficiency through competition gains precedence. The policies of
President George W. Bush's administration in the United States are instructive in
this regard. Government discretionary expenditures actually expanded at a
greater rate than those of any other administration since the Johnson administration in 1967. During Bush's first term in office, total federal spending rose by
29 per cent and employment levels in the federal government were greater than
at any time in history. Yet government programmes for education and health
care (to cite two examples) have been directed toward sponsoring competition
among private-sector agencies for the delivery of these services. *The Economist*
has labelled his policies 'big government conservatism' (28 August 2004,
pp. 22–6). For a comprehensive, empirically grounded comparative approach to
social welfare issues and the concept of the welfare state, see Wilensky (2002).

2. Although the entire business system is of concern here, I am focusing on the
corporation, since this form of business enterprise has set the agenda for most
business-related issues. Privately owned firms, partnerships and owner-managed
firms remain important players but the logic of corporation strategies dominates
their behaviour as well.

3. The concept of 'civil society' remains somewhat amorphous. It conveys the idea
of citizen groups voluntarily organizing to pursue specific objectives. For an historical account of the concept, see Lehmbruch (2001) and Walzer (1998). Taylor
(1990) describes civil society as existing 'over against the state, in partial independence from it. It includes those dimensions of social life which cannot be
confounded with, or swallowed up in the state'. Taylor goes on to note that the
existence of civil society is not likely to be found in societies ruled by ascription
and tradition (see Zelniker, 2001). The concept also assumes some degree of
tension between the state and the larger society not unlike the descriptions
posited by 'conflict theory' in vogue during the 1960s (see Dahrendorf, 1959;
Coser, 1956). Civil society in this sense is defined as the reciprocal of order
imposed by the state or by some other configuration of political power, such as
business interests. It is the source of vested interests that can challenge that
power and influence public policy. In this essay I assume that the concept is
useful not only with respect to the powers of the state but also with respect to
the powers of any dominant institution in society (see also Tilly, 1996).

4. While the case is being made that business interests are currently the dominant
institutions in advanced market economies, this is not to minimize the importance of civil-society movements seeking to redefine the role of the state or to
confront the state on a variety of issues.

5. This tripartite division is currently in common use, especially among those authors arguing for a 'third-way' in realigning the political landscape of western economically-advanced nation-states (see for example, Giddens, 1998).

6. Markets are not self-constitutive; they require rules governing property ownership and rules governing exchange. Nevertheless, current neo-classical economics asserts that markets fundamentally rely on the assumption of the utility-maximizing agent. Thus, it has become common practice to assume that markets differ by degrees of state interventions. Typologies have been advanced plotting different combinations of governments and markets. These can be arrayed along a continuum from government-dominated socialist states where equality is the dominant value through development-authoritarian states and on to types that assert the dominance of markets and market mentality in 'public choice' models (see for example, Block, 1994). But these all represent various ways of constructing the social parameters in which exchanges of scarce resources take place (see Polanyi, 1957).

7. For a more complete account of government labour legislation enacted in response to a variety of citizens groups during the late 19th and early 20th centuries, see Nelson (1975, pp. 136–52). The most popular issue of this early era of social reform was the protection of women and children in the workplace. Fine (1967, pp. 46–52) points to 'social gospelers', social reformers and social scientists as the principal voices opposed to laissez-faire doctrines in the late 19th century.

8. It was during this era that 'community chest' drives (now known as the 'United Way') were organized as a means to coordinate responses to solicitations from voluntary welfare agencies. These were also the years when service clubs for businessmen were founded, such as the Rotary Club, established in 1905, and the Lions Club in 1917. These clubs also strengthened social ties with local community leaders.

9. For a brief account of the Canadian experience, see Dobbin, 1998, pp. 32–48.

10. The head of American Motors declared that 'enlightened self-interest rather than benevolence should be the impelling motive in every relationship between the corporation on the one hand and its employees, neighbours and customers, on the other. After all, it is the job of the corporation to make money for its stockholders. And it so happens that it is good business to be humane and that decency pays in dividends' (Heald, 1970, pp. 155–6).

11. See also Bell, 1960; Myrdal, 1960; Yergin and Stanislaw, 1998, pp. xii–xiii. For an exhaustive treatment of the relationship between economic development and increases in government-sponsored social services, see Wilensky, 2002, especially pp. 214–15.

12. Criticism of the welfare state came from both the political right and left. The right, of course, stressed the need for governments to reduce their interventions in order to increase the efficiencies of market competition (Hayek, 1960, p. 196; Friedman, 1970, 1982; for a recent version of this argument, see *The Economist*, 22 January 2005). The left argued that the welfare state merely promoted 'monopoly capitalism' while containing latent class conflict (O'Connor, 1973; Mishra, 1984; Offe, 1984).

13. Wilensky argues that the 'crisis' was due not so much to a decline in government expenditures for welfare programmes and subsidies for business interests as to a change of priorities (e.g., more funds going to the military and less to welfare programmes during the Reagan administration) and to the shifting of responsibility for welfare delivery from the federal government to states, counties and municipalities (2002, pp. 357–8).

14. This may not be a paradox at all. With fewer welfare services available, subsistence employment of any kind remains the only option available to workers. It is no accident that low-wage jobs in fast-food chains are far more plentiful in the US, with its low minimum-wage levels, than in Sweden, with its higher minimum wage and more generous social provision.

15. This position is one side of an ongoing debate about citizen rights versus citizen responsibilities. The argument for 'need-based' welfare claims to promote responsibility, arguing that unless individuals demonstrate a committed attempt to seek employment, they should not receive public social assistance. An attempted solution to the debate between welfare as a right (thus raising the possibility of 'free riders') and welfare as 'earned' (which raises the possibility of increased social inequality) is the 'third way' (see Giddens, 1998).

16. In Florida, the failure of one school to make a profit for its owners resulted the selling off of its 'assets', such as books and technical equipment, while the students were required to perform janitorial and maintenance work.

17. The history of corporations as legal entities in the United States adds a certain irony to the entire discussion of 'corporate social responsibility'. According to one thesis, they were originally chartered as agencies of government, designed to serve special functions, such as building and maintaining toll-roads, or creating and administering banks. The growing number of these corporations eventually resulted in a shift to the idea of the corporation as an independent profit-making business enterprise, which anyone could form. This transition was further nurtured in the context of a democratic, decentralized state. What was once a structure for public service became a means for private gain (Handlin and Handlin, 1945).

18. It is significant, if somewhat bizarre, that a Microsoft executive has argued that the company must cut costs despite its huge financial reserves of $56.4 billion, in order to improve earnings for its shareholders. Cuts in employee benefits are being proposed as one of the ways to cut costs. Share prices have remained the same over the period 1998 to 2004, even though operating profits have doubled. The executive is quoted as saying, 'The key now to growing our stock price is growing profits even more. If we grow our profits, our stock price is poised to respond' (*Globe and Mail*, 7 July 2004, p. B11).

    In Canada, McNish (2005) reports that 'increasingly take-over negotiations are moving from ... corporate boardrooms to the far-flung offices of money managers who invest on behalf of wealthy individuals, pension and mutual funds.' McNish further notes that 'Spurring the shareholder opposition are recently relaxed corporate laws that make it easier for fund managers to meet and work in unison if they are dissatisfied with a public company transaction. In addition, shareholders say increased cooperation through the Canadian Coalition for Good Governance has encouraged less activist funds to work with more pro-active investors.'

19. Fligstein (1997) notes that financial models for assessing the effectiveness of firms were superseded in the early 1980s by what he calls the 'language of shareholder value'. This was a response to the effects of high inflation rates during the 1970s, when asset values inflated and returns on investment subsequently declined. Institutional shareholders demanded that managers sell off overvalued assets and assume debt as a means to keep firms disciplined. Layers of management were also reduced. They further exerted pressure on managers to buy out competitors and sell off diversified assets. These institutional investors 'of course benefited by making money on organizing and executing mergers' (p. 30).

20. In a survey of 1000 Canadian companies conducted by KMPG in 1999, the most influential reason to invest resources in ethics initiatives was 'protection or enhancement of reputation', which 71 per cent of the respondents ranked 4 or 5 on a scale of 1 (low) to 5 (high) (KPMG, 1999, pp. 1, 11).

21. For more recent examples of the decline in the US government's enforcement of regulations, see Dao (2003) and Pear (2003).

22. Klein (2000, p. 430) argues that the intent of the wave of corporate codes of conduct by corporations with international operations was to silence 'off-shore watchdog' groups. She further notes that these codes were drafted by public-relations firms to ward off media investigations.

23. An example of successful demonstrations is the report that ten of the world's leading banks acceded to demands of protestors to agree to abide by the World Bank's voluntary code of environmental standards when making loans for infrastructure projects.

24. See Djelic (1998) for an historical account of adaptation and resistance by western European countries after the Second World War to the US insistence that they adopt American models. These issues, of course, also challenge the rights of national sovereignty; a problem not unlike the issues raised by supporters of foreign interventionist policies or 'regime change'.

25. Closely related to this framing process is the reification of 'the market' as a causal factor, an observation central to Marx's critique of capitalism. Thus, in the US 'the market' has been held responsible for the increase of executive income from 40 times that of the annual earnings of the average worker 25 years ago to the current level of 400 times the annual earnings of the average worker.

26. There is a body of literature that claims to demonstrate that taking on additional social responsibilities does not necessarily detract from organizations' profitability. But the measures used are so diverse that it is hard to assess these claims (see Margolis and Walsh, 2003).

27. See Margolis and Walsh (2003) for an innovative treatment of this and related issues in their attempt to form a normative theory of the firm. The current popularity of the concept of 'stakeholders' and stakeholder theory suggests that managers are well aware of this dilemma in defining the range of their responsibilities.

References

Allen, M. L. (2001) 'Stake holding by Any Other Name: A Third Way Business Strategy', in A. Giddens (ed.), *The Global Third Way Debate* (Cambridge: Polity Press), pp. 280–9.

Barber, B. R. (2002) 'How to Make Society Civil and Democracy Strong', in A. Giddens (ed.), *The Global Third Way Debate* (Cambridge: Polity Press), pp. 269–79.

Bauman, Z. (1998) *Work, Consumerism and the New Poor* (Philadelphia: Open University Press).

Bell, D. (1960) *The End of Ideology* (New York: The Free Press).

Berle, Adolf A. Jr. (1957) *Economic Power and the Free Society* (Santa Barbara: Center for the Study of Democratic Institutions), pp. 7–12, reprinted in C. Walton and R. Eells (eds), *The Business System: Readings in Ideas and Concepts* (New York: Macmillan, 1967), pp. 1441–5.

Blinder, A. S. (1987) *Hard Heads, Soft Hearts: Tough Minded Economics for a Just Society* (Reading, MA: Addison-Wesley).

Block, F. (1994) 'The Roles of the State in the Economy', in N. Smelser and R. Swedberg (eds), *The Handbook of Economic Sociology* (Princeton: Princeton University Press), pp. 691–710.

Boyer, R. (1996) 'State and Market: A New Engagement for the Twenty-first Century?', in R. Boyer and D. Drache (eds), *States Against Markets: The Limits of Globalization* (New York: Routledge), pp. 84–114.

Bradshaw, T. and Vogel, D. (eds) (1981) *Corporations and Their Critics* (New York: McGraw-Hill).

Chandler, A. (1966) *Strategy and Structure: Chapters in the History of the Industrial Enterprise* (Cambridge, MA: Belknap Press).

Clark, J. (1996) 'Public Nightmares and Communitarian Dreams: The Crisis of the Social in Social Welfare', in A. Warde (ed.), *Consumption Matters* (Cambridge: Blackwell).

Cohn, J. (1971) *The Conscience of the Corporation: Business and Urban Affairs 1967–1970* (Baltimore, MD: The John Hopkins Press).

Coser, L. (1956) *The Functions of Social Conflict* (Glencoe, IL: The Free Press).

Cross, G. (2000) *An All-Consuming Century: Why Commercialism Won in Modern America* (New York: Columbia University Press).

Dahrendorf, R. (1959) *Class and Class Conflict in Industrial Societies* (Stanford: Stanford University Press).

Dao, J. (2003) 'Mine Safety Official Critical of Policies Faces Firing', *New York Times*, 9 November.

Davis, K. (1960) 'Can Business Afford to Ignore Social Responsibilities?', *California Management Review*, II (Spring), pp. 70–6.

Djelic, M. -L. (1998) *Exporting the American Model* (New York: Oxford University Press).

Dobbin, M. (1998) *The Myth of the Good Corporate Citizen: Democracy Under the Rule of Big Business* (Toronto: Stoddart).

The Economist (2003) 'Tough at the Top', 25 October, pp. 3–7.

The Economist (2003) 'Us Versus Us', 8 November, pp. 8–12.

The Economist (2004) 'The Contradictory Conservative', 28 August, pp. 22–6.

The Economist (2005) 'Survey: Corporate Social Responsibility', 22 January.

Eells, R. (1960) *The Meaning of Modern Business* (New York: Columbia University Press).

Esping-Anderson, G. (1994) 'Welfare States and the Economy', in N. Smelser and R. Swedberg (eds), *The Handbook of Economic Sociology* (Princeton: Princeton University Press), pp. 711–32.

Esping-Anderson, G. (ed.) (1996) *Welfare States in Transition: National Adaptations in Global Economies* (London: SAGE).

Etzioni, A. (1988) *The Moral Dimension: Toward a New Economics* (New York: The Free Press).

Fine, B. and Leopold, E. (1993) *The World of Consumption* (London: Routledge)

Fine, S. (1967) 'The General Welfare State in the Twentieth Century', in C. I. Schottland (ed.), *The Welfare State* (New York: Harper Torchbooks), pp. 46–69.

Fligstein, N. (1990) *The Transformation of Corporate Control* (Cambridge, MA: Harvard University Press).

Fligstein, N. (1997) *Markets, Politics and Globalization* (Stockholm: Almqvist and Wiksell International).

Fligstein, N. (2001) *The Architecture of Markets: An Economic Sociology of Twenty-First-Century Capitalist Societies* (Princeton: Princeton University Press).

Forstater, M., MacDonald, J. and Raynard, P. (2002) *Business and Poverty: Bridging the Gap* (London: The Prince of Wales International Business Leaders Forum).

Friedman, M. (1970) 'The Social Responsibility of Business is to Increase its Profits', *New York Times Magazine*, 13 September.

Friedman, M. (1982) *Capitalism and Freedom* (Chicago: University of Chicago Press).

Giddens, A. (1998) *The Third Way: The Renewal of Social Democracy* (Cambridge: Polity Press).

Giddens, A. (ed.) (2001) *The Global Third Way Debate* (Cambridge: Polity Press).

Gilbert, N. (2002) *Transformation of the Welfare State: The Silent Surrender of Public Responsibility* (New York: Oxford University Press).

Handlin, O. and Handlin, M. (1945) 'Origins of the American Business Corporation', *Journal of Economic History*, V (May) p. 223. Reprinted in C. Walton and R. Eells (eds), *The Business System: Readings in Ideas and Concepts* (New York: Macmillan, 1967), pp. 1366–74.

Hayek, F. A. (1960) *The Constitution of Liberty Chicago* (Chicago: University of Chicago Press).

Hayek, F. A. (1967) 'The Corporation in a Democratic Society: In Whose Interest Ought It and Will It be Run?', in C. Walton and R. Eells (eds), *The Business System: Readings in Ideas and Concepts* (New York: Macmillan, 1967), pp. 1434–40.

Heald, M. (1970) *The Social Responsibilities of Business: Company and Community, 1900–1960* (Cleveland, OH: Case Western Reserve University Press).

Hoffman, A. J. (2001) *From Heresy to Dogma: An Institutional History of Corporate Environmentalism* (Stanford: Stanford University Press).

Jackall, R. (1988) *Moral Mazes: The World of Corporate Managers* (New York: Oxford University Press).

Klein, N. (2000) *No Logo: Taking Aim at the Brand Bullies* (Toronto: Vintage Canada).

KPMG (1999) '1999 KPMG Business Ethics Survey: Managing for Ethical Practice' (Toronto: KPMG Canada).

Lehmbruch, G. (2001) 'Germany', in Y. Tadashi and K. G. Ashizawa (eds), *Governance and Civil Society in a Global Age* (New York: Japan Centre for International Exchange).

Lewis, A. (2002) *Morals, Markets and Money: Ethical, Green and Socially Responsible Investing* (London: Pearson Education).

MacIntyre, A. (ed.) (1994) *Business and Government in Industrializing Asia* (Ithaca, NY: Cornell University Press).

Marglin, Stephen A. (2003) 'Development as Poison: Rethinking the Western Model of Modernity', *Harvard International Review* (Spring): 70–5.

Margolis, J. D. and Walsh, J. P. (2003) 'Misery Loves Companies: Rethinking Social Initiatives by Business', *Administrative Science Quarterly* vol. 48, pp. 268–305.

McNish, J. (2005) 'Shareholders Taking a Stand on Takeover Talks', *The Globe and Mail* (Toronto), 19 February, p. B3.

Megone, C. (2002) 'Two Aristotelian Approaches to Business Ethics', in C. Megone and S. Robinson (eds), *Case Histories in Business Ethics* (London: Routledge).

'Microsoft Chief Issues E-mail Prescription for Company's Ills', *Globe and Mail* (Toronto) 7 July 2004, p. B11 (reprinted from the *Wall Street Journal*).

Mishra, R. (1984) *The Welfare State in Crisis* (Brighton: Wheatsheaf Books).

Mintzberg, H., Simons, R. and Basu, K. (2002) 'Beyond Selfishness', *MIT Sloan Management Review*, vol. 44(1), pp. 67–74; also available online at http://sloan-review.mit.edu/smr/issue/2002/fall/7/

Moscovitch, A. and Albert, J. (1987) *The Benevolent State: The Growth of Welfare in Canada* (Toronto: Garamond Press).

Müller, A. (2005) 'Green Mountain Coffee Roasters: Supplier Relations and Community Development', in F. Bird, E. Raufflet and J. Smucker (eds), *International Business and the Dilemmas of Development* (New York: Palgrave Macmillan), pp. 233–54.

Myrdal, G. (1960) *Beyond the Welfare State* (New Haven: Yale University Press).

Nelson, D. (1975) *Managers and Workers: Origins of the New Factory System in the United States, 1880–1920* (Madison, WI: University of Wisconsin Press).

O'Connor, J. (1973) *The Fiscal Crisis of the State* (New York: St. Martin's Press).

Offe, C. (1984) *Contradictions of the Welfare State* (London: Hutchinson).

OECD (2001) *Corporate Responsibility: Private Initiatives and Public Goals* (Paris: Organization for Economic Co-operation and Development).

Osborne, D. and Gaebler, T. (1993) *Reinventing Government: How the Entrepreneurial Spirit is Transforming the Public Sector* (New York: Penguin).

Panitch, L. and Schwartz, D. (1988) *The Assault on Trade Unions Freedoms: From Consent to Coercion Revisited* (Toronto: Garamond Press).

Pear, R. (2003) 'Issue of Competition Causes Widest Split in Medicare', *New York Times*, 10 November.

Pearson, R. and Seyfang, G. (2001) 'New Hope or False Dawn? Voluntary Codes of Conduct, Labour Regulation and Social Policy in a Globalizing World', *Global Social Policy*, vol. 1, pp. 49–78.

Polanyi, K. (1957) *The Great Transformation* (Boston: Beacon Hill).

Powell, W. (1990) 'Neither Market nor Hierarchy: Network Forms of Organization', *Research in Organizational Behavior*, vol. 12, pp. 295–336.

Putnam, R. (2000) *Bowling Alone* (New York: Simon & Schuster).

Schor, J. (1998) *The Overspent American* (New York: Basic Books).

Schwartz, P. and Gibb, B. (1999) *When Good Companies Do Bad Things* (New York: John Wiley).

Smucker, J. (2005) 'Managing for Whom? Foreign Ownership and Management of Korea First Bank', in F. Bird, E. Raufflet and J. Smucker (eds), *International Business and the Dilemmas of Development* (New York: Palgrave Macmillan), pp. 184–98.

Sternberg, E. (2000) *Just Business: Business Ethics in Action* (Oxford: Oxford University Press).

Tadashi, Y. and Kim G. A. (eds) (2001) *Governance and Civil Society in a Global Age* (Tokyo: Japan Center for International Exchange).

Taylor, C. (1990) 'Modes of Civil Society', *Public Culture*, vol. 3, pp. 95–119.

Tilly, C. (ed.) (1996) *Citizenship, Identity and Social History* (Cambridge: Cambridge University Press).

Useem, M. (1993) *Executive Defense: Shareholder Power and Corporate Reorganization* (Cambridge, MA: Harvard University Press).

Wallerstein, I. (1995) *After Liberalism* (New York: W. W. Norton).

Walzer, M. (1998) 'The Concept of Civil Society', in M. Walzer (ed.), *Toward a Global Civil Society* (Providence, RI: Berghahn Books).

Wilensky, H. L. (2002) *Rich Democracies: Political Economy, Public Policy, and Performance* (Berkeley: University of California Press).

Wilson, I. (2000) *The New Rules of Corporate Conduct: Rewriting the Social Charter* (Westport, CT: Quorum Books).

Yergin, D. and Stanislaw, J. (1998) *The Commanding Heights: The Battle for the World Economy* (New York: Simon and Schuster).

Zadek, S. (2001) *The Civil Corporation* (London: Earthscan Publications).

Zelniker, S. (2001) 'Israel', in M. Tadashi and K. G. Ashizawa (eds), *Governance and Civil Society in a Global Age* (New York: Japan Centre for International Exchange), pp. 154–78.

Zijderveld, A. (1999) *The Waning of the Welfare State: The End of Comprehensive State Succour* (New Brunswick, NJ: Transaction Publishers).

4
Toward a Political Ethic for International Businesses

Frederick Bird

Over the last two centuries, international businesses have played a large role in the economically developing parts of the world. Large firms like the English East India Company and British South Africa Company have governed huge colonies. Other large businesses such as the South Manchurian Railway Company and the United Fruit Company have played major roles in relation to political coups in China and Guatemala. International petroleum companies generated much of the wealth that fostered economic development of countries like Nigeria and Malaysia. International trade has significantly affected a large number of developing countries that have organized substantial parts of their economies in conjunction with foreign-dominated supply chains to produce cotton, sugar, coffee, palm oil, tobacco, copper and gold for international markets (Drohan, 2003; Litvin, 2003). In all of these examples, international businesses have directly influenced how governments in developing areas have governed. At times this influence has been excessive. International businesses at various times and in various places have bribed officials, demanded special tax breaks or even dictated public policy.

We may well agree that international businesses should not illegally interfere in the political processes of developing areas. We must nevertheless ask how they should act, given the fact that these businesses in many settings become partners with local governments, dominate local economies and serve as major sources of government revenues. Accordingly, this essay considers the following question. What are the political duties, obligations and responsibilities of international businesses with respect to the national and local governments of the areas in which they are operating?

This question focuses on distinct aspects of the larger discussion about the social responsibilities or social performance of businesses as they interact with established governments. In this essay I will sketch general guidelines for a political ethic for international businesses in developing areas. I will also explore how these guidelines can shed light on a set of perplexing situations, such as the responsibilities of businesses in areas of social conflict as well as the responsibilities of business in relation to weak and autocratic governments. Although this essay will focus on internationally connected businesses in developing areas, much of what I have to say bears upon the practices and responsibilities of all business enterprises with respect to governments in industrialized as well as developing areas.

While considering this question, it is useful to consider several specific situations. Consider, for example, the situation Shell faced in Nigeria, where for most of the period since independence the country has been ruled by military regimes established by coups. The government is the majority owner of the Shell Petroleum and Development Company of Nigeria (SPDC), holding 55 per cent of its shares, though the company was managed and operated by Shell, which holds a 30 per cent interest. At present 12 per cent of the royalties from SPDC's operations are returned to regional governments in the Niger River delta area, where the oil is extracted. For long periods only 3 per cent was transferred to these governments. Initially, as a result of British decrees when Nigeria was a colony, title to the mineral resources under the lands belonging to various ethnic groups in the Niger delta was transferred to the national government. Beginning in the 1970s, the national government used the wealth generated by oil to build a new capital, develop various public works and pay for most government expenses. A number of government leaders and officials amassed great personal wealth in the process. During the 1990s, an extremely autocratic national government cancelled elections, jailed opposition politicians and used excessive armed forces in response to ethnic protests and conflicts. Throughout this period Shell argued that its political obligations consisted in obeying local laws, not offering bribes and not directly getting involved in Nigerian politics. Yet in four decades, during which Shell and other petroleum firms generated hundreds of billions of dollars in wealth, the people in the Niger delta remained as impoverished as ever. In the light of this outcome, Shell might well ask whether it might have conducted its relationship with Nigeria's governments in such a way that more of the wealth from its operations produced would have gone to reducing poverty in the Niger delta.[1]

Consider as well the example of Rio Tinto, which since 1988 has been exploring the possibility of developing a set of mines along the beaches of southeastern Madagascar. Rio Tinto is a powerful and wealthy multinational mining company, and in this case the national government is a junior partner (20 per cent ownership) in the QIT Madagascar Minerals (QMM) company, which will develop and operate the mine. Impoverished and weak, funded in large part through international aid, the government of Madagascar lacks the resources to establish an independent agency to monitor closely the mine's eventual operations. When Rio Tinto sought to explore the possibility of establishing a privately owned, publicly useable port, the government possessed no one with sufficient legal expertise to draw up the appropriate legislation. What are Rio Tinto's political and legal responsibilities in this setting? To what extent should it help the government establish regulatory capacity? And what guidelines should it follow so as to help the government gain strength without seeming to exercise undue political influence?[2]

Consider also the case of Talisman in Sudan. For most of the past 40 years a civil war has sputtered on and off between the national government controlled by the Arabic-speaking population of northern Sudan and the various non-Arab ethnic groups in the southern third of the country, which at various times have sought to secede to form their own country or to become self-governing provinces within a more decentralized and federally structured country. At the same time, the national government has resisted these moves and sought to impose a common body of Islamic regulations on the whole country, including the southern regions in which most people belong to Christian or traditional African religions. Oil was discovered in the area where these two regions divide and overlap. The national government, together with national oil firms from China and Malaysia, began to develop drilling sites and pipelines to transport the oil to a port on the Red Sea. In 1998 Talisman Oil Company from Canada bought a 30 per cent share in the combined oil business. Citizen groups in Canada and the United States staged protests. They argued that by operating in Sudan Talisman was helping to support a morally questionable government that had violated the civil rights of its own citizens, and had even used Talisman airfields to bomb insurgents from the South. Eventually, as a result of these protests and falling share prices, Talisman withdrew from Sudan. Retrospectively, we can still ask what alternative actions Talisman might have taken in its dealings with the Sudanese government?

Questions about the political ethics of business are important but, as these examples suggest, not ones that can be simply resolved.

The conventional approach to political ethics

Many firms have in practice adopted what I shall refer to as the conventional approach to political ethics. This approach requires international business to:

- Obey national and international law
- Stay out of local and national partisan politics
- Neither accept nor offer bribes
- Respect and protect the basic human rights of persons with whom they are directly involved

Each of these guidelines is basic (even obvious) and widely endorsed. For example, consider the first guideline: although many businesses are still frequently cited for violating specific laws on matters as diverse as accounting practices, insider trading, false advertising and pollution, for the most part businesses comply with established legal standards in these areas. There is also widespread public condemnation of bribery, influence peddling and overt human rights abuses (Klitgaard, 1988; ICHRP, 2002). On the other hand, the practices of two branches of the same international firm may well differ with respect, for example, to environmental practices when the laws of different countries, such as Colombia and Peru, establish different expectations (Fossgard-Moser, 1998).

Over time, these standards have become accepted as fundamental norms. This normative acceptance, however does not guarantee that there has been, or will be, universal compliance with these standards, which certain firms (or individuals within firms) will attempt from time to time to skirt or evade. They are likely either to attempt to hide their violations or to clothe their actions in rhetoric or gestures that make them seem acceptable. This is new. When the Belgian mining conglomerate Union Minière directly supported the secession of the province of Katanga from Congo in the early 1960s, it did so blatantly without dissimulation or excuse. Until the past few decades few businesses explicitly acknowledged they had responsibilities for protecting human rights of workers. Over time increasing numbers of firms have overtly invoked these standards and attempted to honour them or to offer good reasons for those situations in which they temporarily failed to comply strictly.

Although the conventional political ethic is not without merit, it provides an inadequate framework for many of the characteristic challenges and dilemmas facing international businesses in developing areas. The inadequacy of this conventional ethic is not primarily a matter of enforcement. Closing the gap between normative standards and actual conduct is a generic moral problem, which is not unique to this widely held political ethic.

We can gain a sense of the inadequacy of the conventional political ethic by reviewing the three examples cited previously. All three firms have attempted to act in keeping its standards in exemplary ways: they have attempted to abide by relevant laws, avoid bribery, not meddle in political process and honour human rights in their practices. Although both Shell and Talisman have been criticized for human rights violations, these abuses were, for the most part, ones for which neither company was directly responsible. In the case of Shell, the abuses were perpetrated largely by government troops whose assistance it had solicited to protect its working sites and pipelines. Similarly, the criticisms of Talisman were for abuses carried out by the armed forces of a government with which Talisman had become a partner. The problem with the conventional political ethic is that it provides few clues for addressing the central political issues raised by these three cases. What kinds of action might Shell have taken so that more of the wealth from the oil extracted from the Niger delta helped to reduce the poverty of this region? What guidelines should Rio Tinto follow as it seeks both to collaborate with and act as a corporate citizen subject to the laws and courts of the government of Madagascar? Apart from divesting, what other actions might Talisman have initiated with the government of Sudan to address the ongoing civil conflict and the needs and rights of the people most affected? The conventional political ethic provides little guidance for these kinds of situations; indeed, as I will demonstrate further on in this essay, it provides little or no basis for determining how much weight should be placed on each of its stipulations in relation to contingent events. As I sketch a fuller, more useful and livelier political ethic for international businesses, I will not abandon the conventional guidelines. I will, however, reinterpret them by placing them in a much wider, more responsive framework.

Designing a relevant and responsive political ethic

Using the three cases mentioned in the previous section as points of reference, we can identify a number of considerations that we would hope an adequate political ethic would address. Thus we would hope that such an ethic would be able to provide guidance as to when and how international businesses ought to act when laws in host countries are in serious conflict either with international laws or the laws of the company's home country. Talisman faced this conundrum in Sudan, as did Shell did in Nigeria – as did a host of firms in relation to the apartheid laws of South Africa. It would be useful to explore what alternatives firms might have in these situations (variants of which occur in many different countries) short of divesting. In summary it would be useful if a political ethic could help firms explore ways of acting politically that were not limited to options of either mute and seemingly loyal compliance with local political directives or exiting because compliance seems unconscionable; that is, options that allowed them to voice or dissent effectively (Hirschman, 1970; Bird, 1996, ch. 2, 7). An adequate political ethic ought to be able not only to identify proscribed behaviours – such as not violating laws, not bribing, not undermining political processes and not abusing human rights – but to occasion imaginative exploration of alternative strategies.

An adequate political ethic should help people to distinguish between moral expectations that call for strict compliance, usually framed as duties and obligations and standards of excellence, usually framed as ideals, aspirations, or objectives. Often, when we discuss ethical issues, we ignore or overlook this important and fundamental moral distinction. We set forth ethical guidelines without spelling out clearly whether a particular guideline is a duty or an ideal, or without distinguishing aspects of these guidelines that call for strict compliance (duties) from other aspects which articulate legitimate desires or objectives (aspirations). When we fail to distinguish between standards of excellence and standards calling for strict compliance, we foster not only moral confusion but also moral deceit (Fuller, 1964). Many written formulations of human rights add to our confusion in precisely this way. An adequate political ethic should help businesses distinguish strict duties from ideals they are seeking to realize; further, this ethic should also help businesses to balance these moral expectations and determine which moral claims have priority at a specific moment in time.

Timing is a major ethical concern. It was, for example, an issue for international firms operating in South Africa during the apartheid era. Many firms asked themselves: should they work for reforms in South Africa over time, or should they divest now? This was also the question for Talisman in Sudan: would it be appropriate to take a long-term view of the situation, or was it important to act decisively in the present? What obligations can be deferred? Which responsibilities should be immediately addressed? Which aspects of current duties can be met part way while other moral tasks are pursued? These questions continuously arise for two different reasons. First, circumstances change. The political situations in which firms find themselves are subject to ongoing transformations as a result of domestic political struggles, economic developments and international political pressure. Second, all moral actors, including international businesses in developing areas, are only capable of responding at any moment to a portion of the moral claims and challenges that involve them. An adequate political ethic should help businesses in particular settings determine the appropriate timing for their responses to the moral issues they face.

We can summarize this discussion concerning the characteristics of an adequate political ethic by stating that such an ethic should especially help businesses in these settings exercise responsible and responsive moral judgements that in turn facilitate effective moral action. An adequate ethic should provide businesses with the vocabularies and models for deliberation, so that they can keep track of contingent developments, set priorities, mobilize people and resources, and take action. Moreover, an adequate ethic must be more than a list of rules and principles. The conventional approach to political ethics fails in part precisely because it is merely conventional – a static set of standards, which does not provide a basis for considering historical contingencies, varying moral resources and differing kinds of moral claims. An adequate political ethic should establish frameworks that would guide us in sizing up situations, imaginatively considering alternatives and developing strategies for action; in other words it should help those involved discuss these matters, weigh alternatives and reach considered judgements.

Elements of an alternative, multidimensional political ethic

In this essay, I will outline the basic features of a multidimensional political ethic designed to help international businesses in developing areas effectively respond to moral issues arising out of their relations with government. This ethic will consider the following four aspects:

1. The basic duties of international businesses as legally defined entities within specific polities
2. Their social obligations, in terms of both formal contracts and ongoing interactions
3. Their civic responsibilities as organizational citizens
4. Their duty to exercise ethically responsible political judgements

Businesses are connected in at least three different ways with the political communities in which they function.

First, they are legal entities expected to comply with diverse statutes in home and host countries. As such, they have certain duties they are expected to fulfil. These duties are *categorical*: they are the same for all businesses in these locales; they are imposed by law, and firms gain licenses to operate only insofar as they acknowledge these duties. There is no bargaining with respect to these duties.

Second, they are often contractual partners with governments, either through negotiated agreements or through less explicitly acknowledged exchanges. International firms act formally as suppliers, customers and collaborators with governments. Insofar as they engage in these overt contractual relations, businesses acquire as well a series of social and political obligations. These obligations represent *hypothetical*: moral expectations affected by the character of the negotiations, agreements and interactions that give rise to them.

Third, international firms and the people who work for them are individually and collectively citizens within these political communities. As such, they are beneficiaries of various public policies and programmes, and they have corresponding entitlements, public goods and rights, as well various civic responsibilities. These responsibilities vary from fairly well-articulated expectations associated with norms of civility to much less clearly formulated expectations regarding philanthropic investments.

The first three elements in the model of political ethics I am sketching grow out of the three different ways in which businesses are embedded in the political communities in which they operate.

1. Basic duties of businesses with respect to governments

The conventional approach to political ethics identifies the basic duties of firms as legal entities. These duties are categorical, not optional; they are the same for all businesses, and are implicit in the charters that give businesses the license to operate; for the most part, they are stipulated in existing statutes. Whenever firms are caught violating these duties, they may be subjected to civil or criminal indictments and corresponding fines and punishments. These basic duties are, as stated previously, that businesses (a) abide by local laws, (b) avoid direct involvement in partisan politics, (c) neither accept nor offer bribes and (d) respect the basic human rights of those whom they directly affect. But none of these duties is absolute. Firms are repeatedly called upon to exercise judgement as to how they should exercise these duties in particular settings, and with due regard to social obligations and civic responsibilities.

Obey local laws. To what degree should firms strictly comply with laws they regard as unjust? A number of international firms considered this question with respect to the apartheid laws in South Africa in the 1970s and 1980s. Should they strictly enforce these laws? Or should they divest? In keeping with the Global Sullivan Principles, a number of firms overtly chose to ignore certain laws requiring separate housing facilities and workplaces. In good conscience, they chose not to comply with these laws.[3] Their actions assumed a mild form of civil disobedience. The government of South Africa made no attempt to penalize these firms. Thus with respect to the duty to obey local laws, firms may well have a range of options and responses, if they consider these laws unfair in terms of their ideals, international standards, or the best interests of the country itself. They may in varying ways selectively abide by particular laws, guided by specific ethical values (Sethi and Williams, 2001).

The issues here are also illustrated by tax laws, customary practices for paying taxes and the strategies firms employ with regard to these laws and practices. In a number of countries, established practices for determining tax rates and collecting payments differ markedly from legally defined rules (Kelly, 1998). In these kinds of settings, current practices may be generally accepted as being, on the whole, normative; or else regarded as questionable, if not corrupt (Klitgaard, 1988); or viewed as an uneasy mixture that is both accepted as customary and yet variously criticized as unfair. To determine their duties in these settings, firms are generally expected to inquire thoroughly into current practices and norms, and seek to abide by these insofar as their own home country's laws and accounting practices would allow. These are not simple matters.

The issue becomes more complicated when we consider alternative accounting practices firms may use to keep track of their income and expenses. These practices are legal. Nonetheless, these figures may vary markedly depending upon how firms register their internal expenses. The taxes firms end up paying sometimes do not correspond to the profits they declare. Many international firms charge excessive prices for resources and services they purchase from foreign units within their own business. Because their profit margins are thereby reduced, so are the taxes they are required to pay. In the 1980s the OECD attempted to establish common guidelines with respect to accounting for transfer prices of these internally exchanged goods and services so that firms operating in different countries in Europe would employ common accounting procedures. A number of European and North American firms operating in developing countries have been accused of using transfer pricing to reduce their tax burden (Tang, 1981; Baro, 2001).

This issue of transfer pricing takes on a quite different coloration in some developing countries where the host governments not only have established excessive rates for taxes and royalties (for example, with respect to resource extraction industries) but also use these revenues disproportionately to pursue the private advantage of government leaders and officials. In these settings, paying the required taxes may have the effect of directly supporting these questionable public expenditures. Should firms in these settings meet the legally required duty to pay taxes fully or should they meet them partway, diverting revenues that might otherwise be taxed into projects that might more directly benefit the public? This is the sort of situation that Shell faced in Nigeria in the 1980s and 1990s. The company conscientiously paid the required taxes and royalties. Without resorting to questionable accounting practices, it might still have considered other alternatives. For example, SPDC might have invested in a variety of local businesses that would be established to generate and deliver electricity, drill for and pump fresh water and construct and maintain roadways not just for Shell operations but for the communities in the Niger delta. Insofar as Shell invested in these kinds businesses, it would have correspondingly realized lower profits and would therefore have paid lower taxes and royalties. In the meantime these investments would have benefited the local economy, strengthened the ties with local communities and provided services from which Shell would directly benefit.

As part of their basic duties, international firms are indeed expected to comply with the laws of the countries in which they operate. They are nonetheless expected to use their intelligence and imagination as they figure out exactly what is morally required of them, especially in settings in which it seems to them that specific local laws are either unjust or generally followed only loosely. For the most part, even in these settings firms are expected to respect and honour the overall system of law. In fact, it is in their interest to find ways of strengthening the institutions and practices associated with the rule of law, since this provides the surest guarantees for the property rights and contractual relationships which are integral to sound business practice (Weber, [1914] 1978, II.8.iii; Berman, 1983; De Soto, 2000). The property and contractual rights of international firms are best protected against arbitrary political or civil interventions in countries that possess systems of law, reinforced by respected independent judiciaries. Insofar as they choose to dissent specific laws that seem unjust or to interpret the meaning or bearing of these laws in ways that differ from current practice, firms are well advised to do so publicly in ways that still respect the overall rule of law (Rawls, 1971, ch. 6). In just this way civil disobedience differs from overtly illegal behaviour: it is undertaken in a public way that calls attention to the injustices sanctioned or condoned by current law. When firms in South Africa adopted the Sullivan Principles, they overtly announced to the government that they were intentionally violating specific apartheid laws regarding the housing and promotion of blacks, laws that they – and the international community – deemed unjust.

Stay out of partisan political processes. In democratic societies, businesses are expected not to involve themselves in partisan political processes. Governments in these societies are expected to be chosen by the votes of citizens. They are expected to govern in ways that seek to promote the best interests of the society as a whole. Most people feel that businesses are out of line when they undermine or manipulate political processes to their own ends. Most democratic societies attempt to limit the monies that businesses can contribute to particular political parties because they do not wish the political processes to be skewed by the excessive influence of wealthy business interests. Pro forma, most businesses endorse the principle that they (and their competitors) ought not to manipulate the political process.

If we were to accept this commitment to non-interference as a full ethical statement in just these terms, we would soon be disillusioned; clearly we must think in broader terms. Most observers would agree that this principle does not, exclude in practice, attempts to influence governments and public policies through lobbying, special pleading and concerted campaigns to shape public opinion. In the industrialized countries, large corporations (and certain wealthy business leaders acting as private individuals) spend billions of dollars in efforts to put pressure on governments. They make campaign contributions, they represent the interest of businesses with respect to legislative debates and they attempt to influence how government agencies interpret and enforce existing statutes. For the most part, these efforts are regarded as legitimate; still, in many areas businesses seem to exercise disproportionate influence. For example, it has been argued that businesses in many countries have acted to retard the enactment of responsible environmental and labour legislation. Still, in a number of settings it might be argued that the problem has less to do with the capacity of businesses to voice their concerns, before national legislatures or international tribunals (such as the dispute boards of the World Trade Organization), than with the inability of labour, community and environmental concerns to lobby on the same scale so as to make their concerns equally well-known.

The principle of non-interference remains important even if it requires a fuller, more sophisticated articulation than it usually receives. Businesses should not directly or indirectly undermine the political processes in the countries in which they operate. They should not help to arrange for coups, as foreign petroleum companies did in relation to the 1954 coup in Iran (Kinzer, 2003). They should not offer huge bribes to government officials as Lockheed did in Japan in the early 1970s. Nonetheless, like community groups and labour organizations, businesses can be expected to communicate their interests to government councils and agencies as persuasively as possible. These kinds of efforts to influence governments should, however, remain public, transparent and civil. Businesses should attempt to respect and, as far as possible, follow current customs when making these kinds of representations. What become morally questionable are secretive and undisclosed efforts at influence, especially when these efforts are connected with gifts of money and other tangible benefits. Public efforts by citizens to communicate interests and concerns to their governments are normal exercises within the wider political processes of all societies, whether democratic or non-democratic.

The initiatives that businesses take to influence governments should be limited by an additional condition, which complements the requirements for civility and transparency: that is, such efforts should be developed in ways that foster reciprocating communications. There are both practical and ethical reasons for this. Businesses, as well as community groups, are much more likely to represent their concerns effectively – to bargain capably for their positions – if they regard their efforts as part of ongoing two-way communications in which they assiduously seek to listen and attend to the interests and concerns of government councils and officials (Bird, 1996, ch. 7).

Avoid corruption. Almost universally it has been argued that businesses should avoid corrupt practices. Both the United States and the European Union have passed laws prohibiting specific forms of questionable payments defined as corrupt practices. Yet corruption still abounds (Klitgaard, 1990; Kwong, 1997; Thomas et al., 2000; Hodess et al., 2001; *The Economist*, 2002). It is clearly easier to lament the extent of corruption, to raise moral outcries in opposition and to pass anti-corruption legislation than it is to find ways of eliminating it. There are a number of reasons why it is probably impossible to stamp out all acts of corruption. When they are faced with situations where it seems possible for them to get away with it, some business people and some government officials will trade in bribery and extortion to advance their interests at the cost of others. This has happened for ages and will continue to do so in part because some people will simply be inclined to take advantage of these situations (Klitgaard, 1988).

There are at least two other reasons for the continued existence of bribery and extortion. One factor has to do with the reasonable limits for regulations and surveillance needed to curb these practices. Zealous attempts to eradicate bribery and extortion would likely increase the intrusive policing powers of governments in ways that would seriously reduce civil liberties and would place the policing officials in positions where some would likely misuse their power for personal advantage. We have seen evidence of both of these tendencies in the so-called war on drugs, especially in the corrosive effect of this war on some police officers.

The second factor limiting the campaigns to curb bribery and extortion results from moralistic and protean ways of thinking about corruption. There is a tendency to define corruption broadly to include all questionable payments, especially all payments not directly itemized in budgets and account records. If we view corruption in this manner, then we may well be led to regard all of the following transactions as corrupt (Banfield and Wilson, 1963; Wertheim, 1964; Mauss, 1967; Scott, 1976):

- Payment of facilitation fees to clear goods through customs or through other often time-consuming logistic procedures
- Gifts to partners, suppliers and other collaborators (even as expected reciprocating customs, e.g., at weddings and funerals in trading partners' families)
- Payment of tips
- The choice of particular suppliers or partners based upon fact that the parties in these ongoing relationships have an educated understanding of how to collaborate effectively
- Continuing and evolving patterns of interactions based upon reciprocating favours rather than impersonal contracts

It is a mistake, I argue, to define these practices as corrupt (Velasquez, 2004). It is true that these practices all involve what might be described as informal or personal rather than formal, contractual, or bureaucratic exchanges. They often involve the use of either discretionary (and therefore not itemized) funds or else the use of discretionary powers, to make certain purchasing or processing decisions. For the most part, however, the types of transactions listed above take place in keeping with widely recognized conventions that treat all involved parties with more or less the same considerations.

The same statements cannot be made with respect to bribery and extortion. Bribery involves making undeclared payments in order to ensure that decisions regarding transactions do *not* follow publicly recognized standards of free market exchanges or reciprocal relationships. Bribery describes situations in which the parties proposing to make the undeclared payments take the initiative. Extortion describes situations in which recipients of these potential payments require them as a condition either of receiving a contract or, sometimes, even being considered for a contract (Carson, 1985). Although these acts may be widely practiced, they are not viewed as normatively acceptable conventions. They have been publicly decried in most countries (Gillespie, 1987; Klitgaard, 1988; Marong, 2002).

We might then be well advised to rephrase this basic duty not broadly in terms of corruption but more narrowly in terms of bribery and extortion. This prohibition against bribery and extortion remains important for a number of reasons. Acts of bribery and extortion undermine the standards of fair competition. They violate local and international law. In practice they divert funds that might otherwise benefit customers, taxpayers, shareholders and employees to those private parties engaging in these acts. As firms attempt to adhere to this rephrased duty, they still must exercise judgement, attempting in complex situations to distinguish proscribed behaviour from ones that seem similar but are not. They are also well cautioned to consider the difference between acts of bribery and acts of extortion. Their situation does not differ appreciably from that of other parties from whom equivalent payments are requested. Hence in some areas in order to operate at all, firms may be forced by circumstances to think twice about whether in the short term they should yield to these requests until, together with other affected firms, they can mount an effective protest.

Do not violate basic human rights. As the 20th century drew to a close, international businesses were being evaluated increasingly in terms of their record on human rights. Companies operating in developing countries were expected to espouse human rights, teach employees to honour them and conduct their operations accordingly. The language and rhetoric of human rights were incorporated into company codes and mission statements. Civil society organizations sought to expose practices that violated human rights.

The language of rights has increasingly been used not only to evaluate business practices but also to think about an ever-wider range of moral issues in the contemporary world. This deference to rights talk is a by-product of what Michael Ignatieff (2000) calls 'the Rights Revolution' (see also Glendon, 1993; Habermas, 1996), which in turn is reflected in the recent emergence of a large number of non-government organizations, local as well as international, devoted to protecting and furthering particular clusters of rights. It is ironic that while most people readily embrace the notion that human rights ought to be respected and protected, they have given much less thought about what specific sets of rights ought to receive pre-eminent attention and what is entailed in preserving these rights. Many of the statements about rights embodied in the Universal Declaration of Human Rights are, for example, not feasible standards but expressions of idealized visions of the world we might try to realize at some future time. Consider the first paragraph in Article 25, which declares that 'Everyone has a right to a standard of living adequate for health and well-being'. Consider as well Article 28, which declares that 'Everyone is entitled to a social and international order in which the rights and freedoms set forth in this declaration can be fully realized'. Neither of these rights can be easily realized in the present. They represent worthy objectives rather than contemporary obligations. Many rights can only be fully honoured in settings where there are sufficient public funds to provide for publicly guaranteed goods. Many low-income countries currently lack the tax base to provide the following goods for their populations: adequate elementary education for all (Article 26); adequate levels of economic security in the event of unemployment, disability, or old age (Article 25); property registries and courts required to insure effectively the right to private property (Article 17) (Holmes and Sunnstein, 1999, ch. 3; De Soto, 2000). In many countries the rights referred to by the Universal Declaration are not and cannot be evenly minimally protected because most low-income citizens in these countries cannot readily secure a 'fair and public hearing by an independent and impartial tribunal' (Article 10). In many countries, the judiciaries that do exist are either not fully independent and impartial (politically and religiously), or else they are not accessible to low-income petitioners. Thus, for a variety of reasons, compliance with the human rights standards remains spotty and uneven. In many cases these failures do not result from deliberate malfeasance, but rather from a failure of impoverished states and underdeveloped institutions to respond to or reflect an idealized formulation.

When thinking about the basic duties of businesses, it is useful to consider Article 23 of the Universal Declaration, which focuses on the rights of workers. This article identifies a number of specific rights, including the right to work, to free choice of employment, favourable working conditions, freedom from discrimination, equal pay for equal work, fair living wages (enough to ensure 'an existence worthy of human dignity' for their families) and the right to form and join trade unions. When we review this article, we are struck by the fact that large numbers of businesses in the industrialized as well as the developing world do not operate in full compliance with these standards. For example, the income of women working at comparable jobs falls short of that of men in many, many businesses. Additionally, in spite of minimum wage laws, many workers receive less than living wages. When we examine this article, we see that it sets forth a number of very basic moral principles; but it is not altogether clear as to which of these standards should be regarded as absolute obligations, generally required stipulations, highly recommended guidelines, or ideals to be pursued. If businesses are to take seriously their duties with respect to workers' rights, they must first re-articulate these principles as (1) minimally obligatory standards, (2) recommended standards, and (3) ideals, and then to state clearly how these might be implemented at (a) present, and (b) in the future.

This proviso holds for other human rights as well. In order to honour these rights as a basic duty, businesses need to exercise judgements determining what responses have priority in relation to present needs, their resources and capacity to act and the economic and institutional development of the societies in which they operate. In order to address their duty in relation to worker rights as well as other human rights, firms cannot simply seek to impose regulations to comply with expressed standards; they must take stock of their current practices, reinterpret and reformulate the standards themselves, realistically assess their own capacities to respond, establish objectives in relation to present and futures possibilities and develop the organizational infrastructures to act accordingly. In addition to whatever else they may commit themselves to undertake, they might well act to strengthen local and national legal systems, which serve as the necessary institutional arena in which human rights must be protected.

Comments

In the paragraphs above I have restated and reformulated the conventional political ethic for international businesses in their dealings with governments. This ethic I have restated as a series of legally binding duties. At the same time, I have indicated that these duties cannot be baldly stated and mechanically enforced. In order to encourage a more serious commitment to these duties, we must guard against a kind of moral fundamentalism, which would expect firms to honour these duties by strict compliance – no more, no less. In order to honour these duties, firms are called upon to exercise imagination and discretion, to allow for thoughtful and sophisticated reflections and to consider timing and contingencies. They must supplement their commitment to respect rules with efforts to mobilize organizational resources, create fitting organizational infrastructures and collaborate with external parties where relevant.

2. The social obligations of businesses with respect to governments

As organized enterprises, businesses interact with governments as well as other social actors and constituencies. Accordingly, business practices give rise to social obligations both insofar as these interactions are contractually defined and insofar as businesses derive material or potential benefit.

In many areas businesses have become formal partners or suppliers of governments. We have mentioned Shell's partnership with the national government in Nigeria, as well as Rio Tinto's with the government of Madagascar and Talisman's with Sudan. Some national governments have established state corporations as partners organized, for example, to extract, refine and market oil, or to manage public utilities. Others have formally hired private sector companies to help develop public works, such as roads, dams, school buildings and port facilities. Practically every government purchases quantities of goods and services from private sector businesses – from large orders of office supplies, vehicles and armaments to thousands of occasional small orders. In all these cases businesses enter into formal contractual relations with governments. By virtue of these contractual relations firms assume a number of both explicit and implicit obligations, including less clearly articulated expectations related to the ongoing relationship between the contracting parties.

The extent to which any business in fact assumes these kinds of social obligations varies considerably with variations in the extent to which (1) they enter into formal contractual relations or engage in informal reciprocating relations with governments, and (2) they directly or indirect benefit from these interactions. Social obligations are not like the duties discussed above, which are the same for all. Particular businesses may have sizeable, moderate, or limited social obligations, depending upon their situation. In the paragraphs that follow I will discuss four specific social obligations that arise out of the contractual or reciprocating interactions of businesses with governments. I will demonstrate why each of these guidelines seems reasonable and justified by their interest and prior commitments as contractual partners.

1. As they enter into relationships with governments, businesses should not coerce or undermine their government partners. There are, to be sure, a number of examples of firms, like the British South Africa Company, that used their wealth and power unduly to influence policies and administrations of local governments (Litvin, 2003, ch. 2). Nonetheless, currently, this obligation is almost universally acknowledged. Misunderstandings arise not with this obligation but with the way firms sometimes interpret the principle that underlies it. Thus, for example, precisely because they seek to avoid either dominating or appearing to unduly influence governments, many firms decide that they should take a strictly neutral role locally or nationally. Despite their duty not to undermine legitimate political processes, as partners in ongoing contractual or interactive relations, firms bear somewhat different responsibilities.

2. Among other things, international businesses have an obligation to undertake those kinds of regular communications that help to maintain, guide and enliven their ongoing interactions with their contractual partners. They need to communicate about any matters, real, possible, or only apparent, that may affect how the relationship unfolds. They need to provide and solicit feedback on how their contractual or informal interactions are working. If they become aware of them, they need to alert governments about contingencies that may well affect how well governments fulfil their commitments. For example, to the degree that managers or employees at Shell could see that the way the national or regional governments in Nigeria used their troops or police to provide protection often had the effect of aggravating ethnic tensions, they had an obligation to communicate this perception as effectively as possible. When businesses attempt to communicate about their ongoing partnerships and collaborations, strictly speaking, they are not lobbying governments; rather, they acting responsibly to support and monitor these interactions and to call for appropriate adjustments. The danger here is that because they do not wish to appear to be intruding in political processes, firms may become morally mute when they should be vocal. From this perspective, Shell in the 1990s had an obligation to voice effectively a wide range of concerns for how their contractual partners in the Nigerian government were mismanaging a host of

issues related to security, the rule of law, environmental policies and the distribution of royalties, since how these issues were being mishandled affected not only Shell's global reputation but also how effectively it could manage its own day-to-day operation in the Niger delta.

Talisman had an equivalent obligation in Sudan. As a partner with Talisman, the Sudanese government undertook a number of actions that undermined or impeded Talisman's capacity to fulfil its own mandate. In violation of strict contractual stipulations the government used the firm's landing strips for military purposes. Rather than seeking accommodation with rebel forces in southern Sudan, thereby generating at least a degree of moderate civil order that would be much better suited for ongoing petroleum production, the government pursued its war in ways that made Talisman seem like an accomplice. As a result of these and other questionable practices and as result of public protests against these practices, the value of Talisman shares fell precipitously. As this situation began to become increasingly aggravated, Talisman itself as a partner with the government had a corresponding obligation to find, as far as possible, effective ways of voicing its concerns and dissenting from these practices.

3. We can further elaborate on this point by observing that firms have an obligation to communicate clearly their needs and interests as contractual partners. Not only are they fully within their rights to voice these concerns, but they also have an obligation, based upon their ongoing responsibilities to their various stakeholders, to protect and, if possible, increase the overall value of their organization. If the governments or agencies with which they are collaborating act in ways that make it difficult for these businesses to fulfil their objectives or that reduce the value of their overall assets, then these firms as contractual partners should explore diverse ways to communicate these concerns and influence governmental policies. Here again, they are not lobbying, as this term in usually understood, but rather communicating and bringing pressure in a process of negotiation to clarify and ensure respect for existing agreements.

If we again look at the position of Shell in Nigeria, we can assume that Shell could most effectively operate if it was in a position to provide minimal levels of benefits to the people living in the Niger delta. Thus it made sense for Shell to petition the national government, as it did repeatedly, so that larger proportions of the royalties and taxes from this business were turned over to regional and local governments. It is important to recognize, nonetheless, that when Shell made these petitions, it was not, as the firm sometimes claimed, fundamentally voicing a civic concern. Rather as a contractual partner, it was voicing this concern because the policy it demanded had the effect of improving the firm's relationship with the surrounding communities, and accordingly, enhanced its capacity to fulfil its basic mission with reduced threats of reprisals from these communities.

4. As contractual or reciprocating partners, firms possess an additional obligation to act in ways that allow or assist the governments with which

they are dealing to fulfil their responsibilities in these relationships. This is a major concern in many developing countries. In many cases governments possess underdeveloped capacities for managing the complex issues related to industrialization and technological change. In many instances modern, independent legal systems are just beginning to be institutionalized. In these settings especially, international businesses have an obligation not to exploit these weaknesses for their own advantages. Rather, as potentially long-term partners, they have a special obligation to help strengthen the emerging political and legal institutions. In a sense, these firms have an obligation to help their partners in government keep the firms themselves in line. This obligation is well illustrated by recent initiatives by Rio Tinto in its partnership with the government of Madagascar. The international mining firm had decided it made sense to build a privately owned port. It had sought financial support for this project from multiples sources including US aid agencies, The World Bank and the Madagascar government. It was important that the Madagascar government be in a position to regulate this port because of its impact on commerce and industry on the island. When the port was proposed, the government lacked people with sufficient skills in maritime law and private utilities to draft laws and administrative rules to govern this situation in ways that would keep the firm and the port answerable to the government. Rio Tinto then decided to use its connections to contract for consultative services from lawyers in France to help officials in the Madagascar government prepare relevant statutes and administrative rules. In the process, the firm was deliberately strengthening the government's capacity to regulate Rio Tinto itself.

While international businesses must seek to avoid becoming, or seeming to become, simply co-opted by national governments, they must also avoid creating such aggravation or distance through their dissent and hard bargaining around government policies that the government decides to expropriate them. This has been a real threat, at times, in a number of countries. To be sure, if situations seem to call for it, businesses in these settings can sell off their operations, as many international businesses did in response to apartheid in South Africa. The challenge is to find the appropriate mix of cooperation and separateness. This challenge has been both especially strong and effectively managed by large numbers of international businesses operating in countries like Malaysia, Taiwan and South Korea where the national governments have played a large role both as regulators of the economy and contractual partners with businesses (Evans, 1995).

3. Civic responsibilities of businesses with respect to governments

Governments make various resources available so that international businesses can undertake the business they were organized to perform. Governments provide licenses to operate, guarantee property rights and validate and help to enforce the contracts they enter into. As a result of their own policing, public works and social welfare programmes, they help to establish a wide range of public goods, such as public order, road networks, power grids, sewage systems, water works, schools and the like. Where they effectively exist, these public goods facilitate business practices. Where these public goods are in short supply, business operations are more difficult.

As beneficiaries of these public goods, businesses, like other organized civic groups possess corresponding civic responsibilities. What are these responsibilities? In the paragraphs that follow I will discuss three different expressions of important civic responsibilities, which arise in addition to international businesses' fundamental duties and social obligations. These responsibilities, however, arise neither out of the company's status as an organized legal entity nor out of its social obligations based on specific contractual or reciprocating interactions. Rather they arise because of the social character of businesses as organizations in society. Businesses are formed so that particular sets of organized interactions – between workers, managers, investors, lenders, suppliers, customers, community groups and the like – create economic value (Freeman, 1984; Williamson, 1990; Bird, 2001). As the creators of economic value, businesses correspondingly possess several different kinds of civic responsibilities, which grow out of both the ways and the extent of economic value they create. Whereas the *duties* of businesses, for the most part, point to activities they should avoid, the *civic responsibilities* identify opportunities and prospects they are called upon to realize.

Basic civic responsibility: To add economic value. The basic civic responsibility for businesses is to add economic value for their organizations as a whole, and to do so in ways that also add value for all those who variously interact with them. Businesses are given licenses to operate in the expectation that they will make use of various resources – from natural and human resources to the public goods of society and the confidence of their investors, lenders and employees – so as to add overall economic value. They are expected not to waste, ignore, or deplete these resources and assets except insofar as they offer fitting compensations. In practice, businesses often create more value through some products, services, manufacturing processes, marketing initiatives, financial schemes than through others. Ideally, the various stakeholders whose investments help businesses to operate should benefit from these operations proportionately to the quality and quantity of the risks and contributions they make and the difficulties in obtaining their contributions. In practice, some stakeholders, such as large investors, usually benefit disproportionately because of their capacity to influence organizational decision-making.

Often the economic contributions of international businesses in developing areas are gauged primarily in relation to job creation and taxes. I adopt a much broader view. The economic contributions should be assessed in terms of how businesses operate as a whole. It is possible to estimate roughly the extent to which businesses add economic value by gauging the extent to which they add to or deplete the overall assets with which they come into contact.

(a) Have they added to the financial assets that they draw upon, from overt investments they attract, the credit they have solicited, the household incomes of their employees and managers and government revenues, balancing in this case taxes and royalties against the expenses for public goods?
(b) Have they added to the productive assets by introducing new technologies and ways of organizing?
(c) Have they added to human assets by helping those involved in their operations learn and utilize new skills?
(d) Have they added to the social assets by fostering new collaborations, new forms of communicating, greater trust and confidence?
(e) Have they added or depleted natural assets by the natural resources they have renewed, reduced, polluted or conserved?

Because these questions can all be answered in fairly clear approximate terms, they should all be raised and addressed. They provide a way of assessing the degree to which businesses are in fact adding economic value for the societies in which they operate. These questions are basic. It is important to stress this fact, because firms may add value to certain stakeholders (for example, profits for investors), while in varying degrees reducing the economic value of their productive, human, social or natural assets for other stakeholders. The basic civic responsibility for businesses is thus a fiduciary one. Businesses are expected to seek to do well at what they are supposedly in business to do: to add economic value to society, by conserving and, if possible, augmenting the overall value of their operations gauged in relation to their financial, productive, human, social and natural assets.

Correlative responsibility: To meet their own needs for infrastructure in ways that also address the infrastructural needs of others. In order to operate effectively to pursue their business objectives, international firms in developing areas require access to resources that may or may not be adequately supplied through local economic, physical and social infrastructures. These include access to fresh water, electricity, roads or waterways that connect with other commercial or industrial or political centres and sewage systems. They also include access to schools for the children of employees and healthcare services for employees and families. Additionally, these resources often include agencies or businesses capable of providing catering services, custodial assistance, taxi and errand services and police protection. In order to engage in business, international firms need to find reliable means of addressing these needs. The challenge facing them varies with the degree that established governments already have acted to provide these resources for their citizens generally.

The challenges become even greater in developing areas where these resources are at best unevenly and inadequately provided. Many firms in developing areas primarily set out to provide these resources exclusively for their operating sites and employees. They do so in part because they argue that it is the responsibility of governments to provide for these kinds of utilities and services for the general public. They do so because, as they correctly point out, they are businesses and not social welfare agencies. Why, they might well ask, should they expend their funds for services that do not directly or indirectly enhance the values of their businesses?

In reply, there are several strong reasons why it is a basic civic responsibility of businesses to address these infrastructural needs more generally, and not just for their own operations.

(a) Insofar as they can find ways of generating these infrastructural services for equivalent costs, for adjacent communities as well as for their own operations, then they should do so. Not to do so in practice and principle alienates businesses from the local societies in which they operate. Often these services can be provided by investing in local agencies and businesses, organized to offer these services as reasonable costs.

(b) By investing in these infrastructural providers, businesses thereby cultivate valuable social assets, that is, networks of communication and trust, which they in turn can draw upon. By undertaking these kinds of initiatives, businesses help to reduce the extent to which their operations may occasion inequalities and social distances.

(c) In the process, businesses strengthen their reputations.

(d) As a result, they render themselves less as targets of public protest.

(e) Given what the neighbouring communities have provided them, in terms of sites to do business, employees willing to work and public goodwill, these kinds of initiatives represent effective reciprocating gestures.

(f) In fact, businesses pay for and help to support the development of adequate infrastructures wherever they operate. The differences have to do with the institutional mechanisms by which they address these needs. In industrialized societies, where business activities as a whole have increased the overall level of wealth, companies help to fund these utilities and services through the increased wages, rents and profits they pay, which are in turned taxed and through property and business taxes they directly pay. In less industrialized societies, they are often challenged to help provide infrastructural services, because governments lack the tax bases and have not yet developed their capacities along these lines.

As it developed its operations in the Niger delta, Shell might well have attempted to develop more of its infrastructural needs by investing in local or regional agencies and firms. Nonetheless it contributed philanthropically to projects providing water, clinics and schools buildings for select communities. It would also have had to contribute skilled labour to initiate these local facilities. In the process, more wealth in the form of wages and productive resources would have been become available to local communities. However, over the long term Shell would probably have developed much stronger collaborative relations with local communities and thereby reduced its security threats (Bird et al., 2005, ch. 1).

It is important to note that I argue for these investments in infrastructure projects as a business interest not as a philanthropic gesture. Businesses can and should invest in these projects because they need to address their own infrastructural needs. Investing in these projects is a way of making sure these needs are met. Meeting these needs by helping to create and maintain local businesses or agencies requires more time and more entrepreneurial impetus at the beginning. It is likely to have a larger payoff over the long haul.

Complementary civic responsibilities: The ideal of civility and social investment projects. Members of political communities are expected to contribute to the overall well-being of these communities by a variety of civic acts that serve to strengthen the sense of community and reinforce and protect the common goods enjoyed by all. These expectations are connected with ideas about civility. Correspondingly, citizens of political communities are called upon from time to time, in response to entreaties from others in their communities, to donate goods or money, extend hospitality to neighbours, seek to resolve disputes amicably when possible, forbear grudges, speak civilly and volunteer to help or serve others from time to time, especially when called upon. These expectations are tacitly understood, evoked by legends and stories and espoused by those who feel called to honour them. They are celebrated often by religious traditions and ethnic heritages. Clearly these ideals of civility are more strongly felt and more vibrant in some societies than in others. Nonetheless, some expressions of these ideas about civility are practically universally found. The fundamental assumption here grows out of the broadest, most basic notions of reciprocity. Insofar as citizens benefit from the social organization of societies as political communities, they are expected to reciprocate through these several ways (Gouldner, 1960). It is worth noting that the ideas of civility are not usually expressed in terms of rigid rules or principles, except with respect to manners and etiquette. Rather in more flexible ways, citizens are expected to respond to requests of others insofar as they are in position to do so and in ways that seem fitting to them. Those with great wealth or more free time may well be expected to be more generous in terms of the amounts they give than those less well off (Gouldner, 1973).

Businesses, as social organizations that benefit from the civility of the larger society, are correspondingly expected to honour these notions of civility. Firms themselves as well as those who benefit from them, through wages, returns on investment, rents or in other ways, are expected from time to time to make donations, volunteer their time and skills, respond civilly to others, offer hospitality and act as good neighbours insofar as their means allow. Because they serve to create added economic value and because they benefit from the civility of the societies in which they operate, international businesses are expected to act civilly – that is, to honour public norms. Many business men and women have expressed their commitment to civility by volunteering in various ways: working on community projects, serving on NGO boards, participating in fraternal business associations and sports events. Yet to speak out on public issues may well be just as important an expression of civility as making a contribution to an annual charity drive.

As an expression of the importance of civility, many businesses develop various forms of social investment: contributions to community projects, donations to the arts and sports, civic endeavours, sponsorships of particular charities. They make these social investments not only for public relations purposes, but also because their managers and employees prefer to live in communities characterized by high civic engagement.

4. The activity of exercising responsible political judgements

The duties, obligations and responsibilities we have discussed amount to little, unless we find ways of putting them into practice. I have indicated the way these duties, obligations and responsibilities emerge out of the ongoing interactions of business, government and civil society within particular political communities. Throughout this essay I have described how the so-called business case for following these directives is intertwined with the social case, which grows out of the obligations and reciprocities of ongoing interactions. Business activities simply could not take place unless those involved most of the time respected the basic norms related to keeping promises, speaking honestly, honouring contracts, respecting the integrity of others and not deliberately wasting valued resources. To be sure, many businesses violate these norms; but it is a testimony to the strength of these norms that there would be little or no reason to pursue these violations if they were the rule rather than the exception. These duties, obligations and responsibilities, then, should not be viewed as extraordinary or exemplary actions, still less as virtuous options that businesses might consider following once they have met their economic objectives. Rather, these duties, obligation and responsibilities are interwoven with ordinary business practices.

Ethical rules, codes and guidelines have a useful life in businesses. They can serve as a way of educating people about relevant moral concerns, and they can define minimal boundaries. But at the core, ethically responsible businesses have to respond to contingent circumstances that often involve conflicting moral expectations, unexpected possibilities and demands and the need to identify priorities. Sometimes but not usually, those involved can invoke moral maxims that apply decisively to some particularly difficult situation. Ordinarily, those involved must weigh alternatives and seek out the counsel of others, while still acting in a timely manner. At its core, ethics involves the act of exercising judgements responsively and responsibly.

These duties, obligations and responsibilities remain morally compelling, even in settings where firms may find it very difficult to fulfil them. This point needs to be underlined. These moral expectations diminish neither when obstacles appear nor when tempting self-aggrandizing alternatives beckon. Nor do they become greater. Businesses' duties, obligations and responsibilities grow out of the way businesses are embedded in political communities. Nonetheless it is important for businesses realistically to assess their political circumstances. If they are operating in a society with an autocratic government, which has violated its own laws and has robbed and oppressed its own people (like the government of Nigeria in the mid-1990s), then businesses must realistically consider their prospects. They may well decide not to abide by what they regard as certain illegitimate laws, based on their understanding of the country's history. They may seek alternative ways of addressing their contractual obligations. As part of their civic responsibilities they may support dissident groups. As they reinterpret the meaning of their duties, obligations and responsibilities, they are called to use their imaginations. If they want to make a difference, they would ordinarily seek to minimize the degree that they would make themselves especially vulnerable. They would need to think strategically, undertaking in the present forms of protest that are likely to be tolerated and deferring temporarily other more overt actions for later times when these seem more likely to realize their desired impact.

It is, in fact, important that firms adopt a strategic attitude toward these legal duties, social obligations and civic responsibilities, which tend to possess a political, if not a partisan, character. As they interact with governments in varied polities, businesses broadly engage in political activities, by which they overtly seek to honour, reinterpret, change or dissent from public policies. These are activities in which they may quite appropriately lobby governments – activities that involve political acts associated with networking, building public consensus and mobilizing public sentiment. While businesses possess a duty not to interfere with or undermine the official political process, this duty does not entail the complete absence of political involvement. As contractual partners and as corporate citizens, businesses are expected to engage in quasi-political activities as they negotiate, petition, bargain with and seek to influence government officials and parties.

In practice, the duties, obligations and responsibilities of businesses differ in substance, depending on their setting. It may well be useful to clarify this point by discussing the particularly difficult situation of international firms that find themselves operating in countries experiencing major social conflicts, like Sudan, since the 1960s. Firms might well decide to exit from these kinds of settings, though in doing so they may aggravate local circumstances socially as well as economically – through lost opportunities for social reform as well as lost jobs. If they continue to operate in these kinds of settings, they must correspondingly reconsider their duties, obligations and responsibilities. Talisman initiated some social investment projects. With respect to the government's human rights abuses, it quietly petitioned the government, although more as a corporate citizen than as a contractual partner. In contrast, it is possible to argue that Talisman, as a contractual partner of the government, had an obligation to petition the government strongly to minimize acts of brutality because these acts had the effect of undermining the firm's estimated value as perceived by its shareholders. As a civic organization, Talisman had a correlative responsibility to work to meet its infrastructure needs in ways that also met the infrastructure needs of communities in the immediate vicinity of its operations. It is not clear that Talisman in any way actively pursued these kinds of options, which would have linked the company much more closely with the Nuer and Dinka peoples living in these areas. Talisman seems to have understood its political duties, obligations and responsibilities in terms of the conventional ethical view. Its critics insisted that Talisman withdraw; the company initially had hoped to stay, while gently persuading the government to adopt a more conciliatory role toward the southern rebels and expanding its social investments. Together with a number of foreign governments, Talisman may have influenced the government to seek an armistice with the south, which would have allowed the government to develop and gain wealth from the oil fields much more effectively. This armistice was in fact signed a few months after Talisman sold off its operations to the national oil company of India.

Conclusion

I have argued in this essay that conventional standards that set forth duties prohibiting certain kinds of practices, such as illegal activities and corruption, for examples, do not provide sufficiently flexible or responsible ethical guidance for international business in their relationships with governments. An adequate political ethic must include not only the social obligations and civic responsibilities of businesses, but also frameworks for interpreting their conventional duties in relation to varying circumstances. Most importantly, a viable political ethics for business should envision ethics as a practice that involves both engaging in responsible action as well as exercising due judgements in response to contingent possibilities and risks. International businesses in developing areas are called upon repeatedly to exercise judgement in the face ethical dilemmas concerning security issues, questionable payments, ways of working with autocratic governments, situations of social unrest and violence unjust or oppressive local laws.[4]

In keeping with the overall theme of this book, I have tried to outline a political ethic for international businesses that would be workable in terms of diverse local moral traditions. The ethics spelled out in this essay do not derive from any particular theory of politics or ethics. Rather, I have first examined common features in the ways international businesses were socially embedded in the diverse political communities in which they have operated. I then set forth guidelines for political duties, social obligations and civic responsibilities that businesses were called upon to honour in keeping with their social position. In this case the relevant norms for business practices grow out of the social characteristics of businesses, as complex, value-creating social organisms, with the potential to both use and abuse their particular powers.

Notes

This is an expanded version of an essay that appeared under the title 'Business as Organizational Citizens: Political Ethics for International Businesses in Developing Areas', in *Wirtschaft, Ethik und Entwicklung* (2005), edited by Gerhard Gad, Stefanie Hiss and Thomas Weinhardt (Berlin: Wissenschaftliche Verlag), pp. 1–42. An earlier draft entitled 'Fostering the Common Good in Developing Countries' appeared in *The Invisible Hand and the Common Good* (2005) edited by Bernard Hodgsons (Berlin: Springer).

1. This case is discussed in Frederick Bird, 'Wealth and Poverty in the Niger Delta: A Study of the Experiences of Shell in Nigeria' (Bird and Herman, 2004, ch. 2).
2. This case is discussed in Frederick Bird, 'Preparing to Mine: The Rio Tinto Venture in Madagascar' (Bird et al., 2005, ch. 6).
3. The text of the Global Sullivan Principles of Social Responsibility is available online at http://www.thesullivanfoundation.org/gsp/principles/gsp/default.asp. For a discussion of Sullivan Principles and anti-apartheid divestment strategies, see E. Raufflet, 'International Businesses in the Political Economy of South Africa' (Bird et al., 2005, ch. 2, pp. 77–82).
4. See F. Bird, 'Dilemmas of Development' (Bird et al., 2005, ch. 1).

References

Banfield, E. and Wilson, J. Q. (1963) *City Politics* (New York: Vintage Books).

Baro, M. (2001) 'Ethics and International Transfer Pricing: Were International Transfer Prices Unethically Established in a Multinational Company During the Period 1988–1996?', Masters thesis, École Nionale des Ponts et Chausées, Paris, and Universidad de Belgrano, Buenos Aires.

Berman, H. J. (1983) *Law and Revolution: The Formation of the Western Legal Tradition* (Cambridge, MA: Harvard University Press).

Bird, F. (1996) *The Muted Conscience: Moral Science and the Practice of Ethics in Business* (Westport, CT: Quorum Books).

Bird, F. (2001) 'Good Governance: A Philosophical Discussion of the Responsibilities and Practices of Organizational Governors', *Canadian Journal of Administrative Sciences*, vol. 18(4), pp. 298–312.

Bird, F. and Herman, S. (eds) (2004) *International Businesses and the Challenges of Poverty in the Developing World* (London: Palgrave Macmillan).

Bird, F., Raufflet, E. and Smucker, J. (eds) (2005) *International Businesses and the Dilemmas of Development* (London: Palgrave Macmillan).

Carson, T. L. (1985) 'Bribery, Extortion and the "Foreign Corrupt Practices Act"', *Philosophy and Public Affairs*, vol. 14(1).

De Soto, H. (2000) *The Mystery of Capital* (New York: Basic Books).

Drohan, M. (2003) *Making a Killing: How Corporations Use Armed Force to do Business* (Toronto: Random House of Canada).

The Economist (2002) 'The Short Arm of the Law: Special Report: Bribery and Business', 2 March, pp. 63–5.

Evans, P. (1995) *Embedded Autonomy: States and Industrial Transformation* (Princeton University Press).

Fossgard-Moser, T. (1998) 'Transnational Corporations and Sustainable Development: The Case of Colombian and Peruvian Petroleum Industries', PhD dissertation, Cambridge University.

Freeman, R. E. (1984) *Strategic Management: A Stakeholder Approach* (Boston: Pitman).

Fuller, L. L. (1964) *The Morality of Law* (New Haven: Yale University Press).

Gillespie, K. (1987) 'Middle East Responses to the U.S. Foreign Corrupt Practices Act', *California Management Review*, vol. 29(4), pp. 9–30.

Glendon, M. A. (1993) *Rights Talk* (New York: The Free Press).

Gouldner, A. (1960) 'The Norm of Reciprocity', *American Sociological Review*, vol. 25(2), pp. 161–78.

Gouldner, A. (1973) 'The Importance of Something for Nothing', in *Sociology: Renewal and Critique in Sociology Today* (Harmondsworth, UK: Penguin Books).

Habermas, J. (1996) *Between Facts and Norms* (Cambridge, MA: MIT Press).

Hischman, A. O. (1970) *Exit, Voice, Loyalty: Responses to Decline in Firms, Organizations and States* (Cambridge, MA: Harvard University Press).

Hodess, R., Banfield, J. and Wolfe, T. (eds) (2001) *Global Corruption Report 2001* (Berlin: Transparency International).

Holmes, S. and Sunstein, C. R. (1999) *The Cost of Rights: Why Liberty Depends on Taxes* (New York: W. W. Norton).

Ignatieff, M. (2000) *The Rights Revolution* (Toronto: House of Anansi).

ICHRP (2002) International Council on Human Rights Policy, *Beyond Volunteerism: Human Rights and the Development of International Legal Obligations of Companies* (Geneva).

Kelly, A. L. (1998) 'Italian Tax Mores', in *Case Studies in Business, Society and Ethics*, Beauchamp, T. L. (ed.) (Upper Saddle River, NJ: Prentice-Hall), pp. 272–4.

Kinzer, S. (2003) *All the Shah's Men: An American Coup and the Roots of Middle East Terror* (Hoboken, NJ: John Wiley and Sons).

Klitgaard, R. (1988) *Controlling Corruption* (Berkeley: University of California Press).

Klitgaard, R. (1990) *Tropical Gangsters* (Toronto: HarperCollins Canada).

Kwong, J. (1997) *The Political Economy of Corruption in China* (New York: M. E. Sharpe).

Litvin, D. (2003) *Empires of Profit: Commerce, Conquest and Corporate Responsibility* (New York: Texere).

Marong, A. (2002) 'Towards a Normative Consensus Against Corruption: Legal Effects of the Principles to Combat Corruption in Africa', *Denver Journal of International Law and Policy*, vol. 30(2); also available online at http://www.law.du.edu/ilj/online_issues_folder/marong.final.9.3.pdf.

Mauss, M. (1967) *The Gift: Forms and Functions of Exchange in Archaic Societies* (New York: Norton).

Rawls, J. (1971) *A Theory of Justice* (Cambridge, MA: Harvard University Press).

Scott, J. C. (1976) *The Moral Economy of Peasants: Rebellion and Subsistence Ethic in Southeast Asia* (New Haven: Yale University Press).

Sethi, S. P. and Williams, O. F. (2001) *Economic Imperatives and Ethical Values in Global Business: The South African Experience and International Codes Today* (Notre Dame, IN: University of Notre Dame Press).

Tang, R. Y. (1981) *Multinational Transfer Pricing: Canadian and British Perspectives* (Toronto: Butterworth).

Thomas, V. et al. (2000) *The Quality of Growth* (New York: Oxford University Press); also available on line at http://www.worldbank.org/wbi/qualityofgrowth/toc.pdf.

Velasquez, M. (2004) 'Is Corruption Always Corrupt?' in Brenkert, G. G. (ed.), *Corporate Integrity and Accountability* (London: SAGE).

Weber, M. ([1914] 1978) 'Economy and Society', in Roth, G. and Wittich, M. (eds) (Berkeley and Los Angeles: University of California Press).

Wertheim, W. F. (1964) *East-West Parallels: Sociological Perspectives on Modern Asia* (The Hague: W. van Hoeve).

Williamson, O. E. (1990) 'The Firm as a Nexus of Treaties: An Introduction', in Aoki, M., Gustafson, B. and Williamson, O. E. (eds), *The Firm as a Nexus of Treaties* (London: SAGE).

5
Global Initiatives to Promote Corporate Social Responsibility in the Mining Sector

Hevina S. Dashwood

Introduction

The launch of the Global Mining Initiative (GMI) in 1998 marked a novel attempt to promote corporate social responsibility within the specific context of the mining sector.[1] The GMI is novel in the sense that it was launched by a group of committed mining company executives from around the world. Made up of non-state actors (in this case, nine major mining companies), without direct involvement on the part of sovereign states, the GMI can be characterized as a global transnational network among mining multinationals.[2]

The GMI represents an attempt by mining companies to shape the discourse on corporate responsibility, and ultimately, to influence the policies and practices of mining companies around the world. Like transnational networks in other fields, the GMI seeks to harness scientific expertise around sustainable mining practices, to transmit information about such practices and to inculcate norms of acceptable corporate behaviour within the mining sector. (In shaping the discourse on corporate social responsibility, member companies have adopted the language of 'sustainable development', a notoriously slippery concept. As such, this study employs the concept of 'corporate social responsibility', as defined in note 7.)

The significance of the GMI lies not so much in its impact, which to date has been modest, as in the influences that drove mining companies to undertake this initiative. This paper will explore those influences, and assess the significance of the GMI from the perspective of the literature on transnational networks. It will be argued that the GMI represents a conscious effort to promote learning and disseminate norms of acceptable corporate behaviour, which will be demonstrated by an examination of the participation of two Canadian mining companies, Noranda (now merged with Falconbridge) and Placer Dome. These companies have global operations in Latin America, Asia and Africa, and are significant players in global mineral markets and in the GMI. The focus of this chapter is on the fact and nature of their participation, as opposed to the manner in which their policies have been implemented in Canada and abroad.

Conceptualizing the Global Mining Initiative

The GMI can be conceptualized within the larger context of the devolution of public (i.e., government) authority to the private sector in certain areas of global governance. Historically, global governance was the exclusive domain of the state; in recent decades, however, non-state actors such as non-governmental organizations (NGOs) and multinational enterprises (MNEs) have come to play an increasingly significant role. Transnational networks such as the GMI have developed around specific issue areas that transcend national boundaries and even bypass sovereign states altogether.

The devolution of political authority from national governments can be understood as an important political by-product of globalization. This devolution has occurred downward, from the national government to the local or municipal level, and upwards to the international and transnational level. Although the diminished or altered role of the state in various policy domains is portrayed as necessary or inevitable, it is in fact an outcome of the various processes associated with globalization – processes which have developed within the political context of the neo-liberal consensus shared by the major industrialized powers. Advocates of neo-liberalism favour trade liberalization, state deregulation and responsible fiscal and monetary policies. In the developing world, governments have been urged to privatize and deregulate, and to liberalize trade. In the developed world, efforts to bring budget deficits under control have generally been associated with, or have served to justify, the erosion of the welfare state.

Another view of the neo-liberal context in which globalization has occurred lends support to the argument that developed states have voluntarily relinquished some of their regulatory powers. The neo-liberal argument for globalization suggests that even if the devolution of political authority is not inevitable, it nonetheless reflects a political consensus that the role of the state should be minimized and a greater role accorded to the private sector. The issue of corporate responsibility is thereby wrapped up in the larger political debate about the appropriate role of the state in society and the economy.

While the role and importance of the state in relation to non-state actors continues to be debated, the complex nature of global governance has clearly opened up space for non-state actors. A number of contributions to the growing literature on global governance are helpful in situating the role of the private sector in advancing corporate responsibility (Hall and Biersteker, 2002; Haufler, 2001a; Cutler et al., 1999). A great deal of this is preoccupied with accounting for the role and influence of international governmental organizations (IGOs) and international non-governmental organizations (INGOs) in various aspects of global governance (O'Brien et al., 2000; Keck and Sikkink, 1998). There are a number of reasons for this. Much of the writing in this vein is taken up with the concept of global civil society (Florini, 2000; Lipschutz and Mayer, 1996; Lipschutz, 2000). INGOs are considered to be important players in an emerging global civil society. They enjoy a legitimacy that is based on their links to national grassroots organizations, and the moral authority of their causes. INGOs are non-profit organizations, and engage in the promotion of human rights and respect for the environment. Keck and Sikkink coined the term 'transnational advocacy network' to denote INGOs that advocate on behalf of others where no self-interested motives can be discerned (1998, pp. 8–10).

Multinational enterprises, because their primary goal is profit maximization, are usually excluded from conceptions of global civil society, although an important exception to this is Lipschutz, who sees it as a 'proto-society composed of local, national, and global institutions, corporations, and non-governmental organizations' (in Hall and Biersteker, 2002, p. 124). On the whole, though, MNEs are seen to lack legitimacy, since they represent the interests of a presumably elite group of shareholders and are motivated by profit maximization. Since MNEs do have, in some cases, a deservedly bad reputation, and because they are deemed to be unable to cooperate either amongst themselves or with other state or non-state actors, they are often excluded from analyses of global governance (Keck and Sikkink, 1998).

There are some good reasons for these assumptions. Multinational enterprises have contributed to environmental degradation, and in some cases, have been complicit in serious human rights abuses, most notably in developing countries. They have also been the disproportionate beneficiaries of economic globalization, and enjoy the protection of international rules covering trade, investment and intellectual property rights, enshrined in international agreements under the auspices of the WTO. In short, their actions often run counter to the liberal values implicitly enshrined in analyses of global governance that rely on notions of global civil society.

A very useful approach that encompasses the role of MNEs is Hall and Biersteker's analysis of private authority in the global realm. Private authority is defined as non-state actors who 'perform the role of authorship (understood as authority) over some important issue or domain' (2002, p. 4). Multinationals are explicitly included in this concept, which is less value-laden then analyses centred around the notion of global civil society. Crucial to the concept of private authority is that such private actors– whether corporations, NGOs or even terrorist groups – are accorded legitimacy by some larger public. It can be empirically observed (as the next section will show) that mining companies are sponsoring policies, practices, rules and norms (phrased in the language of sustainable development) related to issues of corporate social responsibility (CSR). Claims as to the legitimacy of such action, however, must be qualified. While states may be acquiescent in the mining sector's global efforts to promote corporate responsibility, it is not clear that such efforts can be accorded any form of legitimacy, whether by some larger public, or even within the mining sector itself.[3]

What needs to be captured for the purpose of this analysis is the fact that multinationals are participating in the process of global governance around issues of corporate responsibility. For that reason, the concept of a 'multi-layered' process of governance, in which the state, while still an important actor, has relinquished regulatory responsibilities to private agents, is helpful (Scholte, 2000). The fact of corporate participation in aspects of global governance is thereby captured, but without the troublesome connotation of a global civil society. This allows the analysis to move away from prescriptive judgements about whether it is right or wrong for multinationals corporations to be assuming regulatory functions, and to focus on what is in fact happening.[4] All the same, caution must be exercised when including MNEs in analyses of global governance, as their motivations, interests, and the ways in which they interact with other global actors, including states, are likely to be different.

The activities of the GMI suggest that not only does it serve as an organizational nucleus for the gathering and dissemination of information on sustainable mining practices, but that it also constitutes an attempt to promote norms of acceptable corporate behaviour. The literature tends to ignore or discount the possibility that MNEs might play such a role; and since neo-realist theory discounts the existence of norms as sources of influence on state behaviour, the possibility that corporate behaviour may be influenced by norms is likewise discounted.[5] Such a perspective ignores the normative underpinnings of the market within which corporate activity is immersed. Markets would not function but for such norms as the protection of private property rights, the acceptance of money as the medium of exchange and adherence to contracts (Kratochwil, 1989, p. 47). In fact, it is precisely because companies have been so successful in preserving the security of these norms that they are under growing pressure to accept certain obligations around the social, political and economic structures within which they are embedded.

Norms can be defined as inter-subjective beliefs leading to collective expectations about proper behaviour for a given identity (Katzenstein, 1996, p. 54), or of appropriate behaviour as defined in terms of rights and obligations. The study of the influence and role of norms resonates with the constructivist approach to international relations (Wendt, 1999b; Ruggie, 1998). An important area of discussion in this vein is the literature that seeks to explain how and why human-rights-abusing governments, in the absence of traditional power politics inducements, should gradually move to respond to human rights concerns (Risse et al., 1999; Keck and

Sikkink, 1998). Risse et al. (1999) are concerned to show how shifting human rights norms and the efforts of transnational advocacy networks produce changes in the behaviour of human-rights-abusing states, and trace the process – argumentative persuasion, dialogue, even shaming – by which such governments are 'socialized' into respecting human rights norms and gradually move to a point where they have 'internalized' such norms.

There is plenty of evidence to support a shift in societal norms, both domestically and internationally, in support of greater corporate social responsibility (many of which are reviewed in the Business for Social Responsibility web site: BSR, 1999–2005). This evidence can be found in the wide range of responses, many of which emanate from the private sector; responses include company codes of conduct, new industry association standards, international codes of an aspirational (what should be) and issue-specific nature, and global reporting initiatives. Supporting the wide range of company codes are management programmes that oversee the implementation of company codes, such as the Global Reporting Initiative, Social Accountability 8000, the ISO 14000 standards, and AccountAbility 1000 (ibid.). Private agents promoting corporate responsibility include business leaders, NGOs, religious organizations and prominent individuals. They have produced a plethora of organizations, associations and networks, important examples of which include the Prince of Wales Business Leaders Forum (UK), the Caux Round Table (Switzerland), the Business for Social Responsibility and the Interfaith Center on Corporate Responsibility (US).

It is harder to establish whether those norms have been 'internalized' by corporations, but it can be argued that many companies are beginning to engage in dialogue and are learning about the issue of corporate responsibility. Most major companies now have public policies on corporate responsibility, and even though they may be strictly 'voluntary', companies can be held to account if their actions are inconsistent with their words.

To the extent that states operate in a normative environment, it is reasonable to expect that companies must also be responsive to shifting societal norms about acceptable corporate behaviour. Although non-governmental organizations enjoy considerable legitimacy in the promotion of norms-based behaviour, other private actors, even self-interested ones such as corporations, can also play a role.[6]

The Global Mining Initiative

The global context

The Global Mining Initiative is a fascinating example of prominent multinationals coming together with INGOs, international organizations and business associations. Although states are indirectly involved, the dominant players are from the private sector.

The GMI was organized at a time when the anti-globalization movement had achieved considerable momentum. An explanation of the GMI needs to be put in the context of the renewed drive to bring MNEs to account. As the pace of globalization quickened and intensified in the 1990s, concerns came to be voiced from a variety of quarters that seriously challenged the oft-repeated claim that economic globalization was necessarily good and that sooner or later everyone would benefit. It was therefore no coincidence that corporate responsibility should have resurfaced on the global agenda with the rise of the anti-globalization movement.

The international community, through its actions in various international organizations, has long recognized the need to promote corporate social responsibility.[7] However, the various measures did not seem up to the task, in light of the growing power of MNEs under globalization. There is a vast array of international instruments covering various aspects of corporate responsibility, including labour standards through the International Labour Organization (ILO); human rights norms, beginning with the 1948 Universal Declaration of Human Rights; and a host of environmental conventions, as well as the United Nations Environment Programme (UNEP). Trade agreements such as NAFTA also include rules that are intended to promote labour and environmental standards. Organizations such as the OECD have sought to establish rules prohibiting corrupt practices (the OECD guidelines for MNEs). The interests of MNEs are protected through a range of international agreements, such as the WTO-based agreement on Trade Related Investment Measures (TRIMs), and the Chapter 11 provisions of NAFTA.

The re-emergence of corporate social responsibility on the global agenda can be attributed to three interrelated developments. In the past decade, international governmental organizations (IGOs) have spearheaded a number of important initiatives for corporate responsibility. UN Secretary-General Kofi Annan's launch of the Global Compact in 1999 is an example of one effort to encourage multinationals to engage in dialogue on corporate social responsibility. The embracing of CSR as central to the promotion of sustainable development was a significant aspect of the 2002 World Summit on Sustainable Development in Johannesburg. Another vehicle through which CSR norms can be disseminated is the UN Draft Treaty on Transnational Corporations.

International non-governmental organizations such as Transparency International, Human Rights Watch, Greenpeace and Oxfam have played a prominent role in pushing the CSR agenda at the global level. INGOs have exerted their influence in a variety of ways, facilitated by the information revolution and the global reach of telecommunications. Through the Internet they can reach a large audience, and have been able to capture the media's attention through anti-globalization demonstrations at such venues as the WTO meetings or G-8 summits.

Transnational NGOs have become much more influential in international settings that previously were almost exclusively the domain of the state. Recently, a number of important developments within state-based IGOs reflect both the major influence of INGOs, and the renewed prominence of corporate social responsibility on the international agenda. The UN Global Compact explicitly calls upon NGOs and the private sector to engage in dialogue to further the cause of corporate responsibility. At the June 2002 G-8 meeting in Kananaskis, Canada, the non-state sector played a significant role in pushing the issue of corporate responsibility. It was a central issue at the August 2002 Summit for Sustainable Development in South Africa, where both NGOs and the private sector figured prominently. The role of private-sector corporations in promoting sustainable development was explicitly noted and encouraged in the final document (United Nations, 2002, pp. 4, 37–9).

This last remark points to the third development explaining the emergence of corporate responsibility on the global agenda, the growing norms-disseminating role of the private sector. Indeed, it is the private sector from whence some of the most interesting initiatives are coming. Private sector initiatives reflect the larger trend of the state's devolution of its political authority in some areas.

Main features of the GMI

The Global Mining Initiative is, in fact, a series of initiatives that were undertaken starting in the late 1990s. The activities of the GMI have now been subsumed within the organizational umbrella of the International Council on Mining and Metals (ICMM).

There are a number of reasons for the launch of the GMI. The immediate impetus came from the growing awareness that mining companies were suffering from a bad public image, and it was recognized that a global forum was necessary to counter that. The GMI was also an attempt to catch up with the growing number of international voluntary codes and standards, by providing guidelines that would be relevant to the mining sector.

The inspiration for the GMI came in January 1998 at the World Economic Forum in Davos, Switzerland, when a group of nine CEOs from major mining companies reached consensus on the need for global action (MPRI, 2004, p. 7). Under the leadership of Sir Robert Wilson, at that time CEO of Rio Tinto, the original group of companies included Noranda and Placer Dome, Anglo American, Codelco, Western Mining Company (WMC), BHP Billiton, Phelps Dodge (which withdrew in October 2002) and Newmont.

The GMI has fostered a number of initiatives, the largest of which was the Mining, Minerals and Sustainable Development Project (MMSD). In May 1999, through the World Business Council for Sustainable Development (WBCSD), the London-based International Institute for Environment and Development (IIED) was commissioned to conduct a scoping study to set out the terms of a two-year process to study the challenge of sustainable development in the mining sector. In 2000, based on the recommendations of this study, a major programme of participatory analysis and research, the Mining, Minerals and Sustainable Development Project (MMSD) was launched.

A variety of research projects were commissioned, with a view to further understanding of how the mining and mineral sector's contribution to sustainable development at the global, national, regional and local levels could be maximized. The process culminated in May 2002 with the publication of the MMSD's final report, *Breaking New Ground* (MMSD, 2002b). The report assessed the current state of the mining sector, and made recommendations for change, based on the findings of the research. The release of the report corresponded with a major GMI conference hosted in Toronto, which brought together all of the major players within the global mining sector.

A noteworthy feature of the MMSD project was that it was conceived of as a multi-stakeholder consultation process. In this respect, the MMSD was a massive undertaking, bringing in individuals from academia, the sustainable development policy research community, the labour movement, international governmental agencies, non-governmental organizations involved in the environment, development and human rights issues, mining businesses, trade associations, community and indigenous peoples' organizations, consuming industries and financial institutions (IIED, 1999, p. 18).

In an effort to promote genuine engagement, participants were encouraged to set their own agendas for discussion and research. However, given the potential for an exponentially expanding list of issues, a Strategic Planning Workshop was organized in May 2000 in order to identify 'strategic issues' for discussion and research. These issues included the management of mineral wealth, human rights, conflict, corruption, the role of financial institutions, public participation, environmental issues, including land use, biodiversity, waste and mine closure issues, life-cycle assessment, the reporting and verification of information, indigenous peoples' issues and artisanal and small-scale mining (MMSD, 2002b, pp. 7–8). These themes were addressed in 23 global workshops held between 2000 and 2002, involving participants from various stakeholder groups.

The MMSD was equally ambitious in its geographic scope, with regional partnerships established in Australia, North America, South America and Southern Africa. In order to ensure that the consultations were relevant to the specific circumstances in these diverse regions, each regional partner was granted considerable autonomy in setting the agenda and designing the regional research initiatives.

The decentralized nature of the project led to a healthy diversity in terms of the process of consultation and research agendas in each region. In Australia, the project was managed by the Australian Minerals and Energy

Environment Foundation (AMEEF), an independent, not-for-profit organization established in 1991.[8] Nine workshops were held, bringing together a wide cross-section of stakeholders, and seven studies were commissioned covering aspects relevant to the Australian minerals sector, such as research into mining company agreements with Aboriginal communities.

MMSD North America adopted a different approach, where smaller working groups of about 25 individuals were organized around specific topics. Participants were drawn from different interest groups, such as First Nations representatives, NGOs, government and a range of mining companies large and small. The North American process was overseen by the International Institute for Sustainable Development (IISD), based in Winnipeg, Manitoba.

The regional initiatives in South America and Southern Africa were arguably the most impressive in terms of their scope and inclusiveness. In South America, two organizations, the Centro de Investigación y Planificación del Medio Ambiente (CIPMA) and the Mining Policy Research Initiative (MPRI-based at IDRC) were tasked with organizing research and participation, respectively. National teams conducting research and participatory activities were drawn from Bolivia, Brazil, Chile, Ecuador and Peru; together they held about 50 workshops, drawing over 700 participants. In Southern Africa organizers took advantage of the Mining Coordinating Unit of the Southern African Development Community (SADC) to jumpstart the consultation and research process. The overall process was overseen by the University of Witwatersrand and the Council for Scientific and Industrial Research, both based in South Africa, but the consultation process reached widely into the SADC membership base, with focus group meetings held in Botswana, Mozambique, Namibia, South Africa, Tanzania and Zimbabwe.

The MMSD was the most ambitious initiative undertaken under the GMI. Other initiatives were also undertaken to ensure the vision of the GMI be carried forward. The International Council on Metals and the Environment (ICME) was originally tasked to coordinate the various activities of the GMI.[9] In late 2001, the ICME was transformed into the International Council on Mining and Metals (ICMM), so as to provide a more effective organizational architecture within which to manage the GMI. The ICMM has served as the institutional nucleus for coordinating a number of initiatives, including the publication of the ICMM Principles in May 2003 (ICMM, 2003b). What is significant about the ICMM's activities is the growing web of links with INGOs in the promotion of sustainable development in the mining sector. For example, the ICMM set up a dialogue with the World Conservation Union (IUCN), known as the Dialogue Initiative on Mining and Biodiversity. The dialogue resulted in the adoption of a Position Statement on Mining and Protected Areas, which commits member companies of the ICMM to refrain from mining in World Heritage properties that have been designated by the UNESCO World Heritage Committee.

In another example, the ICMM is working with the Global Reporting Initiative (GRI) to establish guidelines that are more relevant to the mining sector. Based on the GRI's 2002 Sustainability Reporting Guidelines (GRI, 2002), the aim is to develop a mining and metals sector supplement. The initiative seeks to embrace a multi-stakeholder consultation process, comprising mining companies, trade unions, and NGOs.

The ICMM's vision and goals are telling in terms of the various motives for the mining sector's global efforts to promote corporate responsibility. The ICMM vision is of: 'A viable mining, minerals and metals industry that is widely recognized as essential for modern living and a key contributor to sustainable development' (ICMM, 2003a). The vision clearly reflects the mining industry's desire to counter its bad reputation, and to promote public awareness about the centrality of mining and metals to maintaining the status of modern industrial society. Appreciation for the importance of mining and metals would then hopefully lead to public acceptance of a reasonable trade-off between reaping the benefits of mining against necessary compromises to the environment (ibid.).

The ICMM's long-term strategic outcomes also reveal a good deal about the concerns that energize the mining sector (ICMM, 2003a):

- Increased trust, reputation and public recognition through enhanced industry performance and responsible stewardship along the entire minerals value chain
- A collective voice on important international policy issues affecting the mining, minerals and metals industry
- Increased sector-wide action in support of ICMM's sustainable development goals
- Continued access to land under clear and equitable rules
- Continued market access and recognition of minerals and metals as materials of choice

The significance of the GMI, with respect to the dissemination of norms, lies in the fact that a process of dialogue and learning is occurring amongst major mining companies. One important indicator of this is that leading mining companies have embraced the idea of sustainable development. The ICMM's statement of principles explicitly adopts the Brundtland Commission's definition of sustainable development as being development that meets the needs of the present without compromising the ability of future generations to meet their own needs. All companies that are members of the ICMM accept the obligation to promote sustainable development.

Sustainable development is a notoriously broad and slippery concept, and this may well be the source of its attraction for the ICMM and its member companies. In the mining and metals sector, sustainable development is understood to mean that 'investments should be financially profitable, technically appropriate, environmentally sound and socially responsible' (ICMM, 2003b). Such a broad and elastic definition leaves plenty of room for interpretation. Yet, it is a significant development that mining companies around the world, as members of the ICMM, have committed to promote sustainable development.[10]

The ICMM principles are indicative of that commitment. Member companies have agreed (ICMM, 2003b) to:

- implement and maintain ethical business practices and sound systems of corporate governance
- integrate sustainable development considerations within the corporate decision-making process
- uphold fundamental human rights and respect cultures, customs and values in dealings with employees and others who are affected by mining activities
- implement risk management strategies based on valid data and sound science
- seek continual improvement of corporate environmental performance
- contribute to conservation of biodiversity and integrated approaches to land use planning
- facilitate and encourage responsible product design, use, re-use, recycling and disposal of products
- contribute to the social, economic and institutional development of the communities in which companies operate
- implement effective and transparent engagement, communication and independently verified reporting arrangements with the company's stakeholders

Motivations behind the GMI

While good public relations are clearly a goal of member companies, it would be an over-simplification to reduce the reasoning behind the GMI to a mere public relations exercise. For that matter, the very act of engaging in public discussions around a company's obligations toward its stakeholders entails a significant shift in thinking. The influences that are inducing companies to adopt socially responsible policies are varied and complex. A brief review of these general influences will help to shed light on the factors motivating companies to support the GMI.

In general, a mix of interest- and norms-based reasons helps to explain the adoption of socially responsible policies. Shifting norms of acceptable corporate behaviour have altered how companies calculate their interests. For some types of businesses, the roles and identities they have crafted for themselves have led them to view corporate responsibility as consistent with their objectives. Although the various influences are interdependent, they fall within the broad categories of political and economic risk considerations (Haufler, 2002b, pp. 167–71).

Longstanding political risks for MNEs with global operations, include the impact of political instability and war and the fear of government regulation. For multinationals operating in developing countries in particular, an additional concern is the mix of regulatory systems from one country to another. While this can work to a company's advantage, there is huge uncertainty for a corporation with transnational operations. There is a range of global instruments (such as the ILO, covering labour, and UNEP, covering environmental standards) that seek to remedy the patchwork quality of national regulations. However, these standards are not uniformly adhered to, so the risk for corporations remains.

Also at play are concerns about 'reputational capital'. Good reputations take years to build, but they can be very quickly destroyed – for example, through the shaming tactics practiced by certain transnational advocacy networks. The success of groups such as Greenpeace in mounting consumer boycotts and media campaigns has been a powerful inducement for some corporations. Shareholder activism, whereby large pension and mutual funds choose to invest in socially responsible funds, has also grown in significance as a source of pressure on corporations.

All of these political risks play directly into the economic risks faced by corporations, the most obvious ones being a company's competitive position and profit margin. Corporations operating in developing countries, where World Bank loans constitute an important part of the financial package in investment decisions, must now consider the fact that the World Bank has developed lending criteria that include CSR considerations.

In the mining sector, there is the further critical risk around what is referred to as the license to operate. Unlike manufacturing MNEs, which have greater mobility, mining companies must base their locations on the presence of commercially extractable minerals. Once an investment has been made, it is critical that company relations with the local communities where they operate be positive. Failure to establish and maintain good community relations makes mining companies more vulnerable to transnational activism. The well-known case of Shell in Nigeria is a case in point. Although Shell did attempt to prevent the execution of Ken Saro Wiwa, the Nigerian activist who had raised concerns about Shell's environmentally destructive practices in Ogoniland, his execution by the Abacha regime did much harm to Shell's reputation. Shell responded by investing millions into cleaning up its image, policies and practices (Bird, 2004).

The political and economic risks outlined above fall within the realm of immediate self-interest for corporations. To what extent can it be argued that there are norms-based reasons for corporations becoming more socially responsible? An examination of Noranda and Placer Dome suggests that both self-interest and norms-based factors have been important in the adoption of socially responsible practices. As will be demonstrated, their decades-long commitment to corporate responsibility weakens claims that the GMI is nothing more than a public relations exercise.

The Role of Canadian Mining Companies

Placer Dome and Noranda

As founding members of the GMI, with well-established policies and practices on corporate social responsibility, Placer Dome and Noranda provide useful insights into the influences shaping that process.[11] For both companies, the adoption of socially responsible practices was an evolutionary process. In the 1970s and 1980s, policies were adopted on worker health and safety issues; in the 1980s and 1990s, policies were adopted on the environment. By the mid-1990s, both companies had come to recognize the importance of being socially responsible in the local communities in which they operate, and both came to embrace the concept of sustainable development as a framework within which to integrate their policies on corporate responsibility.[12]

For Placer Dome and Noranda, CSR policies were seen primarily as a tool for managing a range of political and economic risks, as described above. Both corporations, over the course of the past several decades, learned some difficult lessons about the consequences of poor worker relations, the negative fallout of environmental damage, or the costs of failing to secure local community support for a mine. The development of policies and practices in response to these hard lessons reflects the institutional learning occurring within these corporations.

Up until the mid-1990s, Noranda's and Placer Dome's policies were corporate-driven, in that the impetus for change came from within each individual company. In each case, the company's senior executives spearheaded internal discussions for the development of new CSR policies and management systems to ensure those policies were carried out in practice. No real attempt, however, was made to coordinate policies with other mining corporations so although the two companies were moving in parallel paths, those paths never intersected until the late 1990s.

By the mid to late 1990s, two interrelated processes were unfolding within both corporations. In each case, as they came to understand the importance of addressing social risks, in addition to political and economic risks, both came to recognize the need to develop a framework within which these wide-ranging risks could be addressed as a cohesive whole. The concept of sustainable development provided a useful framework within which social risks could be integrated into already existing policies around environmental and financial risks.

More significantly, perhaps, by the late 1990s both corporations came to recognize that an industry-wide sustainable development approach, rather than individual, corporate-driven approaches, could serve as a vehicle for collective action on corporate social responsibility in the mining sector. The embracing of sustainable development was a recognition that each corporation is but one actor in a complex web of many actors whose roles must harmonize as well as compete. This huge leap in thinking also reflected the realization that global issues as complex as environmental degradation require global action. Individual mining companies could not 'go it on their own'.

Noranda's and Placer Dome's push for the idea of sustainable development within the ICME was met with considerable resistance on the part of other mining companies. They marshalled support for their arguments in the fact that both the European Union and the World Bank had embraced sustainable development by the late 1990s. Some companies were no doubt brought around by the recognition of the fact that the World Bank had introduced sustainability into its lending criteria for mining projects in developing countries.

There were various reasons for this decision to push strongly the concept of sustainable development within the GMI. One major concern was the perceived lack of a global voice on the part of mining corporations on world issues that affected their operations. The 1992 Rio Earth Summit, for example, which was noteworthy for the important contributions of transnational NGOs, left no room for the involvement of MNEs. Mining companies saw the GMI as a means to develop a global voice, and to show that business could make a positive contribution to the goal of sustainable development. By contrast, at the 2002 UNCSD in Johannesburg, business not only had a voice, but the final document acknowledged that business could play a positive role. Participation in such forums puts mining companies in a position to shape future legislation that affects their operations.

Another incentive for the GMI was the need for a collective approach to differentiate between companies that meet socially responsible performance standards, and those that do not. The ICMM also advocates for responsible performance by coordinating the activities of national mining associations, promoting uniform practice, gathering information about what is being done around the world and disseminating information about best practices. Ultimately, member companies are motivated by the desire to ensure access to land, markets and finance.

In effect, Placer Dome and Noranda, together with other corporations committed to sustainable development, such as Rio Tinto, Freeport and Western Mining, were attempting to structure the debates and promote their interpretation of how corporate responsibility should be pursued within the mining sector. With the launch of the GMI in 1998, and certainly with the creation of the ICMM in 2001, sustainable development had gained ascendance as the best means for framing corporate responsibility issues within the mining sector.

The GMI promoted policy learning through the accumulation of scientific knowledge about sustainable mining practices, and through the dissemination of information about best practices in the mining sector. It has been argued, however, that the GMI was not conceived of as merely a vehicle for the dissemination of best practices. It was a forum for debate over a particular interpretation of corporate social responsibility, which its founders hoped would be the source of recognition and legitimation for the mining sector. In other words, the sort of learning taking place involves not just the dissemination of information, but a process of structuring discourse about appropriate CSR norms for the mining sector (Betsill and Bulkeley, 2004, pp. 484–9).

The MMSD process revealed that there was a significant lack of consensus, both among mining companies themselves and between the mining industry and other various stakeholders, about what those norms should be. At one extreme, there were some NGOs that chose not to participate in the MMSD process at all, actively seeking to boycott the consultations (MMSD, 2002b, p. 6). Some of these groups are opposed to mining outright, believing that mining by its very nature contradicts the goal of environmental sustainability. For others, there was a basic lack of trust toward the mining companies, which they feared would seek to control the agenda or manipulate discussions to their advantage.

As is candidly noted in the *Breaking New Ground* report, this lack of trust, or even outright animosity, was obvious to those stakeholder groups that chose to participate (MMSD, 2002b, p. 6). As such, the goal of building confidence between the mining companies and their critics in order to allow honest and open dialogue to take place was compromised from the start. The mining companies, for their part, are hardly a homogeneous group, and there was a diversity of attitudes about the merits of the criticisms levelled against them.

Given this 'crisis of confidence', it is perhaps surprising that the MMSD ever got off the ground. If success is measured by reaching consensus on a range of issues, or else by a dramatic change in mining company practices, then the MMSD would have to be judged a failure. However to expect such a result would probably have been unrealistic, under the circumstances. The scope of the global and regional consultations, the large number of participants and the diversity of reports completed on a range of issues make it reasonable to infer that this massive exercise in multi-stakeholder dialogue produced some positive results. What matters is that a process of dialogue took place, that the various stakeholders learned more about each others' concerns and priorities, and that networks were established or strengthened. The MMSD needs to be seen more as an ongoing process, rather than an end result that needs to be judged.

In the aftermath of the MMSD, there continues to be considerable disagreement among mining companies around the activities of the ICMM. At the moment, direct company membership in the ICMM is limited to the major mining MNEs from the industrialized world. Although the debate on sustainable development appears to have been won, the debate on sustainability goals continues within ICMM, and significant differences remain over the extent of mining companies' obligations, or what form voluntary regulation should take.

The ultimate goal of the ICMM is to push for a uniform reporting regime within the mining sector, complete with external verification. Members currently favour the example of the Responsible Care Codes of Practice, the very successful mechanism in place for the chemical industry, which promotes the responsible storage, handling and distribution of chemicals. As this is part of an ongoing consultation process within the mining industry and with various stakeholders, it is too soon to judge this process in terms of actual outcomes. Still, the stakes are high. One MMSD report concluded: 'Either we will usher in new standards of behaviour and governance as the accepted norm, or we will relapse into a downward spiral of controversy and conflict' (MMSD, 2002a, p. 19).

The example of Noranda and Placer Dome demonstrates that the strong commitment of senior company executives was critical to the launch of the GMI. Institutional maintenance in the form of the ICMM will, in turn, hinge on the support of committed individuals. Beyond that, its success will depend on the extent to which it can be demonstrated that responsible performance on the part of member companies produces results in terms of access to land, markets and finance. While the ICMM does represent a norms-based consensus on appropriate corporate behaviour in the mining sector, its success will also depend on its ability to respond to the instrumental interests of mining companies.

There has clearly been a shift in the identities that mining companies wish to create for themselves. The long-term objectives further indicate that participation in a norms-based dialogue has influenced the companies' perception of their interests, as seen in the recognition that they cannot function if they are denied a 'license to operate'. That license, which requires social acceptance of mining companies, extends beyond the confines of a legal permit, to the need to enjoy legitimacy from the communities within which they operate.

Conclusion

The launch of the GMI in the late 1990s can be traced to the growing potency of the anti-globalization movement and the re-emergence of corporate social responsibility as an issue on the global agenda. At the level of agenda setting, INGOs had a substantial impact, as measured by their success in getting IGOs to undertake initiatives to promote corporate responsibility. The UN Global Compact and the 2002 World Summit on Sustainable Development are examples of that success.

In the late 1990s, mining companies found themselves reacting to pressure from a variety of sources, and the launch of the GMI can be seen in that light. The desire to improve their poor reputation and to foster greater public acceptance of the mining sector led to strategic adaptation on the part of mining companies. In the process of adapting, however, mining companies are slowly being socialized into accepting the need to conform to norms of socially responsible corporate behaviour. What started out as an initially reactive posture has transformed into one of initiation. The formation of the ICMM heralded a determination on the part of leading mining companies to develop the skills, resources and institutional capacity to push corporate responsibility in the mining sector.

The embracing of the concept of sustainable development, as exemplified by the MMSD project, is evidence of the process of dialogue and argumentation taking place among mining companies. The concept of sustainable development served to generate greater coherence amongst corporate initiatives, and provided a catalyst around which mining companies (and their stakeholders) could be brought together. What is interesting in this regard is the fact that it is now 'progressive' mining companies that are engaged in persuading other mining companies, as opposed to INGOs putting direct pressure on them. This paper has demonstrated that mining companies can play a positive role in the promotion of norms of sustainable development. It points to the importance of including corporations in the growing literature on the role of non-state actors in global governance.

Notes

I would like to thank Frederick Bird and Emmanuel Raufflet for their helpful comments on an earlier version of this chapter, which appeared as 'Canadian Mining Companies and the Shaping of Global Norms of Corporate Social Responsibility in the Mining Sector', *International Journal* (Dashwood, 2005).
 1. Although the GMI officially ended in 2002, for ease of discussion, the term is used throughout the chapter. The International Council on Mining and Metals, formed in 2001, now carries forward global initiatives in the mining sector.
 2. A transnational network consists of non-state actors who engage in regular interaction across national boundaries for the purpose of disseminating information, knowledge and norms around a particular global issue or activity. See Betsill and Bulkeley, 2004); Risse-Kappen (1995).
 3. Legitimacy in this sense is understood as non-state actors having authority to formulate and implement policies, practices and rules over a specific issue or domain (Hall and Biersteker, 2002, p. 4). One aspect of the debate centres on whether industry self-regulation is an acceptable substitute for state regulation. For a discussion of the relevant issues, see Kirton and Trebilcock (2004).
 4. The fact of corporate activity in norms and rule-making raises serious questions around legitimacy and democratic accountability. It is not being suggested here that such questions are not valid, but merely that they need to be kept separate from efforts to observe and analyse the implications of what is taking place.
 5. A key assumption of neo-realist theory is that states act in their own self-interest, understood as the maximization of state power. As such, the role of international law and norms as influences on state policy is discounted. For a helpful account of the social constructivist challenge to neo-realist theorizing in international relations, see Ruggie (1998) and Wendt (1992a).

6. For an excellent analysis of the potential of non-state approaches to corporate governance, see Webb (2002).
7. Corporate social responsibility generally refers to the obligations companies have toward their shareholders, employees, customers, local communities and civil society with respect to the conduct and impact of their operations in the areas of human rights, labour standards, and the environment. There is considerable debate about what corporate responsibility should entail in practice. See: Canadian Democracy and Corporate Accountability Commission, (2002) pp. 2–3.
8. The following discussion is drawn from *Breaking New Ground* (MMSD, 2002b; Introduction). Readers interested in greater detail on the regional initiatives may wish to consult this report, or the individual Web sites of the regional partners.
9. Founded in 1991, the ICME's mandate was to promote the development and implementation of environmental and health policies in support of sustainable development. The ICME sponsored a number of conferences and scientific reports throughout the 1990s.
10. At the time of writing, member companies included: Noranda and Placer Dome (from Canada), Alcoa, Anglo American, Anglogold, BHP Billiton, Freeport, Mitsubishi, Newmont, Nippon, Pasminco, Rio Tinto, Sumitomo, Umicore and WMC.
11. The corporate responsibility policies of Placer Dome and Noranda can be found on their respective web sites: www.placerdome.com and www.noranda.com. Note that Noranda merged with Falconbridge in 2005, and at the time of writing, Placer Dome is subject to a take-over bid from Barrick Gold.
12. The following section draws on information gleaned from interviews with senior executives in Noranda and Placer Dome. This section draws especially heavily on the interviews with James Cooney, Placer Dome (30 July 2002), and David Rodier, Noranda, (22 April 2003; 28 October 2003).

References

Betsill, M. M. and Bulkeley, H. (2004) 'Transnational Networks and Global Environmental Governance: The Cities for Climate Protection Program', *International Studies Quarterly*, vol. 48, pp. 471–93.

Bird, F. (2004) 'Wealth and Poverty in the Niger Delta: A Study of the Experiences of Shell in Nigeria', in F. Bird and S. W. Herman, *International Business and the Challenges of Poverty in the Developing World* (London: Palgrave Macmillan).

BSR (1999–2005) Business for Social Responsibility, *Overview of Corporate Social Responsibility*, www.bsr.org/BSRResources/IssueBriefDetail, last updated October, 2003.

Canadian Democracy and Corporate Accountability Commission (2002) *The New Balance Sheet: Corporate Profits and Responsibility in the 21st Century, Final Report* (Toronto: Canadian Democracy and Corporate Accountability Commission).

Cutler, A. C., Haufler, V. and Porter, T. (eds) (1999) *Private Authority and International Affairs* (Albany: State University of New York Press).

Dashwood, Hevina S. (2005) 'Canadian Mining Companies and the Shaping of Global Norms of Corporate Social Responsibility in the Mining Sector', (Autumn), pp. 977–88.

Florini, A. (ed.) (2000) *The Third Force: The Rise of International Civil Society* (Washington, DC: Japan Center for International Exchange and Carnegie Endowment for International Peace).

GRI (Global Reporting Initiative) (2002): www.globalreporting.org.

Hall, R. B. and Biersteker, T. J. (eds) (2002) *The Emergence of Private Authority in Global Governance* (Cambridge: Cambridge University Press).

Haufler, V. (2001a) *A Public Role for the Private Sector: Industry Self-Regulation in a Global Economy* (Washington, DC: Carnegie Endowment for International Peace).

Haufler, V. (2002b) 'Industry Regulation and Labour Standards', in A. Cooper et al. (eds), *Enhancing Global Governance: Towards a New Diplomacy?* (Tokyo: United Nations University Press), pp. 167–71.

ICMM (2003a) International Council on Mining and Minerals, 'About ICMM–Work Programme', http://www.icmm.com/html/work_prog.php (last updated 9 June 2005).

ICMM (2003b) International Council on Mining and Minerals, 'ICMM Sustainable Development Framework: ICMM Principles', http://www.icmm.com/html/work_prog.php (last updated 9 June 2005).

IIED (1999) International Institute for Environment and Development, *Mining, Minerals and Sustainable Development: The Results of a Scoping Project for the World Business Council for Sustainable Development* (London: IIED).

Katzenstein, P. J. (ed.) (1996) *The Culture of National Security: Norms and Identity in World Politics* (New York: Columbia University Press).

Keck, M. and Sikkink, K. (1998) *Activists Beyond Borders: Advocacy Networks in International Politics* (Ithaca, NY and London: Cornell University Press).

Kirton, J. and Trebilcock, M. (eds) (2004) *Hard Choices, Soft Law: Voluntary Standards in Global Trade, Environment and Social Governance* (Toronto: Ashgate).

Kratochwil, F. V. (1989) *Rules, Norms and Decisions: On the Conditions of Practical and Legal Reasoning in International Relations and Domestic Affairs* (Cambridge: Cambridge University Press).

Lipschutz, R. (2000) *After Authority: War, Peace and Global Politics in the 21st Century* (Albany: State University of New York Press).

Lipschutz, R. and Mayer, J. (1996) *Global Civil Society and Global Environmental Governance* (Albany: State University of New York Press).

MMSD (2002a) Mining, Mineral and Sustainable Development, *MMSD: A Process of Consultation*, http://www.iied.org/mmsd/mmsd_pdfs/process.pdf.

MMSD (2002b) Mining, Mineral and Sustainable Development, *Breaking New Ground: Mining, Minerals and Sustainable Development*, http://www.iied.org/mmsd/final-report/index.html.

Mining Policy Research Initiative (MPRI) (2004) 'The Challenges of Transition', in *Global Processes: The Challenges of Mining in a Sustainable Development Framework* (International Development Research Centre), www.iipm-mpri.org.

O'Brien, R., Goetz, A.-M., Scholte, J. A. and Williams, M. (eds) (2000) *Contesting Global Governance: Multilateral Economic Institutions and Global Social Movements* (Cambridge: Cambridge University Press).

Risse, T., Ropp, S. C. and Sikkink, K. (eds) (1999) *The Power of Human Rights: International Norms and Domestic Change* (Cambridge: Cambridge University Press).

Risse-Kappen, T. (ed.) (1995) *Bringing Transnational Relations Back In: Non-State Actors, Domestic Structures and International Institutions* (Cambridge: Cambridge University Press).

Ruggie, J. G. (1998) 'Introduction: What Makes the World Hang Together? Neo-utilitarianism and the Social Constructivist Challenge', in *Constructing the World Polity: Essays on International Institutionalization* (London and New York: Routledge).

Scholte, J. A. (2000) *Globalization: A Critical Introduction* (Houndmills, Basingstoke, Hampshire and New York: Palgrave Macmillan).

UN (2002) United Nations, *Report of the World Summit on Sustainable Development, 26 August–4 September* (Johannesburg, South Africa: United Nations).

Webb, K. (ed.) (2002) *Voluntary Codes: Private Governance, the Public Interest and Innovation* (Ottawa: Carleton Research Unit for Innovation, Science and Environment, Carleton University).

Wendt, A. (1992a) 'Anarchy is What States Make of It: The Social Construction of Power Politics', *International Organization*, vol. 46(2), pp. 391–425.

Wendt, A. (1999b) *Social Theory of International Politics* (Cambridge: Cambridge University Press).

6
Fostering Social Responsibility in Businesses: The Role of Ethical Auditing

Frederick Bird

In the hope of fostering ethically responsible business practices, much effort over the past generation has been invested in developing normative codes of practices and educating business people to know and comply with these standards. Thousands of firms, such as Gap and Levi-Strauss, have developed their own standards (Schoenberger, 2000; Rhone et al., 2004a). Specific sectors, such as chemical producers, forestry and international mining and minerals, have developed their own industry codes (Moffet et al., 2004; Rhone et al., 2004b). A number of important initiatives are under way by groups such as the Caux Roundtable, the Global Reporting Initiative and the Institute of Social and Ethical Accountability to develop internationally recognized standards (Howard, 1998; Caux Roundtable, 2000; Global Reporting Initiative, 2000). Standards of practice have been developed by diverse civic associations, like the Interfaith Centre on Corporate Responsibility, as well as the United Nations Global Compact (TCCR, 1998; McIntosh et al., 2004).[1]

Whether these codes are effective in fostering responsible businesses practices depends not so much on the stipulations of these codes – which are, to be sure, not unimportant – as on how these standards are institutionalized. Are they widely and clearly communicated? Have they received the endorsement of senior business leaders? Are they regularly consulted when boards, managers and employees deliberate about dilemmas or develop business strategies? Most importantly, have firms developed effective procedures for monitoring how well their organizations and stakeholders comply with these standards? If no organized efforts are made to monitor the actual practices of businesses, then codes themselves are not likely to have much impact. They may instead become largely symbolic gestures or public relations initiatives. The means developed by businesses to actually monitor their social and ethical performances has in large part in turn determined both the extent of these efforts to foster responsible practices and the manner in which they are realized.[2]

In this essay I discuss, compare and evaluate different approaches to ethical auditing. I call attention to the diverse approaches for monitoring businesses' ethical performance and highlight some of these differences by focusing on six distinguishable approaches to the ethical auditing process. This typology is not meant to be exhaustive or definitive; it is designed simply for heuristic purposes to illustrate markedly different means by which the actual practices of businesses have been and can be monitored from various ethical perspectives.

I use the term 'ethical auditing' to refer to a broad range of monitoring activities that gauge whether or not businesses are acting in ways that are morally responsible. The social responsibilities of businesses should, I think, be understood in inclusive and comprehensive terms to include how well they utilize the natural and human resources with which they interact so as to add value to their products or services and generate returns for all those who contribute toward their operations – investors, employees, suppliers, creditors, customers, communities and other stakeholders. Businesses fall short of their social responsibilities not only by violating specific contracts and codes but also by failing, as businesses, to utilize resources at their disposal to add value wherever possible. Thus, when we seek to determine how well businesses are fulfilling their social responsibilities, we are interested not only in the social and environmental performances of firms but also in whether they are acting demonstrably as good citizens, whether their practices are demonstrably just, and whether they demonstrably add value as businesses to the societies in which they operate. When we gauge firms in terms of their moral responsibilities, we are just as interested in how they meet their social and environmental bottom lines as in how they meet their economic bottom lines. In this essay I will use the terms 'ethical' and 'moral' to indicate this wider perspective.

With regard to the different approaches for monitoring businesses in terms of their moral responsibilities, I purposefully use the term 'approaches' in order to call attention to the fact that auditing takes place over time as an organized social activity involving many different people. It is not just a technique; the procedures involved are as an integral to this activity as any written reports that may be produced.

Important variables in ethical auditing

The practice of ethical auditing has been undertaken in many different ways, each of which reflects a number of important considerations that are explicitly or implicitly addressed whenever people attempt to monitor human conduct with respect to ethics. I will list and then discuss these considerations as a series of questions.

1. What kinds of ethical standards are we invoking to gauge performances, and how are these standards developed? We can define moral standards in relation both to behaviours and to objectives. With respect to

behaviours, we may use ethical standards to identify what we might best call 'moral minimums': obligatory prohibitions against (among other things) stealing, killing, intentionally harming others and violating legal statutes. At other times we invoke ethical standards to identify 'moral maximums': standards of excellence which we ought to realize: for example, to act with compassion and love, to work industriously, to exercise special consideration for those who are different and to exercise foresight with respect to unanticipated consequences. The distinction between these different kinds of behavioural norms remains fundamental, in spite of the fact that in practice people often set forth moral standards without clearly indicating whether they are to be regarded as minimal obligations or standards of excellence. We can also define moral standards in relation to objectives we seek to attain and goods we seek to realize. A number of observers have argued, for example, that social performances of businesses should be evaluated by the degree to which they add or deplete natural, human, social, productive and financial assets (Zadek, 2001, p. 117; Bird, 2003). It is thus apparent that different businesses may well have different ideas about what constitutes ethically responsible business practice, because they are, for morally legitimate reasons, pursuing this topic with different kinds of ethical concerns in mind.

This point needs to be underlined because of the widespread tendency to presume that when businesses or their critics refer to ethically responsible practices or ethically irresponsible actions, they share a common understanding of what they have in mind. A series of essays in a recent issue of *The Academy of Management Executive* illustrates this assumption. These essays discuss efforts to promote what the authors refer to as ethical behaviour, as well as reasons for non-compliance (Anad et al., 2004; Thomas et al., 2004; Trevino and Brown, 2004). The authors assume that the readers share the same assumptions about what constitutes unethical conduct; they make little or no attempt to distinguish between behaviours that are unethical because they violate strict obligations, fall short of standards of excellence, or undermine valued objectives. Nor do the essays attempt to distinguish between major and incidental acts, sustained actions and momentary lapses, self-serving actions and questionable acts that represent efforts to resolve hard choices. In contrast to the approach taken in these essays, I argue that if we are interested in promoting socially responsible business practices, it is correspondingly important not to oversimplify matters. Rather, it is fitting that we recognize that there are legitimately different perspectives for considering ethical issues (see chapter 1; also Bird, 1981).

2. A second question concerns subject matter. What should be the focus of an ethical audit? Should it attempt to assess a firm with respect to environmental or social issues, interpersonal relations or political activities? In the 1970s, increasing numbers of firms began to develop codes of conduct to monitor the behaviour of personnel with respect to conflicts of interest,

questionable payments and political involvements of firms with their communities and environments. Particular audits might be conducted with respect to quite specific sets of issues, such as promotion opportunities for women workers and managers, the ways a firm supports or undermines local suppliers, work experiences of indigenous employees or the effective engagement of board members. Many favour audits conducted in relation to a comprehensive checklist, while others prefer to monitor with respect to more focused concerns.

3. A third question concerns the timing of audits and their voluntary or obligatory character. Are audits designed to be regularly repeated, occasional or unique exercises? Are they undertaken as compulsory requirements or voluntary exercises? Compelling arguments can be developed for each of these approaches, depending in large part on the purpose of the particular auditing exercise. For example, it is obviously important that certain kinds of fiscal and safety audits be administered regularly as compulsory exercises. In contrast, an occasional, retreat-like setting may provide an excellent opportunity to explore organizational assessments and reflections.

4. A fourth question concerns the process. How will the audit be conducted? Who primarily will perform the audit? For whom is the audit being prepared? When and how are the results of the audit communicated? To begin with, it is important to decide whether the audit is to be viewed primarily as a means of gaining information or as a process of interactive engagement. Many observers argue that an ethical audit is best administered by a third party with little or no connection to the firm in question. Third parties are more likely to take objective positions and to avoid conflicts of interest. Nonetheless, it sometimes makes sense for an organization's members to undertake audits of their own activities. Often those who perform the auditing exercise learn the most in the process. They gain a first-hand sense of the predicaments and possibilities a business faces, as well as the attitudes of various interested parties. Insofar as the auditing process uncovers issues that concern them, those conducting the audits can begin to respond as part of this process. If one of the most important by-products of the auditing process is to facilitate organizational learning and greater commitment to organizational goals, then it can be argued that the auditing processes ought to be a participatory activity that fosters trust and candour, and creates conditions that make it possible to acknowledge shortcomings and cultivate re-commitment (Guba and Lincoln, 1989). Ideally, audits should be prepared for those who are to act effectively in response. Sometimes, of course, audits are prepared for several audiences at the same time. Unfortunately, in some cases audits are prepared for executives, boards, or external agencies that are not prepared to act immediately in response.

5. For what purposes are audits being undertaken? This question is critical. Many think of auditing exercises as a way of policing businesses,

uncovering and penalizing them for evidence of non-compliance; they think of ethical auditing primarily as a way of exposing wrongdoing. For others, it has been a way of attempting to transform the mores and ethos of their organizations – or simply a way of reviewing and enhancing performance. Many businesses have both instituted codes and attempted to monitor conduct as a means of limiting and controlling irresponsible actions by organizational members. More recently, ethical audits have been used to rate and grade firms for those individual investors and pension funds that require the firms in which they hold shares to meet an ethical standard, which these audits confirm. As I will argue in the following pages, these varied purposes for conducting ethical audits are all are morally compelling. They are, however, different in decisive ways.

6. What are the costs of undertaking an ethical audit? Who pays these costs? Ethical auditing entails a number of costs in addition to the fees or stipends for those administering the process. Audits often require the time of many organization members; often they also occasion the additional, and less easily calculable cost associated with the efforts of various individuals and groups to hide from and resist the auditing process. Ideally, auditing process should not be resisted; nonetheless, in some settings they are (Ruggie, 2004). It is therefore useful to develop approaches to auditing that manage the costs of auditing, both expected and unexpected, in effective ways. How much effort do an organization's members expend to keep up appearances? How much conscious covering up and covering over do they engage in? How much unproductive energy is invested in filling out reports that are rarely consulted? How much does the auditing process in unanticipated ways occasion distrust and duplicity?

For comparative and illustrative purposes in considering these questions, I will discuss six possible approaches to ethical auditing. These approaches are not mutually exclusive; they may be combined or undertaken in complementary ways. Two of these approaches – the ones I refer to as 'auditing by exposé' and 'auditing by paying attention' have not usually been thought of as forms of ethical auditing, however I argue that they play a very important role in alerting businesses to ethical issues and moral discrepancies. I also devote attention to 'auditing by means of developmental evaluations' as another form of auditing that has not usually been considered as part of the domain of ethical auditing. In this case I point to affinities between the practices of organizational evaluators and the more teleological approach to ethical auditing used by those who monitor businesses in relation to valued purposes and objectives.

Six possible approaches to ethical auditing

In the remainder of this essay I describe six different and potentially complementary approaches for monitoring businesses with respect to ethical performances:

1. Legally-mandated public audits: the regulatory approach
2. Investigative exposés by civic associations, the media and academics: the prophetic approach
3. Diagnostic surveys using standardized forms: the comparative, 'grading' approach
4. Custom-designed diagnostic audits: the self-appraisal approach
5. Active organizational listening: the attentive approach
6. Developmental evaluations: an approach for internal learning and commitment

After reviewing these different approaches, I will explore how they may be applied in ways that not only complement each other but also serve to reduce resistance to the auditing processes.

1. Legally-mandated public audits: the regulatory approach

Over the years, industrialized countries have enacted legislation that requires businesses to be audited regularly with respect to a variety of activities besides their financial practices. Businesses producing food and drugs are thus monitored to see that their products meet certain minimum health and safety standards. Businesses generally are monitored to ensure that their working conditions meet minimal occupational standards. As a condition of selling shares publicly, businesses have long been required to undergo periodic financial audits. In more recent years, firms have had to undergo regular audits to ensure that they comply with specific environmental codes. Some firms may also be monitored under government regulations or rulings to see whether or not they comply with laws prohibiting discrimination in the workforce. In all of these cases, firms are regularly and publicly monitored by external agencies using objective criteria. In some cases, government agencies directly administer these audits. In other examples, licensed firms undertake these audits, but deliver their reports publicly. In many of these cases, complainants can call for further public investigations by petition to the courts.

Since the beginning of industrialization, the extent and number of these governmental monitoring exercises have steadily expanded. However, beginning in the 1970s, there has been a noticeable movement of resistance to such efforts to regulate and monitor businesses practices, especially their social practices (see chapter 6; also Stone, 1975). The social and ethical practices of firms, it has been argued, should be regulated by voluntary rather than legal codes, and monitored by various industry-based processes rather than by government agencies. This resistance has given rise to a number of significant developments. With several noticeable exceptions, there has been a marked hesitancy to extend regulatory monitoring beyond the areas of business already covered by the law – health, safety, environment, fiscal auditing and some labour practices. The exceptions concern efforts through acts like the federal sentencing guidelines and the Sarbanes-Oxley law in the United States to render managers and boards more legally accountable for their management of fiscal resources (Stith and Cabranes, 1998; Kaplan, 2001; Steers, 2003). However, little effort has been made to adopt as law and therefore legally monitor many of the recommended statutes regarding working conditions developed by the International Labour Organization. Instead most of these statutes have become standard elements in the various voluntary codes promoted by groups like Social Accountability (Pearson and Seyfang, 2001). Similarly, there have been few efforts publicly to monitor firms in terms of their community involvements, the ways they adjudicate internal disputes and complaints, the ways they manage conflicts of interests, and their foreign operations – aside in the latter case from the 1978 Foreign Corrupt Practices Act in the United States and subsequent acts in other countries (Cragg and Woof, 2002). For the most part the regulatory regimes established before the 1980s remain in place. They have, however, not appreciably expanded and have been subjected to foot-dragging compliance, reduced funding and growing rhetorical criticism calling for reduced government involvement (Rodrik, 1999).

This resistance to furthering legally mandated external audits of business practices has arisen for a number of reasons. This kind of monitoring represents an expenditure of public funds in a time when governments have sought to reduce costs. Further, external audits have been viewed by businesses themselves as intrusive and inefficient. The regular and extensive efforts to prepare reports for regulators and to meet with auditors represent significant transactional costs, which many businesses have argued add little or no value to the firm, or return for its owners and investors. Observers began to distinguish between the legal responsibilities of businesses and their social and ethical responsibilities, ignoring in the process the fact that most of the current legal requirements regarding fiscal audits, minimum wages, working conditions and contractual relations were long understood as compelling moral values before they were enacted as statutes (Commons, 1893; Ryan, 1906). Recently, it has been widely assumed that the 'social responsibilities' of businesses are practices that are not covered by existing laws and should not be regulated by future laws. These practices should, various observers have argued, be monitored instead by voluntary efforts, organized by firms, industries, consultancies, ethical investment funds and civic associations (Graves and Waddock, 1994; CPGMWG, 2002; Pellizzari, 2002).

Despite such resistance at this point in time, it is important both to re-affirm the importance of legally mandated external auditing and to specify clearly when and where this form for monitoring the social performances of businesses ought to be implemented. The traditional belief, embodied in the charter of the International Labour Organization, that governments, businesses and trade unions (and today, we might add other civil society associations) should cooperate in identifying certain externally mandated and audited standards, is still morally compelling – as long as we clearly and circumspectly identify the specific areas of business practices that call for this kind of monitoring.

With regard to what areas of business practice is this monitoring strategy called for? In the past, occasioned as much by crusading ideals as by evidence of the exploitation, reformers have zealously sought to extend the range of practices, calling for external monitoring especially with respect to labour practices and environmental issues. These reforming efforts occasioned widespread resistance, in part because monitoring itself sometimes becomes increasingly costly. In order to comply with the recently enacted Sarbanes-Oxley law, which calls for more detailed financial audits of firms, businesses have had to expend time and funds in ways that have occasioned considerable controversy (*The Economist*, 2005). However, it is possible to adopt a more delimited scope for this kind of legally mandated external monitoring. The key feature is to begin with the recognition that governments can legitimately require that certain external monitoring procedures be instituted, especially with respect to practices that can put the public or parts of the public at excessive risk if not responsibly undertaken. The basic issue arises not with respect to the legitimacy and utility of legally mandated audits as such, but rather with respect to the manner in which this auditing processes is institutionalized. Resistance since the 1970s has increased to the degree that governments directly administer these monitoring procedures, and seek to do so in ever more extensive and detailed ways. It is not always necessary or useful to stipulate in minute detail what should be involved in these audits. Several guidelines for external monitoring seem self-evident:

- The practices to be monitored should be ones associated with a clear risk to the public and basic business obligations. For this reason, in the past this kind of monitoring has typically been implemented to deal with practices that present risks to health and safety as well as fraud.
- If the areas to be monitored cannot easily be observed, then the efforts of external auditors can more readily be obstructed. Firms find all sorts of ways of dissimulating. In such cases, it often makes more sense to penalize risky practices after they have resulted in obvious harm than to implement policing investigations that both allow external agents excessive power and indirectly foster duplicity. It often makes sense simply to require that external auditing be undertaken with respect to discrete sets of concerns by responsible agents who will be charged with communicating their observations to concerned parties.

- The reports on these kinds of audits should be publicly available for comment and criticism. The purpose of these kinds of reports, such as fiscal audits as well as most impact assessments, is not primarily to grade organizations for external critics or investors but to provide instructive points of reference with regard to shortcomings, and possible corrective measures to address these concerns.
- External audits should be undertaken in ways that are not excessively intrusive or expensive for the businesses concerned.

These guidelines are easily met by the most widely practiced forms of externally monitoring, as, for example, when firms are required to engage external auditors to review their finances. The guidelines are met as well when firms applying for World Bank financing arrange for environmental and social impact assessments, which they in turn publicly distribute. The traditional uses of external monitoring with respect to health and safety standards meet these guidelines as well.[3]

2. Investigative exposés by civic associations, the media and academics: the prophetic approach

There is a long and honoured tradition associated with a second approach[4] for monitoring businesses with respect to their social responsibilities. This approach has been practiced by media groups, civic associations and academics developing and publicly communicating critical exposés of firms. Throughout the first century of industrialization, we can find examples of these kinds of exposés. Consider, for example, Friedrich Engels's *The Condition of the Working Class in England in 1844*, Harriet Beecher Stowe's *Uncle Tom's Cabin* (1852) or the novels and journalism of the early 20th-century American 'muckrakers' Upton Sinclair, Lincoln Steffens, Ida Turbell and others. Critical exposés of business have played a major role in arousing public attention and generating public protests with respect to specific abuses. They have served to educate citizens and elicit legislative initiatives. In response to these kinds of exposés, such as the Club of Rome's broadside warning in the early 1970s about the world population and the environment, businesses have often initiated reforms or gestures toward reform.

In 1995, Greenpeace initiated a campaign against Shell when the oil company attempted to sink in the North Sea an abandoned an oil rig platform. Although Shell's proposal had received appropriate legal approval as well as support from environmental experts, Shell responded to its critics and did not sink the platform. While Greenpeace later acknowledged that its assessment that the sinking of the platform would result in excessive environmental damage had been wrong, Shell learned a number of important things in the process. The company recognized that it faced a reputational crisis, which could only be effectively managed by attempting to work with civic associations and protest groups like Greenpeace.

Over time, various civic groups, maverick protesters, investigative journalists and inquiring academics have published accounts exposing abuses of particular businesses: financial irregularities, collusion with governments, environmental hazards, workplace injustices and other problems. Many times these exposés have been ignored; at other times they have stirred up a variety of counterattacks, public actions and even internal reforms. In recent years a number of organizations have been purposefully formed to monitor particular businesses and report on questionable practices. Transparency International was formed to expose and seek to limit incidents of corruption in business and government. The Maquila Solidarity was established to keep track of abusive practices of international firms working along the US border in Mexico. Mining Watch was organized to expose overlooked practices in the international mining industry that were either environmentally harmful or degrading to workers. The Forestry Stewardship Council was initiated not only to limit harmful forestry practices but also to promote responsible forest management. Other groups like Human Rights Watch, the Third World Network, and the Amnesty International Business Group in the United Kingdom have been established to monitor practices and expose abuses in international businesses and governments. The number of civil society associations especially formed to monitor business practices has greatly increased since the beginning of the 1990s (see TCCR, 1998; ICHRP, 2002).

Zadek (2001) argues that the active role of these civic associations has helped to give rise to a new form of accountability for businesses, which he refers to as the new system of civil governance. Hardworking, usually idealistic staff members actively keep track of business operations, invite informants to provide confidential accounts, and publicly communicate their analyses. Businesses must ultimately respond to the media attention and public criticism these civil society organizations succeed in generating. It is interesting to examine some of the best-known brand-name producers' and retailers' responses. In order to avoid bad publicity, firms like Nike, Levi Strauss and the Gap have worked to insist that their suppliers produced goods using suitable working practices (Zadek, 2004). They have hired groups like Verité and COVERCO (see chapter 7) to monitor these workshops. At the same time, they have frequently put these workshops at greater distance from their marketing, administrative and design operations by contracting with third-party businesses to manage these operations.

In an increasingly important way, the practices of businesses are being monitored externally in an ad hoc and irregular way by a host of largely self-appointed observers, who tend to assess business according to their own ever-changing criteria. In practice, they tend to look for, and fasten their attention on, 'sinner stories' (reports of irregularities and abuses) complemented by a few 'saint stories' (accounts of especially remarkable achievements). They are inclined to call attention to particular businesses and ignore many others, a number of whom probably would provide bases for even more engaging stories of moral failings and accomplishment. Some of these exposés are likely to be based on thorough and rigorous research and have been remarkably accurate and trenchant. Others are based on surface impressions and have sometimes proved to be seriously misleading.

Overall, what significance should we attach to this increasingly institutionally organized practice of developing exposés of business practices by a diverse assortment of individuals and organizations? Clearly this practice of investigating and exposing questionable (as well as exemplary) business practices possesses considerable merit. In an erratic but often persuasive way, it helps to remind business leaders that their organizations are socially accountable. Over time, this practice has served to unearth and publicize questionable practices overlooked by more standardized government audits. However, some persons engaged in preparing such exposés have been given to developing overly romanticized views of what businesses can and should do – that they might automatically become more humane if they are somehow less governed by the pursuit of economic interests. Nonetheless, these exposés help to make audible, although perhaps with brighter colours and sharper contrasts, the muted voices and sentiments of thousands and thousands of workers, customers, suppliers and community members affected by business practices whose concerns would otherwise go unnoticed.

A number of contemporary writers skilfully practice this art: observers and critics like Lester Brown of the World Watch Foundation; writers for organizations like Greenpeace and the Task Force on Churches and Corporate Responsibility; a number of trade unions; and certain freelance investigators.

Jon Entine is one of the more interesting social critics of business practices. He has made something of a career out of his exposés of The Body Shop. Although some of his criticisms have been exaggerated, misleading or misplaced, he has pointed to a number of examples where actual practices diverged from the especially idealistic rhetoric of The Body Shop (Entine, 1994). From the perspective of The Body Shop, Jon Entine has been an irritant. He has, they argue, at times misrepresented the character and practices of the company and made too much of incidental failings. But his exposés may well have acted as catalysts to help keep the firm on its toes. When Entine began publishing, The Body Shop initiated a set of internal audits and made a number of internal reforms. Although it is difficult to prove a direct causal link, in the larger sense exposés of this sort have functioned to activate a larger civic awareness (Zadek, 2001, ch. 15).

3. Diagnostic surveys using standardized forms: the comparative, 'grading' approach

A number of groups have developed standardized surveys for gauging the social performance of businesses. Survey forms prepared by organizations such as EthicScan Canada, Social Accountability, the Interfaith Centre on Corporate Responsibility in the United States in cooperation with the Task Force on Churches and Corporate Responsibility in Canada, and the Caux Roundtable (see TCCR, 1998; Caux Roundtable, 2000; Pellizzary, 2002; Beschorner, 2005), among others, have been used to gauge the social performance of thousands of businesses. Other surveys for assessing social practices have been developed by private consulting firms as well as industry associations. I have already referred to the self-assessment guidelines developed both by the international mining industry as well as chemical industry.

In order to illustrate typical ways in which standardized instruments have been used, it is useful to review the efforts of EthicScan Canada to survey the social performance of businesses. In a recent issue of the *Corporate Ethics Monitor* (2004), they published their results of surveys of integrated energy companies in Canada. They surveyed human resource policies of these firms by soliciting answers to a number of questions calling for *yes* or *no* answers or simply scaled responses. They asked, for example, whether or not firms had employee assistance programmes, organized re-cycling efforts, offered same-sex benefits, and provided scholarships for the children of employees (EthicScan Canada, 2004). The surveys also scored firms in terms of governance practices, commitment to environmental standards, as well as their sourcing and trading practices. In other surveys, EthicScan Canada asked a comparable range of questions to gauge the social performances of insurance firms, mining companies, food industry companies and even universities. For their analysis of food companies, EthicScan Canada developed eight broad categories:

1. Ethical management and consumer relations
2. Employee relations
3. Equity and family issues
4. Progressive staff policies
5. Sourcing and trading practices
6. Environmental management
7. Environmental performance
8. Community responsibilities

Each category was weighted and subdivided according to more specific criteria. With respect to employee relations, for instance, firms were scored on whether they had worked to mitigate outsourcing; experienced layoffs or work stoppages; reported on training programmes, health and safety statistics, and absentee rates; instituted employee share ownership plans; as well as other related questions. In assessing the performance of these firms, EthicScan Canada used a couple of hundred easily answered questions like these.

Most standardized surveys used to gauge business practices are less detailed than those developed by EthicScan Canada and the specific criteria in relation to which businesses are reviewed may differ significantly. Nonetheless, these standardized surveys tend to be used in comparable ways. Most are designed so that they can be used fairly easily either by external or internal observers. Most ask questions about observable behaviours. Unlike legally mandated audits, these surveys are voluntarily administered – for the most part by people for whom the practice of conducting these surveys is their primary work. Some surveyors are outsiders to the organization; others are insiders assigned this task. Correspondingly, the act of surveying, regarded as an instrumental process, is important only as a way of generating the data found in the survey results. The surveys often gauge performance without clearly distinguishing whether the points of reference are minimal obligations (as in legally mandated audits), standards of excellence, valued objectives or conventional expectations. The chief value of these surveys is that they allow social performances to be assessed comparatively according to common standards recognized by other businesses. Because the data produced are comparable, the surveys can be used to rate and grade the social performances of businesses, while firms can use the data to review and assess their own practices.

Diagnostic surveys produce reports that likewise provide comparative bases for assessing social performance. How valuable these surveys are depends in large part on how the resulting reports are used. Over the past two decades these diagnostic surveys have been utilized for several somewhat different purposes. Investor groups have used them to identify firms worthy of the ethical investments demanded by increasing numbers of investors. A number of investment firms have been established in order to solicit and manage these ethical investments. As a result of concerted efforts, many institutional investment funds, universities and non-profit organizations, as well as concerned citizens, deliberately place ever-larger portions of their investments in these ethical funds (Hutton et al., 1998; Mackenzie and Lewis, 1999; Abbey and Jantzi, 2001). Many investors also invest strategically in order to exercise pressure on less responsible firms to improve their ethical performance.

Diagnostic surveys have also been used by academics interested in gauging social performance and determining to what degree socially responsible businesses perform as well or better than less ethically responsible businesses (Griffin and Mahon, 1997; Waddock and Graves, 1997; Margolis and Walsh, 2003). EthicScan Canada, TCCR and other corporate watch groups have also used diagnostic surveys with some success. The TCCR survey

Bench Marks for Measuring Business Performance (2000) gauged the performance of eight major corporations in Canada: Barrick Gold, Bombardier, Inco, Nortel Networks, Placer Dome, Shell Canada, Suncor and Talisman Energy. The report demonstrated that these firms performed poorly in relation to almost all of TCCR's social and environmental guidelines. Using the survey results as an exposé, TCCR hoped to arouse the public to demand that these firms work forthrightly to become more responsible corporate citizens. In its survey of the Canadian food industry, EthicScan Canada analysed the practices of more than four dozen firms in relation eight broad categories to provide a more balanced, less critical assessment (Pellizzari, 2002); but it hoped that publication of its ratings would arouse consumers to utilize their buying power to influence the surveyed firms to improve their social performance in areas where they scored especially low.

Certain firms have used standardized surveys (or modified versions of these surveys) to assess their own performance. One petrochemical firm I studied in the early 1990s successfully used the information from a survey administered by a consulting firm to gauge its compliance with the chemical industry's Responsible Care guideline and thus strengthen their considerable resolve steadily to improve their performance in relation to all the surveyed categories.

While diagnostic surveys are useful in assessing, comparing and grading firms with respect to designated indicators, they provide little basis for analysing aspects of business performance not covered by their own selected criteria. Diagnostic surveys typically do not attempt to gauge outcomes that are not easily measured by reportable answers to discrete questions or assessable by external observers. They rarely attempt to gauge the ethos of organizations, clearly a feature of businesses integral to any study of ethics. For the most part, these surveys do not attempt to explore the ways and extent to which businesses add to or diminish the value of their various assets through ordinary business activities (Norman and MacDonald, 2004). Further, as I already noted, because diagnostic surveys are valued primarily for their capacity to generate reports, the actual data-gathering process, which might have provided occasions for learning and re-commitment, tends to be regarded as a merely incidental means. As a result, those surveyed often are only superficially cooperative with the investigative process, which initially at least provides them with few occasions to learn or to reposition themselves. They are typically treated as subjects, not as informants or collaborators.

The chief value of diagnostic surveys lies in their subsequent use rather than in the process by which they are generated. They probably have been most effectively used by ethical investment funds instrumentally to promote their own agendas and by firms themselves that treat the surveys as occasions for internal debate and reflection.

4. Custom-designed diagnostic audits: the self-appraisal approach

Many businesses have undergone specially designed self-appraisals to gauge their own overall ethical performance. In the early 1990s, for example, The Body Shop hired an external consultant to gauge how well the company was operating in terms of relevant social, environmental and ethical guidelines. The consultant designed a number of probes, which were then used in interviews with executives, managers, workers, franchisees, customers and outside critics to see how they rated The Body Shop's performance. Responses were tabulated, and the consultant prepared a diagnostic report. This custom-designed ethical audit did not involve the use of standardized scales; although publicly available, it was essentially designed to be read and examined as part of an internal process of self appraisal, which largely focused on The Body Shop's various stakeholders and how they regarded the conduct of the organization, according to a specific set of relevant questions. The report thus brought out into the open a number of views that might otherwise have remained unspoken and unheard. The Body Shop then used this report as the basis for internal discussions, which led, in turn, to efforts by senior management to capitalize on what the firm was doing well, while addressing areas of weakness.

Many other businesses have arranged for or prepared their own ethical self-appraisals. Some firms regularly, usually annually, conduct some kind of self-appraisal survey. For others firms, like The Body Shop, this is a one-time exercise. Typically, businesses solicit assessments of their practice by calling for responses to survey forms, interviews, and sometimes open invitations for comments. In some cases the questions are very restricted. In the early 1990s, for example, a medium-sized pharmaceutical firm sent out 2,000 forms annually to managers and supervisors, asking them to report primarily on questionable practices and possible conflict-of-interest situations. In most cases, however, the surveys invite responses to a much wider range of questions bearing on human resource practices, community involvement and environmental issues.

Since the late 1990s Royal Dutch/Shell International has conducted annual self-appraisals of its social and environmental performance. A set of probes prepared by the firm itself solicits responses not only both from managers of various Shell companies and operations but also from any persons associated with Shell who are willing to comment. This information is collected by the international headquarters, where a summary report is prepared, showing the social and environmental dimensions of Shell's performance alongside its annual report on its financial performance. These reports, which include both complimentary and critical quotes from respondents, provide fairly candid multidimensional appraisals of the how well the organization is addressing social and environmental challenges (Royal Dutch Shell Group, 1998, 1999, 2000, 2001).

5. Active organizational listening: the attentive approach

Although we usually think of ethical auditing in terms of the discrete acts by which a specific audit is conducted, it may also appropriately be thought of as an ongoing activity or as a set of interrelated acts by means of which social practices of firms are regularly monitored and discussed. To a degree, in an almost continuous way the actual practices of businesses, whether these are exemplary or questionable, are in fact regularly observed by various organizational members and stakeholders (Waters, 1978; Waters and Chant, 1982). Such observations are not systematic; nor are they organized in relation to established guidelines. For the most part, they remain ad hoc, contingent and partial. Nonetheless, when they are adequately voiced and heard, these observations are filled with information and viewpoints that are in turn relevant and valuable for those seeking to assess the actual social performance of businesses. Often, however, the observers either fail to voice their concerns with sufficient clarity and force, or other organizational members, particularly senior managers and board members, fail to pay attention to or even deliberately ignore these observations, regardless of the manner of presentation (Bird, 1996, ch. 1–4).

In principle, then, at least one possible strategy for auditing the social performance of businesses is to encourage organizational members and stakeholders regularly to voice their concerns and observations. When these concerns and observations are effectively voiced and attentively heard, organizations can attempt to respond appropriately in a timely fashion before complaints become protests or issues become crises, while mistakes can be easily righted and possibilities for reform can become genuine opportunities. From this perspective, social auditing is not merely a set of periodic interventions to gauge and grade businesses but rather an integral aspect of ongoing conversations by means of which moral concerns are voiced and discussed, and fitting responses are explored. Thus, social auditing, in one authentic form, takes place when organizations foster and facilitate open and reciprocating communications about social and ethical concerns (Bird, 1996, ch. 7).

This vision of social auditing as authentic communication will probably always remain only partially realized. Nonetheless, to the extent businesses fail to attempt to realize this vision, they put themselves at risk. Over the years, many of the most serious moral failings in businesses, from acts of fraud to major safety crises, have occurred because leadership failed to respond when information indicated that something was amiss, or failed to listen actively when others whispered suspicions, asked awkward questions, remained uncomfortably silent or issued troubling reports (Bird, 1996, ch. 3–5). Developing ways to foster better communication within organizations about moral concerns has had the direct effect of making organizations more responsive to social and ethical issues. Indeed, there are a number of ways in which organizations effectively frustrate or block lively and responsive communication (Waters, 1978; Bird, 1996, ch. 6).

These I will consider later as concrete problems (not merely as labels, ratings or scores) for which organizational members can then seek to identify realistic solutions. In this sense, ethical auditing can take place in an unsystematic but active way as an integral aspect of ongoing communication rather than as an isolated assessment exercise. In this sense too it is a lay rather than an expert activity, a responsibility and opportunity for all organizational members and stakeholders, rather than one exclusively assigned to designated auditors and inspectors.

This approach to ethical auditing can be fostered in specific ways. Many organizations have established formal procedures for hearing questions and complaints. Some have established ombudsmen to listen to any concerns from organizational constituents about mistreatment and conflicts and to initiate appropriate actions to resolve the issues in question by raising these concerns with senior organizational officials. An even larger number of organizations have established formal due process systems to hear complaints and adjudicate cases of alleged wrongdoing (Ewing, 1989). Under either system, people tend primarily to speak up about issues where they are personally affected. Nonetheless, they provide a vehicle for voicing concern about wider issues as well, and point out practices that deviate from the organization's norms.

A number of businesses have established anonymous procedures, using protected hot lines, sealed steel boxes or anonymous mailings, to encourage and protect individuals who pass on information about actions by members that deviate from the organization's standards. Other organizations have sought to encourage whistle-blowing by establishing clear rules that protect informants from reprisals (Miceli and Near, 1992). These several procedures are designed to allow for what might aptly be referred to as internal exposés, which are expected to arise from time to time rather than as part of ongoing communications.

Other organizations have taken steps to encourage questions, discussions and debates about ethical business practice by slightly altering and expanding sessions devoted to performance appraisals, contract negotiations and renewals, discussions among colleagues in working units and board meetings. In each case, initiatives have been taken to render discussions more open-ended and reciprocal so as to offer all parties at least a modest agenda-setting role (Culbert and McDonough, 1980; Westley, 1990; Isaacs, 2000). One of the more successful examples of this practice occurred at a newly developed petrochemical plant in Alberta in the 1980s. All new employees were required to participate in a three-day workshop on conflict resolution. The fact that all managers and employees participated in these workshops had a measurable impact on the culture of this business. People felt freer to raise problems and more compelled to listen when others spoke. One unexpected result was that people spoke about moral concerns quite readily, whether to complain, invoke ideals, reflect on dilemmas or affirm their existing commitments.[5]

6. Developmental evaluation: an approach for internal learning and commitment

Ethical auditing can also be viewed primarily as a process for fostering organizational learning and cultivating renewed and altered organizational commitments. The orientation of auditing shifts away from a policing role, exposing wrongdoing, or from the production of reports which gauge and grade performances. Rather the auditing process leads those directly involved through a step-by-step reassessment of their specific objectives and current activities, thus enabling them to take immediate action to alter relevant practices in order better to realize their aims. This approach to ethical auditing is what those in the field of organizational evaluations call 'developmental evaluation'. Patton (1997) notes, for example, that a great many conventional evaluations produce reports that are largely ignored. Such reports often have had much less impact than expected because they were prepared by outsiders for administrators or supervisors, who were subsequently expected to implement the reports' recommendations in the face of resistance on the part of those directly involved. What Patton refers to as 'utilization-focused evaluation' proceeds in a markedly different way. The evaluation is designed by the people involved – supervisors, subordinates, colleagues, stakeholders – who also participate in the investigations, analysis and response through ongoing consultations and workshops. People have an opportunity to confront the evidence directly, explore alternative responses and commit themselves in direct communication with each other to mutually agreed-upon courses of action (Guba and Lincoln, 1989). To the degree that organizations monitor their own performances by means of these developmental evaluations, they also thereby create occasions for organizational learning (Senge et al., 1994) in environments where people can acknowledge shortfalls and mistakes without putting their jobs at risk. This developmental view of ethical auditing as an internal, consultative, interactive learning process also has a classical, Aristotelian aspect in that it directly encourages participants both to review the ends they are seeking to realize – ethical goods or end values – as well as the ways in which current practices support or frustrate the realization of these ends (Bird, 2003).

It is possible to point to a number of contemporary examples of this consultative, development approach to ethical auditing. Most of the American firms operating in South Africa that adopted the Global Sullivan Principles monitored their compliance through a consultative approach.[6] At the outset the Principles were stated very generally – more as objectives to be aimed at rather than strict behavioural norms. Cooperating firms committed themselves to work to realize these objectives. Moreover, the principles themselves underwent further changes: they became both more specific and assumed more the form of performance standards. Throughout this time, firms monitored their own performances, but their audits were checked by outside consultants and the firms received general grades for their overall efforts. For the most part, consultants' evaluation reports remained private and internal. A number of the cooperating firms used these accounts as bases for their own internal reforms. Some firms took the Sullivan Principles much more seriously than others (Sethi and Williams, 2001). For example, after having received a mediocre rating in the late 1980s, Otis Elevator made a concerted effort to reorient its management practices and enhance the opportunities for black employees.

Among civic associations, there have been a number of efforts to promote a consultative, developmental approach to ethical auditing. Both the United Way in the United States and the Canadian Centre for Philanthropy have developed handbooks to help local organizations successfully move themselves through internal auditing processes. In both cases the processes include the active participation by representatives from all relevant stakeholders. In both cases, participants in the auditing process are asked to address a series of questions, and their various answers are then used to foster discussions. These discussions consider how well the organization is performing, how the participants have contributed to this situation, and what they and others in the organization might now do to more closely realize organizational goals (United Way, 1999; Mollenhauer, 2000).

The Institute for Social and Ethical Accountability has taken the lead in developing a consultative approach to ethical auditing. Although the Institute developed a common standard in much the same way as Social Accountability (another European initiative), its approach to ethical auditing has been quite different. The standard, known as the AccountAbility 1000, is not an objective template, but a set of interactive processes that involve ongoing interactive discussions and debates between a firm and its stakeholders, assessing the firm's ethical performances in relation to a set of standard questions. Firms are encouraged to modify and elaborate on these standards with respect to their own particular circumstances. They are then expected to adopt a problem-solving mindset to assess both current performance and options they might pursue collaboratively to realize their valued objectives (Gonella et al., 1998; Howard, 1998; Zadek et al., 1999; Beschorner, 2005).

In their own way, consultative, developmental audits can be fairly systematic and rigorous. They have occasioned wide-ranging investigations as well as thought-provoking self-assessments and personal soul-searching. They have often given rise to thoroughgoing organizational self-analysis. Indeed, they may well foster more extensive and more personally engaged reflections than either diagnostic surveys or external audits. The outcomes they produce are less tangible but more profound than those produced by other auditing strategies. Although they rarely produce reports by means of which organizations can quantifiably compare their performance to that of others, they frequently help to give rise to new as well as renewed commitments and altered or reaffirmed practices.

Conclusion: Why multiple approaches to ethical auditing make sense

Each of the approaches to ethical auditing discussed in this essay possesses its own strengths and weaknesses. The regulatory and diagnostic approaches use more objective criteria. The prophetic strategy is undertaken with great moral energy. The developmental approach is more likely to foster learning. The standard diagnostic approach is the most systematic while the strategy of paying attention is the most closely integrated with ongoing organizational activities. There are many reasons why organizations and their critics might favour one approach more than other approaches. Many people favour external audits or diagnostic surveys because they produce reports that can be reviewed by outsiders. Many people remain deeply suspicious of the reliability of auditing processes that are voluntary. They point to the ways these auditing processes allow those being investigated to choose what kinds of evidence to submit for review. In contrast, advocates for internal, consultative audits note that the reports produced by external auditors are often loudly extolled but usually only selectively implemented. Many champions of voluntary audits talk as if few contemporary businesses have had to undergo legally mandated external audits – overlooking fiscal, health and safety audits required by modern government.

Much of the current debate about ethical auditing proceeds on the assumption that firms ought to institute a single effective means to monitor their social and ethical performance – *the one* approach that suits them best. One good reason for adopting this assumption is that organizational members are likely to resist efforts to put them through multiple ethical investigations that assume similar organizational forms in practice. They may reliably ask why one auditing exercise isn't enough, and will probably respond hesitantly and superficially to further inquiries, indeed they might well respond by opting for whichever audit exposes them to the least risk and exposure. There is also the danger that in the course of different ethical audits a firm's actual performance may well be over-analysed and ultimately misunderstood. Clever managers may also play off the findings of one audit against others, to their own advantage (Norman and MacDonald, 2004). More information, especially uncoordinated information that has been gathered from different angles, does not necessarily produce greater clarity or sharper perspective. Thus, it is understandable that ethical auditing has usually been thought of as a unique organizational exercise to be undertaken according to a single, permanent model.

Nevertheless, this assumption is misplaced. To a significant degree, these different approaches to ethical auditing are neither competitive nor redundant. They operate largely independent of each other, embedded in different organizational domains and different organizational practices.

At least two of these approaches to auditing – the regulatory and the prophetic – have existed for a long time. To be sure, they have sometimes been broadly unappreciated. Nevertheless, they have served as important vehicles for conveying useful information about social performance to businesses and their critics. Both of these forms of ethical auditing are initiated, organized and largely funded by groups that are independent of the business world – governments, media and voluntary-sector organizations. It is worth noting that both of these approaches to ethical monitoring play vital clearly circumscribed roles. The regulatory approach has worked best in evaluating health and safety risks and cases of fiscal impropriety – common problems to which business activities in industrialized societies give rise. The prophetic approach has alerted businesses and society generally to unseen dangers, unrecognized hypocrisies and longstanding injustices. Thus the regulatory and prophetic approaches to ethical auditing provide occasions for what social psychologists refer to as anticipatory socialization.

It can be argued that the basic elements that allow for 'attentive' auditing are already in place in most businesses. To the extent that adequate provision for voicing and hearing ethical concerns have in fact been instituted, businesses are well situated to identify serious social and ethical problems and nip them in the bud. They are also able to support the moral commitments of their constituents (Bird, 1996, ch. 5 and 6). The problem is that in a large number of businesses many of the elements that might facilitate the attentive approach to ethical auditing remain dormant.

Given the steadily growing interest in ethical investing as well as the interest of firms in securing and maintaining their good repute, we can expect that diagnostic audits will continue to be used. These are not very intrusive; they provide a quick and relatively easy means of assessing relevant aspects of the social performance of firms, and as the diagnostic scales become ever more multidimensional and finely tuned, they are also able to provide increasingly reliable characterizations. These diagnostic scales, however, are reliable only to the extent that those consulting them keep in mind that a diagnostic only gauges what it is designed to measure, and may omit certain quite important aspects of a business's social performance. It is important to recognize that these surveys are not developmental evaluations. They do not cultivate the settings for organizational learning and renegotiated commitments that are integral to organizational renewal.

Ironically, the form of ethical auditing that has probably received the least attention is the consultative strategy associated with developmental evaluations. This is unfortunate because this approach allows the most opportunity for organizational learning and strengthening organizational commitment.

These several distinct auditing practices comprise interrelated aspects of what several different observers refer to as the new patterns of public governance. According to these observers, increasingly public governance is being exercised by governments in concert with businesses and voluntary-sector associations. As societies industrialize, the structures of public administration and accountability include ever-larger numbers of non-governmental organizations working as contractors, collaborators and advocates seeking the attention of governmental agencies and offices (Salamon, 2002; Webb, 2004, ch. 1–5). These several different forms of ethical auditing we have discussed reflect and embody these diverse and multifaceted emerging forms of accountability. Nonetheless, though we may become more appreciative of the diverse forms of ethical auditing that may be undertaken, it does not follow that we should be uncritical of how these several forms of auditing are put into practice. At present we are painfully aware of the many ways in which these diverse forms of auditing fail in practice to foster responsible business practices. It may well be, however, that we will be better equipped to address the current situation when we recognize that we can work to enhance responsible business practices not by seeking to impose one form of auditing on all businesses but rather by strengthening those particular approaches to auditing that seem best positioned in particular settings to be viable and most likely to foster learning and commitment.

Notes

1. For a useful survey of a large number of relevant codes of practice, see McKague (2003).
2. This study applies to international businesses but does not especially focus on them. In two ways, the situations of international businesses call for special attention. (1) Many international operations, because of their distance from corporate headquarters, seem able to evade ordinary auditing processes. Businesses and community groups have correspondingly worked harder to keep track of these distant operations (see chapter 7). (2) Specific operations may be audited from the perspective of both host and home countries, which may have different concerns. For a discussion of ways to manage these differences, see chapter 1.
3. The Stock Exchange in Johannesburg, South Africa, requires that all listed firms undertake an annual audit of their environmental practices (van der Lugt, 2004, p. 143).
4. In the *Concise Oxford Dictionary* (8th edition, 1991) the word 'exposé' has two meanings: 'an orderly statement of facts' or 'the act or instance of revealing something discreditable'. I use 'exposé' largely in the first sense, recognizing that in practice orderly statements of the facts about businesses often involve revealing discreditable information.
5. The information for this example comes from field research I conducted in the early 1990s.
6. See also E. Raufflet, 'International Businesses in the Political Economy of South Africa' (Bird et al., 2005, ch. 2, pp. 77–82). The text of the Global Sullivan Principles of Social Responsibility is available online at http://www.thesullivan-foundation.org/gsp/principles/gsp/default.asp.

References

Abbey, D. and Jantzi, M. (2001) *The 50 Best Ethical Stocks for Canadians: High Value Investing* (Canada: Macmillan).

Anad, V., Ashford, B. and Joshi, M. (2004) 'Business as Usual: The Acceptance and Perpetuation of Corruption in Organizations', *The Academy of Management Executive*, vol. 18(2), pp. 39–53.

Beschorner, T. (2005) 'Global Governance and Social Standards', in G. Gad, S. Hiss and T. Weinhardt (eds), *Wirtschaft, Ethik und Entwickling* (Berlin: Wissenschaftliche Verlag), ch. 2.

Bird, F. (1981) 'Paradigm and Parametres for the Comparative Study of Religious and Ideological Ethics', *Journal of Religious Ethics*, vol. 9(2), pp. 157–85.

Bird, F. (1996) *The Muted Conscience: Moral Silence and the Practice of Ethics in Business* (Westport, CT: Quorum Books).

Bird, F. (2003) 'The Value Added Approach to Business Ethics', *Zietschrift fur Wirtschafts- und Untenehmensethik*, vol. 4(2), Autumn.

Bird, F., Raufflet, E. and Smucker, J. (eds) (2005) *International Business and the Dilemmas of Development* (London: Palgrave Macmillan).

Caux Roundtable (2000) *The Caux Round Table Self-Assessment Process*, Draft 3 (unpublished).

Commons, J. R. (1893) *The Distribution of Wealth* (New York: Macmillan).

CPGMWG (2002) Consumer Protection in the Global Market Working Group, *The Desirability and Feasibility of ISO Corporate Responsibility Standards*. Report to the ISO Consumer Policy Committee (unpublished).

Cragg, W. and Woof, W. (2000) 'Legislating Against Corruption: International Markets and the Story of the FCPA' (Toronto: York University) (unpublished).

Culbert, S. A. and McDonough, J. J. (1980) *The Invisible War: Interests at Work* (New York: John Wiley and Sons).

The Economist (2005) 'Adecco', 19 May.

Entine, J. (1994) 'Shattered Image', *Business Ethics*, September–October, pp. 23–8.

EthicsScan Canada (2004) 'Integrated Energy Companies: Ethical Performance Comparison', *Corporate Ethics Monitor*, vol. 16(2), pp. 18–24.

Ewing, D. W. (1989) *Justice on the Job: Resolving Grievances in the Non-union Workplace* (Boston: Harvard Business School Press).

Global Reporting Initiative (2000) *Sustainability Reporting Guidelines on Economic, Environmental and Social Performance* (Boston).

Gonella, C., Pilling, A. and Zadek, S. (1998) *Making Values Count: Contemporary Experience in Social and Ethical Accounting, Auditing, and Reporting* (London: Certified Accountants Educational Trust).

Graves, S. B. and Waddock, S. A. (1994) 'Institutional Owners and Corporate Social Performance', *Academy of Management Journal*, vol. 37(4), pp. 1034–46.

Griffin, J. and Mahon, J. (1997) 'The Corporate Social Performance and Corporate Financial Performance Debate: Twenty-five Years of Incomparable Research', *Business and Society*, vol. 39(1), pp. 5–31.

Guba, E. and Lincoln, Y. S. (1989) *Fourth Generation Evaluation* (Thousand Oaks, CA: SAGE).

Howard, K. et al. (1998) *The Practice of Social Reporting for Business: Linking Accountability, Sustainability and Reputation* (London: AccountAbility).

Hutton, R. B., D'Antonio, L. and Johnsen, T. (1998) 'Socially Responsible Investing: Growing Issues and New Opportunities', *Business and Society*, vol. 37(3), September, pp. 281–305.

ICHRP (February 2002) 'The International Council on Human Rights Policy', *Beyond Volunteerism: Human Rights and the Development of International Legal Obligations of Companies* (Geneva).

Isaacs, W. (2000) *Dialogue: The Art of Thinking Together* (New York: Currency).

Kaplan, J. M. (2001) 'The Sentencing Guidelines: The First Ten Years', *Ethikos* (November–December).

van der Lugt, C. (2004) 'Growing Big, Learning that Small is Beautiful', in M. McIntosh, S. Waddock and G. Kell (eds) *Learning to Talk* (Sheffield: Greenleaf).

Mackenzie, C. and Lewis, A. (1999) 'Morals and Markets: The Case of Ethical Investing', *Business Ethics Quarterly*, vol. 9(3), July, pp. 439–52.

Margolis, J. D. and Walsh, J. P. (2003) 'Misery Loves Companies: Re-thinking Social Initiatives by Business', *Administrative Science Quarterly*, vol. 48, pp. 268–305.

McIntosh, M., Waddock, S. and Kell, G. (eds) (2004) *Learning to Talk* (Sheffield: Greenleaf Publishing).

McKague, K. (ed.) (2003) *Compendium of Codes of Conduct and Instruments of Corporate Responsibility* (Toronto: Voluntary Codes Research Group, York University).

Miceli, M. P. and Near, J. P. (1992) *Blowing the Whistle: The Organizational and Legal Implications for Companies and Employees* (New York: Lexington Books).

Moffet, J., Bregha, F. and Middelkoop, M. J. (2004) 'Responsible Care: A Case Study of a Voluntary Environmental Initiative', in K. Webb (ed.), *Voluntary Codes: Private Governance, the Public Interest, and Innovation* (Ottawa: Carleton University Press), pp. 177–208.

Mollenhauer, L. (2000) *Benchmarks of Excellence for the Voluntary Sector: Facilitator's Guide*. Co-sponsored by ALS Society of Canada and Health Canada (Toronto: Canadian Centre for Philanthropy).

Norman, W. and MacDonald, C. (2004) 'Getting to the Bottom of "Triple Bottom Line"', *Business Ethics Quarterly*, vol. 14(2), pp. 243–62.

Patton, M. (1997) *Utilization-Focused Evaluation* (Thousands Oaks, CA: SAGE).

Pearson, R. and Seyfang, G. (2001) 'New Hope or False Dawn?' in *Voluntary Codes of Conduct, Labour Regulation and Social Policy in a Globalizing World* (Thousand Oaks, CA: SAGE).

Pellizzari, P. (2002) *Conscious Consumption: Corporate Social Responsibility and Canadian Grocery Giants* (Toronto: Ethics Scan Canada).

Rhone, G. T., Clarke, D. and Webb, K. (2004a) 'Two Voluntary Approaches to Sustainable Forestry Practices', in K. Webb (ed.), *Voluntary Codes: Private Governance, the Public Interest, and Innovation* (Ottawa: Carleton University Press), pp. 249–72.

Rhone, G. T., Stroud, J. and Webb, K. (2004b) 'Gap's Code of Conduct for Treatment of Overseas Workers', in K. Webb (ed.), *Voluntary Codes: Private Governance, the Public Interest, and Innovation* (Ottawa: Carleton University Press), pp. 209–66.

Rodrik, D. (1999) *The New Global Economy and Developing Countries: Making Openness Work* (Washington, DC: Overseas Development Council).

Royal Dutch/Shell Group (1998) *Profits and Principles: Does There Have To Be a Choice? The Shell Report* (London).

Royal Dutch/Shell Group (1999) *People, Planet, and Profits: An Act of Commitment: The Shell Report* (London).

Royal Dutch/Shell Group (2000) *How Do We Stand? People, Planet, Profits: The Shell Report* (London).

Royal Dutch/Shell Group (2001) *People, Planet and Profits: The Shell Report* (London).

Ruggie, J. G. (2004) 'The Theory and Practice of Learning Networks: Corporate Social Responsibility and the Global Compact', in M. McIntosh, S. Waddock, and G. Kell (eds), *Learning to Talk: Corporate Citizenship and the Development of the UN Global Compact* (Sheffield, UK: Greenleaf Publishing Ltd).

Ryan, J. A. (1906) *A Living Wage: Its Ethical and Economic Aspects* (New York: Macmillan).

Salamon, L. M. (2002) 'The New Governance and Tools of Public Action: An Introduction', in L. M. Salamon (ed.), *The Tools of Government: A Guide to the New Governance* (Oxford: Oxford University Press).

Schoenberger, K. (2000) *Levi's Children: Coming to Terms with Human Rights in the Global Marketplace* (New York: Atlantic Monthly Press).

Senge, P. et al. (1994). *The Fifth Discipline Field Book* (New York: Doubleday).

Sethi, S. P. and Williams, O. F. (2001) *Economic Imperatives and Ethical Values in Global Business: The South African Experience and International Codes Today* (Notre Dame, IN: Notre Dame University Press).

Steers, J. (2003) 'The Sentencing Commission's Implementation of Sarbanes-Oxley', *Federal Reporter*, vol. 15(4), pp. 263–69.

Stith, K. and Cabranes, J. (1998) *Fear of Judging: Sentencing Guidelines in the Federal Courts* (Chicago: University of Chicago Press).

Stone, C. (1975) *Where the Law Ends: Social Control of Corporate Behaviour* (New York: Harper and Row).

TCCR (1998) Task Force on Churches and Corporate Responsibility, *Principles for Global Corporate Responsibility: Bench Marks for Measuring Business Performance* (Toronto: Interfaith Centre for Corporate Responsibility).

TCCR (2000) Task Force on Churches and Corporate Responsibility, 'Benchmarks for Measuring Business Performance', unpublished report (Toronto: Interfaith Centre for Corporate Responsibility).

Thomas, T., Schermerhorn, J. R., Jr. and Hienhart, J. W. (2004) 'Strategic Leadership of Ethical Behaviour in Business', *The Academy of Management Executive*, vol. 18(2), May, pp. 56–66.

Trevino, L. K. and Brown, M. E. (2004) 'Managing to be Ethical: Debunking Five Business Ethics Myths', *Academy of Management Executive*, vol. 18(2), May, pp. 69–81.

United Way (1999) *Achieving and Measuring Community Outcomes: Challenges, Issues, Some Approaches* (United Way of America); also available online at http://national.unitedway.org/files/pdf/outcomes/cmtyout1.pdf.

Waddock, S. A. and Graves, S. B. (1997) 'The Corporate Social Performance-Financial Performance Link', *Strategic Management Journal*, vol. 18(4), pp. 303–19.

Waters, J. A. (1978) 'Catch 20.5: Corporate Morality as an Organizational Phenomenon', *Organizational Dynamics*, Spring, pp. 3–19.

Waters, J. A. and Chant, P. D. (1982) 'Internal Control of Management Integrity: Beyond Accounting Systems', *California Management Review*, vol. 24(3), pp. 61–6.

Webb, K. (2004) *Voluntary Codes: Private Governance, the Public Interest and Innovation* (Ottawa: Carleton University Press).

Westley, F. (1990) 'Microdynamics of Inclusion: Middle Managers and Strategy', *Strategic Management Journal*, vol. 11, pp. 337–52.

Zadek, S., et al. (1999) *AccountAbility 1000 (AA 1000) Framework: Standards, Guidelines, and Professional Qualifications* (London: Institute of Social and Ethical Accountability).

Zadek, S. (2001) *The Civil Corporation: The New Economy and Corporate Citizenship* (London: Earthscan Publications, Ltd.).

Zadek, S. (2004) 'The Path to Corporate Responsibility', *Harvard Business Review*, (December), pp. 1–8.

7

Monitoring Labour Conditions of Textile Manufacturing: The Work of COVERCO in Guatemala

Sylvie Babarik

A number of initiatives have sought to monitor companies' adherence to corporate codes of conduct. These range from large, multi-stakeholder initiatives to the more modest efforts of non-governmental organizations (NGOs). This study focuses on one of the latter; a small NGO referred to as COVERCO. Its full Spanish name is 'Comisión para la Verificación de Códigos de Conducta' or 'Commission for the Verification of Codes of Conduct'. The group emerged in Guatemala for the purpose of promoting the rights of workers in clothing manufacturing plants. COVERCO has also conducted studies of the working conditions of workers in Guatemala's coffee and electrical sectors. It proposed to do so by monitoring adherence to corporate codes of conduct, particularly those of its two most important clients: the American companies Gap Inc. and Liz Claiborne Inc., which hired COVERCO to monitor the Guatemalan factories of some of their East-Asian-owned suppliers, and worked with the group for a number of years. This paper looks at COVERCO's operations during the period between 1999 and 2002.

Though the scope of the COVERCO experience may seem limited, it illustrates some of the tensions NGO monitors must work with, as well as the difficulties involved in developing and adapting a monitoring methodology. COVERCO's experience also offers some important lessons about the enforcement of corporate codes of conduct.

Codes and textiles

The 1990s saw an increase in anti-corporate campaigns aimed at highlighting poor working conditions in many clothing factories in developing countries. European and North American consumers heard repeated tales of abuses of workers by brand-name manufacturers, or by those manufacturers from which the brands were buying their products. Scandals spread from companies like Nike and Gap, to Cathy Lee Gifford's brand of clothing. Many were accused of profiting from sweatshops.

In the United States, politicians stepped in with initiatives like President Clinton's 1997 Multi-fibre Agreement. It demanded that companies work with other stakeholders, in the name of organizational or social learning (Utting, 2002). Europeans were quick to pick up the issue with similar initiatives. As a result, a number of new associations (among others, the Fair Labor Association (FLA) in the United States) were formed to bring the players together: brand-name companies, organized labour and advocacy and church groups. Their first task was often to draw up a code of conduct and standards by which behaviours could be measured. Their second task – to develop methods of verifying that codified rules were being respected – proved to be more difficult.

Multi-stakeholder initiatives were not the beginnings of corporate codes of conduct. Prior to the upsurge of popular pressure, some companies had drawn up their own internal regulations to uphold decent standards, as they defined them. When codes of conduct were presented as an alternative to increased government intervention, many businesses approved. Though advocacy groups would have preferred obligatory measures, many also accepted the idea of codes of conduct for their promise of speedier improvements. New national and international laws would have taken much longer to implement and might never have been passed at all. As for governments, even if there had been political will for tougher regulations under existing legislation, enforcement would have been a problem. In some countries, where business alliances were valued above the rights of workers, there would not even be the will to enforce new regulations.

What independent code initiatives quietly eroded was the idea that all workers should enjoy the same protections. Where they exist, most codes contain similar standards on matters such as minimum working age, abuse, and discrimination. However, there is little consistency among the different initiatives on matters of freedom of association, occupational health and safety, training, and health services (Pearson and Seyfang, 2001; Jenkins, 2001; Utting, 2002). As the production of corporate codes of conduct became a small industry, companies adopted various sorts of principles. Assuming they were being seriously implemented, workers in the same country, working for different corporations, would have different codified assurances.

An additional problem with many codes of conduct is that their content does not necessarily reflect the conditions and concerns of many of the workers whom they are supposed to protect. Most codes are written by people living in wealthy northern countries. As a result, they emphasize the values of such societies, overlooking the priorities of the southern workers whose interests need protection. For example, in situations where there are many female workers finishing their shifts late in the evening, transportation becomes a particularly important issue, especially in places without a safe and reliable public transportation system. However, few codes take this need into account. In Guatemala, most factories are not located in the cities, but rather are situated within a 100-kilometre radius of the city centre. Most factories therefore provide bus service for their workers; but provisions to ensure that the service is not arbitrarily discontinued are rarely included in factory codes of conduct. When COVERCO documented problems of workers being denied busing services, there was no way to file a written complaint. COVERCO had to try and convince the brand-name companies, Gap and Liz Claiborne, that even though their codes of conduct had not been violated, the factories should provide reliable busing for workers.

Without adequate verification methods, even the most perfectly drafted corporate code of conduct always risks becoming a dead letter. In 1998, the International Labour Organization (ILO) published a report that suggested that company codes were not being monitored in a convincing manner (ILO, 1998). A review in 1999 found that 41 per cent of the codes of conduct made no mention of monitoring, while 44 per cent of the companies that did mention it used self-monitoring instead of third-party monitoring. (Kolk et al., 1999). A year later, the Organization for Economic Co-operation and Development (OECD) reviewed 246 codes. It found that only 10 per cent of codes included provisions for monitoring by external, independent parties (OECD, 2000). Such findings fed into the perception that corporations were drawing up codes of conduct simply to placate their critics.

COVERCO's first years

COVERCO came along during the period of debate on allegations of workers' rights abuses in Guatemala's growing textile industry[1] and the elimination of sweatshops through code of conduct initiatives. It was founded in 1997 by a handful of Guatemalan professionals whose fields included education, sociology, business administration and communications. They recognized that proving the existence of and extent of abuses was an important first step to change given that Guatemalan factories are closed to observers, including regular watchdog groups such as unions and rights activists.

As members of COVERCO began to outline the group's mandate, methodology and principles, they sought help from US labour experts.[2] Those relationships led to contact with US corporations, beginning with Liz Claiborne Inc. The American apparel company had been trying to monitor operations in its foreign suppliers with the help of a company monitor. However, given a climate where internal monitors were looked upon with suspicion, the Liz Claiborne decided to experiment with third-party verification of its code of conduct. For its pilot project, in 1999, it hired COVERCO to monitor two Guatemalan factories.[3]

One of the challenges in initiating the project was gaining the effective cooperation of factory managers. Though usually responsive to the desires of their American client, the managers were not actually employed by Liz Claiborne. Most were at the service of larger supplier companies based in Asian countries.[4] Moreover, none of the managers were eager to operate under regular scrutiny. They had enjoyed a climate in which visits by the Guatemalan Ministry of Labour were rare. The only other party able to question the state of working conditions was the Liz Claiborne representative, whose main concern was for the American firm, not for the workers. What COVERCO was proposing was to conduct frequent visits over a prolonged period of time, with emphasis placed on the well-being of workers. Managers likely foresaw that having labour rights monitors in the factories was going to change the work environment in a way that they might not like. They opposed the monitoring at the outset.

Given their initial resistance to the project, managers were not particularly cooperative with COVERCO monitors when the work began. Though they usually granted access to the factories, the managers did their utmost to hinder free interaction between monitors and workers. When monitors asked to review employment documents, factory managers frequently made them wait or found excuses to deny them all the files that they needed. Liz Claiborne had to step in to right the situation a few times. However, with time, and with pressure exerted on the factories by Liz Claiborne, some of the tensions were reduced. When COVERCO began to work with Gap in 2000, similar problems arose initially, but they too were solved with intervention from the company.

COVERCO's methodology

Before COVERCO began working with Gap and Liz Claiborne suppliers, the companies had to convince their suppliers to tolerate independent monitors inside factories.[5] Unfortunately, COVERCO was not privy to the types of negotiations that went into setting up monitoring projects. The group was also kept in the dark about factories that rejected a brand-name company's request for independent monitors. Gap had roughly a dozen Guatemalan factories regularly producing garments; but COVERCO was able to monitor only six. Therefore, conditions in other factories remained a mystery. As casual observers, COVERCO workers would read news items referring to fairly widespread worker mobility and vocal complaints from workers when a factory abruptly shut down – all these might raise suspicions; but clear cases of ill-treatment were not the sort of information the brand-name companies were quick to share with the NGO.

Once all parties agreed to a monitoring project, COVERCO's first step was to meet with factory bosses to explain the monitoring process. Factory managers were told about the types of problems that would be recorded and were informed about the lines of communications: COVERCO would deal with the brand company, leaving problem resolution up to negotiations between the brand company and the factory. Managers were told that they must comply with all reasonable requests for information and grant the monitors unrestricted access to facilities and workers. Monitors, for their part, promised to avoid interrupting production and to respect rules of confidentiality about production methods or names of workers and managers. These ground rules were often reiterated and fine-tuned as the monitoring projects took their various courses.

Following the meeting with factory officials, the next step was a general meeting with all workers. Monitors introduced the project to hundreds of workers in group meetings, without any managers present; this helped people differentiate between COVERCO and the factory. Monitors told workers how they could report problems and promised to protect the identity of all of those who brought complaints forward. They indicated that the more information the brand was given about the factory environment, the more improvements would be possible. At the same time, monitors stressed that their role was not to act as workers' representatives: their job was to record incidents, not lobby directly for change. However, they would indicate existing complaint mechanisms that workers might use to solve some of their problems.

Once past the initial stage, monitors visited factories every two weeks to observe and document conditions inside.[6] They typically spent about six hours on location examining the physical state of the factory, gathering information from workers and studying administrative practices. Because it was impossible to cover all areas of the work environment during every visit, monitors drew up agendas. Priority was usually given to investigating complaints brought by workers. Monitors also tried to follow up chronic problems and searched for previously undetected issues.

Most COVERCO visits were unannounced to prevent managers from creating artificial working conditions in advance. However, there were occasions when monitors warned a factory of an upcoming visit so as to ensure adequate access to specific information or facilitate interviews.

Monitors usually gathered complaints from workers during the factory lunch break to avoid disrupting production. However, there were investigations that demanded that interviews be conducted while people were still on the job. In such cases, COVERCO selected a sample of workers to help conceal the identity of a person who had complained. Interviewing samples was also a useful way to get a larger sense of a particular problem or allegation.

Monitors also used a sampling method in reviewing a factory's employment documents. For instance, when looking for problems like unsigned contracts, improper payment of wages or special requests for time off (particularly for medical appointments), they would ask managers to provide the files of 5 to 10 per cent of the workforce. COVERCO always made the sample selection to ensure that they were not shown files that were better than the norm. Another way to avoid managerial interference was to try and conceal from factory officials the nature of investigations. Afterwards, monitors wrote up and submitted their reports to the brand which then had the responsibility of lobbying the factory to make improvements or correct problem situations. However, the brand was denied the right to actually hand over a COVERCO report to a factory. It also had to guarantee that workers who complained would remain anonymous in discussions with the factory.

Aside from document review and worker interviews, monitors also conducted occasional interviews with managers. These were necessary in cases where a worker's version of an event had to be compared to that of someone in charge. In other instances, monitors got a better sense of operations in a factory when they assessed a manager's reaction to a problem. Interestingly, the longer monitors spent in most factories, the more common it was to find informal, cordial relationships developing between the managers and the monitors. However, monitors were taught to beware of getting too friendly with managers, some of whom would offer meals, gifts and other favours that might have compromised the monitors' position.

COVERCO's most important relationship was with the brand-name clients. Interactions usually centred on the information gathered in the factory, with monitors sending the brand-name client their written reports. There were also telephone exchanges and occasional meetings where discussions included some fine-tuning of the monitoring process. For example, Gap and COVERCO jointly developed new tools to better report and codify labour violations. Part of the success of the interactions came from the fact that Gap had its own internal monitors, who understood workers' rights. Gap had created an actual department within the company to monitor the conditions in its supplier firms, with its own representatives specifically mandated to make sure factories around the world were following the law and Gap's code of conduct. The Liz Claiborne representative's job, on the other hand, was mainly to ensure that the partner factories, which he visited only occasionally, were meeting the brand's production needs; attention to worker rights remained a real but, a secondary concern.

When it came to identifying problems, COVERCO referred to four written standards: (1) the factory's internal regulations, (2) the brand-name company's corporate code of conduct, (3) national labour laws, and (4) international labour treaties. Using all four types of documents ensured that regulatory loopholes were fairly well sealed. For example, there was some confusion about what Guatemala's labour code considers to be the maximum number of overtime hours. This could have become an area of contention between the brand-name companies and COVERCO, since brand-name companies' codes of conduct were no more specific. Monitors therefore turned to an International Labour Organization treaty, signed by Guatemala, in which hours of work were capped at 60 per week. From there, they had a good footing to argue about excesses when they occurred.

COVERCO used the data it gathered to produce two types of reports during a monitoring period: confidential and public. The confidential reports were used to record initial observations and findings, and were handed over solely to the brand-name client, never to the factory. Such reports remained confidential from other parties as well because they potentially contained information about individual workers and supervisors, and could have revealed operational details that could have compromised a company's competitive position. Their main purpose was to indicate to a brand where problems existed and to encourage it to work with the factory to find solutions. Each subsequent report typically provided information on whether there has been successful remediation.

At the end of a monitoring period, COVERCO would take the information contained within the private reports and weave them into public ones. These were then distributed to all interested parties in the hopes of contributing to the discussion of working conditions.

COVERCO's findings

COVERCO monitors found that conditions varied a fair bit inside factories. Some of the most common problems were verbally abusive behaviour, mistreatment of women, poor industrial hygiene, constraints of freedom of association, confusing pay schemes and excessive working hours. In monitoring the Liz Claiborne plants and Gap facilities, the most common type of worker complaint was that managers or supervisors were abusive. The problem for COVERCO was that these charges were some of the hardest to prove. Examples of abusive behaviour ran the gamut from rare accusations of sexual abuse to common claims about supervisors shouting at workers. In a three-year period between 1999 and 2002, monitors recorded dozens of complaints about verbal abuse. Familiarity with a factory and its employees was key to figuring out if such complaints were well founded. When evidence was hard to come by, monitors waited to collect a series of similar complaints so as to suggest the likelihood of a pattern of abuse. Unfortunately, monitors were not in the factory often enough to observe many problems first-hand. As a result, they sometimes dismissed claims for lack of proof.

Treatment of women was another area where monitors found frequent problems. From 1999 to 2002, between 62 and 84 per cent of the workers in COVERCO-monitored factories were women. Still, managers did not always respect Guatemalan laws relating to gender, particularly with respect to pregnancy and motherhood. For example, some workers in Gap and Liz Claiborne factories complained that managers avoided hiring pregnant women. Monitors could not find any smoking gun to back the claim. However, during the year 2001, monitors noticed that at one factory some workers had written on their job applications that they were not pregnant. As such information cannot be part of a person's application form, it must have been solicited by the factory. Monitors also heard rumours of certain factories forcing applicants to undergo pregnancy tests. However, other than the generalized verbal reports, there was no evidence of such a practice.

Despite the fact that Guatemalan law protects pregnant workers from being fired, COVERCO recorded a few cases where expectant mothers were dismissed. Most were let go during their trial period, saving the factory from having to justify the cause of the firing. Monitors also recorded situations where managers undertook measures that negatively affected pregnant workers: denying women their legally mandated breaks, denying them overtime opportunities, and shifting them into departments where they would earn lower wages. COVERCO's theory was that managers were trying to discourage pregnant workers so as to make them quit their jobs voluntarily.

In the seven factories where COVERCO has had a regular presence, monitors heard of only a few cases of sexual harassment or abuse. In one instance, groups reported that a worker who was allegedly assaulted by a supervisor was pressured into quitting when she could not prove her story. COVERCO did not succeed in having her reinstated. In a different factory, there was a period of time during which workers repeatedly complained that the staff doctor was touching patients in inappropriate ways. It took the factory a couple of months to react to the allegations brought forth by COVERCO, but eventually the doctor was dismissed.

Investigating wage problems was another tough task for monitors. Factories often used confusing methods to determine a worker's pay, which consisted of Guatemala's legal minimum wage, plus a number of factory bonuses and some national bonuses. Problems arose because of apparent subjectivity of many of the factory bonuses and the way that the factories interpreted the legally mandated one. Moreover, record-keeping was very poor, complicating the job of breaking down a pay-envelope.

Guatemalan law states that it is illegal to force, or try to force a worker into working overtime. However, at all factories monitored by COVERCO, there were complaints that overtime was mandatory. When monitors investigated the matter, management would usually deny coercing people to stay late. There was one exception when, in a time of heavy production, a top manager at a Liz Claiborne supplier said that worker 'cooperation was required'. There were also a couple of cases where managers admitted to abuses of the law, but laid the blame on individual supervisors.

The factories to which COVERCO had access appeared to be fairly safe and well maintained. However, monitors did come across problems in certain factories, ranging from issues of cleanliness to safety. Washrooms were an area where standards of hygiene were sometimes neglected. However, in a couple of factories, what really troubled workers was controlled access to washrooms. Though Gap and Liz Claiborne have codes of conduct that should protect workers from such limitations, some factories controlled how long each worker spent in the washroom, apparently so as to avoid production slowdowns. In one factory, there were complaints that three minutes was the maximum time for a trip to the toilet. In a couple of other instances, the problem was long waits for washroom permissions. Supervisors controlled who could go and relieve themselves and when by way of a system of permission slips.

Typical safety problems concerned excessive noise levels in the factories, inadequate attention to the use of protective equipment, use of potentially dangerous chemicals for stain-removal, passageways blocked by boxes of finished goods or bolts of fabric, and blocked or locked emergency exits. Because COVERCO did not employ a professional industrial hygienist or safety engineer, proving these violations was sometimes difficult. When COVERCO was able to document a physical problem with a factory's installations, change was often slow. A review of the monthly confidential reports sometimes showed an almost comical repetition of the same problems. Broken stall doors in bathrooms, dirty cafeteria tables, or locked emergency exits were the type issues that seemed to reoccur regularly in some factories.

In July of 2001, freedom of association became the focus of COVERCO monitoring at the two factories producing for Liz Claiborne. Some of the workers there formed unions.[7] Trouble began as soon as the union leaders sought accreditation. A small number of their peers on the production line began threatening them, apparently encouraged to do so by supervisors and managers. At the height of the tensions, about a dozen union members were allegedly forced to resign. It took international attention and intervention by the Guatemalan Ministry of Labour to obligate the factories to hire back the workers. COVERCO interceded with Liz Claiborne representatives to ensure that union workers were hired back and that they be spared further intimidation. COVERCO argued that if the factory did not ensure a safe working environment the alternative could be seen as passive encouragement of the anti-union movement. The monitoring group also asked Liz Claiborne to draft a letter to workers stating that it would not cancel its contract with the factory as a result of the union. Some factory officials had been scaring employees with the idea that Liz Claiborne was anti-union and would therefore cancel its contract with the factory.

During the height of the unionization shake-up, COVERCO briefly found itself in an uncomfortable position of being resented both by management and by the union. At one point, union representatives suggested that

COVERCO monitors could not be trusted because of the relationship with Liz Claiborne officials. At other times, the union leaders accused COVERCO monitors of trying to take their place, acting as worker-representatives. Interestingly, there was a similar charge from managers, who suggested that it was the example of COVERCO that encouraged workers to seek union accreditation. Eventually, harsh feelings on both sides did die down, though the apparent weakness of the union may have been partly responsible.

COVERCO's principles

COVERCO identified several principles that it sought to uphold in its work. It tried to be independent, 'non-substitutive', transparent, multidisciplinary and accurate. Aside from helping to describe the group's ideals, referring to these principles is a useful way to evaluate its work.

The principle of 'independence' describes the organization as seeking to place itself apart from the process it seeks to monitor. COVERCO operated by communicating with all members of the economic community: workers, employers, other NGOs and union groups. However, it tried to keep some distance from each of these types of players so as to avoid charges of bias. However, statements about independence did not guarantee that the ideal was realized. For example, although COVERCO laid claim to its findings and publications, it could not have operated without the support of its brand-name clients. The group received most of its income from the fees it charged for monitoring services. If COVERCO's two main clients, Liz Claiborne and Gap, had decided to stop using its services it is hard to imagine how the group would have survived. Moreover, the end of a relationship with a brand would also have meant the end of access to factories – leaving COVERCO in the position of a being a monitoring group with no factories to monitor.

The idea of being 'non-substitutive' is connected with the issue of independence. The term is used to suggest that COVERCO would not act as a representative of the factory management, the brand-name company, or the workers. It tried to avoid direct involvement in factory issues, observing, studying and documenting events at arm's length. However, this ideal was more complicated in practice than in principle. For example, when disgruntled workers brought a problem to the attention of COVERCO, they sometimes had the expectation that monitors would act on their behalf. And in a sense they were right, for the very act of recording and announcing the existence of a problem is a form of advocacy, in fact if not in name. By bringing forward the workers' concerns, COVERCO was acting as a de facto representative; by recording and airing complaints, it was pressuring the factories to make changes.

Though COVERCO might pride itself on coming up with the idea of being 'non-substitutive', there were others who did not value the principle as highly. Bob Jeffcott, of the Maquila Solidarity Network, a supporter of

COVERCO, has questioned the usefulness of taking an arm's-length stance. Interviewed in May 2003, Jeffcott said that he would like to see COVERCO become more involved in helping workers understand their rights through overt labour rights training. He cited GEMIES, a monitoring group in El Salvador, as an example of how monitors can more directly help workers defend themselves against rights abuses. Though Jeffcott understood the idea that an arm's-length stance could put COVERCO in a better light as far as the brand-name and the factory were concerned, he questioned whether the monitoring group was doing enough, given its interest in workers' rights.

Another COVERCO principle was transparency. The group managed to partially accomplish this objective with the publication of findings on its monitoring experiences. Such data were useful for making comparisons with other scenarios and for getting a sense of changes in the area of labour rights and working conditions. COVERCO also pursued transparency by making public its methodology and opening itself up to the scrutiny of all sorts of observers. On the other hand COVERCO had to struggle to meet this ideal, failing to publish reports as regularly as it had planned. It fell behind its targets in 2001, 2002 and 2003, when it was late in publishing both its Liz Claiborne and its Gap public reports. The effect was that other parties could not review the monitoring work in a timely manner.

With regard to being multidisciplinary, COVERCO acted as much the part as it could. Its monitors tried to be accountants, social scientists, lawyers, health and safety experts, and journalists; however, the best the group could afford were staff members able to learn enough about these areas to serve them in their inspections of factories. The group's board of directors was somewhat diversified, but many of its members did not remain active in COVERCO's regular functioning. Therefore, the claim to being multidisciplinary was not very strong.

Accuracy in reporting was the final COVERCO principle. Though it was taken very seriously, monitors sometimes struggled, due to a lack of knowledge and necessary tools. The area of industrial hygiene provides clear examples of that: monitors were not able to recognize dangerous chemicals in stain-removal departments. Monitors likewise lacked the means to measure noise pollution, something they suspected to be a problem in a number of factories. At the time when this essay was written, monitors were still without noise meters.

Upholding the principle of accuracy was also a problem when it came to details of clothing production. In the years under consideration, COVERCO had no expertise in forensic accounting. Its monitors knew how to read time sheets and payroll records, but not how to estimate production hours according to input and output. In other words, they didn't know how to calculate the time required to transform a certain number of bolts of fabric into a garment, something that would have helped in detecting excessive hours of work. Unless workers complained about excessive overtime or covert night shifts, COVERCO had no means of detecting abuses of this sort.

The COVERCO experience

Despite the difficulties that COVERCO encountered in trying to improve the working conditions of factory employees, its years of operations still bore fruit. To begin with, managers were made acutely aware of the importance that their brand-name clients placed on the treatment of workers. It was clear to monitors that the factory did have to answer to Liz Claiborne and the Gap whenever COVERCO reported problems. Moreover, factory officials were well aware that their client companies were actually paying to get such reports.

One of the clearest signs of a change of managerial attitude came through an official at one of Gap's production factories, who told two monitors that his factory had improved overall as a result of contact with COVERCO; he even asked if he could hire monitors when the Gap contract was over. On an observable level, every factory made improvements following COVERCO's reports; for example, most factories found ways to better protect those working in the hazardous areas.

COVERCO also appeared to have a positive impact on workers. With time, many grew confident enough to report problems to COVERCO, and apparently appreciated having their concerns recorded. Others were able to learn more about the channels at their disposal if they felt their rights had been violated. Monitors often reminded workers of the existence of an internal factory complaint mechanism and explained to people how they could appeal to the Guatemalan Ministry of Labour or to the courts, if necessary. Still, such information was shared with workers more on a case-by-case basis, rather than as part of a training programme. That meant that those who did not first turn to COVERCO might not learn where to go next. If COVERCO changed its position on the education of workers, it might indeed have seen an erosion of its privileged position with the factory. However, the organization might have been able to avoid the activist role by insisting that some other party train workers. It could then monitor the content of labour rights workshops, as well as their frequency and their accessibility to workers.

Despite improvements in the factory conditions, COVERCO members have themselves admitted to certain shortcomings. The group's leaders have taken measures to develop reporting skills and improve the information gathering process. For example, COVERCO took part in organizing training sessions on health and safety issues for its own monitors, as well as for those of other Central American groups. It was also planning to purchase equipment to help evaluate certain suspected problems like excessive noise.

COVERCO's experience offers several lessons about the monitoring of labour codes. It points to the delicate position of monitors in a factory setting, all the while suggesting that a long-term presence is important to earning the trust of workers. It also seems clear that the lack of professional skills among its monitors may have allowed problems to go undetected. Still, COVERCO is a rare model of the way that NGO monitoring can avoid antagonistic relationships all the while benefiting workers. In trying to facilitate reflection about the workplace, and how to improve it, COVERCO has managed to become a broker of ideas: besides assisting the development of new ideas in the factory, it has been solicited for input about code initiatives in a larger sphere: specifically, members of the Fair Labor Association found COVERCO directors to be important voices on the issue of codes of conduct and monitoring.

Finally, whatever its critics (or supporters) may say, COVERCO cannot be expected to do the job of a government. Guatemalan authorities are those who should demand improvements in working conditions and teach factory workers about their rights. 'Even the strongest code of conduct is unlikely to achieve results in countries where governments fail to enforce basic employment rights' (Watkins and Fowler, 2002). Guatemala's laws look good on paper; but they are poorly enforced. They certainly helped COVERCO argue for workers' rights, at least as much as any corporate code of conduct. However, they translated into incentives for good corporate conduct without independent monitors. They were designed to allow for penalties in the face of abuses. Punishing a factory or a brand-name corporation is something far beyond the means of a small NGO.

Notes

An earlier version of this essay, translated into Portuguese, appeared in M. Griesse and F. Bird (eds) Forthcoming (2006) *Responsabilidates Sociais: Practicas de Empresas Internacioais na America Latina* (Perciciba, Brazil: Editora UNIMEP).

Most of my knowledge of COVERCO comes from a nine-month period of working with the group between August of 2001 and May of 2002. In that time I became familiar with some of the views of the group's directors as well as those of the factory monitors. As my task was to assist in the writing of both confidential and public reports, I became aware of most of the complaints that the group had recorded. I was also in a position to observe some of the reactions that COVERCO documents elicited from representatives of brand-name companies, union leaders, and other NGOs. A year after leaving the group, I was able to supplement my first-hand knowledge through document research and interviews with other member of the labour rights community.

1. Though agriculture remains the greatest source of income and the largest employer in the country, the Guatemalan government has embraced textile manufacturing as a way to provide employment. By 2002 the sector comprised some 228 apparel factories, generating over 97,000 jobs, in addition to 36 textile mills and 260 supplying accessories or providing related services (VESTEX, 2003). In 2003 the Guatemalan Export Association estimated that textiles accounted for 68.8 per cent of the country's exports (AGEXPRONT, 2003).

2. Two strong influences in the group's foundation were Business for Social Responsibility and the International Labour Rights Fund.
3. Some retail brands will hire corporate consultants to do monitoring work. Unlike COVERCO monitors, the consultants report only to their client firms, and may not have any particular mandate relating to workers' rights.
4. COVERCO has agreed to keep the names of the factories and their owners confidential.
5. Most of the information in this section can be found in COVERCO reports, dated 1999, 2000 and 2001.
6. COVERCO's target is to have monitors visit a given factory for at least six months. However, the group spent almost three years monitoring the two initial Liz Claiborne supplier-factories, and later spent two years in two Gap suppliers.
7. Until July of 2001, there had only been one successful attempt at establishing a union in a textile manufacturing plant in Guatemala. However, it was a short-lived success. In 1997, after a six-year campaign by workers, a Guatemalan factory that produced clothing for the Phillips-Van Heusen label signed a collective bargaining agreement with its employees. The factory shut down its operations a year later.

References

AGEXPRONT (2003) *Asociación Greminal de Exportadores de Productos No Tradicionales* (website), http://www.quetzalnet.com/agexpront.

COVERCO (1999) Commission for the Verification of Codes of Conduct, 'First Public Report: Independent Monitoring Pilot Project with Liz Claiborne Inc.', http://www.coverco.org/eng/media/media-2194.pdf (accessed 16 July 2005).

COVERCO (2000) Commission for the Verification of Codes of Conduct, 'Second Public Report: Independent Monitoring Pilot Project with Liz Claiborne Inc.', *Coverco* (website), http://www.coverco.org/eng/media/media-2195.pdf (accessed 16 July 2005).

COVERCO (2001) Commission for the Verification of Codes of Conduct 'First Public Report: Gap Inc. Suppliers in Guatemala', *Coverco*, http://www.coverco. org/eng/media/media-2197.pdf (accessed 16 July 2005).

COVERCO (2001) Commission for the Verification of Codes of Conduct 'Special Report: LCI's Standards of Engagement and the Unionization of Two Supplier Factories in Guatemala', *Coverco*, http://www.coverco.org/eng/monitoring.

Griesse, M. and Bird, F. (eds) Forthcoming (2006) Responsibildades Sociais: A Admininstracado de Empresas em Paises em Desenvolvimento Pericicabo, Brazil: UNIMEP.

ILO WP/SDL (1998) International Labour Organization, Working Party on the Social Dimensions of the Liberalization of International Trade, 'Overview of Global Developments and Office Activities Concerning Codes of Conduct, Social Labelling and other Private Sector Initiatives Addressing Labour Issues', 273rd session: Geneva, Switzerland, http://www.ilo.org/public/english/standards/relm/gb/docs/gb273/sdl-1-a1.htm.

Jenkins, R. (2001) 'Corporate Codes of Conduct: Self-Regulation in a Global Economy', *United Nations Research Institute for Social Development*, http://www.unrisd.org (accessed 16 July 2005).

Kolk, A., van Tulder, R. and Welters, C. (1999) 'International Codes of Conduct and Corporate Social Responsibility: Can Transnational Corporations Regulate Themselves?', http://papers.ssrn.com/sol3/papers.cfm?abstract_id=182830.

OECD (2000) Organization for Economic Co-operation and Development, 'Codes of Conduct: An Expanded Review of their Contents', Working Party of the Trade Committee (Geneva).

Pearson, R. and Seyfang, G. (2001) 'New Hope or False Dawn? Voluntary Codes of Conduct, Labour Regulations and Social Policy in a Globalizing World', in *Global Social Policy* (London: SAGE).

Utting, P. (2002) 'Regulating Business via Multistakeholder Initiatives: A Preliminary Assessment', in *Voluntary Approaches to Corporate Responsibility: Reading and Resource Guide* (Geneva, Switzerland: UN Non-Governmental Liaison Service).

VESTEX (2003) Comisión de la industria de vestuario y textiles, http://www.vestex. com.gt.

Watkins, K. and Fowler, P. (2002) *Rigged Rules and Double Standards: Trade, Globalisation, and the Fight Against Poverty* (London: Oxfam, 2002).

Part III

Acting Responsibly in the World As It Is and As We Hope It Will Become

Introduction

Frederick Bird and Manuel Velasquez

We have written this book in the hope that international businesses can make a positive difference in economically developing areas of the world today. These areas, which comprise more than half the earth's human population, suffer from high rates of poverty, malnutrition and disease. People have lower life expectancies and lower levels of educational achievement. For over a century international firms have been doing businesses in these areas – extracting minerals and oil, purchasing crops and goods, retailing products, constructing factories and physical infrastructures. In recent years the number of international firms working in these areas has increased; still more, hoping to find 'fortune at the bottom of the pyramid' (to use a phrase coined by management Professor C. K. Prahalad), are being encouraged to invest in these areas.

In order to make a constructive difference, these businesses must first realistically examine the situations in which they find themselves. Those who hope to address social problems, reduce injustices and help the people they encounter to enhance their capabilities (Sen, 1999; Nussbaum, 2000) must first assess the world as it is and see what is really possible.

Because the situations international businesses face are diverse and changing, it is not realistic to assume they can responsibly proceed by following the same set of normative guidelines everywhere in the developing world. It is not enough to invoke ideals. Nor is it useful to grade businesses against detailed sets of benchmarks for ethical and social performance, because almost all will fail the test. Rather, as an initial step toward any programme of reform, it is important to get a full sense of the world as it is, appreciating both limitations and possibilities present in each situation.

While working with community groups in impoverished areas of the United States and Canada, the community organizer John McKnight developed an approach which he called the 'asset identification' method for 'building communities from the inside out' (Kretzmann and McKnight, 1993; McKnight, 1995). The asset identification method calls for reformers to start with a thorough analysis of the local situation. The word *thorough* is crucial, as far too many studies of poor communities, whether in North America or in the developing world, focus predominantly on the problems and deficits people face, while overlooking existing assets that could be mobilized among individuals, groups and institutions in these areas. If international businesses are going to make a positive difference in developing areas, they must begin realistically to assess the world they find at their doorsteps.

The essays in Part III, which were written as companion pieces to the case studies presented in this book and its associated volumes, attempt to map dominant features of the world as it is against a normative background with regard to poverty, globalization and contrasting views of equity. Frederick Bird and Joseph Smucker write from a sociological perspective; Russell Daye, on the other hand, writes from the perspective of theology. Nonetheless all three writers seek to address the world as it is and on this basis to conjecture both about current trends and the possibilities for constructive action.

In chapter 8, 'Perspectives on Global Poverty', Bird asks what obligations businesses have in the face of global poverty. He begins by discussing the key causes of the impoverishment of households, arguing that household poverty is found where economies are underproductive either because of resource deprivation, crises (war, disease) or lack of development. Despite these obstacles, economies can become more productive through the introduction of innovative improvements in local production processes. Some innovations, such as skills development, provide capabilities that generate further development. Also of primary importance is the development of physical, social and economic infrastructures. Bird notes, however, that development efforts have not reduced poverty when based on opportunistic wealth, unsustainable resource consumption or productive innovations that remain disconnected from indigenous industries. Bird then examines the structural causes of household poverty including unemployment, low access to credit and insufficient protections for property. International businesses, Bird argues, can help alleviate the effects of these various causes of poverty. First, he suggests, business investments in developing nations can spur development, provided that such investments create 'multiplier' effects: introducing new skills or ways of accessing resources, or involving local businesses as suppliers, partners or customers. Businesses can also help reduce structural impediments by providing access to credit and contributing toward improving political infrastructures.

In chapter 9, 'Theological Responses to Economic Globalization', Russell Daye examines the role of multinationals from the perspective of a Christian theologian with extensive experience in a variety of different cultural contexts including India, Mexico, the South Pacific and South Africa. Daye sets out a Christian hermeneutics for evaluating globalization and multinationals according to three principles: (1) Everything in the created order has inherent value, (2) God has special empathy for the poor, (3) Just community is fundamental. Daye argues that multinationals and the forces of globalization have created environmental harms that have significantly violated the first of these principles. Although globalization and multinationals may have advanced the second principle by lifting many out of poverty, they have also violated it by increasing inequality, countenancing low wages, withholding life-saving HIV/AIDS drugs from the poor and creating trade imbalances. On the other hand, though globalization and multinationals have violated the third principle by destroying cultural communities, they have also created new economic opportunities, which have liberated people from certain unjust communal restrictions.

In the final essay, 'Markets, Development and Equity: Lessons from South Korea', by Joseph Smucker, we can see how moral demands can significantly affect the course of a nation's development. Smucker notes that South Korea's rapid economic development has given rise to increasing levels of dissent and social unrest focused on justice, i.e., on 'matters of equity, of competing definitions of what constitutes just procedures and just outcomes in the distribution of wealth and the distribution of citizens' rights'. Smucker describes how the authoritarian South Korean government between 1945 and the 1970s encouraged the rise of business conglomerates, the large and powerful *chaebol*, which then pushed South Korean economic development toward growth and efficiency at the expense of equity and justice. As South Korea developed, however, the resources became available to create a middle class and an increasingly active civil society that has now challenged the power of the *chaebol*. Smucker describes how these demands for social justice have led to widespread protests against unjust wages, against growing inequality and the unfair distribution of wealth. Further adding to the social disquiet has been the increase of direct foveign investments and foreign linkages with Korean enterprises since the economic crisis of 1997–1998. These developments have exposed the difficulties in resolving differences in both business objectives and cultural interpretations. Illustrating this problem is Smucker's description of contractual negotiations between a South Korean and Canadian firm. Finally, Smucker introduces the concept of *time*, arguing that individuals may endure privations in the interests of a better future, as thay were promised in South Korea, but eventually, unmet expectations will also promote social unrest.

Several basic assumptions inform these essays. One common theme involves respect for historical contingencies. As Smucker demonstrates in his essay about social changes in Korea, and, as Bird argues with respect to economic development, as countries pass through varied phases of industrialization, they face different kinds of moral challenges. The issues that have become prominent for Koreans in the 1990s were quite different than those that attracted attention 20 years earlier, when Korea was a much less industrialized society. One of the limitations of standardized approaches to ethical issues is that they overlook these historical differences.

A complementary theme is that social change of any sort, even positive social change, is inherently disruptive. As societies urbanize and industrialize, they typically become more productive in ways that raise household incomes and standards of living. In many areas international businesses have helped occasion these changes. But these changes also disrupt people's traditional patterns of life and loosen former bonds of social cohesion. Well-intentioned people who hope to enhance the standard of living in developing areas must recognize the disruptive aspects that often accompany even positive changes and seek ways make the transition less troubling. (In a similar vein, Daye notes that the changes associated with globalization leave many people, especially those concerned about social justice, feeling ambivalent.) Many business investments in economic development do not, in fact, improve productivity and some may actually reduce it. It is very important, therefore, that businesses distinguish at the outset between constructive changes and other, possibly destructive, outcomes that may be associated with these positive changes.

Sometimes international businesses operating in developing areas have aggravated local problems by sheer inattention. They often miss significant opportunities to alleviate poverty, sometimes as a result of short-term cost minimization and sometimes through mere lack of imagination. At other times, they have acted egregiously: destabilizing local governments, carelessly ravaging environments, paying suppliers unconscionably low prices, bribing officials, employing forced labour and using clever accounting to avoid taxes. They have aligned themselves with oppressive regimes, allowed or encouraged security forces to use excessive violence and exacerbated social tensions. If today some international businesses seek to act in more constructive ways, they must recognize that there are reasons why their best intentions are not always accepted at face value.

These essays take a somewhat sceptical view of the current discourse around globalization, which often seems too simple and not nearly 'global' enough. A genuinely global perspective would view all human activities, including international businesses, from the perspective of how they utilized and interacted with all of the living things and mineral systems that make up the earth as a whole. Clearly, as Bird observes, it is important to recognize that the natural resources of the earth are limited. A truly global perspective would need to begin by recognizing that much of the developing world has not yet been really incorporated into the expanding, interconnecting web of worldwide communication and commerce. From this perspective the world is unbalanced rather than flat, divided rather than borderless. From this perspective the so-called globalized world looks like a fairly large but exclusive club of industrialized countries and local elites exploiting or marginalizing those outside the charmed circle of membership.

In his *A Treatise of Human Nature* (1972), David Hume famously describes how ethicists seem in subtle ways to begin writing about the world as it is and then surprisingly move on to talk about the world as it ought to be – from statements of facts to statements of value. Interestingly, Hume himself was a master of this move. In constructing his own ethics, he begins by noting that humans everywhere in quite different ways have developed codes (many of which Hume considers arbitrary). Nonetheless, he further observes, shifting attention from the stipulations of these codes to their larger social function, they do so in order to foster beneficial ways of living. Having called attention to this common feature, Hume argues for an ethic that identifies right and wrong actions in terms of whether they promote or undermine human well-being. Hume's move was not accidental. Ethics that move people to act responsibly must be more than pious statements of ideals. They must find ways, as Hume did, of connecting their moral ideas with the world as it is, both by calling attention to the deficiencies of existing moral guidelines and by finding ways to ground any proposed moral agenda in existing human sentiments and institutions.

In this book we have been arguing that it is important for international businesses to take account of the world as it is: to learn from the positive examples and missed opportunities of other businesses, yet seek to realize their task in development by building on their assets as businesses, not as social welfare agencies. This seems integral to the process of bringing into being a world that is less unbalanced by poverty and injustice.

References

Hume, D. (1972) *A Treatise of Human Nature: Books Two and Three*, (ed.) P. S. Ardal (London: Fontana Collins).

Kretzmann, J. P. and McKnight, J. L. (1993) *Building Communities from the Inside Out: A Path Toward Finding and Mobilizing Community Assets* (Chicago: ACTA Publications).

McKnight, J. (1995) *The Careless Society: Community and its Counterfeits* (New York: Basic Books).

Nussbaum, M. (2000) *Women and Human Development: The Capabilities Approach* (Cambridge: Cambridge University Press).

Prahalad, C. K. (2005) *The Fortune at the Bottom of the Pyramid: Eradicating Poverty Through Profits* (Philadelphia: Wharton School Publishing).

Sen, A. (1999) *Development as Freedom* (New York: Anchor Books).

8
Perspectives on Global Poverty
Frederick Bird

Introduction

The proportion of the world's population that is impoverished today is somewhat smaller than it was half a century ago. However, as the world's population has dramatically increased during this time, the total number of impoverished households has at best only very marginally declined (Deaton, 2005). If we count as impoverished all those households that have incomes of less than $2 a day per person, then there were 2.3 billion poor people as the 21st century began. The existence of this many impoverished people – one out of every three human beings on earth – is outrageous in a world that has witnessed such a dramatic increase in wealth in all the industrialized and industrializing countries over the past 50 years. This increase has benefited billions, who as a result have come to enjoy appreciably higher standards of living, better health care, longer lives and more opportunities. But what about the poor? Why have they not benefited in comparable ways from the same processes of economic expansion?

Of course, many who were poor 50 to 70 years ago are no longer impoverished. There has been an appreciable decline in poverty in wealthy countries like the United States, in quickly developing countries like Taiwan, China and Malaysia and even in certain slowly developing countries such as Ghana and Nicaragua. The reduction of the extent of poverty has been especially noticeable in China in the past quarter of a century, as the country introduced markets and free-enterprise mechanisms into large areas of its economy (Tenev and Caudry, 2004). But many other areas of the world have not fared so well. Even in rural China, there is still extensive poverty, as there is in rural India and much of sub-Saharan Africa. There remain disturbingly large minorities of impoverished households in most industrialized countries as well.

In this essay, I first outline a comparative framework that will allow us to identify the factors that seem to be most influential in occasioning or reinforcing poverty, both generally and in particular contexts. I then discuss what initiatives are most likely to help reduce the extent of poverty. Clearly, the causes of poverty are not the same in all settings. If we hope to reduce the extent of poverty significantly – in keeping, for example with the UN's Millennium goal of halving the rate of poverty by the middle of the second decade of this century – then we are well-advised to explore a framework that will help to determine what kinds and combinations of efforts and policies are likely to have the most leverage in reducing poverty in various contexts.

As an editor of this book I am interested especially in what role businesses, both national and international, can play and have played either in reducing or aggravating problems of poverty. A number of groups and authors, from the UN Global Compact and the International Business Leaders Forum to economists like Nobel laureate Amartya Sen, have called upon businesses to address this challenge (Sen, 1999; Forstater et al., 2002; McIntosh et al., 2004). Professor C. K. Prahalad has especially called upon businesses to extend their operations in areas of poverty. In *The Fortune at the Bottom of the Pyramid* (2004), he has argued that businesses can make good profits while helping to eradicate poverty. Later in this essay, I will examine these arguments at greater length For the most part, however, I will be examining how larger societal factors affect the conditions and rates of poverty. The efforts individual poor people have made on their own behalf have frequently made a marked difference, but there are limits to what they can do. During the 1940s and 1950s, for example, millions of Americans, through hard work, thrift and clever ideas, overcame the poverty in which they had found themselves during the Depression years of the 1930s. They were able to do so as well because the overall economy grew, credit was extended, social insurance programmes were initiated and expanded, governments subsidized or invested in particular industries and new economic opportunities developed. At the same time, many Americans remained impoverished as a result of factors that were largely beyond their capacity to influence positively. In ways that I will later analyse in more detail, many of those who remained impoverished were unable to obtain regular full-time employment or qualify for the most generous publicly funded transfer programmes and inexpensive forms of credit.

For the purposes of this study I will focus on the economic condition of households, since this chiefly determines whether individuals – especially children, the elderly or handicapped persons – are poor or not. Members of impoverished households are much more likely to suffer from ill health, to die in infancy, to live shorter lives, to receive inadequate nourishment and to suffer from a lack of education.

There have been many different perspectives on how to define when a household is poor. Observers have defined poverty in relation to relative or absolute income standards, minimally acceptable levels of nourishment, health care, clothing and housing, as well as arbitrary daily per capita income standards such as those used by the World Bank. For the purposes of this study I will use the word 'poverty' to indicate households living on less than US$2 per day per person and 'abject poverty' to indicate households living on less than US$1 per day per person (World Bank, 2000/2001). In practice, I think poverty is more aptly defined as such a weak command over economic resources over time that households are unable to supply themselves with adequate nourishment, clothing, housing and health care to live minimally decent lives. This minimally adequate command over material resources varies from place to place and time to time. It cannot strictly be gauged by ordinary income figures. Nonetheless, in this essay I have utilized the World Bank's figures even though they both underestimate and overestimate the extent of actual poverty in particular areas.

There are a number of reasons why the existence of such extensive poverty is today so disturbing, indeed outrageous. First, there are at present sufficient physical and technical resources globally to ensure, even while some households enjoy affluence, that no other households need suffer the degree of deprivation that defines poverty. This possibility exists now, and it has existed for some time. Before the industrial revolution it was not really possible to think of a world without extensive poverty, which indeed was the general condition in which, for centuries, most humans probably lived. Because humans now have the resources markedly to reduce poverty, it seems inhumane not to work effectively to realize this possibility. Second, the existence of so much poverty in a world of plenty is destabilizing, often not so much for the abjectly impoverished who have lost hope as for those who imagine that by force of arms they can seize a bit more goods, land, minerals or revenues for themselves and their people. To be sure, it is not necessary to be poor to be caught by these imaginings. Still, out of the conditions of poverty people are more likely to be recruited to movements prepared to use violent means to address perceived injustices (Stern, 2003). Third, poverty in many settings is occasioned by unjust transactions between those with power and wealth who seize, control and exploit the land and labour of impoverished people without due compensation for the wealth and resources they have thereby gained. Numerous examples might be cited in support of this observation, from the dispossession of lands by conquering armies and subjections of slaves to the poverty wages paid to tenant farmers, migrant workers, miners and domestics in many settings.

In a technical sense, poverty differs from powerlessness, inequality and dependency, even though it is often associated with these things. The poor often lack power to realize their own objectives and to counter and limit the hegemony of others who effectively control their resources. This lack of power is both a cause and a consequence of poverty, and many who are not impoverished may still possess only marginal power; nonetheless the dynamics and variations in this relationship are best understood by analysing poverty and powerlessness as distinguishable (if not always clearly distinct) yet interrelated realities. The relationship between poverty and *inequality* is much looser. The poor are often unequally treated; but many who are affluent also suffer from unequal treatment. Even when people are equally treated, we often believe that it is appropriate to reward them unequally in terms of the contributions they make or risks to which they are exposed. Some of the poor are dependent. But in many cases it is precisely by becoming dependent in some ways, whether upon family members, social insurance remittances, or even wages from government-subsidized industries, that individuals are able to safeguard themselves from poverty.

Overall, in relation to these immediate causes, households are likely to become or remain impoverished (1) because the economies in which they live are impoverished; or (2) because they live in households that remain marginal to otherwise flourishing economies, or for both of these causes. I will refer to the first condition as *general* causes of poverty, and to the second as *structural* causes. There is a serial relation between these different types of immediate causes. It is difficult, if not impossible, to reduce poverty by addressing the structural causes until efforts are undertaken to address the general causes of poverty.

Table 8.1   Major Causes of Global Poverty

Immediate causes	Critical factors
	These are the factors that give rise to the immediate causes. These factors vary from society to society and over time. In most cases these factors must be addressed in order to be able to alter the immediate causes
1. General Causes Impoverished households have inadequate incomes because they live within economies that are depressed as a result of: a) Deprivations and Crises b) Underdeveloped Economies	
2. Structural Causes Impoverished households have inadequate incomes because they remain or have become marginal to, or excluded from: (a) The labour force (b) The most generous forms of welfare (c) The least expensive forms of credit (d) Systems that provide adequate protection of their possessions	

General causes of poverty

Most households are poor because the economies in which they live are impoverished: that is, these economies do not produce sufficient wealth in the forms of jobs, income, goods or services so that most households can live with adequate material resources. These are, in a word, underproductive economies. In very broad terms, these economies are unproductive either (1) because of various deprivations and crises; and/or (2) because they are underdeveloped or underproductive economies. In these settings the immediate cause of poverty is a depressed economy. The critical factors are those variables that cause these economies to be depressed.

Deprivations and crises

The economies in many areas have become or remain impoverished as a result of various deprivations and crises. I have already referred to how the Depression of the 1930s impoverished millions of households throughout the industrialized countries.

This is just one well-known example of a wide range of deprivations and crises, which would include both natural factors like droughts as well as political factors like wars, that have severely depressed the economic opportunities of many local economies.

Natural factors have placed a number of areas at greater risk of poverty. For example, the likelihood that economies will be exposed to poverty is increased in areas where there is little arable land, potable water is difficult to obtain, rain is either absent or arrives in torrents, or oceans are inaccessible or distant (Landes, 1998, ch. 1, 2; Diamond, 1999, p. 44; Thomas et al., 2000, ch. 4). To be sure, it is possible to overcome some of these handicaps. Diamond (2005, ch. 7, 9) cites the examples of the Inuit in northern Canada and Greenland as well as the highlanders in Papua New Guinea who learned over many centuries to survive with meagre resources in harsh climates by working together without exhausting natural resources. Although these peoples survived, they remained impoverished. Cities like Hong Kong and Singapore have, to cite a different kind of example, learned how to thrive as commercial and manufacturing centres in spite of the absence of arable land or mineral resources. Nonetheless, these options are not available for many areas, which lack other resources or which have sought to develop at later historical times when they are at a competitive disadvantage with respect to already-developed areas. With some exceptions depressed economies are more likely to persist in places that are subjected to natural deprivations, or have experienced frequent droughts, floods, epidemics and other natural disasters (Sachs et al., 2001). To be sure, episodic droughts do not necessarily occasion famine or depressed economies. As Sen (1981) and others have argued, much depends upon how humans respond to these natural disasters, how in particular they distribute available food (see also Davis, 2001).

Nonetheless, areas regularly exposed to droughts are less able to maintain productive agricultural sectors, which in turn can disadvantage their economies generally. Epidemics are another matter. Braudel (1980) has argued that the Black Death of 1348 had a depressing impact on European economies for centuries. The epidemic diseases carried by European conquistadors and settlers were devastating to the indigenous populations of the Americas, who lacked natural resistance to these diseases; not only local economies but also entire societies collapsed as a result. Certainly the contemporary AIDS epidemic is likely to have a permanently depressing impact on the economies in southern Africa and perhaps in other areas of the world in the future (Landes, 1998, ch. 6, 8; Berger, 1999, ch. 1–3; Diamond, 1999, ch. 11).[1] As a result of these kinds of natural factors, many areas have been handicapped. They have fewer natural resources to utilize in their efforts to generate lively economies.

These conditions cannot be easily ameliorated by the dominant strategies used in most cases to overcome poverty, namely efforts to promote economic development or efforts to overcome structural factors that marginalize the impoverished in relation to otherwise productive economies. Rather, these natural deprivations and crises are best addressed directly, through endurance, mutual cooperation, hard work and aid programmes (whether mutual or philanthropic). Alternatively, many households have improved their economic prospects in these settings simply by migrating away from the areas subject to these persistent natural deprivations and crises (Galbraith, 1979; Williamson, 1999, p. 41). Not all of these out-migrants have done so well. Urban centres in the developing world have attracted large numbers of people, currently living in slums, who might fittingly be described as the displaced victims of rural poverty.

Humans have at times acted to render these natural deprivations and crises even more damaging. In the past a number of societies have exhausted their weak supply of natural resources through practices that have led to excessive deforestation, degradation of soil and depletion of freshwater reserves (see Diamond, 2005, ch. 2, 4, 5, 8). Other factors occasioned by more intentionally provoked causes have also been influential. In Africa, countries such as Sudan, Uganda, Angola and Congo have experienced prolonged periods of civil conflict resulting in widespread death, injury and property damage that have undermined ordinary patterns of commerce and industry. The longer the period of civil strife, the more profoundly and permanently impoverished the area becomes (World Bank, 2003, ch. 1). In other countries, government leaders have directly acted to depress local economies through excessive spending on pet public projects that have no direct or indirect benefits to their overall economies, and by privately pocketing public funds (Klitgaard, 1988; Cohen, 1998, pp. 9–14; Diamond, 1999, ch. 14). A number of governments have impoverished rural areas by policies that have kept agricultural prices artificially low

(Cohen, 1998, ch. 1). In many cases, publicly defended economic policies have had the effect, often not especially intended, of dramatically depressing local economies. For example, in the late 19th century the British imperial policies that forced farmers in India to switch from growing rice to growing cotton that could be sold to British textile manufacturers made it impossible for regions of the subcontinent to meet their own domestic economic needs and thus rendered them much more vulnerable to drought. While serving the needs of British industry, this policy had the effect of depressing the Indian economy (Davis, 2001, ch. 1, 2, 4, 5). Although they have proven beneficial in some areas, the Structural Adjustment Policies of the International Monetary Fund have been criticized for undermining local economies in a number of Latin American and African countries. In these settings the local economy declined as local government spending on infrastructure dropped off and as North Atlantic countries were able to utilize trade liberalization policies in targeted developing countries to sell goods at lower prices than local farmers and merchants (Ghai, 1991; Chossudovsky, 1997; Stiglitz, 2002).

The factors that give rise to these kinds of humanly caused crises are multiple and diverse and it is impossible to develop any one over-arching strategy to prevent their occurrence. To some degree, we can hope that governments, which have played a disproportionate role in giving rise to the actions causing these crises, will learn by thoughtfully reviewing past experiences. While we can argue that these kinds of crises are avoidable, it is probably the case that humans will continue to be subjected to them and those living in weak economies will be more vulnerable than those living in more robust economies. We cannot altogether eliminate the possibility of these humanly occasioned crises, whether through efforts to foster economic development or initiatives to overcome structural inequalities. Understandably these kinds of crises give rise to calls for compassion. They also occasion anger as others call for the end of government abuses though direct action.

Underproductive economies

In many situations local economies become or remain depressed because they are underproductive: that is, the people and institutions that make up these economies are unable to make full use of existing natural and human resources. From the perspective of the much more productive highly industrialized economies, we often refer to these economies as being 'undeveloped' or 'developing'. From this perspective, we assume that they can discover ways of using given human and natural assets more effectively to produce more goods and services. To be sure, for countless centuries humans supplied their basic economic needs by hunting and gathering. Later, after the discovery of agriculture and the domestication of animals, humans discovered ways to utilize given natural and human resources more effectively so they could supply more abundant goods and services. As a result of subsequent developments, humans have discovered more productive ways of utilizing available resources. This capacity to produce ever-increasing surpluses increased as links of commerce multiplied, technological discoveries unfolded and manufacturing expanded. The modern industrial revolution with its concomitant features, including the greater use of new energy sources, the application of scientific discoveries, the increased skill development of workers and the organization of factories and mass production, has even more dramatically increased productive powers (Weber, 1923/1961, parts III, IV; Braudel, 1984; Landes, 1998, ch. 13–16). It is from this perspective that we are in a position to observe economies where given human and natural resources seem by our standards to be less efficiently organized to meet the human needs and wants of local or national populations. Of course, the degree to which any specific economy is 'underproductive' varies considerably; nor should we assume that economies must necessarily develop systems of commerce, manufacturing, science and education like those found in currently industrialized societies, whether they follow Swedish, French, Japanese or American models. Nonetheless, these 'underdeveloped' economies might become more productive in any number of ways, whether in terms of past and current models, or perhaps through experiments as yet untried.

By and large, the processes of economic development are cumulative. Particular changes in the processes of production, such as introduction of modern systems of transportation, set the stage for further changes, such as the development of vertically integrated firms. Those changes that possess the greatest significance, such as the introduction of mechanization, rail and air transport, the automobile, modern accounting systems and electronic communication, are those which provide the bases for many further developments. From this perspective, the innovations that matter the most in any locale have been those with the greatest leverage for fostering further developments, such as effective literacy and training initiatives, rather than those which might produce the most income in the short term.

Productivity is best measured not by comparing profit margins, return on investment or changes in per capita national income levels. Rather, it is best measured, I argue, by gauging how effectively given natural and human resources are utilized, by comparing over reasonable periods of time all the *inputs* of resources, assessed in terms of quantity and quality, for any productive activity (from farming to manufacturing), with the *outputs* of those activities. A full accounting would examine how over specified periods of time all assets – gauged in relation to financial, productive, human, social and natural capital – were utilized, whether in the process those assets grew or diminished, and what benefits and utilities resulted (World Bank, 2003, ch. 2). If a business were to produce high returns for investors while allowing its productive assets to become worn out or obsolete, we would appropriately judge that the firm's overall level of productivity was at best mixed, assuming in the process that at least it treated its employees with dignity.

When an economy is underproductive, it fails to utilize human and natural assets so that these assets yield benefits and utilities in quantities and qualities less than we now know they are capable of yielding. In language favoured by some observers, these economies *under-appreciate* and *underdevelop* human capabilities (Nussbaum, 1999; Sen, 1999). These economies typically under-appreciate and underdevelop natural capabilities as well; as a result, they fail to produce enough goods and services such that most households in these areas are unable through their own work and investments to mobilize sufficient material resources so as to achieve a standard of living that is no longer impoverished. In varied and complex ways, which I will analyse later, these underproductive economies give rise to poverty, and a large proportion of the world's impoverished households are located in economies that have long been, or have become, underproductive. When economies become more productive, existing human and natural resources can be utilized more effectively to produce quantitatively and qualitatively greater benefits and utilities.

Economic development should not be gauged primarily in relation to higher levels of per capita income, a figure that provides only an average for a society as a whole. Per capita income may rise quite markedly because a small number of elites have been able to generate excessive wealth through their control over some lucrative segment of the economy (such as the mining of a particular mineral) while the rest of the economy operates on quite unproductive modes of labour and production. In recent years the per capita income of a number of countries has risen because one or more export-oriented enclaves has produced extensive wealth for small minorities who have been able to exploit these opportunities. However, this rise in per capita income has not reflected what has been happening in these societies generally (Broad, 1988). Overall income levels sometimes have risen because of windfall earnings or changes in exchange rates unrelated to any significant changes in overall productivity.

Economic development is best viewed in relation to changes that provide means for groups of people to make more effective and more fruitful uses of resources at their disposal in sustained ways over time. The critical factor is not just whether they produce more benefits and utilities, but whether they are developing, or have developed, the means that allow them to continue to generate from given resources these expanded outputs, and perhaps even greater outputs over time. Societies establish the 'means' that foster development both by helping members of their societies to develop their capabilities and by discovering ways to put given natural resources to more productive uses. Clearly educational and training programmes that allow people to develop their skills make a difference. So do the introduction of technological innovations that allow people to utilize given skills for more extensive and diversified operations.

It is also important to look at these 'means' from an institutional perspective, which focuses attention on those kinds of social arrangements that enable people to learn, develop skills and undertake a number of other activities integral to any advanced economy. We use the term 'infrastructures' to refer to these institutional arrangements, which multiply and assume diverse forms as societies develop and industrialize. For example, we can speak of physical infrastructures to describe transportation and communications systems as well as the water, electrical and sewage systems. We can also speak of *social* infrastructures to point to public and semi-public institutionalized social arrangements that provide education, social insurance for the aged and unemployed, welfare and access to health care. We can also, I think, usefully refer to *economic* infrastructures to identify those institutions and social arrangements – those legal institutions, offices, and commercial associations – that establish local and regional markets for trade and commerce, access to credit, rules and institutions to protect property and contracts, and that provide information about employment and investment possibilities. No less than physical infrastructures such as highways, canals and schools, these social and economic infrastructures are produced by various socially constituted agencies, organizations and networks, supported both by governmental policies and funding as well as business and voluntary initiatives (Weber, 1914/1978, pp. 666–752; Weber, 1923/1961, part IV; De Soto, 2000; Stackhouse, 2000; World Bank, 2000/2001, ch. 5, 6). To the degree that societies develop these varied physical, social and economic infrastructures, they thereby help to establish the means to foster sustained and productive utilizations of natural and human resources over time.

Generally economic development, viewed in relation to increased productivity, has been correlated with reduced rates of poverty. I have already referred to the example of the way poverty levels were steadily reduced in the United States between the 1930s and the 1960s as the overall American economy expanded. Between 1949 and 1969 there was a 27 per cent reduction in the number of impoverished households, and 80 per cent of this reduction was effected not by government spending but by economic growth, which resulted in doubling the real median family income levels (Danziger and Gottschalk, 1995, p. 102). We can observe similar patterns in other industrialized societies during this period (Dollar and Kraay, 2001). Poverty rates have markedly declined as well in countries like South Korea, Malaysia and Thailand as these countries have fairly rapidly industrialized during the second half of the 20th century.[2] As Europe industrialized over the course of the 18th, 19th and 20th centuries, the extent of poverty correspondingly receded (Braudel, 1984). Generally, economic development through higher productivity adds to the wealth and assets of societies.

Rates of poverty are much lower in societies that have been correspondingly enriched by developmental processes.

Currently those areas of the world that are least economically developed also experience the highest rates of poverty. Measured in per capita income terms, those countries with the lowest level of income are those with the least developed infrastructures commercially and industrially. They experience high rates of poverty in part because of natural deprivations as well as natural and political and crises and in part because their economies remain so unproductive. They tend as well to be those countries least connected by trade and commerce with the industrialized countries (Group of Lisbon, 1995; Legrain, 2002; UNCTAD, 2002).

Most industrialized countries contain areas with local depressed economies. These depressed locales are more likely to be found in rural areas and urban slums as well as areas populated by indigenous people (Taub, 1970; Wilson, 1987; Duncan, 1992; Milanovic, 1999). It can be instructive to identify these locales as discrete economies, which are in turn depressed and underproductive, but which possess the potential of becoming more productive. Nonetheless, in many cases these areas have become or remained underproductive because of structural factors, which I will analyse later in this study.

It is important to recognize that economic development, even when defined in relation to enhanced capabilities and infrastructural institutions, does not automatically result in lower levels of poverty. In a number of settings, economic developments have occasioned increased overall inequalities, so that while general rates of poverty have modestly declined, the relative differences in income between low-income and high-income households have become more marked (Lal and Myint, 1996; Milanovic, 1999). In some countries, economic development has been associated with modest increases in the extent of poverty, as those with the greatest wealth have used their influence to claim disproportionate shares of the rewards made possible by economic growth (Frank and Cook, 1995; Aghion, 1999, p. 39; Davis, 2001). In some places the increased buying power of these advantaged groups has driven up prices for essential goods and services, thereby reducing further the relative economic power of disadvantaged groups (Evans, 1979). Even though most industrialized countries experienced generally sustained periods of economic growth from early 1980s through the late 1990s, in these countries economic inequality generally increased and the overall extent of poverty has not appreciably changed (Danziger and Gottschalk, 1995; Milanovic, 1999). During this period, economic development in industrialized countries has not reduced poverty in the way it did between 1930 and 1970.

It is useful to reflect further on circumstances where economic development has not operated to reduce poverty. I will discuss four such circumstances.

1. There is a complex relation between growth in population and economic development. Suffice it to note that the early phases of industrialization seem to be associated with population increases, in part as death rates decline. However, as societies become highly industrialized, birth rates (with some exceptions) characteristically decline. As a result, fewer new households form and the number of households competing for the pool of societal utilities and benefits stabilizes. Where the population continues to increase and the number of households likewise grows, the corresponding competition for utilities and benefits results in a situation where fewer resources are available for the average household. Poverty rates and levels may thus remain stable or even increase, even though the general economy is becoming more productive. In highly populated areas especially, steady high rates of population growth can act to thwart the benefits of economic development. Steadily increasing population growth, for example, certainly had an impoverishing impact upon Rwanda during the 1970s and 1980s as extant arable land had to be utilized by increasing numbers of households. As plots sizes were further reduced, many households lacked sufficient land to produce adequate sustenance or income. Struggles over the land increased (Diamond, 2005, ch. 10).

Considerable controversy surrounds the topic of population policy. Should countries directly seek to limit population growth, as China has done? Or are there viable alternative strategies? In general, a case can be made for working to foster industrialization both as a valuable objective in itself as well as an effective means to slow population growth. To be sure, there are other non-intrusive ways of reducing birth rates; probably the most effective is the provision of more opportunities for women to receive education, as increased levels of education for women are correlated roughly with reduced birth rates.

2. Another factor that seems to have played a decisive role in blocking or dampening the expected benefits of increased productivity has been opportunistic wealth. I use this phrase to describe more broadly what others have discussed both in relation to the so-called 'resource curse' and the 'Dutch Disease'. In all of these cases societies have gained a great deal of wealth fairly quickly by the exploitation of mineral resources or advantageous market opportunities. This excess wealth enters the economy for reasons largely unrelated to local institutions and patterns of work. In the 16th century, for example, Spain gained enormous wealth opportunistically as a result of its conquests in the New World. More recently countries like Nigeria, Saudi Arabia and Kuwait have gained immense wealth by the discovery, extraction and marketing of oil. Other countries, such as South Africa, have gained large amounts of wealth by exploiting various minerals found in their territories. When these countries gain significant additions of wealth over short periods of time, several outcomes are likely. First, many of those directly benefiting from the increased wealth have been

prone to expend it on consumables or luxury items rather than invest it in ways more likely to help their economies develop productively over the long term. This is widely exemplified by traditional practices among many ruling elites, labouring classes and peasants (Weber, [1905] 1958, ch. 2). Second, in times of opportunistic wealth, many of those in positions of political authority have been inclined to use their offices and access to power to influence how this extra wealth will be distributed, invested, consumed or saved. Many governments have discovered that they can meet a large share of their expenses by taxes and royalties levelled on opportunistic wealth. In the process, a variety of people and institutions, both public officials and governments themselves, devote excessive portions of their time competing for and living off these supplies of opportunistic wealth, instead of seeking more diverse and long-term sources of government income and developing additional industries. Third, opportunistic wealth has often had an unbalancing impact as it enters local economies. As those with access to this wealth spend their earnings, these expenditures have had the unanticipated effect of raising overall price levels, thus forcing many businesses and households to pay more to secure the goods and services they ordinarily use. As their purchasing power declines, so does their capacity to live within their means. As a result of these several factors, genuine economic development accompanied by opportunistic wealth has seldom resulted in more productive overall economies and lower rates of poverty (Auty, 1993; Asher, 1999; Landes, 1998, ch. 12, 15; Auty, 2001).

3. It is possible to identify instances where supposed patterns of economic development have become unsustainable. Economic practices (such as mining) that deplete or exhaust particular natural resources can only be described as productive to the extent that they add sufficient economic value in the form of wages, taxes, royalties, products and marketable skills to compensate for the depletion of natural assets, provided that this depletion does not place the society at risk. One can mount a provisional case for mining operations as productive activities but only by demonstrating that these activities augment existing assets in various beneficial ways. Humans have excessively fished, hunted, lumbered and grown crops; they have drained aquifers and paved over arable lands; all these activities involved the loss of natural assets. Other such losses have resulted from the pollution of lakes, the air and the soil. Historical examples of unsustainable economic practices include the over-utilization and degradation of arable lands among the ancient Mayans, the deforestation of Easter Island and the over-grazing of lands in Australia over the past two centuries (Diamond, 2005, ch. 2, 5, 13).

It is possible to develop parallel arguments with respect to how human resources are employed. The overall productivity of economic activities that exhaust or damage their own workforces remains questionable, even if those operations result in highly valued products that generate high profits. If these activities – like the labour practices in early industrial factories of Europe – were rigorously assessed, the cost in terms of the degradation of workers should be subtracted from whatever other values these activities produced. In all of these instances, we find examples of unsustainable economic practices that reduce or degrade natural, human and social assets, with only the semblance of increased productivity.

4. In many instances investments have been made in developing areas to foster the growth of particular enterprises and industries that remain largely disconnected from indigenous industries and enterprises. For example international firms have frequently invested in developing countries in order to obtain a valued resource at a low cost, often without attempting in any way to connect these operations with local commercial networks. These kinds of internationally initiated operations existed largely as economically unconnected enclaves, in ways exemplified by (but not limited to) many of the sugar plantations in the Philippines, oil enterprises in Angola, mining operations in Papua New Guinea and *maquila* assembly plants in Mexico (Broad, 1998; Diamond, 2005, ch. 15). Correspondingly, while these operations may have generated considerable wealth, as have oil enterprises in the Middle East, gold mining in South Africa and diamond and copper mining in the Congo, these enterprises have contributed very little toward the development of local economic infrastructures (Drohan, 2003). These insular and unconnected enterprises have in places produced wealth for those few able to benefit directly or indirectly from their operations. In so far as they produced tax revenues that are then effectively invested to develop social and physical infrastructures, they have also indirectly helped to make possible conditions that can render their local economies more productive. However, these kinds of insular investments have seldom occasioned public investments (Evans, 1979).

The status of economic development in such contexts is, at best, ambiguous. From the perspective of the larger societies, these kinds of expanding economic activities, with their opportunistic wealth, unsustainable production practices, and poorly integrated enterprises have not appreciably augmented overall productivity. They have tended to generate wealth for small groups within these societies without significantly strengthening institutional arrangements, enhancing economic infrastructures or expanding the opportunities for members of these societies to develop their varied capabilities. In these instances, particular investments and enterprises have temporarily increased the amount of wealth generated in societies; but they have done so without at the same time rendering the overall economies of these societies measurably more productive.

With these examples in mind, a number of observers have argued that economic growth measured by increases in per capita income alone rarely serves to reduce poverty (Galbraith, 1979, ch. 1, 30). Development occasions underdevelopment especially in those areas that are marginal to the centres of increasing industrialization, commerce and finance. There is considerable evidence to support this claim. Many of the most impoverished areas in the world – sub-Saharan Africa, rural areas in South and East Asia and Latin America, and urban shanty-towns and slums – are not underdeveloped territories, rather they are areas whose lack of development has been reinforced by debts they cannot repay, trade obstacles to marketing their agricultural products, marked absence of investment, supply chains that under-pay and keep them trapped in unproductive work, and lack of effective political representation (Stiglitz, 2002, ch. 3; Sejjaaka, 2004). What we have in these areas is not genuine economic development but a chimera that appears like, and is sometimes mistaken for, economic development

Nevertheless, a strong case can be made that economic development that avoids these problems generally works to increase the productivity of economies and thereby to reduce the incidence and extent of poverty. By generating added wealth, economic development and industrialization also make it possible for governments to fund varied social welfare programmes – from old-age pensions and unemployment insurance to manpower training programmes and health insurance – which in turn reduce the rates and impact of poverty for low income households. Economic developments provide a basis for taxes that can in turn be used for social welfare (Holmes and Sunnstein, 1997). Acknowledging the importance of the exceptions just discussed, the strongest case for this argument emerges out of the overall historical trends. As economies of nations have developed over longer stretches of historical time, gradually interconnecting webs of local and far-flung commerce, and as they have become industrialized, the overall rates of households living in poverty have declined.

Broadly viewed, economic developments tend to engender a number of benefits: not only more productive uses of natural and human resources but also higher standards of living and lower overall rates of poverty. However, as the changes in productive systems and patterns of commerce are instituted, they occasion a number of characteristic societal changes, many of which are experienced as disruptive. Such are the economic developments that are typically associated with urbanization: increased mobility; the separation of the household from the places where family members work; and the increased economic risks occasioned by unemployment, irregular employment, work-related accidents and retirement (Polanyi, 1944). Eventually, industrialized countries have almost universally instituted various public and private social insurance schemes, from workmen's compensation and unemployment benefits to old-age pensions, to provide the basic means to support those especially put at risk as labour forces are industrialized (Titmuss, 1958; Wilensky, 1975). The beginning stages of industrialization are associated with considerable social dislocation, as people seek out employment in new jobs in different areas. While economic developments generally allow more households to enjoy higher overall household incomes, they also often occasion increases in inequality and insecurity.

If my argument thus far has been convincing, or at least plausible, then it is possible to conclude that the immediate causes of current levels and rates of poverty in a number of areas result from economies that are depressed and underproductive because these economies are in turn undeveloped or underdeveloped. This observation is important. It helps to establish priorities for poverty reduction strategies. However, we still need to consider the factors that most decisively in any area cause these economies to remain as they are. Since these factors vary greatly for different societies and different historical periods, it is critical to determine for each area what variables have exerted the weightiest influences in the past and which are most likely to leverage constructive change in the future. One of the persistent criticisms of development policies and programmes is that they are frequently imposed upon particular societies in ways that do not take adequate account of the strengths and weaknesses of their existing economies. Some critics point to the urban bias of development planners, who seek to develop modern industrial operations without trying first to reform and to make more productive the agricultural bases of these societies (Lifton, 1977). In many areas investments aimed at development have been undertaken without first working to strengthen appropriate physical, social and economic infrastructures. Several critics have argued as well that policies of fostering development by strengthening the export-oriented sectors of local societies have had the effect, at the same time, of weakening patterns of commerce and industry integral to the domestic economy (Evans, 1979; Chossudovsky, 1997; Stiglitz, 2002). Development strategies, therefore, clearly need to be constructed anew in relation to particular assets and power arrangements that play a critical role in each developing area.

At the same time, it is possible to generalize about the importance of several critical factors, which play a decisive role in all settings. These include: investment in education and skill training programmes; fostering local commerce, strengthening local legal systems, eliminating corruption, removing causes of civil strife, the development of infrastructures and the development of credit.

Over time, the scourge of poverty has been most effectively reduced through policies and practices that strengthen local economies and make them more productive. However, there have always been limits with respect to how far any economy can develop. This is especially true today. Given the size of the earth's population and its probable increases over the next half-century, there are limits to how far the economies of nations can grow. There are limits to arable land and fresh water, as well as to oil and gas as energy sources. The earth does not now possess sufficient known resources so that all of the countries of the world could consume these resources on the scale of present-day industrialized states (Brown, 1995; Diamond, 2005, ch. 16). Even if development in today's impoverished countries remains far below that of the most industrialized nations, such development will increase the overall demand upon the planet's limited resources. This increased demand, as evidenced for example in the contemporary increase in the worldwide demand for oil as increasing numbers of Chinese begin to own cars, may increase the cost of the assets in ways that disadvantage low-income countries. Although the economic development of impoverished areas aggravates the pressure on these limited resources, it is not possible morally to argue against the development of these areas, as long as such development functions to reduce general rates of poverty as well as to reduce hunger, disease and illiteracy. In the face of these limits to growth, the most highly developed nations must re-examine their own rates of consumption.

The structural causes of poverty

Whether households experience poverty to a considerable degree is affected as well by how their economies distribute resources and benefits, utilities and risks. Many households experience poverty not primarily because the overall economy is underproductive. Rather their poverty results from the unequal and unjust manner in which wealth and income are distributed – as well as the opportunities to gain wealth and income. We may use several different models for attempting to describe overall systems of economic distribution and to diagnose how effectively and how fairly they work. By comparing the income levels of the households with the highest incomes with households with the lowest incomes, economists have established overall indicators of inequality. When we compare many counties using these indices, we discover, for example, that Brazil and South Africa are among societies with the highest discrepancy between income levels at the top and the bottom. For the purposes of this study I have adopted a different perspective. I focus attention especially on impoverished households as a kind of economic class – what might be referred to as an underclass – with a comparable relation to the sources of wealth. What characterizes these households when they are viewed from this perspective is that they face similar impediments in terms of their access to the major sources of income and wealth. Thus, I address the larger questions about how effectively and how fairly economies distribute resources and benefits by examining as a more focused subject of attention the structural factors that affect the opportunities of impoverished households to gain income and wealth. Accordingly, I do not attempt to determine whether particular political systems or economic philosophies are more effective or fair as systems of distribution. Rather, I call attention to structural factors that frustrate and impede the opportunities of the poor.[3]

In developed and developing economies alike, many households remain or become impoverished because of social factors which render these households external or marginal to the economy of their own society.

I describe and analyse these factors as the structural causes of poverty. As in the previous discussion, I will distinguish between the structural causes that directly marginalize impoverished households and the critical factors that give rise to these structural causes. I define and discuss the structural causes of poverty in relation to factors that immediately affect household budgets, looking for the most part at the relationship of households to the basic sources of income and wealth – namely, employment, transfer entitlements, access to credit and protections for property – as well as variations in household expenses. The income and wealth of impoverished households may suffer from one or more of these causes. Typically these factors are cumulative and mutually reinforcing in ways that render them difficult to overcome.[4]

1. Many households become or remain impoverished because they receive little or no income from employment. Members of impoverished households experience disproportionately higher rates of unemployment and under-employment. Viewed comparatively, members of impoverished household spent significantly fewer hours per year working for pay, at whatever levels, than do members of non-impoverished households. Insofar as they are able to find employment, members of these households are much more likely to work part-time or part-year. Over the past two decades, the under-employment problem, where workers in conditional labour markets work part-time or part-year, has become much more severe (Butless, 1990; Parker, 1994; Klein, 2000, part 3). Official unemployment rates frequently obscure this problem. Over the course of several years, members of these households are often periodically employed and unemployed and under-employed. Their overall household income levels occasionally rise above and fall below the official poverty lines. Over time, they generate few assets. When members of these households do work, whether full-time or part-time, they frequently receive much lower wages (Levitan et al., 1993; Cohen, 1998, ch. 4, 5). It is important to observe, at this point, that in all of these cases the incomes of impoverished households are reduced primarily as a result of factors associated with the character and number of jobs at which they are employed or not employed, rather than with the characteristics of the workers themselves. To be sure, members of impoverished households disproportionately end up in these jobs. Nonetheless it is the jobs themselves that produce inadequate flows of income because they are too few in number, offer limited hours for working and pay low wages.

Often observers commenting on the labour force participation of people from impoverished household focus not on the character of these jobs but either on characteristics of the poor themselves or on the patterns of discrimination from which they suffer. These are, to be sure, relevant considerations with regard to factors affecting the supply of workers to jobs. It is important to recognize that poor people have lower labour force participation rates in part because their households are disproportionately constituted by adults who cannot readily work for pay – in large part because the adult members who might seek employment are old, handicapped or already busy caring for children. Even the available members of these impoverished households are less able to compete successfully for employment positions due to lower levels of education, less developed skills, irregular work histories and fewer useful employment-creating contacts. Such adults often face appreciably higher levels of discrimination, based on their racial, ethnic and social class backgrounds, as they compete for jobs with longer annual hours and higher wages. In an oft-cited study conducted in the early 1970s, Jencks et al. documented how children from black households in the United States suffered from discrimination at every new competitive level as they sought to achieve in school, find employment, obtain wages and gain promotions (Thurow, 1969, p. 37; Jencks et al., 1972; pp. 226–7). Businesses can address these problems by working to recognize and reduce unannounced patterns of discrimination in the employment practices.

However, these factors do not in any way affect the major problem here, which concerns the character of the supply of jobs for people seeking employment. In many industrialized societies the supply of jobs does not adequately meet the demand of workers for employment. In the late 20th century, job markets in industrialized economies increasingly produced situations where many workers are periodically unemployed, under-employed or must work at jobs that pay poverty-level wages. If no efforts are made to address the way jobs are supplied, this problem will remain even if discrimination were to be eliminated and previously poor workers were to receive better education. Members from previously impoverished households might compete more effectively for the limited number of full-time, year-round, adequately paying jobs. But overall the number of workers who were periodically unemployed or under-employed, or who would have dropped out of the labour force, would not appreciably change. The demographic character traits of impoverished households might alter slightly while numbers of these households probably would not be significantly different.

A number of industrialized countries have variously recognized and taken steps to respond when their economies have produced inadequate supplies of full-time, year-round jobs for workers seeking employment. They have developed public works programmes and initiated tax incentives to encourage investments in new economic enterprises. They have deliberately acted to provide tax breaks and subsidies to particular businesses and industries. Beginning in the late 1930s, the United States government, for example, sought to reduce the unemployment and under-employment through major tax breaks for producers and consumers in the housing construction industry. It has been persuasively argued that these tax concessions for mortgage interest payments represent one of the major welfare programmes in the US. In addition to its probable welfare function for middle-class households, the mortgage interest tax-relief policies have also helped to stimulate the construction industry in ways that expanded job opportunities.

The problem of under-employment has not received the same kind of public attention as the problem of unemployment. Nonetheless, increasingly large numbers of workers are employed part-time or seasonally in jobs with little future and little or no fringe benefits. Typically these jobs pay wages that result in yearly incomes at or below the poverty line. They provide, at times, marginal opportunities for learning employable skills, but little or no basis for career planning. Although governments in industrialized countries have established compensatory unemployment benefits for many of these workers between jobs, they have not explored ways to address the underlying policies that lead year-round and not seasonal businesses to develop and expand their part-time, seasonal or temporary employment practices.

2. A second structural cause of poverty emerges out of the typically marginal relationship of impoverished households to public welfare programmes, even where these are readily available, as in modern industrialized states. Although one would naturally suppose the poor to be the major beneficiaries of welfare programmes (Simmel, 1965), impoverished households actually receive much less from welfare systems than what is usually assumed. Modern welfare systems include a wide range of publicly mandated and supported programmes by which economic value is transferred from governments to households in a variety of forms. These include cash payments, in-kind benefits, insurance disbursements, tax rebates, tax credits and subsidized services. Defined as public transfer programmes, modern welfare encompasses much more than assistance to the indigent and needy. Modern welfare programmes also include old-age pensions, workmen's compensation, subsidized education, subsidized medical care, tax credits for mortgage interest payments, tax credits for charitable giving, subsidized pre-school programmes, unemployment benefits, subsidized water systems, old-age assistance, family assistance and general assistance. These programmes vary from country to country in their character, the names by which they are known, and the flow of assistance they provide. Over the course of the 20th century the amount of public funds devoted to these welfare programmes has greatly expanded. In 1928–1929 all governments in the United States were expending 3.1 per cent of the country's gross national product on these programmes. Even though the economy had greatly expanded in the meantime, by 1974 these central, state and local governments were spending 17.6 per cent of GNP on these programmes (Plotnick and Skidmore, 1975). The proportion of the total economy devoted to welfare programmes was proportionately larger in most of the northern European states.

How do we explain this sizeable increase in public spending? Most observers do not think that this expansion reflects an appreciable increase in the extent to which these countries have become more charitable. Rather, the citizens of industrialized societies have come to look to their governments to provide, on the basis of diverse taxing schemes, an increasingly wider range of services and benefits. To a large extent publicly supported welfare programmes, broadly defined, have expanded in order to address a number of concerns that have become more prominent as societies industrialize. For example, three large modern welfare programmes, namely, worker's compensation, unemployment insurance and old-age social insurance schemes, were introduced in Germany in the 1880s and in other industrialized countries somewhat later to address the economic insecurities and corresponding needs of previously employed workers who were no longer able to work. Because urban households were almost exclusively dependent upon wages as their source of income, they were correspondingly put at risk when wage earners became unemployed through accidents, fluctuations in labour markets and retirement. In varying degrees these kinds of welfare programmes have been established in all industrialized societies. It is worth noting that the impetus to create these programmes arose not only in order to manage the increased economic insecurity occasioned by periodic economic crises characteristic of industrial economies but also in order to manage the economic insecurities occasioned by the increased inter- and intra-generational distance between kinship-related households. This social distance between kin-related households, a by-product of increased occupational and geographic mobility as well as the value asserted for individual choice, renders particular households markedly more economically vulnerable whenever their employment-generated income is cut off. They no longer expect to receive most of their assistance from other members of their extended kinship networks. Most industrialized societies have devoted as well considerable public funds to provide medical care services to their citizens. For a variety of reasons, then, public spending on welfare programmes has greatly expanded (Rimlinger, 1975; Romanyshyn, 1971; Wilensky, 1975).

Additionally, in order to assist particular valued industries, most industrial societies have either acted to subsidize local producers in these industries or used public law to protect them from foreign competitors. For example, a number of North American and European countries support local farming enterprises through a combination of means, including supplying them with water at highly reduced costs, purchasing their products at inflated costs, and setting tariffs to keep out competitors, thereby indirectly taxing customers.

Impoverished households have benefited greatly from these programmes in all industrialized countries and the proportion of the population living in poverty would be much larger without them. Without publicly subsidized medical programmes, unemployment insurance and old-age pensions, there would be more impoverished households and these households would be worse off. In the United States, in 1972, various welfare programmes reduced the total number of households that would have had incomes below the poverty line by 7.7 million or 44 per cent. Aged households were especially helped by these programmes. Without these programmes three-fifths of the households headed by elderly people, 5.5 million out of 8.6 million households, would have had incomes below the poverty line, rather than the one fifth of these household that actually had poverty incomes in that year. It is worth noting that 71 per cent of the otherwise impoverished households that benefited from these welfare transfers in that year were households headed by elderly people (Plotnick and Skidmore, 1975, pp. 91, 112, 139, 147).

After all these varied welfare transfers – direct assistance, insurance benefits, tax credits – had been disbursed, almost 10 million households remained poor in 1972 by the US government's official measure. In that year the government had expended an estimated $185 billion on welfare programmes, broadly defined. If funds had been given directly so that the incomes of impoverished households were raised to the poverty line, it would have required about $34 billion, less than one-fifth of that total, but instead the funds were expanded to further a wide range of objectives, associated with modern welfare state systems, from providing education to helping the elderly, from supporting farmers to aiding child care programmes. Reducing poverty was simply one objective among others, not these programmes' primary goal (Plotnick and Skidmore, 1975, pp. 56, 68, 140).

To explain this situation, it will be useful to analyse welfare programmes in greater detail. Thus, it is possible, for heuristic purposes, to distinguish between regular public welfare programmes directed to assist varied households, whether they are impoverished or not, and poor peoples' welfare programmes directed exclusively to help impoverished households. The regular welfare programmes include all the social insurance schemes, including old-age pensions, unemployment insurance, Medicare for the elderly and worker's compensation; most educational subsidies; most manpower programmes; and mortgage interest tax credits. Although these programmes helped poor households in significant ways, they were not especially aimed at helping the poor; rather, they variously sought to strengthen civil society as a whole. The poor people's welfare programmes include public assistance, family assistance, public housing, Medicaid and some special training and educational programmes (Tussing, 1975). In 1974 regular welfare programmes in the United States paid an average of $925 per person for all eligible households. In the same year the poor people's welfare programmes paid $200 per person for all the eligible households (Plotnick and Skidmore, 1975, p. 112). The regular welfare programmes were clearly more generous and many impoverished households received assistance from these programmes. Households headed by elderly people benefited much more from these regular welfare programmes, including especially from social security and medical assistance.

Modern welfare programmes in the United States have operated moderately to reduce the extent of poverty. However, for the most part these programmes aid those who are not impoverished. More than 80 per cent of the total welfare budget is expended in ways that assist households that are not poor. Those households who remain poor do so, in part, because they simply benefit less from publicly funded welfare programmes. This is not entirely surprising when we consider the wide range of purposes these programmes seek to realize, as well as specific stipulations attached to many of the regular welfare programmes. Thus, for example, members of impoverished households benefit less from employment-related old-age pensions and medical assistance because more than others they have had comparatively unstable employment histories. They benefit less from mortgage interest tax credits because they are less likely to be in a position to purchase their own homes.

To be sure, the degree to which impoverished households remain marginal under the most generous welfare programmes varies from country to country. Some countries have developed more generous welfare programmes than others. The overall character of public welfare programmes reflects the varied purposes and values that countries have sought to honour by means of these programmes. For example, a recent study of poverty rates in Germany, Great Britain, Canada and the United States examined the risk of poverty faced by single-parent households with small children in these countries in the 1990s. In all these countries the chances that these household would be at least temporarily impoverished was very high, because most could count on income only from very irregular employment supplemented by alimony and child support payments that were also often irregular. However, the risk of poverty for these household was much lower in Germany and somewhat lower in Great Britain, simply because these countries provided more welfare support for these kinds of families (Valetta, 2005, p. 18).

3. Members from impoverished households historically have faced excessive barriers trying to obtain financial credit, which handicaps these households in several ways: it is much harder to make major household purchases, including housing, cars and appliances, except at very steep interest rates. Low-income households often buy into extremely expensive credit schemes, thereby appreciably adding to the cost of their purchases. Because of their credit difficulties, members of impoverished households historically have had a much harder time securing loans to invest in their own economic future through educational loans as well as small business loans, insurance, equipment and commercial space, and other facilities that make entrepreneurial initiatives possible (Caplovitz, 1967).

4. In many areas of the world, impoverished households also suffer from barriers that make it difficult to protect their belongings as their own legally recognized property. In a word, they lack effective property rights. Millions of low-income households in the developing world have built or purchased their own dwellings, regularly cultivated their own lands and developed their own shops and businesses without any legally binding guarantees that these dwellings, lands and enterprises constitute their own property. To the degree that these belongings are unrecognized as property, these belongings are at risk in a number of ways. They are vulnerable both to arbitrary seizure or defacement; they may be unexpectedly appropriated by others who are able to claim legal ownership; and it is impossible to recognize them as assets on the basis of which their owners might obtain credit so as to improve their economic condition. This lack of enforceable property rights disadvantages large numbers of impoverished households (Landes, 1998, ch. 15, 20; De Soto, 2000).

In both industrialized and developing economies, many households are impoverished in part because of structural impediments that make it difficult for them to generate sufficient income by means of their access to labour markets, public transfers, systems of credit, land or possessions they can claim as their own. None of these structural factors are inherent by-products of economic development. They are not integral to industrial social organization. Depending upon the setting, these structural factors – which are the immediate causes of poverty – have gained force because of impacts of other influences, which in turn constitute the critical causes of poverty. I will discuss several of these.

1. Wherever these structural impediments exist, they do so, in part, because governments have not been willing or able to act to make a difference. Governments enact labour legislation that shapes labour markets. They develop and fund social welfare programmes. They affect the character of credit and the legal status of property. Governments are in decisive positions either to reinforce or to reduce these impediments. Depending on the country, governments in industrialized and developing societies have initiated programmes and laws to increase employment opportunities, to raise minimum wage levels, to support social insurance programmes, to make credit more available to low income households and to strengthen property rights of the poor. However, because they have been variously influenced by particular political philosophies, the self-aggrandizing actions of their leaders, or their own political weaknesses, governments have also acted in ways that have reinforced these structural causes of poverty.

2. These structural causes of poverty persist, in part, because many of those with power and wealth resist changes and reforms that would reduce the influence of these factors. To a degree, improving the life chances for impoverished households may cost those with wealth and power. More

generous welfare programmes targeting low-income households are likely to occasion modest tax increases. However, these increases are likely to be decidedly much lower than the much higher tax raises that have, for example, been collected to pay for thousands of nuclear weapons in the half-century after Second World War – weapons that have never been used (Schwartz, 1998).[5] It is not clear that reforms to improve poor people's access to jobs, credit or property will measurably affect the life chances of the affluent. Nonetheless, it is probably accurate to surmise that many affluent households fear that such liberalizing reforms will be purchased at their expense. Especially in the years since the Depression of the 1930s, many people have argued that government should not expend tax dollars to create job opportunities for the poor. These kinds of expenditures have been described as make-work jobs, as examples of socialism and as contrary to the fundamental principles governing free market societies. People who make these arguments often do so inconsistently, in so far as they support government involvement in their economies through mortgage interest tax breaks; tax benefits for particular industries and firms, from corporate agriculture to defence contractors; government subsidized industry research and development; as well as the sale of water for industry and agriculture below actual cost levels. For these and many other reasons, those with power and wealth have often resisted reforms that might reduce the structural causes of poverty.

In a number of developing countries comparatively small numbers of well-to-do households have been able to exert disproportionate amounts of power and gain access to disproportionate wealth. In countries as diverse as Brazil, Nigeria, Indonesia and Congo, elites have been able claim extensive tracts of land, gain control over the wealth produced by particular extractive industries and effectively influence government practices. Where they have held extensive power, elites in many of these developing countries have resisted efforts to share this power and wealth more widely and to institute, for example, progressive tax systems or genuine land reforms. Efforts to invest in these countries often have further reinforced these systems of inequality.

3. To a degree, the structural causes of poverty have persisted because they have remained unnoticed and unidentified, and therefore unopposed. As the economies of the industrial nations greatly expanded during the 19th and 20th centuries, members of many formerly impoverished households gained jobs, access to credit and social benefits that enabled them to raise their household incomes and appreciably augment their assets. Particularly over the course of the half-century from the Depression of the 1930s until the affluence of the 1980s, many people journeyed from poverty to wealth – from what seemed like rags to what seemed like riches. For many this journey seemed to be universally possible; it seemed that poverty could be overcome individually, as each person or each family

worked, saved, invested and sought to make the most of their circumstances. If others were less successful, then this could be explained by their lack of industry or bad luck. What this perspective fails to recognize are the structural inadequacies of labour markets and their inability to create enough full-time jobs with career possibilities to match the supply of job seekers. This perspective also fails to see the uneven and limited character of welfare systems. Most people in industrial societies continue to imagine government welfare services or social programmes as being directly aimed at aiding the poor, even though most public transfer programmes have been created, as I have already indicated, to promote a much wider range of economic or political objectives and to manage the risks faced by middle- and upper-class households. These structural factors that render many impoverished households marginal to the major sources of income remain unnoticed. Because rates of poverty are attributed to other factors such as slowdowns in economies or the lack of enterprise, industry and thrift among the poor – factors that may still have some impact – the steps to address and to alter these structural impediments have been minimal in a number of industrialized countries.

4. Structural causes of poverty have been reinforced by patterns of prejudice and discrimination. In many settings members from impoverished households have probably competed less effectively for work and wealth because they suffered from discrimination on the basis of personal and social characteristics. They were discriminated against because of their age, gender, racial or ethnic background, and their lack of social or business connections. Many old people, young people, minorities and women have been discriminated against in their pursuit of education and work. The impact of such discrimination has been huge.

5. Many have argued that structural causes of poverty are reinforced by the very ways members of impoverished households respond to various economic opportunities. The poor have often been regarded as lazier, less industrious, or less frugal than others. Following the narrative studies of impoverished Mexican families, even as sympathetic an observer of the poor as Michael Harrington has argued that the poor were influenced by a 'culture of poverty' that rendered them less future-oriented, less likely to save and less likely to invest in long range training programmes (Harrington, 1962, ch. 5). This description of the outlook of the poor is clearly a misleading caricature, especially when we think of millions of impoverished agrarian households whose working lives have traditionally been linked to the recurrent patterns of the changing seasons. Clearly, these households planned in relation to their futures in ways that seemed reasonable. Nonetheless, in many settings where opportunities to improve life chances in progressive ways seem extremely improbable, it has probably made sense to remain present-oriented and to look for episodic lucky breaks. In these kinds of situations, particular cultures of poverty have

emerged as an understandable response to existing conditions. Thus, we may well regard the influence of cultures of poverty from different perspectives: as much the consequences and correlates of poverty as inherent outlooks that render many able-bodied members of impoverished households disinclined to recognize and take advantage of realistic opportunities for work, training and investment. No matter how much sympathy we may feel for impoverished households, we must still acknowledge that in some cases their poverty may be reinforced by these kinds of cultural attitudes, which prevent them from exerting themselves on their own behalf.

The role of international businesses in reducing poverty

Even though significant progress has been made in reducing the extent of poverty in a number of areas since the early 20th century, the factors that work to maintain poverty remain powerful. All too frequently the potential benefits from industrialization and the growth of commercial interconnections have been undermined by either higher rates of population increase or by factors that resulted in restricting benefits of development to particular sectors and classes of society. There have been far too many cases in which the rich and powerful have resisted tax reforms, land reforms, welfare programmes, higher wages and other efforts which, if implemented, would have markedly improved the life chances of impoverished households. In *The Nature of Mass Poverty*, Galbraith describes mass poverty as a state of equilibrium where various improvements, such as higher wages or more productive agricultural practices, often lead to population increases and practices, such as spending increased income on consumables, which tend to perpetuate poverty. 'The tendency of the rich country *is* to increasing income; the tendency of the poor country is to an equilibrium of poverty' (Galbraith, 1979, p. 46). Overall, we can probably best predict whether any household is likely to be impoverished by simply asking whether the adults in that household grew up in households that were impoverished.

Looking at the comparatively successful efforts of the most affluent groups to increase their wealth over the past 25 years and the corresponding increases in inequality both nationally and globally, one is inclined to become pessimistic about the current prospects for reducing poverty. Nonetheless, I think this pessimism is misguided. If we hope to reduce the rates of poverty, we must be realistic and we must pay close attention to the factors that make it difficult to reduce the extent of poverty. In fact, I think we can be cautiously optimistic. Historically, with increased industrialization and with various state reforms that resulted in social insurance programmes, minimum wages, fairer taxes and the like, poverty rates have declined. It is therefore realistic to assume that further progress is possible. However, progress will not transpire if we aim our efforts in directions not likely to yield promising results. The discussion above with respect to the general and structural causes of poverty provides points of reference for deciding what kinds of initiatives are likely to pay off.

For the purposes of this study, I am especially interested in the contributions that internationally connected businesses have made and can make toward the reduction of poverty. I make several assumptions. First, these businesses are not the only players; stakeholders of many other sorts are involved. Whether or not the extent of poverty is reduced over time in any given area depends on actions by governments, civil society associations, local enterprises, international agencies and members of impoverished households themselves. Poverty rates are affected as well by the international economy and geographical factors. Second, there are no panaceas. Initiatives that once worked easily may at later times prove much less useful. Third, the problems of poverty have to be addressed differently in different countries, depending on their own cultural traditions, levels of economic development and existing resources.

Using the prior discussion as a point of departure, I believe that the best chances for reducing the extent of poverty involve (a) the promotion of increased productivity within local economies in ways (b) that help to foster the social and economic interconnections among the households and businesses participating in those economies, thereby moderating the influence of structural causes of poverty. Using these principles as basic points of reference, it is possible to suggest a series of initiatives that are likely to work toward the reduction of poverty.

1. The most important contribution that international businesses have made in the economies of impoverished areas is to invest in these economies in ways that function so as to generate development. As I have already noted at the outset, those areas of the world which are least connected by trade and investment with other countries are also the most impoverished. Prahalad (2004) argues that businesses can indeed thrive while doing business in economically underdeveloped areas. Prahalad focuses primarily on strategies and techniques, such as flexible approaches to packaging, marketing, sourcing and staffing. He demonstrates how investments in these can assume varied forms, including often-overlooked opportunities in retailing, health services and banking. Prahalad's study encourages international businesses to think in practical terms about investing in economically developing countries. In the following pages, I will examine why these kinds of investments are important and how they are likely to make a difference.

It is worth reiterating the traditional argument that international investments in developing countries have often helped the economies of these countries develop by offering jobs to workers, taxes and royalties to governments, and skill training opportunities to employees. These investments have grown more significant in the late 20th century as they grew in number and size (Culpeper et al., 1997; Thomas et al., 2000; Legrain, 2002). Nonetheless, it is important to recognize that not all forms of investment foster genuine sustainable economic development. The pursuit of opportunistic wealth, disconnected or enclave-like investments and other unsustainable investments have rendered the overall economies of less developed areas less productive. With quite mixed results, such investments have generated income, wealth and power to certain groups, while more generally depleting overall natural resources, exacerbating inequalities and aggravating social tensions. These kinds of investments should be strenuously avoided.

2. The most effective forms of investments are those which have a multiplier effect on local economies, that is, they provide means to add to or make more accessible the productive, human, social, natural and financial resources of these developing areas. The investments that have had these effects are those that foster new and more effective patterns of work, make use of new technologies, raise skill levels of workers, foster collaboration among and between enterprises, open up previously inaccessible natural resources and cultivate new lands in sustainable ways.

Consider the following cases. HLL, the Indian subsidiary of Unilever, greatly expanded its retail sales by training women to market their products door-to-door. As the firm expanded its sales, it also raised the skill levels of these women, now trained to act as members of a dispersed sales staff. The Bank of Madura expanded its business into low-income areas by working with groups of villagers, who, in order to qualify for loans, had to organize ongoing local credit groups and initiate and keep track of individual savings. As the Bank's business increased, the villagers developed skills at organizing meetings, initiating community actions and bookkeeping (Prahalad, 2004, ch. 1, 4). The Body Shop has made a successful business of purchasing substantial amounts of raw materials and goods from a number of community producer groups in the developing world during the 1990s. This community trade initiative succeeded because The Body Shop worked effectively to train members of these groups in managerial and marketing skills, thereby enhancing the productivity of these local operations (Fostater et al., 2002, ch. 4, 5).[6] When Hewlett-Packard invested in a computer firm in China in the 1980s, as a matter of standard practice it gave the Chinese partner complete access to its technologies. This technology transfer greatly enhanced the Chinese firm's capacity to make and market its products (Velasquez, 2002). In all of these examples investments not only created jobs but also helped raise the skill levels of those involved and foster new forms of social cooperation.

International investments have a much larger multiplier effect in developing areas to the extent that firms interconnect their operations with local businesses as suppliers, partners or customers. Making these kinds of connections is often challenging and calls for imagination. One of the strengths of Unilever's investment in developing areas has been its commitment to purchase as much of its supplies locally as possible (Puplampu, 2004). In many settings, however, international businesses have failed to meet this challenge. Shell's operations in Nigeria over the past 45 years are a particularly clear example.[7]

In his review of international business operations in China, Santora (2000) contrasted firms that pursued their interests in terms of cost minimization or asset development. These firms, which naturally sought to market appreciable portions of their products locally, were much more likely to use local suppliers, invest in training programmes for workers and work with local partners. Firms that adopt asset development strategies have also been more likely to invest in ways that also strengthen the assets of the areas in which they are operating (Bird, 2003).

3. Some of the most noteworthy investments in developing areas have helped reduce or eliminate structural impediments that restricted the economic opportunities of impoverished households. Of particular importance have been the various efforts to provide credit to low-income families. The best known of these have been the micro-credit programmes developed by the Grameen Bank in Bangladesh and similar systems in other countries (Yunnus, 1999). Prahalad cites a number of other initiatives. He describes how the Brazilian retailer, Casas Bahia, greatly expanded its business to more than 350 stores and 70,000 employees by developing a system that allowed low-income customers to make purchases they could not otherwise afford through installment payments. The Mexican cement company Cenmex offered credit so that low-income households could pay for home improvements over time. The ICICI bank in India in 1996 developed a programme of lending to self-help groups; by 2002, the bank was working with almost half a million such groups (Prahalad, 2004). These examples highlight the capacity of businesses to succeed and grow while offering useful services to low-income households. Prahalad is less clear in details about the extent to which impoverished households were able to access this credit for investments in education and their own businesses. Nonetheless it seems certain that reducing credit barriers made it easier for many impoverished household to make these kinds of investments on their own behalf. In some areas, impoverished households have similarly benefited by gaining access to cellular phones, which have made communication less expensive and easier to access. When, for example, the price of cell phone services was reduced to a level affordable by low-income households in Uganda, some of the latter used this opportunity to develop their own entrepreneurial initiatives (Mutoigo and Sejjaaka, 2004).

In a number of areas international businesses have worked to incorporate workers from impoverished households more fully into the labour force. In South Africa, in response to national legislation, many firms including Toyota South Africa, Otis Elevator and Saldahana Steel have worked to create more opportunities for blacks to improve their skills and gain promotions.[8] Falconbridge developed training programmes to offer Inuit workers in northern Quebec skilled jobs in the company's mining operations at Raglan.[9] In 1999, at a time when unemployment rates in South Africa were running nearly 20 per cent, Placer Dome's South Deep mine at Westonia laid off 2,650 workers. It then decided to work to reintegrate these workers into the labour force – or their proxies, in cases where the workers had become too ill because of the HIV/AIDS epidemic. In this very interesting initiative, Placer Dome Canada extended itself to help workers the company had laid off. Through Project Care, funded in part by the Canadian International Development Agency, Placer Dome contacted the laid off workers in villages all over South Africa and neighbouring countries and offered them training in financial life skills and relevant business skills. Project Care then helped some ex-workers find new jobs and helped even more to start their own businesses as farmers, crafts workers or service providers. By the end of the project in 2003, nearly two-thirds of those who participated in the programme had found a new line of work. Additionally, Project Care had the correlative impact of persuading the mining industry in South Africa to develop a range of progressive HIV/AIDS programmes and services (Placer Dome, 2003). More importantly than offering them decent severance packages, this project helped these ex-workers develop skills and resources and find or create new work.

What has been especially noteworthy about these examples, whether in terms of the multiplier effect or of reducing structural impediments, is that they have functioned to a considerable extent to foster and facilitate investment by and for the people living in low-income areas. Surplus wealth, above and beyond that returned to international shareholders, was introduced into these areas from outside, and thus encouraged and made possible additional investments in the forms of collaborations, entrepreneurial activities, savings and training among the populations of these developing areas. These initiatives have played a catalytic role.

4. Because the Earth's natural resources are limited, international businesses must face the challenge of using these resources as efficiently as possible. As the economies of developing countries expand, there is a corresponding increase in demand not only for consumer goods but also for the natural resources required to produce these goods. The problem is that international businesses have been involved in using up a number of non-renewal resources – minerals, gas and oil in particular. Humans have also exhausted, or have come close to exhausting, potentially renewable resources such as arable lands, underground aquifers and fish stocks. Access to other natural resources, including potable water and fresh air, has been put at risk by current patterns of industrialization, urbanization and consumer practices that are not sustainable over the long term (Brown, 1995; Diamond, 2005; Millennium Ecosystem Assessment, 2005). Despite certain controversies, we can see that for the present and near future at least, it has

become increasingly important that international firms use whatever natural resources they are working with as efficiently as possible, lest they jeopardize their own businesses by permanently eliminating assets that could be eventually used to foster economic development (Heath, 2001). Ordinarily, efficiency is regarded as a good business practice; why then do international businesses tend to operate in less than efficient ways? Part of the problem has to do with ways of estimating efficiency, which is often gauged in terms of financial resources, and calculated in terms of profit and returns on equity. I have argued instead that efficiencies should be gauged by examining how effectively businesses utilize natural and human resources. Efficiencies are increased by making multiple uses of existing resources and by conservation measures to increase effective utilization.

5. One of the most important contributions that international businesses can make toward the reduction of poverty is to join the struggle against corruption. A number of areas characterized by high poverty rates also suffer from high rates of corruption. When they offer or accept bribes or yield to extortion, international businesses act to divert to private ends wealth that otherwise might have been used to benefit workers, consumers, shareholders or taxpayers, as well as public education and social welfare programmes As I have noted in chapter 4, reducing this problem and fostering transparency is not a simple matter. But the current costs of these illegal payments remain high, not only in terms of public revenues lost, but also in the depletion of social capital that corrupt practices occasion – eroding public trust, diverting attention from the pursuit and protection of common civic goods and breeding widespread resentment (Klitgaard, 1988; Marong, 2002; Young, 2005).

6. While initiatives by international businesses can make a difference, they cannot act alone. In several decisive ways, governments of developing and industrialized nations must act on the principle that international business initiatives must make lasting improvements. There are several basic strategic actions that international businesses and civil societies associations can undertake, and must continue to campaign for. The first is to strengthen the rule of law and politically neutral judicial systems. Only where there are minimally reliable independent tribunals is it possible to make legitimate claims with respect to human rights. Claims with respect to property rights, so fundamentally vital to the poor, can only have effect in settings where there are courts that will hear these claims without prejudice and duly and deliberately consider them. It is also the court's role to adjudicate and protect contractual rights. It is clearly in the interest of businesses that developing countries institute reliable systems of law, even if the courts thereby established might from time to time rule against these businesses. To be sure, in many developing countries it will not be easy and may take considerable time to develop effective judiciaries and legal systems that operate in terms of the rule of law. Nonetheless, this remains a valuable objective both in the immediate and long term, because any

progress along these lines is likely to be beneficial (see Prahalad, ch. 5). Second, international businesses can help the economies of developing countries by supporting efforts to remove trade barriers in the industrialized north to agricultural goods produced in developing areas. The industrialized countries have worked to reduce trade barriers for their goods in developing countries through the trade liberalization guidelines built into the structural adjustment programmes of the International Monetary Fund. Yet many of these same countries have retained trade barriers with respect to agricultural produce and products. This is an unjustifiable restriction on international development (Oxfam International, 2002). Finally, international businesses, through their involvements in developing countries, can strengthen social and commercial infrastructures in the developing world as integral features of their basic business strategies.

Notes

1. Generally it is true that economies are comparatively disadvantaged if they are located in areas lacking access to mineral resources (especially, in the past, areas without coal or iron, or, in the present, areas without access to a wide range of industrial and precious minerals). Access to minerals has often served to create wealth that can be variously invested to stimulate affected economies. However, as this essay shows, the exploitation of mineral resources has acted to unbalance local economies as various actors compete to appropriate the royalties, taxes and profits these resources generate (Asher, 1999; Auty, 1993, 2001).
2. See J. Smucker, 'The Formation of Business Practices in South Korea' (Bird et al., 2005, ch. 8).
3. This section draws upon research I have previously undertaken on poverty in the United States from 1870 to the 1990s. In 1972 I completed a doctoral thesis, 'The Poor Be Damned: American Perceptions and Responses to Poverty, 1885–1970'. I later updated this thesis as an essay on 'The Political Economy of Poverty' (1997; unpublished).
4. In industrialized societies, many more households temporarily experience periods of poverty rather than chronic poverty (Valletta, 2005). These temporary periods of poverty, especially if they are recurrent, may permanently prevent these households from acquiring or building assets, investing in education or even maintaining family stability.
5. In the 50 years prior to 1998, the US government spent more on nuclear weapons than on education, law enforcement, agriculture, natural resources, general science, space and technology, job training, community and regional development combined (Schwartz, 1998).
6. See F. Bird, 'International Trade as a Vehicle for Reducing Poverty: The Body Shop's Community Trade Programme' (Bird and Herman, 2004, ch. 13).
7. See F. Bird, 'Wealth and Poverty in the Niger Delta: A Study of the Experiences of Shell in Nigeria' (Bird and Herman, 2004, ch. 2).
8. See E. Raufflet, 'The Mixed Blessings of Paternalism: The Case of San Rafael (1893–1991)' and E. Kotze, 'Green Steel: A New South African Steel Company's Response to Internal and External Challenges' (Bird et al., 2005, ch. 3, 4).
9. See F. Bird and R. Nixon, 'Collaboration and Cultural Difference: The Raglan Mine and Nunavik Inuit' (ibid., ch. 12).

References

Aghion, P. (1999) 'Inequality and Economic Growth', in P. Aghion and J. G. Williamson (eds), *Growth, Inequality, and Globalization: Theory, History, and Policy* (Cambridge: Cambridge University Press).

Asher, W. (1999) *Why Governments Waste Natural Resources: Policy Failure in Developing Countries* (Baltimore, MD: John Hopkins University Press).

Auty, R. M. (1993) *Sustaining Development in Mineral Economies: The Resource Curse Thesis* (London and New York: Routledge).

Auty, R. M. (ed.) (2001) *Resource Abundance and Economic Development* (Oxford: Oxford University Press).

Berger, T. (1999) *A Long and Terrible Shadow: White Values and Native Rights in the Americas Since 1492* (Vancouver and Toronto: Douglas and McIntyre).

Bird, F. (1972) '"The Poor Be Damned": American Perceptions and Responses to Poverty, 1885–1970', doctoral dissertation, Berkeley, CA: Graduate Theological Union.

Bird, F. (1997) 'The Political Economy of Poverty' (unpublished).

Bird, F. (2003) 'The Value-added Approach to Business Ethics', *Zeitschrift fur Wirtschafts- und Entenehmenethik*, vol. 4(2) (Autumn).

Bird, F. and Herman, S. (eds) (2004), *International Businesses and the Challenges of Poverty in the Developing World* (London: Palgrave Macmillan).

Bird, F., Raufflet, E. and J. Smucker (eds) (2005) *International Business and the Dilemmas of Development* (London: Palgrave Macmillan).

Braudel, F. (1980) *The Structures of Everyday Life: The Limits of the Possible. Civilization and Capitalism 1500–1800, Vol. 1.* tr. by S. Reynolds (New York: Harper and Row).

Braudel, F. (1984) *The Perspective of the World. Civilization and Capitalism 1500–1800, Vol. 3*, tr. S. Reynolds (New York: Harper and Row).

Broad, R. (1998) *Unequal Alliance: The World Bank, The International Monetary Fund and the Philippines* (Berkeley: University of California Press).

Brown, L. (1995) *Who Will Feed China? Wake Up Call for a Small Planet* (New York: W. W. Norton).

Burtless, G. (ed.) (1990) *A Future of Lousy Jobs? The Changing Structure of U.S. Wages* (Washington, DC: Brookings Institution).

Caplovitz, D. (1967) *The Poor Pay More: Consumer Practices of Low-Income Families* (New York: The Free Press).

Chossudovsky, M. (1997) *The Globalization of Poverty: Impacts of the IMF and World Bank Reforms* (London: Zed Books).

Cohen, D. (1998) *The Wealth of the World and the Poverty of Nations*, tr. J. Lindenfield (Cambridge: Cambridge University Press).

Culpeper, R., Berry, A. and Stewart, F. (eds) (1997) *Global Development: Fifty Years After Bretton Woods* (New York: St Martin's Press).

Danziger, S. and Gottschalk, P. (1995) *America Unequal* (New York: Russell Sage).

Davis, M. (2001) *Late Victorian Holocausts: El Niño Famines and the Making of the Third World* (London: Verso).

Deaton, A. (2005) 'Measuring Poverty in a Growing World (or Measuring Growth in a Poor World)', *The Review of Economics and Statistics*, MIT Press, vol. 87(1), pp. 1–19.

De Soto, H. (2000) *The Mystery of Capital: Why Capitalism Triumphs in the West and Fails Everywhere Else* (New York: Basic Books).

Diamond, J. (1999) *Guns, Germs, and Steel: The Fates of Human Societies* (New York: W. W. Norton).

Diamond, J. (2005) *Collapse: How Societies Choose To Fail or Succeed* (New York: Viking).

Dollar, D. and Kraay, A. (2001) 'Growth is Good for the Poor', *Policy Research Working Paper 2587*, World Bank Development Research Group (April), *The World Bank: Documents and Reports*, http://www-wds.worldbank.org/servlet/ WDS_IBank_Servlet?pcont=details&eid=000094946_01042806383524.

Drohan, M. (2003) *Making a Killing: How and Why Corporations Use Armed Force to Do Business* (Toronto: Random House Canada).

Duncan, C. (ed.) (1992) *Rural Poverty in America* (New York: Auburn House).

Evans, P. (1979) *Dependent Development: The Alliance of Multinational, State, and Local Capital In Brazil* (Princeton: Princeton University Press).

Forstater, M., MacDonald, J. and Raynard, P. (2002) *Business and Poverty: Bridging the Gap* (London: Prince of Wales International Business Leaders Forum).

Frank, R. H. and Cook, P. J. (1995) *The Winner-Take-All Society: Why the Few at the Top Get So Much More Than the Rest of Us* (New York: Penguin Books).

Galbraith, J. K. (1979) *The Nature of Mass Poverty* (Cambridge, MA: Harvard University Press).

Ghai, D. (ed.) (1991) *The IMF and the South: The Social Impact of Crisis and Adjustment* (London: Zed Books).

Harrington, M. (1962) *The Other America: Poverty in the United States* (New York: Simon & Schuster).

Heath, J. (2001) *The Efficient Society: Why Canada Is As Close to Utopia As It Gets* (Toronto: Penguin Books).

Holmes, C. and Sunnstein, C. R. (1997) *The Cost of Rights: Why Liberty Depends on Taxes* (New York: W. W. Norton).

Jencks, C. et al. (1972) *Inequality: A Reassessment of the Effects of Family and Schooling in America* (New York: Basic Books).

Klein, N. (2000) *No Logo* (London: HarperCollins).

Klitgaard, R. (1988) *Controlling Corruption* (Berkeley: University of California Press).

The Group of Lisbon (1995) *Limits to Competition* (Cambridge, MA: MIT Press).

Lal, D. and Myint, H. (1996) *The Political Economy of Poverty, Equity and Growth: A Comparative Study* (Oxford: Clarendon Press).

Landes, D. (1998) *The Wealth and Poverty of Nations: Why Some are So Rich and Some are So Poor* (New York: W. W. Norton).

Legrain, P. (2002) *Open World: The Truth about Globalization* (London: Abacus).

Levitan, S. A., Gallo, F. and Shapiro, I. (1993) *Working But Poor*. Revised Edition. (Baltimore, MD: John Hopkins University Press).

Lifton, M. (1977) *Why Poor People Stay Poor: A Study of the Urban Bias in World Development* (London: Temple Smith).

Marong, A. B. M. (2002) 'Towards a Normative Consensus Against Corruption: Legal Effects of Principles to Combat Corruption in Africa', *Denver Journal of International Law and Policy*, vol. 20(2), pp. 99–129.

McIntosh, M., Waddock, S. and Kell, G. (eds) (2004) *Learning to Talk: Corporate Citizenship and the Development of the UN Global Compact* (Sheffield, UK: Greenleaf Publishing).

Milanovic, B. (1999) 'True World Income Distribution, 1988 and 1993' (World Bank Development Research Group).

Millenium Ecosystem Assessment (2005) *Ecosystems and Human Well-Being* (Washington, DC: Island Press).

Mutoigo, I. and Sejjaaka, S. (2004) 'Seeking a Better Connection: Mobile Telecommunications Networks and Social Responsibility in Uganda', in F. Bird and S. Herman (eds), *International Businesses and the Challenges of Poverty in the Developing World* (London: Palgrave Macmillan).

Nussbaum, M. (1999) *Woman and Human Development: The Capabilities Approach* (Cambridge: Cambridge University Press).

Oxfam International (2002) *Rigged Rules and Double Standards: Trade Globalization and the Fight against Poverty* (Washington, DC: Oxfam).

Parker, R. E. (1994) *Flesh Peddlers and Warm Bodies: The Temporary Help Industry and Its Workers* (New Brunswick, NJ: Rutgers University Press).

Placer Dome Canada (2003) *Final Activity Report: Project Care: South Deep Mine, Westonia, South Africa* (Johannesburg, SA: Placer Dome Canada/Western Areas Joint Venture).

Plotnick, R. and Skidmore, F. (1975) *Progress Against Poverty: A Review of the 1964– 1974 Decade* (New York: Academic Press).

Polanyi, M. (1944) *The Great Transformation* (Boston: Beacon Press).

Prahalad, C. K. (2004) *The Fortune at the Bottom of the Pyramid: Eradicating Poverty Through Profits* (Upper Saddle River, NJ: Wharton School Publishing).

Puplampu, B. B. (2004) 'Capacity Building, Asset Development, and Corporate Values: A Study of Three International Firms in Ghana', in F. Bird and S. Herman (eds), *International Businesses and the Challenges of Poverty in the Developing World* (London: Palgrave Macmillan).

Rimlinger, G. V. (1975) *Welfare Policy and Industrialization in Europe, America and Russia* (New York: John Wiley and Sons).

Romanyshyn, J. (1971) *Social Welfare: Charity to Justice* (New York: Random House).

Sachs, J. D., Mellinger, A. D. and Gallup, J. L. (2001) 'The Geography of Poverty and Wealth', *Scientific American* (March), pp. 70–6.

Santora, M. (2000) *Profit and Principles: Global Capitalism and Human Rights in China* (Ithaca, NY: Cornell University Press).

Schwartz, S. (1998) *Atomic Audit: The Cost and Consequences of U.S. Nuclear Weapons Since 1940* (Washington, DC: The Brooking Institution).

Sejjaaka, S. (2004) 'From Seed to Leaf: British American Tobacco and Supplier Relations in Uganda', in F. Bird and S. Herman (eds), *International Businesses and the Challenges of Poverty in the Developing World* (London: Palgrave Macmillan).

Sen, A. (1981) *Poverty and Famines: An Essay on Entitlements and Deprivation* (Geneva: International Labour Organization; Oxford University Press, 1982).

Sen, A. (1999) *Development as Freedom* (New York: Anchor Books).

Simmel, G. (1965) 'The Poor', tr. C. Jacobson. *Social Problems*, vol. 13(2).

Stackhouse, J. (2000) *Out of Poverty* (Toronto: Random House Canada).

Stern, J. (2003) *Terror in the Name of God: Why Religious Militants Kill* (New York: HarperCollins).

Stiglitz, J. E. (2002) *Globalization and its Discontents* (New York: W. W. Norton).

Taub, W. K. (1970) *The Political Economy of the Black Ghetto* (New York: W. W. Norton).

Tenev, S. and Caudry, O. (2004) 'Scaling Up: Private Sector Models for Poverty Reduction', A Report of Field Visits in Sechuan and Zhejian Provinces, China (International Finance Corporation), www.ifc.org/publications/paths_out_of_ poverty.pdf.

Thomas, V., Dailami, M., Dhareshwar, A., Kaufmann, D., Kishor, N., Lopez, R. and Wang, Y. (2000) *The Quality of Growth* (Oxford University Press. Published for the World Bank).

Thurow, L. (1969) *Poverty and Discrimination* (Washington, DC: The Brookings Institution).

Titmuss, R. (1958) *Essays on the Welfare State* (London: Unwin).

Tussing, A. D. (1975) *Poverty in a Dual Economy* (New York: St. Martin's Press).

UNCTAD (2002) United Nations Conference on Trade and Development, *Escaping the Poverty Trap: The Least Developed Countries Report 2002* (New York and Geneva: United Nations).

Valletta, R. (2005) 'The Ins and Outs of Poverty in Advanced Economies: Poverty Dynamics in Canada, Germany, Great Britain and the United States'. Income Research Paper Series (Ottawa: Statistics Canada)

Velasquez, M. (2002) 'H-P China and Legend Computer: A Case of Just Technology Transfer' (unpublished essay).

Weber, M. (1905/1958) *The Protestant Ethic and the Spirit of Capitalism*, tr. T. Parsons (New York: Charles Scribner's Sons).

Weber, M. (1923/1961) *General Economic History*, tr. F. Knight (New York: Collier-Macmillan).

Weber, M. (1914/1978) *Economy and Society*, G. Roth and C. Wittich (eds) (Berkeley: University of California Press).

Wilensky, H. (1975) *The Welfare State and Equality: Structural and Ideological Roots of Public Expenditure* (Berkeley: University of California Press).

Williamson, J. (1999) 'Globalization and the Labour Market: Using History to Inform Policy', in P. Aghion and J. C. Williamson (eds), *Growth, Inequality and Globalization: Theory, History and Policy* (Cambridge: Cambridge University Press).

Wilson, W. J. (1987) *The Truly Disadvantaged: The Inner City, the Underclass and Public Policy* (Chicago: University of Chicago Press).

The World Bank (2000/2001) *World Development Report 2000/2001: Attacking Poverty* The World Bank Group, *PovertyNet*, http://web.worldbank.org/WBSITE/ EXTERNAL/TOPICS/EXTPOVERTY/0,,contentMDK:20195989~pagePK:148956~piPK:2166 18~theSitePK:336992,00.html.

The World Bank (2003) World Development Report 2003: Sustainable Development in a Dynamic World – Transforming Institutions, Growth, and Quality of Life (World Bank/Oxford University Press); available online at http://www-wds.worldbank.org/servlet/WDSContentServer/WDSP/IB/2002/09/06/000094946_020824040 15854/Rendered/PDF/multi0page.pdf.

Young, S. B. (2005) *How to End Poverty in Africa Forever* (CAUX Roundtable).

Yunnus, M. (1999) *Banker to the Poor: Micro-lending and the Battle Against Poverty* (New York: Public Affairs).

9
Theological Responses to Economic Globalization

Russell Daye

Like most Christians who respond to economic globalization through action, sermons or theological writing, I see both the benefits and the wreckage. We struggle to decide which is greater and, more importantly, to know how to advocate in a way that could cause the benefits to grow and the wreckage to diminish. This kind of interpretation requires a hermeneutic, of course and for Christians such a hermeneutic follows from what we understand to be God's will for the world – including all its communities and biospheres. What follows are brief attempts to (1) articulate such a hermeneutic; and (2) apply it to the current dynamics of economic globalization.

The context in which this essay is written is one of considerable ambivalence. There is scepticism among economists and critics about the meaning and even the validity of the term 'economic globalization'; there is ambivalence within the global Christian communion (including its theologians) about the processes to which the term 'globalization' refers – and I must admit to ambivalence of my own about those same processes. Let us look at each in turn.

'Globalization' is an ambiguous term, which appears to mean different things to different groups of people. While its usage has become increasingly common, the term has been criticized both for its imprecision and for its inevitable association with the ideological and polemical hostilities of the globalization/anti-globalization debate (which accounts in no small part for the imprecision). The same can be said of the term 'economic globalization'. But there is no denying that the economies of countries in all corners of our globe are being subject to a number of shared and integrating economic processes. These include (but are not limited to):

- *Industrialization* (while there are signs that Western economies are becoming more service-based and less driven by industrial manufacturing processes, these developments come in the wake of an extended process of industrialization – a process that is still on the rise in many parts of the world)

- *Commercialization:* the expansion of market capitalism
- The great *increase in international trade*, with agreements that sanction and facilitate such trade and the establishment of organizations to monitor adherence to those agreements
- The growth of *multinational corporations (MNCs)*, sometimes called 'transnational corporations', whose presence often has a profoundly transformative affect on nations
- The increased importance of *para-governmental agencies and non-governmental organizations (NGOs)*, including (among the former) the World Bank, the International Monetary Fund (IMF), the World Trade Organization (WTO) and the International Labour Organization (ILO); and (among the latter) OXFAM, CARE International and Jubilee South
- The expansion of systems of communication and transportation, facilitating and accelerating exponentially the transfer of people, goods, information, money and culture

Let us turn to our second source of ambivalence. To say that Christians are varied and conflicted in their responses to global economic transformation would be an understatement. I recently attended, as a guest, a meeting of a committee that is charged with the oversight of a large Protestant denomination's mission work, both at home and overseas. Part of the agenda was given to the church's critique of the 'global economic system'. Both in the reporting by one of the church's national staff people and in the discussion that followed, there was an almost unqualified denunciation of that system and its 'major players': MNCs and the WTO, IMF and World Bank. The consensus in the room was that globalization was making a small minority of people obscenely rich and powerful while pushing a large percentage of their fellow humans into poverty and marginalization as well as doing great harm to the biosphere. The harm done by economic globalization was seen as greatly overshadowing its benefits.

This kind of rhetoric is frequently encountered among clergy and social activists within mainline churches, both Protestant and Roman Catholic. It grows out of a longstanding suspicion of market economies, a disposition that was prevalent among 20th-century theologians. Theological giants like Paul Tillich and Karl Barth showed affinities to socialist ideas and protagonists in the social gospel and liberation theology movements articulated severe critiques of capitalism. The realm of 'mammon' – the sphere of economic activity – was seen as fraught with greed and exploitation. In the 1990s, as the 'anti-globalization' movement took shape, church groups became important participants and allies, often voicing the concern that mammon was being unleashed to wreak havoc in a frightening array of new ways and places.

On the other hand, there are many Christians who believe that economic globalization is unfolding according to the will of God. They see the riches generated by the expansion of market capitalism as a concrete form of God's blessings upon humanity. In recent years, a growing number of theologians have articulated similar, if more nuanced, points of view. William Schweiker explains this change of perspective (2000, pp. 115–16):

This shift rests on an acknowledgement of the sinfulness of mammon, but also the insight that the 'world of mammon' taken descriptively is the fact of globalized, differentiated social systems. These systems are a more or less orderly reality (a cosmos) needed to sustain human life in our age; they are also (more or less) consistent with democratic politics. More than one scholar has noted that the 'corporate economies' and personal rights and freedoms tend to go hand in hand. Protestant theologians, like Max Stackhouse, David Krueger and others, as well as the U.S.A. Roman Catholic Bishops and moral theologians Dennis McCann and David Hollenbach have reopened the question of the moral assessment of the market. Even Pope John Paul II, in his encyclicals on labour, makes a proper, if limited, place for the growth and expansion of the market.

The contours of my own ambivalence mirror those of the larger church and its theological debate, but I am of two minds mostly because of first-hand encounters with economic realities in the developing world. In India, Mexico and a host of other countries, I have met many peasants who have been forced off land farmed by their families for generations in order to make way for large-scale agribusinesses or other development projects. Many of them now eke out a living in horrific urban slums. In the South Pacific, I met survivors of Papua New Guinea's civil war, which started in the Bougainville Province, spurred in no small part by the social and environmental damage caused by the operations of an international mining company. In Southern Africa, I saw the heavy social costs of migrant labour – including family breakdown, the spread of AIDS and communal violence – where hundreds of thousands of men leave their homelands to work the gold mines and other export-oriented projects.

I have been shocked by the juxtaposition of shanty-towns and the luxurious, gated communities where the expat managers of MNCs live. I have met garment factory workers who, after long months of service under trying conditions, showed up for work one morning only to find the gates locked by expat managers who had fled the country without paying overdue wages. I have watched poor people struggle to pay for water, education and health care as prices rise due to 'structural adjustment' programmes. There is definitely an underside to economic globalization, and much of the time it looks to be the greater side.

But I have also seen a better side. In Fiji, where there is protracted discord between indigenous Fijians and Indo-Fijians, I encountered internationally connected business corporations that were intentionally hiring equal numbers of employees (and managers) from these two ethnic groups, and were working hard to build trust and cooperation between them in the workplace. In the same country, I met expat managers of international businesses that were giving time, energy and money to reconciliation efforts in the wake of the 2000 coup. I also met Fijian managers and engineers in international businesses whose place in the professional class came as a result of informal employment equity programmes run by expat executives. In South Africa, I studied a transnational automobile company engaged in groundbreaking employment equity and social investment programmes. Its operations were generating a kind of cross-racial social capital that is invaluable in the wake of apartheid (Daye, 2005). And, of course, I have seen the great wealth generated around the world by MNCs – wealth that could not be spawned without the communication and transportation systems, trade agreements, international capital exchanges and technology transfers that are key elements of economic globalization.

The economy of God

Perhaps the most straightforward way to provide a theological interpretation and evaluation of current economic realities is to compare them to the 'economy of God'. From its inception, the church has been concerned with economic questions, but the ancient world in which the church was born had a very different understanding of 'economy'. The Greek word from which we derive 'economy' is *oikonomia*, which is a compound of *oikos* (household) and *nomos* (law, or management). Economy for the early church communities meant the management of the household. But 'household' also had a different meaning than what we give it today. M. Douglas Meeks explains:

> Many of the biblical traditions represent God as engaged in creating, sustaining and recreating households. *Household* can refer to the people of Israel or the church of Jesus Christ, to families, to a royal court or dynasty, to a place of God's abode, or, in the most comprehensive sense, to the whole creation. God has made God's self responsible for the households of Israel and the Church, the households of the nations and the household God has brought into being. (Meeks, 1989, p. 4)

These biblical traditions convey the values and principles by which Christians interpret the world and act in it. The first principle is that the whole world and all its households (all levels of human community and all systems within the created order) are God's. They came into being through God's acts of creation and they are being transformed by continued acts of divine creation. There is a divine intention for them: God desires that they find livelihood and well-being that is physical, communal and spiritual. God's economy is marked by 'households' that embody these blessings. People are well fed, doing productive and meaningful work and rooted in strong community. These are the marks of the *reign of God* – often called the 'Kingdom of God'.

This then, is the starting point for a theological evaluation of global economic transformation. The yardstick by which Christians measure globalization's goodness is not, ultimately, the amount of wealth generated or the extent to which it advances the interests of our nation or its effectiveness in spreading Western-style democracy. Ultimately, the virtue of the series of processes that, taken together, we call economic globalization is judged according to the extent to which it advances or impedes livelihood and well-being for the infinitely layered households in God's creation.

To flush out further these notions of livelihood and well-being, I offer below a number of principles that are central to Christian theology and belief.

Everything in the created order has inherent value

The very first chapter of the Hebrew Bible offers a creation story that is of fundamental importance for the way Christians see the world in which they live.

In the beginning when God created the heavens and the earth, the earth was a formless void and darkness covered the face of the deep ... Then God said, 'Let there be light'; and there was light. And God saw that the light was good ... And God said, 'Let the waters under the sky be gathered together into one place and let the dry land appear'. And it was so. God called the dry land Earth and the waters that were gathered together he called Seas. And God saw that it was good. Then God said, 'Let the earth put forth vegetation ...' The earth brought forth vegetation: plants yielding seed of every kind and trees of every kind ... And God saw that it was good. (Genesis 1:1–12, NRSV)

The story goes on with God putting lights in the sky and creating fish in the waters, birds in the air and animals on land. After each step in creation the text carefully points out that God 'saw that it was good'. There is a strong statement of valuation here: the natural systems and the creatures created by God are important in and of themselves. They are things of beauty – God's handiwork; they are not to be valued only as resources for human sustenance and development.

Later in the story human beings are created and are told their role in the created order: 'Be fruitful and multiply and fill the earth and subdue it; and have dominion over the fish of the sea and over the birds of the air and over every living thing that moves upon the earth' (Genesis 1:28b NRSV).

The use of the term 'dominion' in this passage can be interpreted (and has been, lamentably) to justify the view that the rest of nature exists only to serve humanity. Theologians are adamant, however, that this is a false and destructive interpretation (Berry, 1988; Hallman, 1992). The correct interpretation, they say, makes the opposite claim: 'dominion' is to be understood to mean, not a freedom to lord it over creatures and natural systems, but rather a *responsibility* to care for them, ever to suffer and sacrifice for them. Douglas John Hall (1982, p. 111) makes the case forcefully:

> We are (yes, why should we not use this word?) to 'have dominion'. But what does that mean in the full perspective of biblical religion? Does it mean only what the word *literally* connotes? Trampling and being heavy handed and dominating? Why should it? Why should we want to be so *literal*? Who (biblically speaking) is our *model* of dominion? Is it Caesar? The Pharoah [*sic*]? Or even the divinely-approved Cyrus? No, it is the one whom we call 'Lord' – *Dominus*: Jesus the Christ ... 'and him crucified'! *His* dominion, far from being a trampling over everybody and everything, seems to have involved his being trampled upon.

Human beings are to relate to the created order as Jesus related to them – through love, service and sacrifice. Hall and a number of other important theologians argue that we should see our relationship to creatures and ecosystems as one of *stewardship* (Hall, 1982, 1985, 1986; Hallman, 1992). This point of view obviously makes claims upon human economic activity. Ecosystems are households of God; as such their well-being must be considered when humans plan for and engage in economic activity. The influential ecotheologian, Father Thomas Berry (1988, p. 74) puts it this way: 'The primary objective of economic science, of the engineering profession, of technical invention, of industrial processing, of financial investment and of corporation management must be the integration of human well-being within the context of the well-being of the natural world'. In other words, all human institutions must be marked by our divinely granted vocation of stewardship. The vast resources of the natural world and the systems that constitute it are there for us to employ; but we are obliged to use them in a way that fosters well-being not only for all human beings, but also for those systems themselves. We are to be guardians that protect eco-communities from death – gardeners who ensure that all that which lives does so abundantly.

God has special empathy for the poor

This principle, sometimes more controversially expressed as 'God's preferential option for the poor', is a fundamental tenet of liberation theology – the school of theology that began in Latin American and grew to have global influence during the last four decades of the 20th century. Gustavo

Gutierrez, perhaps the most influential liberation theologian, expresses the principle this way: 'The reciprocal relationship of God and the poor person is the very heart of biblical faith' (1983, p. 8).

Certainly, poverty is a theme given consistent and profound attention, both in the Hebrew Bible (the Old Testament for Christians) and in the New Testament, where the texts that capture Jesus' self-understanding and the essence of his teaching speak directly about poverty. Early in the Gospel of Luke, as the reader is getting to know Jesus and the mission to which he is called, Jesus returns to his home town and is asked to read scripture in the Synagogue. He chooses a passage from Isaiah (chapter 61), 'The Spirit of the Lord is upon me, because he has anointed me to bring good news to the poor. He has sent me to proclaim release to the captives and recovery of sight to the blind, to let the oppressed go free, to proclaim the year of the Lord's favor' (Luke 4:18–19, NRSV). The reference to 'the year of the Lord's favor' is meant to evoke the Jubilee – a time when the poor would be forgiven their debts and have their lands returned to them.

Why does Jesus (God) have such deep concern for the poor? The reasons are both obvious and subtle. The poor suffer; it is not a surprise that a compassionate divinity would be moved by, and even share, those sufferings. In our time, we can also say with confidence that there is divine outrage spurred by the fact that one third of the human race lives in poverty (according to the World Bank Standard of less than US$2 income per day per person) in a world that has generated so much wealth.

Beyond being objects of sympathy and causes for moral indignation, however, the poor are valued by God because they have an important role in history. Their very existence means that God's purposes for the world are being thwarted: the households of God are not receiving livelihood and experiencing well-being. Because of their sufferings, poor people are in a special position to see the ways in which social, political and economic reality is contrary to God's intentions. They can see how humanly-created systems are out of step with the divinely willed order (God's reign); and they can take action toward restoration. The Argentinean theologian, Enrique Dussel argues that the eyes of the poor are opened as they suffer domination and exploitation: 'as the poor grow in awareness, they hear the voice of the other, the other poor among the people and they are transformed into subjects, agents, of the reign – its primary builders, its principal protagonists' (1986, p. 54).

Just community is fundamental

For a forthright statement of our next principle, we turn again to Dussel. Referring to a biblical text that describes Jesus' apostles living together in close-knit community, Dussel (p. 7) writes: 'This text recalls for us that the essence of Christian life is *community*: being together with others. This is also the essence of the reign of God: to be together with God, face-to-face with God in community'. Community is not just valuable because it sustains individuals – helping them to meet their needs and to grow. Community (relationality, a web of relationships – a word very close in meaning to 'household' as that word is used in this essay) is what makes human beings human from the Christian point of view. It is also the locus of the incarnation of the body of Christ, the place where God comes alive in human society.

Of course, not all communities humanize human beings; nor do all communities embody the kind of relationality celebrated in Christian scriptures and theology. Communities marked by oppressive power relationships, marginalization of minorities or extreme inequality obviously do not fit the bill. So, what are the marks of the kind of community cherished in biblical texts – what we might call *righteous community*? This is a topic dealt with by many Christian writers. One of the most evocative and influential treatments in recent years has been that of the biblical scholar Walter Wink.

A central concern of Wink's work is *domination*. He believes that the early Christian communities that produced the New Testament texts were particularly insightful on the subject of domination because of their oppression under the Roman Empire. These texts, he maintains, juxtapose the socio-political system of the Roman Empire against the communal order willed by God, which Christian communities sought to embody (Wink, 1984, 1986, 1992). The former he calls the 'Domination System' and the latter 'God's Domination Free Order'. Turning his attention to the social/economic/political realities of today's world, Wink argues that many manifestations of the Domination System can still be found. He then attempts to outline the marks of a community or society that would embody the opposite nature – God's Domination Free Order (God's reign) (1992, pp. 46–9):

- The Domination System is marked by vertical power relationships and competition. God's Order is marked by partnerships, competition and cooperation
- The Domination System is marked by the economics of greed, exploitation and inequality. God's Order is marked by sharing, responsibility and equality
- In the Domination System relationships are marked by hierarchy, patriarchy, classism and rigidity. In God's Order relationships are marked by flexibility, deep linkages and equality of power and opportunity
- The Domination System is marked by the politics of conquest and authoritarianism. God's Order is marked by decentralization and democracy
- In the Domination System, transformation happens through force, violence, war or an imposed suppression of conflict. In God's Order transformation happens through non-violent action and conflict resolution

A community that exhibits the characteristics Wink ascribes to God's Domination Free Order could be considered a righteous community or a household living in harmony with the divine intention.

A key issue here is whether a household – one as small as a nuclear family, or as large as the 'global village' – provides its members with the opportunities, freedom, challenges and resources necessary to grow and change in dynamically creative ways as individuals and groups. Communities marked by domination provide these things to some members but not most. Sometimes, especially in cases of strident oppression, even the dominant classes lack the intellectual freedom to be truly creative: there is too much risk that the products of that creativity will undermine or unmask institutionalized injustice. This brings up another seminal issue: the *world view* that shapes the ethos and action of a community. Is it a world view in harmony with the values of God's Domination Free Order, or does it embody antithetical values?

The economy of the world

A Christian theological response to the processes and developments that we together call (with some ambivalence) 'economic globalization' requires an evaluation of the extent to which these processes are in harmony with the marks of 'God's economy'. In this section I will attempt to articulate such a response by looking at economic globalization through the lens of each of the three principles outlined in the previous section.

Economic globalization and the inherent value of the created order

To what extent have industrialization, commercialization, the growth of MNCs, the expansion of communication and transportation systems and other globalizing economic processes advanced human stewardship of ecosystems and other species? To what extent have they impeded or even eroded such stewardship? It seems clear that much ground has been lost during the era of globalization. We need only look at the impact humans are having on creation's other creatures. During the decades (in some cases centuries) that these processes have been expanding, the well-being of many, many non-human species has become much more precarious. Hundreds of species have disappeared from the world forever and thousands more are under threat.

In some cases the negative effects of human economic activity have gone beyond the extinction of species to the destruction of whole ecosystems. Acid rain has killed whole lakes. Rising seawaters are swamping atolls. Diversion of water has created deserts. To convey the just how profound is the environmental crisis, we could examine such threats as the damaging effects of pollution produced by manufacturing processes; the smog, effluent and dangers of transportation processes; or the impacts of large-scale agriculture on soil, water tables and species diversity. But one phenomenon by itself can capture the magnitude of the human threat to life on earth. That is, of course, global warming.

According to the Intergovernmental Panel on Climate Change, global warming due to the human production of greenhouse gases will raise the average surface temperature of the earth by as much as 5.8 per cent during the 21st century. No increase of this magnitude has occurred in the past 10,000 years. This increase will radically alter precipitation patterns, speed the retreat of glaciers and raise sea levels by as much as 0.88 m. Projected affects of these changes include: increased threats to health for humans and other species (e.g., cold and heat stress, alteration of disease vectors such as mosquito populations or water-borne pathogens), especially in lower-income tropical or subtropical countries; threatened food sources; increased risk of species extinction; desertification; and inhabitability of some islands and atolls (IPCC, 2001).

According to the biblical tradition and Christian theology, the right relationship between non-human and human households (it is important to understand that humans and other species are members of the same households, as observation of almost any regional ecosystem will prove) is one of *stewardship*. Human beings are to be the stewards, but we have to confess that we have largely abused that role. We have pilfered, squandered and despoiled many of the riches entrusted to us. Of course, economic globalization cannot be blamed for all this abuse. Deforestation, species extinction, dirty industrialization and other kinds of ecological damage have also occurred outside of globalizing processes; but economic globalization has undoubtedly contributed to the depth and breadth of the devastation that we witness today.

Is there another side to the story? Perhaps there is a sign of hope in the observation that globalization has helped us to see and to begin to respond to the great harm that it itself has helped bring about. Because of technologies generated during the period of economic globalization, we are better able to measure carbon dioxide levels, sea levels, or levels of ultraviolet radiation; we are also better able to transport the technicians and equipment to the appropriate sites, store and analyse their data and communicate their findings. People concerned about those findings are in a better position to network and advocate with others equally concerned, to organize for change and to lobby governments, corporations and para-governmental agencies. While the speed with which progressively integrating economies have sent the world into ecological crisis is breathtaking, the pace at which those economies have begun to change in response to the crisis is not altogether unimpressive. Signs of that change include the Kyoto accord; environmental components of codes of corporate responsibility (such as the Organization for Economic Co-operation and Development's Guidelines for MNCs or the UN's Global Compact); cooperation between corporations and environmental NGOs (Toyota Motor Corporation working with the World Wildlife Fund to respond to an oil spill in the Galapagos Islands, for example); and the acceptance by some MNCs that 'the environment' is a stakeholder with rights that must be accounted for in planning processes.

It appears that a notion of stewardship is beginning to creep into our economics. While this can be celebrated as a positive development, perhaps even a small first step in the direction of God's reign, we are a long time away from the day when we can rejoice over the amount of ground gained. Limited liability corporations by nature (and according to the laws that sanction them) are still beholden more to the interests of shareholders than to the interests of other stakeholders, including biospheres. Governments are still much more responsive to the voices of 'the business community', consumers and labour than they are to the groans of nature. Institutions that are key to the governance of international trade, like the WTO, still place economic concerns ahead of environmental protection (Singer, 2002, pp. 57–70, 90). When looking at the world through the lens of God's concern for all creatures and biospheres, we can only conclude that the economy of the world lives more as a contradiction of than an expression of God's economy.

Economic globalization and God's special empathy for the poor

Here the good news is not so overwhelmingly overshadowed by bad; but neither does it completely emerge from gloom. Debates over the extent of poverty on our planet and the effect of globalization on levels of poverty are difficult to settle because the defining and measuring of poverty is so complex. In *One World: the Ethics of Globalization*, Peter Singer provides a careful and balanced analysis of the data available (2002, pp. 79–90) yet this is his conclusion (pp. 89–90):

> No evidence that I have found enables me to form a clear view about the overall impact of economic globalization on the poor. Most likely, it has helped some to escape poverty and thrown others deeper into it; but whether it has helped more people than it has harmed and whether it has caused more good to those it has helped than it has brought misery to those it has harmed is something that, without better data, we just cannot know.

Singer's conclusion rings true on both counts: we cannot be overly confident in the data on poverty; but it does appear that globalization is helping many people escape or ameliorate poverty while pushing others further into it. In chapter 8 of this volume Frederick Bird describes the situation in similar fashion (although he seems a little more confident in the data). Bird argues that over the last 50 years the proportion of the world's people living in poverty has declined considerably. Particularly impressive progress has been made in China and the 'tiger' economies, but there has also been significant progress in slower-developing countries like Ghana and Nicaragua. But he also points out that poverty has become even more deeply entrenched in some regions, most notably sub-Saharan Africa.

So far we have been discussing *absolute* poverty which can be defined as the lack of the financial and physical resources needed to meet an individual's or a household's most basic needs. Also important is *relative* poverty, which is the experience of people existing on meagre resources but living in proximity to others who enjoy much greater privilege. This juxtaposition and the self-perception of living a life of a lower standard causes mental suffering and very often spawns social ills like crime, drug use or family violence. There is no question that we live in a time of great inequality. In recent years there have been some dramatic descriptions of this. The 1999 UN *Human Development Report* stated that the assets of the world's three richest individuals were greater that the combined Gross National Products of all the world's least developed countries (600 million people) (Singer, 2002, p. 81). The same report asserted that the ratio of income received by the fifth of the world's population living in the world's richest countries relative to that received by the fifth living in the world's poorest countries grew, from three to one to 74 to one between 1820 and 1997 (Singer, 2002, p. 81).

These dramatic comparisons may only be part of the picture when it comes to the ways globalization is affecting economic equality. There is some evidence that economic globalization is both reducing inequality (between the top and bottom *thirds* of global income recipients) and increasing inequality (between the top and bottom *tenths*) (Singer, 2002, p. 4). As with absolute poverty, the relevant data are complex and incomplete.

For the purposes of this study, however, better data are not needed. The debate about whether economic globalization is doing more harm than good is not our debate. Our issue is whether or not economic globalization is doing *enough* to move the least privileged households of this world toward the state of being that God wills for them. Are livelihood and well-being for the poor, to whom God directs special empathy, being fundamentally established? No, they are not – not fundamentally. If they were, we would not countenance the paying of such low wages – sometimes as low as ten cents an hour – to factory workers in Bangladesh or Indonesia. If it were, we would not countenance the withholding of life-saving drugs from Africa's poor in order to maintain the profit margins of pharmaceutical companies. Nor would highly-developed nations be imposing tariffs on food imported from 'the South'. Livelihood and well-being for the poor are not being established in a profound way; and anything less than a profound change cannot meet the call of the gospel.

I am not arguing that economic globalization is a complete contradiction of the reign of God. Some aspects of it, like the movement of millions of Asians out of poverty, are in harmony with that reign. But so much more could be done to increase that harmony. Here is a partial list of such measures:

- Implementing an international minimum wage
- Making low-interest credit more broadly available to poor people
- Giving greater punitive powers to the ILO and making its conventions legally binding
- Revisiting legislation regarding limited liability corporations so that they become more responsible for their impact on non-shareholder stakeholders
- Re-working regulations regarding currency exchanges and the 'virtual economy' such that there is greater incentive to invest in sectors that generate employment
- Advancing debt relief for developing countries (even holding the G8 to its commitments would be a big step)
- Sensitizing multinational businesses to issues of culture such that their operations can be moulded to fit the rhythms of a greater variety of work cultures

Fundamental reform in just one area of the global economy could make an enormous difference; I am referring to international trade. Oxfam (2002, p. 5) describes the situation this way:

> There is a paradox at the heart of international trade. In the globalized world of the early twentieth-first century, trade is one of the most powerful forces linking our lives. It is also a source of unprecedented wealth. Yet millions of the world's poorest people are being left behind. Increased prosperity has gone hand in hand with mass poverty and the widening of already obscene inequalities between rich and poor. World trade has the potential to act as a powerful motor for the reduction of poverty, as well as for economic growth, but that potential is being lost. The problem is not that international trade is inherently opposed to the needs and interests of the poor, but that the rules that govern it are rigged in favour of the rich.

Oxfam claims that tariff barriers in highly developed countries cost developing countries $100 billion a year – twice as much as they receive in aid. When rich countries export to poor countries, they generally face much lower barriers – partly because of IMF and World Bank 'structural adjustment' programmes, which require poor countries to open their markets. Equally damaging are agricultural subsidies paid by governments to farmers in Europe and the US.

The values of the reign of God call for trade rules to be *skewed in favour of poor nations*. An example would be trade agreements that allow least-developed nations to protect and encourage the growth of local industries by imposing certain import barriers, without having similar duties imposed on their exports to more highly developed nations. But just redressing the current imbalance in favour of rich nations would be a great improvement.

The fact that such an imbalance exists is a sign that current economic realities are dissonant with God's Domination Free Order (to use Wink's term). I explained above that, according to liberation theology (and also to many theologians who belong to other schools as well) the poor have a special place in history because they are well positioned to see how historical realities contradict God's reign. It would be helpful to take a glimpse at how liberation theology – which comes as close as anything in the world of theology to being the voice of the poor – is responding to economic globalization.

Leonardo Boff, a liberation theologian whose influence matches any other, considers the current nature of globalization to be the extension of a process that began in 1592, when Ferdinand Magellan circumnavigated the globe. Colonization, according to his line of thought, was the first stage of globalization. Boff calls that stage the 'iron age of globalization' and argues that it laid the foundations for the kind of global integration that we see today (Boff, 1999). Globalization today may not be as overly brutal as it was during the colonization of Africa, Asia and Latin America, but Boff believes that it continues to be a process deeply marked by domination. This domination comes about through the unwarranted ascendancy of the rights of capital, making private acquisition of profit and the maximization of income the most important elements. As a consequence, the masses are excluded (Boff, 1999).

> Disproportions like this demonstrate clearly that this type of market is fundamentally anti-social. It does not produce in order to meet human needs, but in order to meet the needs of the market itself. Liberation theologians are not against a market that is a central institution in a modern society, but we cannot accept a market that brings death to the majority of the human race. If world hunger continues to grow, we will have to alter the nature of the world economy in order to survive and we will have to learn to see it not just in terms of material growth, but as an instrument for satisfying the needs of all human beings and all other creatures. (Boff, 1999)

Given the data being generated about economic globalization, one might be able to argue with Boff about whether or not it 'brings death to the majority of the human race'. But we would be unwise to ignore Boff's last point: that globalization has been driven by an economics obsessed with material growth to the exclusion of other human needs and dimensions. This raises the issue of core values, which is central to our examination and application of the third of our three Christian principles.

Economic globalization and just community

This is another extremely complex and paradoxical topic. My own thinking on the subject has been greatly influenced by my experience of one context: present-day Fiji, which was recently my home for three years.

It looked to me that globalization was simultaneously destroying community and freeing some people to engage in new kinds of community in Fiji. Like the societies of other Pacific Island countries, Indigenous Fijian society (upon which alone these remarks are intended to comment) has been characterized by very strong, very traditional community. The ties of family and clan have run extremely deep for most Indigenous Fijians, giving them weighty cultural and economic responsibilities to other members of their community. The benefits of these responsibilities have included an extremely rich culture expressed in ritual, music and dance; the economic security that comes with communal sharing of resources; and firm and clear narratives of identity construction, which can afford the peace of mind that comes from knowing one's place in society and the cosmos. Traditional Christian religion brought by 19th-century missionaries has been an integral part of this society.

Today, all of these features of society still exist, but are undergoing striking change. With the influx of movies from Hollywood and 'Bollywood', as well as Western television, less and less time is spent experiencing and learning traditional stories, songs, dances and rituals – especially by young people. Under pressure from politicians and other leaders to save their wealth for investment and entrepreneurship, Fijians are retreating from the communal sharing of resources. Attracted by new professional opportunities in business, law and communications, more and more young Fijians are eschewing their traditional community roles as fishers, homemakers, builders, etc. Drawn to new religious movements planted by the latest round of missionaries or expat workers, a great number of Fijians have left the Roman Catholic and Methodist churches that were such key institutions in their society. Many thousands of Fijians, each affected by his or her own mix of these dynamics, have left their villages for urban centres.

The combined effect of these developments is profound. On the negative side, village life and traditional community have been eroded. Some results of this are growing crime rates, rising rates of sexually transmitted diseases and teenage pregnancies, increased use of alcohol and illegal drugs, the growth of an urban homeless population and the introduction of ethnonationalist rhetoric into social and political discourse.

On the positive side (not all Fijians would agree) are the growth of new kinds of community and new freedoms to engage in non-traditional community. One new community, still found only in urban areas and mostly in the capital, is the gay community. Another is the inter-racial community, found in some workplaces, churches, sporting clubs, artistic associations and urban neighbourhoods. Also growing are connections to international networks through NGOs, sporting bodies, the academic community and professional associations. Women are experiencing new freedoms to leave their traditional roles and participate in these kinds of community. Especially noteworthy is the prominence of women in the NGO sector and academia.

For a Westerner shaped in a society that champions individual freedom and human rights, these changes seem extremely valuable. Today Fijians are much more free to choose the destiny they want to pursue and the kind of community in which they want to make their place (although, on balance, they are not yet as free as North Americans or Europeans). But even a Westerner can discern within Fijian society a profound regret for the loss of the cohesion and cultural vitality that used to mark traditional society.

There is a growing debate in Fiji over the cultural impact of globalization. Of course, this debate is not unique to that country. The UN devoted an entire chapter of its 2004 Human Development Report to 'Globalization and Cultural Choice' (UNDP, 2004, pp. 85–105). The chapter highlights three crucial issues: indigenous peoples, extractive industries and traditional knowledge; trade in cultural goods; and immigration. The report notes (p. 88):

> The extreme positions in these debates often provoke regressive responses that are nationalistic, xenophobic and conservative: close the country off from all outside influences and preserve tradition. That defence of national culture comes at great costs to development and to human choice. This report argues that these extreme positions are not the way to protect local cultures and identities. There need not be a choice between protecting local identities and adopting open policies to global flows of migrants, foreign films and knowledge and capital. The challenge for countries around the world is to design country-specific policies that widen choices rather than narrow them by supporting and protecting national identities while also keeping borders open.

The UN report recognizes that global flows of goods, ideas, capital and people can threaten local and national cultures, eroding traditional values and practices and destabilising the economy upon which traditional culture is based. It argues, however, that attempts to close a country off from outside influences lead to other problems: cultural exclusion and economic weakness. The proper response to the cultural threats of globalization, it argues, is multiculturalism based on four principles:

1. Defending tradition can hold back human development
2. Respecting difference and diversity is essential
3. Diversity thrives when people have multiple identities, belonging at once to community, nation and world
4. Addressing imbalances in economic and political power helps to ward off threats to the cultures of weaker and poorer peoples (UNDP, 2004, p. 88)

The 2004 Human Development Report is commendable in its identification of the threats that globalizing processes hold for poor countries, indigenous peoples and local or national cultures in general. One can witness the disruption of culture and the emergence of identity crises in contexts as heterogeneous as Fiji, Quebec and outport Newfoundland in Canada, Afrikaner communities in South Africa, African communities in the same country, or any number of European cities. The temptation to 'restore' identity through the generation of ethno-nationalist narratives is omnipresent in these contexts and these narratives always identify an 'other' who must be excluded. Often, as with the rejection of Indo-Fijians, the targeted other is not the primary source of cultural threat but rather a locally present scapegoat. Such a situation provides just the right growing conditions for racism, demagogic leadership and communal violence.

Much of what the UN report advocates as a proper response is admirable. I agree that respecting diversity is important, that contemporary humans must learn to develop and harmonize multiple identities (though this is no mean task, especially for people living economically mean lives) and especially that addressing imbalances in economic and political power is a very good way to defuse threats of cultural imperialism. The report takes a generally positive view of cultural globalization because of the diversity of broader cultural choices that it affords; and this, no doubt, has been a blessing to many, including gays and lesbians, women in patriarchal societies and individuals whose creative potential could not be embraced or channelled by their traditional or local cultures.

But in the final analysis the UN report is somewhat naïve. In a world with such great imbalances of economic power, it is a bit facile to say: 'There need not be a choice between protecting local identities and adopting open policies to global flows of migrants, foreign films and knowledge and capital'. Some countries (the US is the foremost example, but India, China and certain European countries qualify as well) have such powerful cultural industries that smaller countries and especially developing countries, must resort to protective measures to bolster local identities and cultures. These include state subsidies for homegrown cultural industries, tariff barriers for cultural products, foreign content limitations for radio and television and restriction of 'split-run' magazines. But these measures are often difficult to implement under the rules of the WTO or bilateral and multilateral trade agreements, which developing nations usually negotiate from a position of weakness.

One problem that the UN report explains well is the exclusion of traditional knowledge from global regimes for intellectual property. It criticizes these regimes for focusing too much on individual property rights in a way that fails to recognize communal ownership and the spiritual dimension of traditional knowledge, especially that of indigenous peoples (UNDP, 2004, pp. 88, 93). This often leads to the awarding of rights to the wrong interests. The classic examples here are medicines identified through the study of traditional healing practices. The report here puts its finger on a larger issue that is the source of a growing and intense debate: the world view (with its assumed values) at the heart of economic globalization. Today throughout Africa, Asia and Oceania there is much protest about the influx of 'Western values'. Politicians, clerics, NGOs and academics argue that these values corrode local cultures and spiritualities, thereby enfeebling community. The values in question – individual freedom and rights, the rights of capital, heightened concern for economic growth and consumer choice – might not be recognized by some in Europe and North America as 'Western values' but rather as the values of economic globalization or, more precisely, the liberal economic philosophy which seems to be at its core. In the West too it is argued that this value set and its associated world view destroy community.

In *Unequal Freedoms* (1998), the Canadian philosopher John McMurtry offers an extended deconstruction of the global 'market value system'. He asserts that the global economy is undergirded by a set of beliefs woven together to form a value structure that is assumed and therefore unchallenged – an interesting parallel to Wink's Domination System.

> When we approach a value structure as global and as universally practiced as 'the market value system', with an immense edifice of technical experts, government ministries, national and international banks, transnational corporations and international trade regimes all promulgating and implementing its prescriptions, we are faced by an especially difficult value programme to investigate and question. Still it is important to make the effort to do this investigation, this questioning. If a value system is simply presupposed and obeyed as the given structure of the world that all are made to accept and serve, it can become systematically destructive without our knowing there is a moral choice involved. (McMurtry, 1998, p. 10)

Some of the values embraced by the market system are efficiency of factor allocation, increased GDP performance and annual incomes, high returns on investment, market freedom from government interference, the growth of international trade and unrestrained movement of capital. Each of these can be understood as a good; but their elevation over other priorities and unquestioned adoption by governments and economists as a value set for the guidance of public policy, development and societal organization also leads to environmental destruction, unsustainable development, unemployment, poverty, labour exploitation and heightened inequality – a cocktail of effects that is extremely destructive of community (ibid.).

McMurtry maintains that the market value system is broadly adopted despite the severe consequences because its tenets and promises have taken on a 'theocratic' character (p. 16). The 'invisible hand' of the market will solve our problems. 'Sacrifices' may be necessary, but 'market miracles' will follow. The invisible hand can also mete out worldly rewards and punishments to those who serve or fail the faith.

McMurtry is far from alone in arguing that belief in the market system has become a quasi-religion. A number of writers have identified the discipline of economics as generative of a theology (or anti-theology) (Berry, 1988, p. 75; Korten, 1995; Kroeker, 1995). David Korten (p. 70) identifies in neoclassical economics a set of fundamental assumptions that serve as the core elements of this faith:

- Humans are primarily motivated by self-interest focused on financial gain
- The action that produces the greatest financial gain for an individual or a firm is the best one for society
- Competitive behaviour is more rational than cooperative behaviour
- Human progress is best measured by increases in the value of what members of society consume

While taking seriously the views of Christian ethicists and theologians who see the market value system in a more positive light and argue that its wealth-generating and democratizing effects are compatible with God's reign (Stackhouse, 1987; Krueger et al., 1997; Schweiker, 2000), I have become convinced that McMurtry has a strong point. In country after country where I have studied, worked or carried out field research (Daye, 2003, 2004, 2005), I have encountered a totalizing economic discourse that was transforming societies' institutions, whether political, educational, welfare-oriented or cultural. The people I met who were naming and condemning this trend included post-apartheid South Africans lamenting the ANC's forfeiting of its socialist ethos in favour of economic neo-liberalism; Canadian farmers being forced to choose between abandoning the family farm or upscaling it into an agribusiness; Papua New Guineans who had been displaced by mining operations in Bougainville and Micronesian church leaders who explained that they were losing members to new American churches that promised to help converts gain work visas for the US.

There is no doubt that the paradigm at the heart of economic globalization is a threat to community and particularly just community, in many ways. But, as the 2004 Human Development Report points out with regard to cultural choice, globalization is also providing opportunities that can liberate people from communal restrictions that are stifling and themselves unjust. I have also witnessed this. Blacks in South Africa who were escaping economic apartheid through employment equity practices of MNCs and women in the South Pacific who were rising to leadership positions in international, or internationally funded, NGOs are examples that come immediately to mind.

Our examination of the impact on community of economic globalization and its world view shows that, as with poverty, its effects are legion, are both constructive and destructive, and are interconnected in very complex ways. To articulate a Christian response, it might be helpful to revisit Wink's schema that juxtapositions the Domination System with God's Domination Free Order (see above).

Economic globalization appears to embody both domination, on one hand and aspects of the divinely-willed order, on the other. Of particular concern is the anthropology of the economic theory that drives globalization, and which portrays human beings as driven by self-interest focused on material gain. This is a complete contradiction of the anthropology implicit in the biblical tradition's portrayal of God's economy, in which the highest human concern is for relationship and the highest good is sacrifice for others. Lamentably, the anthropology of neo-liberal economics does appear to be shaping people in many parts of the world. The spread of consumerism gives witness to this.

Equally disturbing is neo-liberal economic theory's philosophy of history. The belief that progress is best understood as advance in the quality of goods consumed and is best fostered through intense competition is an equally robust contradiction of God's will for human households. There is no doubt that one expression of globalization, the remarkable intensification of the presence of MNCs in communities around the world, has amplified economic competition, but competition is a catalyst of conflict as well as growth, and it is clear that rivalries between international businesses have fuelled conflicts in developing contexts. The diamond wars in Central and West Africa serve as prime examples. But in certain other contexts such competition appears to have positive effects. Transnational automobile companies in South Africa are challenging each other to enact better affirmative action and social investment programmes, for example. Such efforts can generate wealth and social capital for marginalized groups in a way that fends off conflict.

Wink recognizes that there is room in God's Order for competition, as long as it is expressed in a larger framework of cooperation. A key issue with regard to MNCs is whether they cooperate with governments and para-governmental organizations to advance democracy and the rule of law or whether they under cut these things. This kind of undercutting not only happens through corporate action that is blatantly illegal; when a corporation, especially a large one functioning in a developing context, strategizes without a good understanding of, or concern for, the social, political and environmental dynamics of the country in which it operates, it can unwittingly cause havoc. Shell's contribution to political corruption and oppression by its paying of enormous oil royalties to Nigeria's Abacha regime made this clear (Bird and Herman, 2004).

In general, economic globalization appears to play a very mixed role in the generation, mediation and resolution of conflicts. Thomas Friedman (2000) argues that global economic interests force governments to be accountable and to foster social stability for the sake of attracting investment, thereby reducing conflict. On the other hand, Amy Chua (2004) argues that economic globalization generates ethnic violence and communal conflict by creating privileged minorities who become lightning rods for the discontents of other groups. Both arguments are to some extent true.

A critical issue is how economic institutions respond to conflict or potential conflict. Do they seek to establish order and protect themselves through the use of armed force, or do they engage in relationship building and conflict mediation in an effort to find non-violent solutions?

With regard to Wink's assertion that in the Domination System relationships are marked by hierarchy and rigidity, while in God's Order relationships are marked by flexibility and equality, there appears to be reason to hope that economic globalization can be a kind of solvent that weakens traditionally dominating and exclusive relationship systems in some countries. The UN argument (UNDP, 2004) that globalization presents citizens of many countries with greater cultural choice is relevant here. Again, the role of MNCs is important. When these businesses open operations in hierarchically or patriarchally organized societies, they sometimes reinforce traditionally rigid delineations of social roles by adjusting their hiring practices and other policies so as to conform to local norms; but they sometimes engage in behaviour that defies these norms for example, by promoting women or members of marginalized groups to important positions. Such practices have a doubly deconstructive effect: they give economic power to those who previously had little and they model alternative norms.

Unfortunately, the value of this solvent appears to be lost in many contexts: sometimes because MNCs or other agents of globalization conform to the norms of undemocratic societies, reinforcing vertical power relationships; at other times, because they establish new kinds of vertical power relationships. Important here is the working culture of MNCs or other bodies: are they decentralized, empowering workers and managers to take initiative and be creative, or are they marked by rigid hierarchies and the concentration of authority? Especially odious are organizations that place expats in rarefied positions at the top of a pyramid, while local employees languish at the bottom with little power and paltry remuneration.

From the point of view of just community, there is good reason to conclude that economic globalization is a contradiction of God's Domination Free Order (God's reign) – but not a complete contradiction. In some ways it advances that order, or at least drives fissures into domination systems such that there are opportunities for advancement.

Conclusion: Judgement

According the biblical and theological traditions that guide Christians, what is a proper, holistic response to the vast and profoundly transformative set of processes that together are being called economic globalization? Jesus taught, 'Judge not, that ye not be judged' (Matthew 7:1). In the biblical tradition, however, God's judgement was spoken through a spokesperson, a prophet such as Moses or John the Baptist. An outstanding example can be found in the opening chapter of the book of the prophet Amos: 'The Lord roars from Zion and utters his voice from Jerusalem ...' (Amos 1:2). Amos voices God's denunciation of the nations surrounding Israel for their various transgressions. He then, in a masterful shift that startles the reader, turns his displeasure on Israel itself: 'Thus says the Lord: For three transgressions of Israel and for four, I will not revoke the punishment; because they sell the righteous for silver and the needy for a pair of sandals – they who trample the head of the poor into the dust of the earth and push the afflicted out of the way' (Amos 2:6–7a, NRSV). The harsh words of the prophet are meant to call the nation back to righteousness; in this case righteousness means a halt to the exploitation of poor people and a return to the duty of caring for the afflicted.

In light of our comparisons of God's economy and the economy of the world, what might be a prophetic response to economic globalization? To what changes is the household of humanity, with its rapidly changing and ever integrating economy, being called? The word 'repent' in its biblical usage means to turn around 180 degrees and to live in the opposite way. Summing up the reforms outlined in the discussions above, I would like to suggest three ways the whole household of humanity and each person and institution in proportion to his or her economic power, is being called to repent. First, we are called to see other creatures as our brothers and ecosystems as our own communities, and to treat them with the care that we treat our own families. Second, we are called to give globalization's losers the honoured place in our global village and to fundamentally reform our *oikonomia* so that they get a bigger share of resources and opportunities. Third, we are called to value community above production and consumption, adopting a perspective like that of the African notion of *ubuntu*, which holds that each person's very humanity is engendered by her web of relations with others (Battle, 1997; Tutu, 1999).

References

Battle, M. (1997) *Reconciliation: The Ubuntu Theology of Desmond Tutu* (Cleveland: The Pilgrim Press).

Berry, T. (1988) *The Dream of the Earth* (San Francisco: Sierra Club Books).

Bird, F. and Herman, S. (eds) (2004) *International Business and the Challenges of Poverty in the Developing World* (London: Palgrave Macmillan).

Boff, L. (1999) *Liberation Theology and Globalization*, http://www.volny.cz/christian-peace/cpc/info/wn001a.thm, accessed 14 June 2005.

Chua, A. (2004) *World on Fire: How Exporting Free Market Democracy Breeds Ethnic Hatred and Global Instability* (New York: Anchor Books).

Daye, R. (2003) 'Finding a Model of Reconciliation in Fiji', *Fijian Studies*, vol. 1, pp. 177–92.

Daye, R. (2004) *Political Forgiveness: Lessons from South Africa* (Maryknoll, NY: Orbis Books).

Daye, R. (2005) 'Responsible Change in the Wake of Apartheid: The Case of Toyota South Africa', in F. Bird, E. Raufflet and J. Smucker (eds), *International Businesses and the Dilemmas of Development: Case Studies in South Africa, Madagascar, Pakistan, South Korea, Mexico and Columbia* (London: Palgrave Macmillan).

Dussel, E. (1986) *Ethics and Community* (Maryknoll, NY: Orbis Books).

Friedman, T. (2000) *The Lexus and the Olive Tree* (New York: Anchor Books).

Gutierrez, G. (1983) *The Power of the Poor in History* (Maryknoll, NY: Orbis Books).

Hall, D. J. (1982) *The Steward: A Biblical Symbol Come of Age* (New York: Friendship Press).

Hall, D. J. (1985) *The Stewardship of Life in the Kingdom of Death* (New York: Friendship Press).

Hall, D. J. (1986) *Imaging God: Dominion as Stewardship* (Grand Rapids: Eerdmans/Friendship Press).

Hallman, D. (1992) *A Place in Creation: Ecological Visions in Science, Religion and Economics* (Toronto: United Church Publishing House).

IPCC (2001): Intergovernmental Panel on Climate Change, *Change 2001: Synthesis Report Summary for Policy Makers*, http://www.ipcc.ch/pub/un/syreng/spm.pdf, accessed 13 June 2005.

Korten, D. C. (1995) *When Corporations Rule the World* (West Hartford: Kumarian Press).

Kroeker, P. T. (1995) *Christian Ethics and Political Economy in North America: A Critical Analysis* (Montreal & Kingston: McGill-Queens University Press).

Krueger, D. A., Shriver, D. W. Jr. and Nash, L. (1997) *The Business Corporation and Productive Justice* (Nashville: Abingdon Press).

McMurtry, J. (1998) *Unequal Freedoms: The Global Market as an Ethical System* (Toronto: Garamond Press).

Meeks, M. D. (1989) *God the Economist: The Doctrine of God and Political Economy* (Minneapolis: Fortress Press).

Oxfam (2002) 'Rigged Rules and Double Standards: Trade, Globalization and the Fight Against Poverty', http://www.maketradefair.com/en/index.php?file=03042002121618.htm, accessed 9 July 2003.

Schweiker, W. (2000) 'Responsibility in the World of Mammon: Theology, Justice and Transnational Corporations', in M. L. Stackhouse and P. J. Paris (eds), *God and Globalization: Religion and the Powers of the Common Life* (Harrisburg, PA: Trinity Press International).

Singer, P. (2002) *One World: The Ethics of Globalization* (New Haven and London: Yale University Press).

Stackhouse, M. L. (1987) *Public Theology and Political Economy: Christian Stewardship in Modern Society* (Grand Rapids: Eerdmans).

Tutu, D. (1999) *No Future Without Forgiveness* (London: Rider).

UNDP (2004): United Nations Development Program, *Human Development Report 2004: Cultural Liberty in Today's Diverse World*, http://hdr.undp.org/reports/global/2004, accessed 9 June 2005.

Wink, W. (1984) *Naming the Powers: The Language of Power in the New Testament* (Philadelphia: Fortress Press).

Wink, W. (1986) *Unmasking the Powers: The Invisible Forces that Determine Human Existence* (Philadelphia: Fortress Press).

Wink, W. (1992) *Engaging the Powers: Discernment and Resistance in a World of Domination* (Philadelphia: Fortress Press).

10
Markets, Development and Equity: Lessons from South Korea

Joseph Smucker

Introduction

Most development theorists regard South Korea (the Republic of Korea) as a success story. Guided in large part by a strict, authoritarian state, the history of its rapid economic development appears to be an example of nearly flawless execution. South Korea, starting from an annual per capita income of $87 at the end of the hostilities of the Korean War in 1953, currently has an annual per capita income of over $10,000. In 2005, South Korea had the twelfth largest economy among the nations of the world (*Korea Times*, 2005a).

However, this transformation has not been achieved without considerable dislocation and social unrest. Periodic outbursts of dissent against the authoritarian policies of both governments and large business conglomerates have accompanied South Korea's economic development. These incidents of social unrest are not surprising. Apart from the authoritarian controls, the fast pace of change itself caused enormous shifts in social relations and distributions of wealth and status. What is more intriguing is the fact that expressions of dissent have increased, rather than subsided, as South Korea has taken its place among the 'developed' countries of the world.

It is the thesis of this essay that incidents of dissent are a part of the emergence of an increasingly active civil society.[1] At the core of the recent episodes of social turmoil are matters of equity, of competing definitions of what constitutes just procedures and just outcomes in the distribution of wealth and the distribution of citizens' rights.

A variety of groups, including rice farmers, environmentalists, student groups, labour groups, consumer groups, religious-affiliated groups, business associations and anti-corruption movements, have emerged within South Korea, expressing in different ways their concerns about the distribution of the costs and rewards of economic development and growth. Social movements and other public expressions of dissent have gradually increased in frequency and intensity since the mid-1970s and they gained momentum following the Kwangju Riots in 1987. Led by labour and student groups, the riots of 1987 resulted in the start of the so-called era of 'democratization'. An increasingly active civil society has forced the state to become more responsive to social demands and less dictatorial in the execution of its policies (Han, 2001). Meanwhile, large business interests have been left with far less government support than they once enjoyed, and they have had to adjust to a more critical and sophisticated public.

South Korea's experience provides a vivid example of the changing definitions of equity in the distribution of costs and rewards incurred during the process of rapid economic development. Market economies require individuals to act in a rational, self-serving manner in the pursuit of their economic objectives. But, paradoxically, this behaviour is possible only if there exists a deeper structure of cooperation and equity that binds society together and fosters networks of trust.[2] In a fundamental sense, questions of equity in market-based economies are questions that maintain a focus on the continuing strains between these two requirements.

In this study, I first review a number of reasons why the question of equity in the distribution of rewards and costs of economic development has become so prominent in the current public discourse of Korean society. I then cite two examples that illuminate the different ways in which questions of equity have been articulated: (1) issues of equity in labour-management relations, and (2) issues of equity in negotiating contractual relationships with foreign interests. In the final section, I consider the dimension of time as an underlying factor in forming perceptions of equity and social justice.

Questions of equity within public discourse

Table 10.1 provides a timeline of significant events in the economic development of South Korea.

The left column of the table depicts significant economic events aligned along a horizontal scale of increased generation of wealth. The right column lists significant political events and events indicating an increasingly active civil society.

Economic development, by definition, requires ongoing realignments of social institutions. How these realignments are implemented depends very much on the reciprocal roles of business and government, the former oriented primarily to the pursuit of private gain, the latter to the maintenance of the public good. But in market-based economies there is a high degree of variation in the roles played by governments in maintaining the public good. Governments may serve as 'umpires', ensuring that rights to private property are upheld, that rules of exchange are honoured, and that honesty and integrity predominate in the conduct of business affairs. But govern-

Table 10.1 Major Events in the Economic Development of South Korea

Economic growth scale	Major political events
(GDP per capita ppp*)	
Less than US$87 ... More than $US10,000	
+US foreign aid	1945 End of Japanese Occupation.
+Gov't patronage system; import substitution strategy	1948 Division of Korea; Syngman Rhee heads gov't (1st Republic).
+Landowning yang-ban class destroyed	1950 North Korea invades South Korea.
	1953 Armistice signed between North and South Korea.
+Chaebol conglomerates established	1960 Student-led revolts end Rhee regime; 2nd Republic established.
	1961 Military coup; Park Chung Hee administration (3rd Republic).
+Close chaebol-gov't strategy	1965 Relations normalized with Japan.
+Japanese direct investments in electronics	1972 Yusin Constitution (4th Republic).
+Decline in financial aid from US	
+Japanese pull out most of their direct investments	1979 Park Chung Hee assassinated
+Attempted reforms of chaebol	1980 Chun Doo Hwan takes over presidency. Further constitutional amendments (5th Republic).
+Continued restrictions of labour	1981 Martial law lifted but autocratic gov't continues; first balance of payments surplus.
+High rate of economic growth	1987 Kwangju Riots; downfall of Chun regime. Roh Tai Woo elected president; constitution revised (6th Republic); beginning of increased civil rights to general population; efforts to co-opt labour in gov't policies.
+Labour unrest; serious student-led riots; general civil unrest	1992 Kim Young Sam first civilian elected president since 1961. Major reforms against chaebols attempted; efforts to curb corruption.
+Financial crisis; IMF bailout	1997 Kim Dae-jung elected; greater rights to civil society; major economic reforms to accommodate IMF loans.
+Radical restructuring of financial sector and chaebol	
+Dramatic increase in FDI	
Dramatic economic recovery+	

Table 10.1 Major Events in the Economic Development of South Korea *continued*

Economic growth scale	Major political events
(GDP per capita ppp*)	
More than $US10,000	**2001** World trade downturn; increased activity among groups in civil society.
Less than US$87	
Slow-down in rate of economic growth+ Increase in wealth disparities+ Corporate restructuring+ Increased media attention on gov't and corporate corruption+	**2003–2005** Roh Moo-hyun elected president; continuing efforts toward democratization and economic restructuring; threats from North Korea followed by negotiations; trade sanctions from US and Euro community; increased exports of automobiles and high technology products. Continued activism in civil society. May, 2005 Korea hosts 6th UN- sponsored forum on 'Reinventing Government'.

* ppp = Purchasing power parity, a comparative measure of living standards (in this case, relative to the US)

ment may also serve as a leading actor, determining the course of economic development and the manner in which its rewards and costs are distributed. The latter role roughly describes the nature of government policies in South Korea's economic development, although there has also been a considerable oscillation between the influence of governments on the strategies of business firms and the influence of big business on successive governments (Moon, 1994, 1999; OECD, 2000a; You, 1995).

This oscillation, some observers maintain, has occurred when the state plays an active role in pursuing economic growth or 'accumulation' while also attempting to maintain its popular support. Faced with this dilemma, the state must choose between ensuring its legitimacy among the larger population and simply imposing its policies by force. Unfortunately, as numerous examples among nations have demonstrated, efficiencies in economic development do not ensure equity in the distribution of its costs and rewards among the population. If the state seeks legitimacy, it must at least attempt to ensure procedural and distributive justice, which may preclude the maximization of economic development and growth.

During the formative years of South Korea's economy, from 1945 through the 1970s, the state played the major role in directing the course of development by encouraging the development of the huge business conglomerates known as *chaebol*, and influencing their business strategies through governmental control of most of the institutions in the financial sector. Once in place, however, the giant *chaebol* were often able to influence the decisions of the state. In addition, an increasingly independent and influential government bureaucracy emerged as a major player in influencing development strategies. These three groups of institutional players – politicians, *chaebol* and bureaucrats – were not completely distinct; rather, social networks of influence based on kinship, region or school linked them together.

Left out of the roster of actors in the drama of South Korea's economic development was civil society. The authoritarianism of the governments was deeply entrenched, beginning with the Syngman Rhee government installed by American occupation troops after World War II and continuing through the years of the Park Chung Hee regime and finally the Chun regime that lasted until 1987.

Ironically, the economic success of these coercive policies ultimately created the resources for an increasingly active civil society, challenging the legitimacy of authoritarian regimes. In the labour movement, for example, there appears to have been an increase in the number of incidents of unrest with the shift from light fabricating industries, staffed largely by low-waged women employees from rural areas with high turnover rates, to heavy industry staffed by an increasingly urbanized, skilled and stable male labour force.

Abetting these movements was a growing middle class, ever sensitive to the distribution of wealth, especially during economic downturns. Following the assassination of the authoritarian president, General Park Chung Hee, in 1979, the regime of General Chun Doo Hwan attempted to exert even tighter controls over labour and to outlaw any movements of dissent from students or other groups emerging from the middle class. As economic growth slowed, the newly emerging middle class grew more emboldened, creating, as it were, articulate voices challenging the mode of operations of the government as well as the *chaebol*. General Chun, in an effort to gain some legitimacy with the newly emerging and vocal civil society, sought to control the power and influence of the *chaebol* by removing many of the government supports and putting into place neo-liberal market reforms. These policies were ostensibly designed to make the *chaebol* more efficient and more competitive as they became increasingly involved in world markets. But the policies were also designed to reduce the political influence of big business.

A major unintended effect of the shifts in government policies was the increase, rather than decrease, in the power and influence of the *chaebol*. Reduced support from the government also meant greater economic freedom and greater influence in the economy for business interests. These shifts in alignments over the past 20 years have resulted in a three-way struggle among the state, big business and social justice groups from the emergent civil society. Voices from a more self-confident civil society have been challenging the hegemony of the *chaebol* and the state while the government, in an effort to maintain its legitimacy, attempted to control the growing independent power and influence of the giant *chaebol*. The *chaebol* in turn, united through their umbrella organizations, the Federation of Korean Industries and the National Employers' Association, have sought to protect their interests against challenges both from the state and from civil society. Over recent years, the most remarkable development in South Korean society has been the emergence of a myriad of special interest groups challenging the authoritarian regimes of the state and the influential power of big business (Han, 2001).

These are not merely internal developments. As the large *chaebol* sought growth at the expense of profits, intricate and unstable links with foreign financial institutions were established. Short-term loans were readily obtained, backed by increasingly vast production assets. But the fragility of these links was dramatically exposed when South Korea was drawn into the Southeast Asian financial crisis of 1997–1998. Since then, and in part as a result of the strictures imposed on Korea by the International Monetary Fund as a condition for receiving its financial aid, Koreans have had to contend with the effects of direct foreign investment in their domestic economy. These developments have introduced another source of disquiet over issues of fairness and equity among the Korean population. Many

Koreans are dubious about the long-term effects of foreign direct investments in their economy as well as the effects of being drawn into Westernized styles of contractual relations, whether these are relations between firms or between management and employees (*Korea Times*, 2003a, 2003b). Although South Korea began allowing limited foreign direct investment in 1962, it was not until 1998, following the large-scale restructuring of the economy, that direct foreign investments were actively encouraged by the state. The vigorous support of the Foreign Investment Promotion Act in 1998 signalled a significant shift in government development policies. Foreign investments in 2003 rose 97.4 per cent to $12.77 billion. In 2004 there were 16,181 foreign-invested companies in South Korea, accounting for 11 per cent of the country's total sales (*Korea Times*, 2005b).

These two developments – the growth of a more vocal and influential civil society and increased contact with foreign firms – have encouraged public debates over issues of equity within Korean society.[3] In the next two sections, I present examples of these concerns.

Establishing equity in labour-management relations

The changing relations between management and labour represent a prime example of the concern for fairness in the distribution of responsibilities as well as of rewards. In pursuing an export-led model of economic development, successive authoritarian governments attempted to keep labour costs as low as possible, and were active in controlling and eliminating expressions of labour unrest. These repressive labour policies were further reinforced by an ideological rhetoric that constantly reminded the general population of their obligations to create a strong, independent nation able to compete, first, as a supplier to more advanced economies and, second, as a world-class producer competing with other industrial nations in world markets for finished goods. Further, successive governments linked their development policies with the need to maintain military preparedness in the face of possible military incursions from North Korea.

But as the nature of industry moved from the manufacture of basic goods to highly sophisticated finished goods such as automobiles, appliances, computers and communications equipment (Hobday, 1998), all of which required a more highly skilled labour force, the emphasis upon a highly disciplined, militaristic model of managing labour proved to be counterproductive for innovative strategies; in any event, it was increasingly resisted by employees. Demands by labour, often abetted by student groups, for more equitable distribution of economic and social returns and for a greater voice in implementing changes increased in intensity from the late 1970s through the 1980s and have continued into the present (Ahn, 1996, pp. 41–2, 1998).

The relationships of the *chaebol* with the state have also shifted, as the government, in order to maintain its legitimacy and authority in the face of an increasingly self-conscious civil society, has taken on the task of reforming traditional business practices of the giant *chaebol*. Prodded by the IMF, following the financial crisis of 1997–1998, the government has also reduced much of its active role in the market economy, especially in relaxing its control of the financial sector.

Meanwhile, traditional strategies of business firms and their traditional forms of organization have been changing as a result of the exigencies of international competition. In the past, large Korean firms offered their employees such benefits as job tenure, housing subsidies, leaves of absence for family obligations and generous cash awards upon retirement (Kim, Ch. S., 1992). Such benefits were provided as part of a patrimonial management style based on traditional Confucian values of loyalty, responsibility, allegiance and discipline. Although there were few opportunities to express dissent, there was considerable security in employment. But it is now questionable whether this model is economically viable in an atmosphere of intense international competition (Kim and Lee, 2000).

Norms of management obligation to workers in exchange for their personal loyalty to the firm are now competing with new, imported models of labour deployment that stress 'flexibility' and the ability to hire and lay off workers as market demand fluctuates (Hamilton and Biggart, 1988; Chung et al., 1997). Since the 1997–1998 financial crisis, when the IMF required that South Korea open its domestic markets to direct foreign investment, Korean firms have attempted to improve their competitiveness by adopting many of the practices of their foreign competitors. But there remain differences about the degree to which foreign practices should be assimilated (Lee, 2004; *Korea Times*, 2004a, 2005c). Nevertheless, many of the larger firms have been reducing the number of their permanent employees while increasing their part-time and contingent workers (Genda and Yee, 1998). Changes to labour laws have made it easier for employers to lay off workers. In 1996 only 1.5 per cent of Korean firms used 'contract-based' employment strategies. By 2001, this had increased to 21.8 per cent of Korean firms (Ministry of Labour, reported in KPMG Consulting, 2002, p. 21). In addition there have been growing concerns about increased outsourcing of employment by major firms, especially those in the electronics and automobile sectors. The increased unemployment rates among younger workers appear to be one consequence of this (*Korea Times*, 2004d).

It is no longer certain that employees will be rewarded for their loyalty to the firm as they had been in the past (Kim, Ch. S., 1992; Kim, B. W., 1992). A number of researchers have noted that with the decline in the proportion of permanent workers, the ranks of dissatisfied workers have increased (see for example, Park, Park and Yu, 2001; *Korea Times*, 2003b). There have been attempts to fuse past patrimonial practices with the contemporary emphasis on 'flexible' hiring. Permanently laid-off workers, for example, may be called 'honourable retirees' in an attempt to convey the idea that unemployment is their personal sacrifice for the good of the firm and the nation. Some may receive support in searching for new employment, but this is meagre recompense for the loss of their permanent jobs and many have come to view this practice as merely a whitewash on the personal costs of such dislocation.

In the spring of 2000, part-time and contingent workers accounted for 34 per cent of the total number of paid workers (Federation of Korean Trade Unions, 2001, p. 7). These workers have few, if any, of the benefits of long-term core workers (*Korea Herald*, 2004). Further, among small and medium-size firms, employment remains very unstable; in many cases it is also highly exploitative. Many of these firms are parts suppliers to larger firms (Lim, 1999, pp. 117–25).

During the period from 1997 to 2001, the average monthly income for urban workers increased 14.8 per cent. But the average monthly income for the lowest 10 per cent of income earners increased only 3.9 per cent while income earners among the top 10 per cent increased by 30.8 per cent (*Digital Chosun Ilbo*, 2002b). These inequities in both wages and working conditions have become new additions to the list of labour grievances and have become the focus of concern for reform groups in the larger civil society.

Labour organizations have directed their protests against both firms and the state. In 1997, apparently as a conciliatory response to labour, the government headed by the elected president, Kim Dae-jung, established a Tripartite Commission consisting of representatives from business groups, labour and government. But despite its official presence on the commission, organized labour remains unconvinced that complaints of social injustices have been adequately addressed (see *Korea Times*, 2003b, 27 June). Employment is increasingly precarious and labour-management relations continue to be fractious (Judd and Young, 2000; *Digital Chosun Ilbo*, 2002c).

Meanwhile, wealth disparities among the general population have been increasing (Leipziger et al., 1992; *Digital Chosun Ilbo*, 2002b). In 2003, a survey among a sample of adults, conducted by the Samsung Economic Research Institute and Seoul National University, revealed that 59 per cent of the respondents felt that the 'conflict level between the haves and have-nots in Korean society were very serious'. Sixty-four per cent agreed with the statement that 'Korea gives too much recognition and financial rewards to the winners' and more than 70 per cent viewed corruption as a 'serious problem'. More than half of the respondents in their twenties and thirties would immigrate if 'given the chance' (*Digital Chosun Ilbo*, 2003b). In 2005, the top 10 per cent of the population earned a monthly average 18 times the monthly average of the lowest 10 per cent. The effects of these discrepancies are indicated in the ability of this top tenth to spend considerably more for education and medical care (*Korea Times*, 2005a).

Social activist groups that challenge the distribution of wealth and privilege are gaining significant recognition in the press and within the government. Yet they are not necessarily hoping to emulate a Western model, since a major part of their social criticism is aimed against the incursion of Western practices. It is not unusual to see student groups denouncing increasing foreign (especially American) direct investments and their practices.

Many commentaries in the increasingly unrestrained public media also attribute this social turbulence to the growing presence of foreign interests in the Korean economy. Not only has foreign direct investment increased, but so have foreign portfolio investments in Korean firms, including financial institutions (*Korea Times*, 2005b). Foreign interests have demanded steady returns on their investments rather than underwriting riskier expansion policies that had marked the past strategies of the Korean *chaebol*. Thus the emphasis has been on efficiencies in production, on redefining production units themselves as saleable commodities (Lee, 2004). When corporations adopt these policies, labour bears a very high cost relative to other corporate stakeholders (You, 1995; *Korea Times*, 2003c; *Korea Herald*, 2004). On the other hand, Korean firms have had a reputation of inefficient management in the past.

These are significant institutional changes in the larger society and significant changes within business enterprises. Trust in the employment contract has weakened as employment has become less secure. Support for government policies has weakened in the absence of a compelling rationale for the inequities in the distribution of wealth or the deprivations formerly endured in the era of mobilization for rapid industrialization. The current era of 'democratization' is really an era of civil debate over establishing appropriate structures that can ensure a 'just' distribution of rewards and obligations.

Establishing equity across cultural divides: negotiating contractual relations

Ever since the Age of the Enlightenment, there has been a tendency in the West, as Saussy points out, to assume that a kind of 'universalism' is possible in defining the character of all societies; that all of humankind have similar desires and values hidden behind diverse veneers of culture, and that there is a sort of Hegelian ideal State, to which all societies aspire. 'The notion that preserving, not reducing, the otherness of others is our most demanding ethical task ... runs counter to millennia of moral training' (Saussy, 2001, p. 92). This 'ethical task' becomes very apparent in negotiating contractual relations between firms from different cultures. The issue is creating trust with a foreign 'other', without requiring the 'other' to become a member of one's own 'tribe'. One result of an increasing foreign presence in South Korea has been an increased awareness of differences in the meanings attributed to the concept of equity, and differences in what constitutes just relationships. If diversity is to be respected, successful contractual negotiations with foreign 'others' require the creation of bonds of trust; agreements about what constitutes equitable rewards, responsibilities and returns in the contractual relationship; and assurances that these agreements will be honoured in the future. In a certain sense, this is a process of creating a 'mini-culture': a system of behaviour and meanings that is unique to the negotiating parties.

One cultural feature of Korean society that was an ever-present force during its period of rapid economic development was the role played by clan-like relationships. These social networks, based on family, region or educational institution, were a vital means of ensuring trust among the parties to any social or economic transaction.

Korea is not unique in this regard. Such relationships are also predominant in other societies such as Japan, Taiwan and China in which Confucianism has been a major influence. But there are variations in the nature of these associations among cultures in which they play a significant role. For example, a number of observers have noted a higher degree of individual competition within clan-like associations in Korean society in contrast to Japan, where individual competition is far more muted.

Some observers have noted that in Korea, individualism is most strongly expressed within the circumscribed clan-like group. Thus, there can be heated debates among individuals within a defined collectivity, but a unified stance will be likely when the same individuals confront an outside group. Further, loyalty appears to be most strongly directed toward the leader of a group rather than to fellow members (see for example, Hamilton and Biggart, 1988; Kim, B. W., 1992; Chang and Chang, 1994, pp. 45–57; Chung et al., 1997; Paik and Sohn, 1998).

These social units of trust and exclusivity can also foster considerable wariness toward outsiders and it is especially noticeable in establishing business relationships with foreigners. Of course, Korea's past history of foreign occupation likely reinforces this sense of distrust. When it comes to establishing contractual relationships with Western firms, the process of establishing trust becomes an extremely complex matter since business negotiators must deal with a Western model of market relationships, which is based on quite different assumptions and criteria.

Almost every Western commentator on establishing contractual relations with Korean companies has noted the difficulties in reaching agreements of mutual advantage that both parties agree are fair and equitable (Genzberger et al., 1994; Country Business Guides, 1995). Since foreign negotiators are not part of any traditional network of trust in Korea, an underlying problem in negotiating contractual relations is to arrive at a common set of criteria by which trust can be established. In relations with foreign business enterprises, the issues that provoke the most difficulty in establishing trust appear to be (1) the degree of importance to be assigned to the attributes of the individual negotiators themselves, in contrast to their respective firms, and (2) the degree of authority to be assigned to the contract itself.

Personal attributes are important, of course, in any negotiation process. A negotiator needs to know that the opposite party is reliable, trustworthy and has the authority to speak for his or her firm. But cultures may differ markedly in the set of attributes they require to establish this trust. The North American negotiator is typically responsible for acting on behalf of his or her 'office' or position in the firm; the office is divorced from the person as such.[4] The traditional Korean negotiator, on the other hand, represents a fictive clan, in the sense that the negotiator is responsible for upholding the reputation and honour of the collective membership in his or her firm and the senior officers in it. He or she is therefore likely to assume that the individual Western negotiator, not his or her position, is the main referent in the negotiation process. The position represents the 'field' within which the negotiator acts, and it bestows a mark of status on the negotiator. But the person acting as a negotiator remains the primary referent. Exchanges take place between actors who first establish a personal relationship, before they deal with the interests of their respective firms. This process of establishing interpersonal trust may be time-consuming; but once it is established, implementation of the agreement can be relatively swift.

The second issue concerns the meaning of the contract itself. From a Korean perspective, a contract is embedded in personal relations and norms of respect and social honour. Just as these relationships may change over time, so might the interpretations of a contract. The North American, on the other hand, tends to assume that the contract itself is inviolable as a legal document specifying rights and obligations.

In unravelling the implications of the distinction between the North American and the South Korean business negotiator, one can draw on Weber's account of the idealized themes of the 'Protestant ethic' and the 'formal bureaucracy' in the West, in contrast to his description of Confucianism and the patrimonial bureaucracy of ancient China. In the former case, the actors are guided solely by the most efficient and effective means of attaining a given end, and they are judged by impersonal criteria, defined in large part by their position in a rational and independent organization. In the latter case, the actors must always take into account the degree to which their actions support or add to the welfare of the larger social unit. The patrimonial form of bureaucracy, as Weber once pointed out, operates on the principle of honour and respect for individual actors who are one's superiors (Weber, 1914/1978, pp. 726, 1047–51; Biggart, 1991). The Confucian tradition stresses loyalty, honour and respect toward individual actors who in turn are presumed to be acting in the best interests of other individual members of the group whether family clan, a firm or even the country as a whole.[5]

The idea of personal responsibility for the collective welfare is deeply embedded in Korean culture, even in the conceptualizations of everyday language. According to the dean of a school of management in Seoul, 'Korean expressions are never personally possessive in a singular sense. For example, one never says "my mother" but "our mother". It's always "ours", never "mine". That is what the Confucian ethic is all about.'[6]

In contrast, Weber's Puritan is concerned not so much with the collective welfare as with working out his personal salvation – or expressed in secular terms, personal achievement. In Adam Smith's more liberal formulation, the public good is assured if each individual seeks to maximize his or her own returns – assuming that this is done in a morally responsible manner. Thus one can act one way as an agent for one position and another way for another position, as long as one advances the objectives appropriate to either position. The public good is treated as a by-product of one's success in these achievements.

These differences create daunting challenges for Korean managers, since increasingly they must negotiate with unknown agents who, if they are from the West, especially North America, operate on a market model that stresses self-interest and competitive behaviour within an impersonal legal framework. This model also informs appropriate behaviour within a Western business firm. In the past, Korean business networks have served the South Korean economy well. They have been integrated into a grand social effort to attain greater heights of economic well-being. In dealing with foreigners, especially North Americans, this network-based model comes into direct conflict with the more impersonal market-based model.

In network modes of transactions, individuals are engaged in 'reciprocal, preferential, mutually supportive actions' (Powell, 1990, p. 303). The assumption is that 'one party is dependent on resources controlled by another and that there are gains to be had by the pooling of resources' (ibid.). A socially just agreement, in this sense, is not merely a matter of arriving at mutually acceptable terms of economic exchange. It is also a matter of ensuring that social honour, respect and trust are in place among the individuals within the 'community' of negotiators. Favours and gift-giving are accepted rituals in establishing and reinforcing these relationships. In effect, the Korean approach is 'multi-stranded', in the sense that it includes both the personal attributes of individual agents and the firms to which they are responsible. If the relationship does not incorporate these elements then one is negotiating with an imperfectly known party, toward whom one must be wary.

Finally, it should be remembered that even if individual competition is the hallmark of a market economy, a 'deeper structure' of cooperation provides a supporting framework (Birchall, cited in Young and Schuller, 1988, p. 7). Cooperation, in turn, assumes that there is an agreement about the terms of equity in the distribution of rewards and responsibilities. How this agreement is to be established is the essence of contractual negotiations. The following account of a Canadian firm's negotiations with a Korean firm and also with South Korean government officials illustrates a number of these dilemmas.[7]

In 1990, the South Korean government was seeking to modernize its military communications equipment for use by army ground units. Its main concern was that the contract should eventually be awarded to a Korean firm that could meet advanced standards of technology. A medium-sized Korean firm had been manufacturing both military and commercial communications equipment and it sought to win the government contract by forming an alliance with a foreign firm that could provide the technology to meet these standards.

At the same time, a Canadian communications equipment company, which had had experience in South Korea since 1977, was also looking for an alliance with a Korean firm. It had formed a working relationship with a major Korean conglomerate, a *chaebol*, to supply 'line-of-sight' tactical radio units for the Republic of Korea Armed Forces, but by 1990 the alliance was coming to an end as a result of disagreements between the two partners over pricing policies.

The Canadian firm began searching for another partner in South Korea in order to maintain its presence in the Korean market and to expand into other far eastern markets, especially those in China and Taiwan. Contacts between the Canadian and Korean firms were made through the services of a broker. After each firm had evaluated the other, following a set of desired criteria, they entered into negotiations over the terms of a licensing contract.

Negotiations between the two companies, and subsequently with the Korean government, continued for about eight years before a final agreement was reached in 1998. In the encounters between representatives of the Korean and Canadian companies an extended period of time was required in order to establish a sense of trust between the individual negotiators, as well as to establish the nature of the intent of each of the firms. The leader of the Canadian negotiating team reported that it became very clear that as an outsider, seeking a long-term contractual relationship for his firm, he was constantly put in a position of proving the authenticity of his credentials. The pattern that emerged during the negotiation process required the Canadian negotiating team to take responsibility for suggesting solutions to problems, while the Koreans could decide their relative merits. In effect, the Canadians had to demonstrate *why* royalties must continue at a given rate; *why* cost accounting had to follow a given formula; and *why* the word of a negotiator required written confirmation.

From the Korean point of view, the Canadians may have had the upper hand in terms of their control of sophisticated technology, but with that control came the responsibility for providing solutions while respecting the status of the Korean negotiators. In Korea, such respect is integral to the sense of trust that ensures the continuity of the relationship; it is thus extremely important to understand one's opposite in negotiations as *a person*, including his or her personal reactions in various contexts. Thus ostensibly social occasions such as dinners, golf outings or conversations on issues apparently unrelated to the contract itself are in fact crucial to the progress of the negotiations. As the principal negotiator for the Canadian firm, an individual well-versed in Korean culture put it, 'Personal relationships are paramount. Many key decisions are made privately at dinner or in the car or during a golf game. Then everything is re-discussed during a formal meeting the next day. Loss of face is something to be avoided at all costs, and they dislike lawyer talk very much.'

What is involved here is the establishment of a code of equity that involves not only the formal matters of licensing technology but also interpersonal relations. This, in turn, involves establishing a system of social honour and respect that provides the framework for the allocation of responsibilities and rewards.

The North American model, based on competition in an impersonal market, is highly dependent on a legal framework that stresses property rights and stipulates the grounds for litigation should these rights be violated. This might result in a speedier conclusion to contractual negotiations, but the implementation of agreements based on this model can be slow and cautious. In contrast, the Korean approach may entail lengthy and complicated negotiation processes; but the emerging bonds of trust can ensure quicker implementation of policies and can be more flexible in meeting unexpected demands.

Koreans tend to regard North Americans as cold and calculating, interested only in costs and returns rather than in establishing the broad-based trust that Koreans regard as an essential for dealing with unexpected changes and future exigencies. As one young Korean sales manager of a small high technology firm put it, 'Americans only want to talk about costs. That's it. For us, trust is the most important part of a relationship. Without trust, how can you continue in a relationship?' He went on to point out that Europeans seemed to understand this better than North Americans:

> The Europeans are more concerned than Americans about the social conditions of any business relationship. And they are more concerned about the quality of a product. The Americans do not consider, nor place any importance on, relationships in business deals. Their only concern is with getting products cheaply. They often make impossible demands on price while wanting products to meet their own standards.

What is interesting in this comment is that the quality of personal relations is perceived to be an index of the *quality* of contractual conditions, and even of the products involved, in an exchange relationship. Indeed, in commenting on the comparative merits of market, hierarchy and network models of exchange, Powell notes (1990, p. 304):

> Networks ... are especially useful for the exchange of commodities whose value is not easily measured. Such qualitative matters as know-how, technological capability, a particular approach or style of production, a spirit of innovation or experimentation, or a philosophy of zero defects are very hard to place a price tag on. They are not easily traded in markets nor communicated through a corporate hierarchy.

The protracted length of time spent in negotiating for the licensing contract (eight years) is not altogether unusual. However, in this particular case there were a number of factors that contributed to the lengthy process. First, there were three changes of government during this time, 1990 to 1998. In addition to negotiations between the Korean and the Canadian firms, with each change of government the negotiations had to be reviewed with new government officials under new mandates. A second reason for the delay was that another foreign competitor linked to a Korean *chaebol* was quite successful in influencing senior government officials to prefer its products. It had, according to the Canadian informant, presented arguments that exaggerated its products' capabilities while stressing the limitations of the products of the Canadian firm. It took three very expensive field trials before the Canadian company was able to establish, for the government officials, the superiority of its technology.

A third reason for the lengthy negotiations was uncertainty about patterns of influence within government ranks.[8] Despite the fact that a broker was hired to sort this out, the Korean company found it difficult to predict how different government officials would respond to the proposed alliance with the Canadian firm.

In a final effort to win the government contract, the Korean firm hired an ex-general and former chief of staff – who happened to be the uncle of an advisor to the chief executive officer of the Korean company – to represent the joint project to the government. In the meantime, however, the government had decided against the bid. The Korean-Canadian partners appealed four times, with the ex-general playing a key role in these appeals. In the final negotiations, his powerful presence, his experience in the field and finally his assumption of personal responsibility for the merits of the bid eventually won the contract for the partnership. The vice president of the Canadian firm observed that throughout the entire process the quality of personal relations in negotiations between the Korean and Canadian firms and the process of establishing personal credibility with government representatives were decisive factors in securing the final contract.

But signing a contract does not finish the process; continuing a contractual relationship means continual negotiation over the terms of the contract, since, as the Koreans are likely to see it, conditions never stay the same and new insights or interpretations may emerge. A contract itself is defined as merely a thing created at a given time, under circumstances that may well have been unique; it can never therefore be viewed as unalterable. Defined in these terms, it is the *trust* built up between the parties, not the verbal formulation, which is the essence of the contract. Trust flows through changing conditions, something a static, written document can never accomplish; as long as the trust holds, modifications are always possible, according to changing needs.

From the point of view of North Americans who deal with Korean firms, the matter of continual negotiations is often taken to mean a reworking of past agreements and continual nit-picking over details. As one executive with a Canadian accountancy firm in South Korea put it, 'The Koreans are "grinders". They constantly go over every detail of a contractual agreement. They make agreements and then come back with more demands.'

Westerners, and North Americans particularly, tend to assume that there is a sort of universal acceptance of business values; that everyone is, at heart, a utility maximizer. If there are cultural differences, these are only veneers overlaid upon this basic human drive (see Marglin, 2003). Clearly this view is far too simple; it denies the culturally embedded nature of economic exchange and definitions of equitable contractual relations.

The dean of the Korean management school cited earlier argued that the emphasis on the quality of interpersonal relationships can no longer compete with merit-based systems which stress only economic performance. As he put it, 'The main problem in Korea is its "protectionist mentality". The emphasis on "groupness" tends to stifle risk-taking and creativity and innovation. This has a long history and the good thing about globalization is that it forces Korea to open up its economy and make it more efficient as a producer.'

Countering these assertions, however, is the argument that market-based models, especially those oriented toward financial interests, are highly unstable and often untrustworthy, and that to insist on their pre-eminence is to overlook the advantages of network-based models, especially those oriented toward increasing production capacity. Further, to insist on the superiority of one model is to overlook the fact that business transactions are not culture-free nor are they immune to change over time. Meanwhile, it remains the responsibility of negotiating parties to start with a respect for cultural differences and then to work out ways to accommodate them in a socially just manner. How this is to be done remains problematic for each encounter, but the process begins with finding mutually acceptable ways to establish relationships of trust and reliability.

Time and perceptions of equity

One can note the consequences of institutional change accompanying processes of economic development and growth, but 'time' as a factor in assessing procedural and distributional fairness is often overlooked. Theories of economic development implicitly include the concept of time – of present activities leading to future states; neoclassical economic theory is consistent with this perspective. If, as this theory assumes, individuals are rational utility maximizers, they are also future-oriented. There can be no such thing as an enduring present (Gell, 1992, see especially pp. 175–220). There is, in this assumption, a promissory theme: the notion that future economic returns represent a reward for the sacrifice of immediate gratifications; that individuals are willing to endure personal hardships and lost alternative opportunities in their pursuit of 'satisfactory', if not maximal, economic returns.

In the ongoing operations of market economies, time is a dimension of efficiency in the manufacture of goods and the provision of services; it is, in its own right, a unit of value.[9] Employees, for example, are hired for the use of their abilities and skills over time with the promise that rewards – the payment of wages or salaries will follow. There is, in this arrangement, a 'wage-effort' bargain between the employer and the employee. The former seeks some assurance of acceptable levels of effort during the time of employment; the latter seeks an acceptable level of payment for that effort and the sacrifice of time that could have been spent in other activities.

On a broader scale, time is a crucial variable in theories of 'modernity' and 'post-modernity'.[10] In considering the effects of economic development over time, there has been a tendency to equate them with the correlative development of Western-style democratic civil societies. The five stages of economic development enunciated by Rostow over 30 years ago are illustrative of this approach (Rostow, 1971). But the fact that this model flows from Western perceptions of the 'desirable' creates, in Fabian's view (cited in Saussy, 2001, p. 94), a kind of ethical trap by putting different societies on a timeline where they occupy places formerly held by advanced Western societies. The trap lies in assuming that the hegemony of the Western powers actually represents a superior social and ethical system. The historical interpretations of Hegel and Marx further illustrate this approach: both attempt to interpret human history as a process leading to the ultimate creation of just societies in which the ideals of equity and freedom are simultaneously achieved (ibid.). But even among advanced Western industrialized countries there is a considerable difference in their definitions of the rights and obligations of citizens, and of what constitutes a just society. This diversity should caution one against succumbing to the allure of this convergence thesis.[11]

The experience of rapid economic development in South Korea suggests that individuals may be willing to forego control over their personal time if they believe that their sacrifices are equitably shared and that rewards will be ultimately forthcoming and equitably distributed. But the longer the interval of time between effort and reward, and the greater the disparities in rewards, the higher is the cost in the perceptions of individuals. We have already noted the emergence of a more active civil society with the creation of an articulate, well-educated middle class and a more robust labour movement in South Korea. In a sense, these movements have drawn strength from their extreme experiences of past repression while pursuing greater social and economic equity in the present.

Promises of the future rewards of disciplined obedience in the face of military threats from North Korea; promises of future prosperity and security, of overtaking international competitors – all have been themes constantly articulated by both the state and big business throughout South Korea's development process. These themes have emphasized to workers and the general public the necessity of delayed gratification as they contribute their time and effort for these social benefits. But it is not at all clear why the population should continue indefinitely to endure economic and social privations in the name of continued advanced economic development. Individuals may differ in their perceptions of what a more just society might mean, but they tend to agree that many of those conditions that made rapid economic development possible have become obsolete, and that economic and social privations cannot continue in the face of advanced collective wealth. An older generation may recall with some nostalgia the more 'disciplined' years of early development as an era of social unity, cohesiveness and camaraderie; but they are also aware that the outcomes have benefited some sectors of society more than others.

Exhortations to continue working long hours seem unjust when the wealth this produces is not equitably distributed. Promises that living standards will improve become ineffectual when there are few social welfare measures to protect the unemployed. Some have argued that the increased insecurity of employment has had a direct impact on family units, changing them from protective networks for communal welfare during a time of collective effort to units of competitive achievement within a more wealthy, consumer-driven society, the promises of which, for many, have turned out to be illusory. One indication of this has been the effects of the introduction of credit cards. Their widespread use, together with increasing numbers of family loans from banks, have transformed South Korean society from one of high savings rates to a society of increasing proportions of individuals carrying large-scale debt (*Digital Chosun Ilbo*, 2003a; *Korea Times*, 2004b, 2004c). A variety of groups and social movements have been pressing the state to meet social obligations across a wide spectrum, including legislation to ensure better working conditions and a five-day work week, reforms of a rigid education system, and a more comprehensive welfare system (Judd and Young, 2000; see also *Digital Chosun Ilbo*, 2002a; *Korea Times*, 2003e). It was not until 1988 that a pension system for the aged was put in place (OECD, 2000b).

South Korea's social expenditures as a percentage of Gross National Product have been among the lowest among member countries in the OECD. In 1997, just before the last financial crisis, only 5 per cent of GNP was allocated to these expenditures. Canada, by comparison, spent 17 per cent, the United States, 16 per cent, Sweden, 33 per cent, Denmark, 31 per cent, France, 30 per cent and Germany spent 28 per cent of GNP.[12] The immediacy and prominence of social welfare issues are indicated by the greater attention labour unions today are directing toward government policy, above and beyond their relations with corporate management (*Korea Times*, 2003b).

Meanwhile, the middle class, losing ground relative to the wealthiest, have become increasingly vocal in their criticism of government favouritism and its tendency to give in to demands from the large *chaebol* (Judd and Young, 2000; see also Han, 2001). Further, in the midst of greater insecurities in employment, the middle class are becoming more critical of inequities in the workplace, including gender discrimination in wages and working conditions.[13]

Increased demands for more immediate responses to the problem of inequities in the distribution of economic and social rewards have also been directed against the exclusive nature of clan-like relationships.[14] In the past, these relationships have permeated not only business enterprises but also government bureaucracies. While these social networks have been the foundations of trust among economic and political actors, they have also been susceptible to practices of cronyism and political influence peddling. For example, many of the hopes for greater democratization with the election of the former dissident, Kim Dae-jung, in 1997, turned to disillusionment when he recruited his closest advisors from his home province of Cholla-do and sought special favours for an airline based in his home province (see also *Korea Herald*, 2002; *Korea Times*, 2003d). His attempts at limiting the influence of the *chaebol* and fostering more transparency in the finance sector had mixed results. In the face of these ongoing problems many reform-minded voices are calling for a more comprehensive and neutral legal system. According to one Korean informant, 'We need to move to a system based more on law so that the government does not act arbitrarily and citizens have recourse to action through class action suits. Government by law provides more predictability which you need if you want to attract investment.'

However, from the point of view of a Canadian executive based in Seoul, laws and government regulations are not the real issue; the problem lies rather in the way they are applied. 'Government regulations are always somewhat negotiable in their application. The government comes out with a hard stance and then usually backs off through compromises. The issue is not "rules" but how the rules are enforced.' Indeed, it is not unusual for prominent businessmen to receive leniency in cases of fraud or influence-peddling.[15] In contrast, outspoken political dissenters in the past have been dealt with harshly by the courts (see also OECD, 2000c).

The government of President Roh, elected in 2002, appears to be committed to addressing many of the problems associated with the unequal distribution of wealth and social welfare. But these issues remain the focus of considerable social turmoil and Roh has been finding it difficult to make good on his promises, while having at the same time to design government policies to deal with processes of advanced industrialization and create the conditions in which those processes are to become embedded in Korean society.

It is perhaps significant that in May 2005 South Korea hosted the Global Forum on Reinventing Government, a conference sponsored by the United Nations. In his welcoming address to the conference, President Roh stated that his government had 'made a great leap in building a transparent society devoid of corruption. We no longer have the linkage of corruption between politics and business.' He also pointed out that his government had recently signed a 'social covenant' with 'political and business circles and civic groups' to 'get rid of corruption'. He further declared that it was the aim of his government to build 'an effective, transparent, and decentralized government which serves and is with the people' (*Korea Times*, 2005c). If these words are more than mere political rhetoric, they represent a significant shift in the role of the government and in the influence of a recently 'unbound' civil society in establishing new standards of social and economic equity.

Conclusion

Economic development and economic growth are seldom smooth social processes. Inequities in both procedural and distributive justice inevitably appear, in part because development influences social institutions in different and unsynchronized ways, and even alters conceptions of time itself (Laslett, 1988). Development and growth can continue only if governments and business interests can offer persuasive arguments for their support among the general population. These arguments typically include the promise of a future system of equitable distribution of rewards and responsibilities.

Because of its relatively short period of economic development, South Korea provides an exceptionally clear example of the difficulties in maintaining a just allocation of rewards and costs in the collective pursuit of wealth accumulation in conditions of considerable, even extreme, privation and sacrifice on the part of the general population. But it is increasingly difficult to justify why those sacrifices should continue. Indeed, what were once considered as 'honourable' sacrifices are increasingly thought of as social injustices. Observers have noted that managers of both international and Korean firms in South Korea must be sensitive to these problems and, if possible, use their positions of influence so as to contribute toward solutions (see Kirk, 1999; Kluth, 2001).

Systems of legitimation, whether rooted in a Protestant ethic or in neo-Confucianism, can be easily moulded to legitimize powerful business or government interests. On the other hand, they also offer clues about the solutions to problems of inequity (Hahm, 1999; see also Mo and Moon, 1999; Moon, 1999). This further suggests that there are different formulae for achieving a more just society and that the outcomes may be considerably different from those historically experienced by the West. Part of the reason for these differences has to do with definitions of citizens' rights and obligations and the governments' roles in ensuring their legitimacy.

The social outcomes of economic development depend on the cultural and institutional heritage of each individual society and the manner in which its institutions are affected. It is only recently that international economic development agencies such as the International Monetary Fund and the World Bank have recognized the importance of these national variations. This recognition has come as a result of severe social costs in nations on which universalist economic principles based on the historical experience of the West have been imposed. Justice in contributing to and benefiting from the distribution of rewards and responsibilities of economic development and growth may take different forms. It will continue to evolve in its expression depending on each economy's historic values and norms, and on the outcomes of ongoing relationships between systems of authority and civil society. Western views of individual freedom and the institutional contexts required for this to take place may be quite inappropriate in those societies whose institutions are structured so as to favour and encourage cooperative economic and social activity. What is required in dealing with questions of equity is to line up what Saussy (2001, p. 97) calls the 'relevant pasts and presents' of evolving institutional structures and systems of meaning that justify their existence, both of which define the manner in which the costs and rewards are allocated among the population (see also Weller, 1999).

Notes

1. The term 'civil society' has no precise definition; rather it refers to emergent politically and socially active groups from among the general public. The London School of Economics Centre for Civil Society defines it as 'the arena of uncoerced collective action around shared interests, purposes and values' (http://www.lse.ac.uk/collections/CCS). For a more complete account of the formation of 'publics' and the idea of civil society, see Taylor (2004), pp. 166–7.

Non-government organizations, volunteer organizations, special interest groups and social movements are expressions of an active civil society. 'New' social movement theory also captures much of the nature of these emergent groups (see for example, Tarrow, 1994). Carothers and Ottaway (2002) view 'civil society' as a collective term characterizing the emergence of national and international non-government, not-for-profit organizations. Finally, it is well to keep in mind Barber's observation about the three obstacles to civil society as 'the mediating domain between the government and the private sector: government itself, when it is arrogant and overweening; market dogmas, when they presume that private individuals and groups can secure public goods; and the yearning for community, when it subordinates liberty and equality to solidarity' (Barber, 2001, p. 269).

2. Birchall (1988, p. 195) offers the following poetic description of this paradox: 'While the competitive individualists are learning how to examine the habits of the rest in order to exploit them, there is always the possibility of a counter-tendency, that the cooperators examine their habits too, and in the end refuse to cooperate. The survival of the fittest can only be assured when the whole species cooperates to support them'.

3. The concept of equity in this paper does not imply equality; rather it refers to the ongoing concern for justice in the distribution of rewards and obligations across society. Underlying any debate on equity is the question of the ideologies or belief systems that justify the distribution of rewards and obligations, as well as the nature of the distribution itself. For example, the high salaries of many CEOs may be viewed as just rewards for their education, cumulative experience and ongoing responsibilities; but there is a point when their salaries may be viewed as excessive or unjust, no matter how important the services they provide.

4. See Jackall (1988) for an account of the difficulties American managers experience in dealing with the demands of their positions; demands which may contradict their own sense of ethical behaviour. See also Bird (1996).

5. It is interesting to compare Korean and North American corporate mission statements. The former invariably make reference to their contributions to the betterment of Korean society, while the latter merely state their commitment to create quality products or services to enhance the abilities or performance of individual consumers.

6. From an interview conducted in Seoul, 18 May 2001.

7. The following account relies heavily on several interviews with the Vice-President of Asian Operations of the Canadian company conducted during 2001 and 2002, and on interviews conducted in South Korea in the Spring of 2001. While in South Korea, I conducted interviews with senior officials of a Korean firm specializing in facilitating negotiations between Korean and foreign firms and which was involved in these specific negotiations. (I was unable to get clearance to interview officials at the Korean electronics firm because of its sensitive role as a supplier of military equipment.) I also conducted interviews with additional Korean business people, Korean academics, Canadian and American executives stationed in Seoul and experts on the staff at the Canadian Embassy. I also observed production operations in an electronics assembly plant. Additional information and clarification was facilitated by email subsequent to my interviews in South Korea.

8. Some might view this problem as one of corruption, which may well be true; but there is a fine line between networks of influence and outright corruption, as Western democratic governments have demonstrated many times.

9. The commercial value of time in European societies preceded the Industrial Revolution. Time and its measurement, including the manufacture of elaborate clocks, was a prominent preoccupation during the Mercantile Era, beginning with 14th- and 15th-century Florence and continuing through mercantilist expansion prior to the 19th-century Industrial Revolution. The successful merchant during that era had to be as obsessive about his time as he was about his money (Grafton, 1995), and was not unlike the modern-day industrialist who has embarked on a 'just in time' system of production.

10. Crucial to the idea of modernity is the separation of time from space, and the transformation of both into 'empty dimensions'. This permits a wider scope of coordination both for business organizations and governments (Giddens, 1990, pp. 17–21). If 'modernity' connotes a sense of unilinear progression, 'post-modernism' argues that progress itself creates oppositions, which result in unanticipated consequences. New technologies, for example, distort realities and create new ones; thus the idea of any sort of linear progression toward a desirable future is constantly undermined (see Lash, 1990). Yet the idea of 'post-modernism' is impossible without the societal processes encompassed in the concept of modernity. A different tack is taken by Fukuyama (1992), who argues that modernity has created the union of political liberalism with free-market capitalism – an enduring state of post-modernism.

11. For an account of a process of 'modified' acceptance and outright resistance by European countries to American models of industrial reconstruction after the Second World War, see Djelic (1998).

12. Social expenditures, as defined by the OECD, include programmes that provide benefits for old age and disability; occupational injury and disease; family services; unemployment insurance; active labour market programmes; and health benefits (OECD, 2000b, p. 126).

13. In 1990, Amsden reported that for most years since the Korean War, ended in 1953, South Korea led other countries in wage growth, but also had one of the highest rates of discrimination against women workers in terms of both access to desirable jobs and wage levels (Amsden, 1990, pp. 85–6). Genda and Yee (1998, pp. 72–107) reported that while wage differences associated with gender, age, education and occupation were declining, wage differences associated with firm size were increasing.

14. A recent newspaper article reported the comments of a government legislator from the Democratic Labor Party who criticized the standard practices of large firms whose hiring policies required detailed information about job applicants' family backgrounds. He intended to introduce legislation to abolish this traditional practice.

15. Leniency continues. In June 2005, a Seoul court suspended a three-year jail term for the head of the SK Corporation. In 2004, top executives from Samsung Electronics, Hyundai Motor and Korean Air, all of whom were convicted of violating campaign-financing laws, had their jail sentences suspended. In June 2005 the founder of the collapsed Daewoo Group, Kim Woo-chong, returned to Korea after having fled the country six years earlier, in order to escape arrest for fraud amounting to approximately $80 billion. Current speculation is high about his ultimate fate. What makes these cases interesting is that these are individuals who are also portrayed as major contributors to the development of the South Korean economy. There may be an analogy here to the late-19th-century American 'captains of industry', who were also characterized as 'robber barons' (Times OnLine, 2005).

References

Ahn, P. S. (1996) 'Mature Industrialisation and Democratisation: The Role of Korean Trade Unions in a Double Transition', PhD dissertation, Faculty of Law, Environmental and Social Sciences, University of Newcastle upon Tyne.

Ahn, P. S. (1998) 'The Role of Trade Unions in the Economic Crisis of Korea', House of Culture, International Conference: 'Calvin vs. Confucius', Berlin, 7–10 May.

Amsden, A. (1990) 'South Korea's Record Wage Rates: Labor in Late Industrialization', *Industrial Relations*, vol. 29, pp. 77–93.

Barber, B. R. (2001) 'How to Make Society Civil and Democracy Strong', in A. Giddens (ed.), *The Global Third Way Debate* (Cambridge: Polity Press), pp. 269–79.

Biggart, N. W. (1991) 'Explaining Asian Economic Organization: Toward a Weberian Institutional Perspective', *Theory and Society*, vol. 20, pp. 100–232.

Birchall, J. (1988) 'Time, Habit and the Fraternal Impulse', in M. Young and T. Schuller (eds), *The Rhythms of Society* (London: Routledge), pp. 173–97.

Bird, F. (1996) *The Muted Conscience* (Westport, CT: Quorum Books).

Carothers, T. and Ottaway, M. (2002) 'Defining Civil Society', *World Bank*, http://www1.worldbank.org/devoutreach/winter02/article.asp?id=142 (accessed 2 August 2005).

Centre for Civil Society (2005) 'Civil Society Organizations', London School of Economics (website), http://www.lse.ac.uk/collections/CCS (accessed 3 August 2005).

Chang, Ch. S. and Chang, N. J. (1994) *The Korean Management System* (Westport: Quorum Books).

Chung, K. H., Hak, Ch. L. and Ku, H. J. (1997) *Korean Management: Global Strategy and Cultural Transformation* (New York: Walter de Gruyter).

Country Business Guides (1995) *Korea Business* (San Rafael, CA: World Trade Press).

Digital Chosun Ilbo (2002a) 'More School Children Opting for Overseas Schools', 18 January.

Digital Chosun Ilbo (2002b) 'Income Disparity Widens to Alarming Level', 3 March.

Digital Chosun Ilbo (2002c) 'IMF Recommendations Draw Criticism', 25 September.

Digital Chosun Ilbo (2003a) 'More Firms Following Western Recruiting', 15 January, http://www.english.chosun.com/service/archives.html (accessed 31 July 2005).

Digital Chosun Ilbo (2003b) 'Young People Want Out, Survey Says', 23 April.

Djelic, Marie-Laure (1998) *Exporting the American Model: The Postwar Transformation of European Business* (New York: Oxford University Press).

Federation of Korean Trade Unions (2001) Federation of Korean Trade Unions, 'Industrial Relations and Increasing Globalization', *International Relations Bureau*, Seoul (unpublished).

Fukuyama, F. (1992) *The End of History and the Last Man* (New York: The Free Press).

Gell, A. (1992) *The Anthropology of Time: Cultural Constructions of Temporal Maps and Images* (Oxford: Berg Publishers).

Genda, Y. and Yee, S. Y. (1998) 'Korea: Wage Determination and Labour Turnover', in T. Tochibanaki (ed.) *Wage Differentials: An International Comparison* (New York: St. Martin's Press), pp. 72–107.

Genzberger, C. A. et al. (1994) *The Portable Encyclopedia for Doing Business with Korea* (San Rafael, CA: World Trade Press).

Giddens, A. (1990) *The Consequences of Modernity* (Stanford University Press).

Grafton, A. T. (1995) 'Chronology and Its Discontents in Renaissance Europe: The Vicissitudes of a Tradition', in D. Owen Hughes and T. R. Trautmann (eds), *Time: Histories and Ethnologies* (Ann Arbor: University of Michigan Press).

Hahm, C. (1999) 'The Confucian Tradition and Economic Reform', in J. R. Mo and Ch. I. Moon (eds), *Democracy and the Korean Economy* (Stanford, CA: Hoover Institution Press), pp. 35–54.

Hamilton, G. and Biggart, N. W. (1988) 'Market, Culture and Authority: A Comparative Analysis of Management and Organization in the Far East', *American Journal of Sociology*, vol. 94, Supplement, pp. S52–94.

Han, S. J. (2001) 'Modernization and the Rise of Civil Society: The Role of the "Middling Grassroots" for Democratization in Korea', *Human Studies*, vol. 24, pp. 113–33.

Hobday, M. (1998) 'Latecomer Catch-up Strategies in Electronics: Samsung of Korea and ACER of Taiwan', in C. Rowley and J. Bae (eds), *Korean Businesses: Internal and External Industrialization* (London: Frank Cass), pp. 48–83.

Jackall, R. (1988) *Moral Mazes: The World of Corporate Managers* (New York: Oxford University Press).

Judd, K. L. and Young, K. L. (eds) (2000) *An Agenda for Economic Reform in Korea* (Stanford, CA: Hoover Institute Press).

Kim, B. W. (1992) *Seniority Wage System in the Far East: Confucian Influence Over Japan and South Korea* (Aldershot: Avebury).

Kim, Ch. S. (1992) *The Culture of Korean Industry: An Ethnography of Poongsan Corporation* (Tucson: The University of Arizona Press).

Kim, D. I. and Lee, J. H. (2000) 'Changes in the Korean Labor Market and Future Prospects', in K. Judd and Y. K. Lee (eds), *An Agenda for Economic Reform in Korea* (Stanford, CA: Hoover Institution Press), pp. 341–73.

Kirk, D. (1999) *Korean Crisis* (New York: St Martin's Press).

Kluth, A. (2001) 'In Praise of Rules: A Survey of Asian Business', *The Economist*, 7 April, pp. 1–18.

Korea Herald (2002) 'GNP Again Calls on Prosecutors to Arrest President's Second Son', 10 June.

Korea Herald (2004) 'Irregular Workers Find No Relief in New Workweek', 15 March, http://www.koreaherald.com/archives/result_detail.asp (accessed 31 July 2005).

Korea Times (2003a) 'Korea's Pain in Transition to Anglo-Saxon Economic Model', 27 June.

Korea Times (2003b) 'South Korea Worst in Labor Relations', 27 June.

Korea Times (2003c) 'Major Trends in the Labor Market', 25 June.

Korea Times (2003d) 'Overseas Educational Spending Reaches Half of Trade Surplus', 7 May.

Korea Times (2003e) 'Micron Faces Boomerang from Hynix', 23 April.

Korea Times (2004a) 'FKI Wants Korean-Style Corporate Reform', 11 May.

Korea Times (2004b) 'Bankruptcy Threatens 39% of Small Firms', 3 May.

Korea Times (2004c) 'One Out of 13 in Their 20s Faces Bankruptcy', 23 April.

Korea Times (2004d) 'Globalization Raises Concern Over Job Exodus', 15 April.

Korea Times (2005a) 'Rich Earn 18 Times More than Poor', 25 May, The Korea Times, http://times.hankooki.com/service/listmore/kt_archive.php?media=kt&page=1&strSec=&strItem=&type= (accessed 31 July 2005).

Korea Times (2005b) 'Foreign Firms' Contribution to Korea's Total Sales Reaches 11%', 24 May.

Korea Times (2005c) 'Competitiveness Through Decentralization, Deregulation', 24 May.

KPMG Consulting (2002) 'Foreign Direct Investment in Korea', KPMG Samjong, http://www.aspac.kr.kpmg.com (accessed 20 December 2003).

Lash, S. (1990) *Sociology of Postmodernism* (London: Routledge).

Laslett, Peter (1988) 'Social Structural Time: An Attempt at Classifying Types of Social Change by Their Characteristic Paces', in Michael Young and T. Schuller (eds), *The Rhythms of Society* (London: Routledge), pp. 17–36.

Lee, Ch. (2004) 'Confucianism and Hostile M & As', *Korea Times*, Supplemental, 15 April.

Leipziger, D. M., Dollar, D., Shorrocks, A. F. and Song, S. Y. (1992) *The Distribution of Income and Wealth in Korea* (Washington, DC: The World Bank).

Lim, Y. (1999) *Technology and Productivity: The Korean Way of Learning and Catching Up* (Cambridge, MA: MIT Press).

Marglin, S. (2003) 'Development as Poison: Rethinking the Western Model of Modernity', *Harvard International Review* (Spring), pp. 70–5.

Mo and Moon (1999) 'Epilogue', in J. R. Mo and Ch. I. Moon (eds), *Democracy and the Korean Economy* (Stanford, CA: Hoover Institution Press), pp. 171–98.

Moon, Ch. I. (1994) 'Changing Patterns of Business-Government Relations in South Korea', in A. Macintyre (ed.), *Business and Government in Industrialising Asia* (Ithaca, NY: Cornell University Press), pp. 142–66.

Moon, Ch. I. (1999) 'Democratization and Globalization as Ideological and Political Foundations of Economic Policy', in J. R. Mo and Ch. I. Moon (eds), *Democracy and the Korean Economy* (Stanford, CA: Hoover Institution Press), pp. 1–34.

OECD (2000a) Organization for Economic Co-operation and Development, *OECD Economic Surveys: Korea* (Paris: OECD Publications).

OECD (2000b) Organization for Economic Co-operation and Development, *Pushing Ahead with Reform in Korea: Labour Market and Social Safety-Net Policies* (Paris: OECD Publications).

OECD (2000c) Organization for Economic Co-operation and Development, 'The Fight Against Bribery and Corruption', *OECD*, http://www.oecd.org/ dataoecd/ 3/6/1918235.pdf (accessed 2 August 2005)

Paik, Y. and Sohn, J. H. (1998) 'Confucius in Mexico: Korean MNC's and the Maquiladoras', *Business Horizons*, vol. 41(6) (November–December), pp. 25–34.

Park, D. J., Park, J. and Yu, G. -C. (2001) 'Assessment of Labor Market Response to the Labor Law Changes Introduced in 1998', in F. Park, Y. -B. Park, G. Betcherman and A. Dar, *Labor Market Reforms in Korea: Policy Options for the Future* (Seoul: Korea Labor Institute). Ch. 7.

Powell, W. W. (1990) 'Neither Market Nor Hierarchy: Network Forms of Organization', *Research in Organizational Behavior*, vol. 12, pp. 295–336.

Rostow, W. W. (1971) *The Stages of Economic Growth: A Non-Communist Manifesto* (Cambridge: The University Press).

Saussy, H. (2001) *Great Walls of Discourse and Other Adventures in Cultural China* (Cambridge, MA: Harvard University Press).

Tarrow, S. G. (1994) *Power in Movement: Social Movements, Collective Action and Politics* (New York: Cambridge University Press).

Taylor, C. (2004) *Modern Social Imaginaries* (Durham, NC: Duke University Press).

Times Online (2005) 'Daewoo Chief to Face £39 Billion Music', 14 June, http://www.timesonline.co.uk (accessed 2 August 2005).

You, J. I. (1995) 'Changing Capital-Labour Relations in South Korea', in J. B. Schor and J. I. You (eds), *Capital, The State and Labour* (Aldershot, UK: United Nations University Press), pp. 111–51.

Weber, Max (1914/1978) *Economy and Society: An Outline of Interpretive Sociology*, 2 vols, G. Roth and C. Wittich (eds) (Berkeley and Los Angeles: University of California Press).

Weller, R. P. (1999) *Alternate Civilities: Democracy and Culture in China and Taiwan* (Boulder, CO: Westview Press).

Index